The picture you saw here in Vol. 3 was of my editor, which I used a computer to alter and make him look like Komui. It is not a picture of myself. My editor was at a loss for words. And what you see above is a portrait of Katsura Hoshino drawn by my older sister.

—Katsura Hoshino

Shiga Prefecture native Katsura Hoshino's hit manga series *D.Gray-man* has been serialized in *Weekly Shonen Jump* since 2004. Katsura's first series "Continue" first appeared in *Weekly Shonen Jump* in 2003.

Katsura adores cats.

D.GRAY-MAN
VOL. 4
SHONEN JUMP Manga Edition

STORY AND ART BY
KATSURA HOSHINO

English Adaptation/Lance Caselman
Translation/Toshifumi Yoshida
Touch-up Art & Lettering/Elizabeth Watasin
Design/Yukiko Whitley
Editor/Urian Brown

Printed in the U.S.A.

Published by VIZ Media, LLC
P.O. Box 77010
San Francisco, CA 94107

10
First printing, February 2007
Tenth printing, November 2022

viz.com

SHONEN JUMP MANGA EDITION

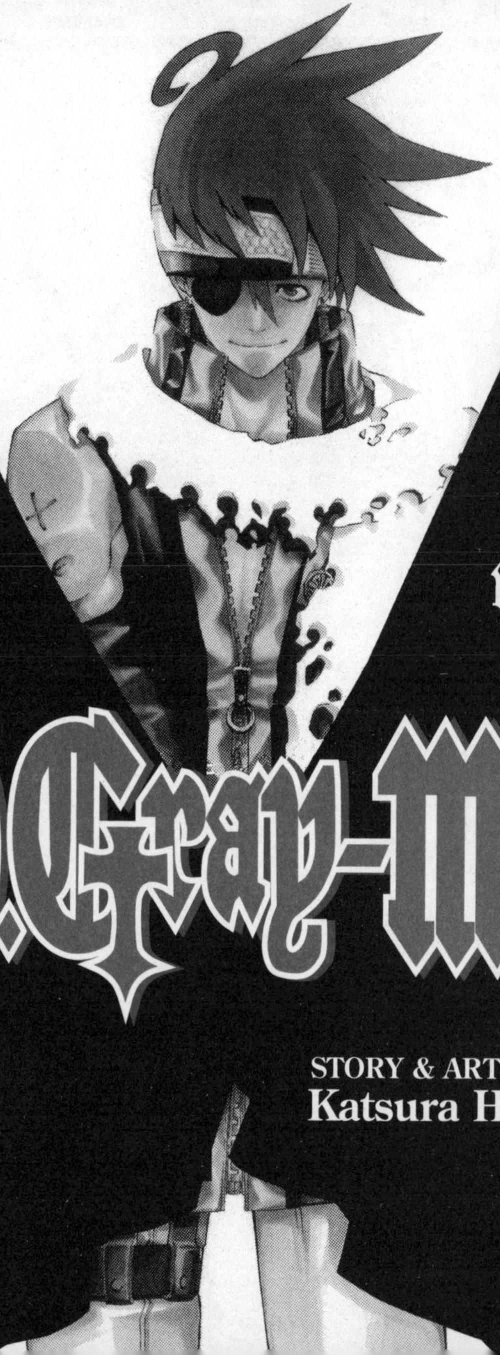

vol. 4

D.Gray-man

STORY & ART BY
Katsura Hoshino

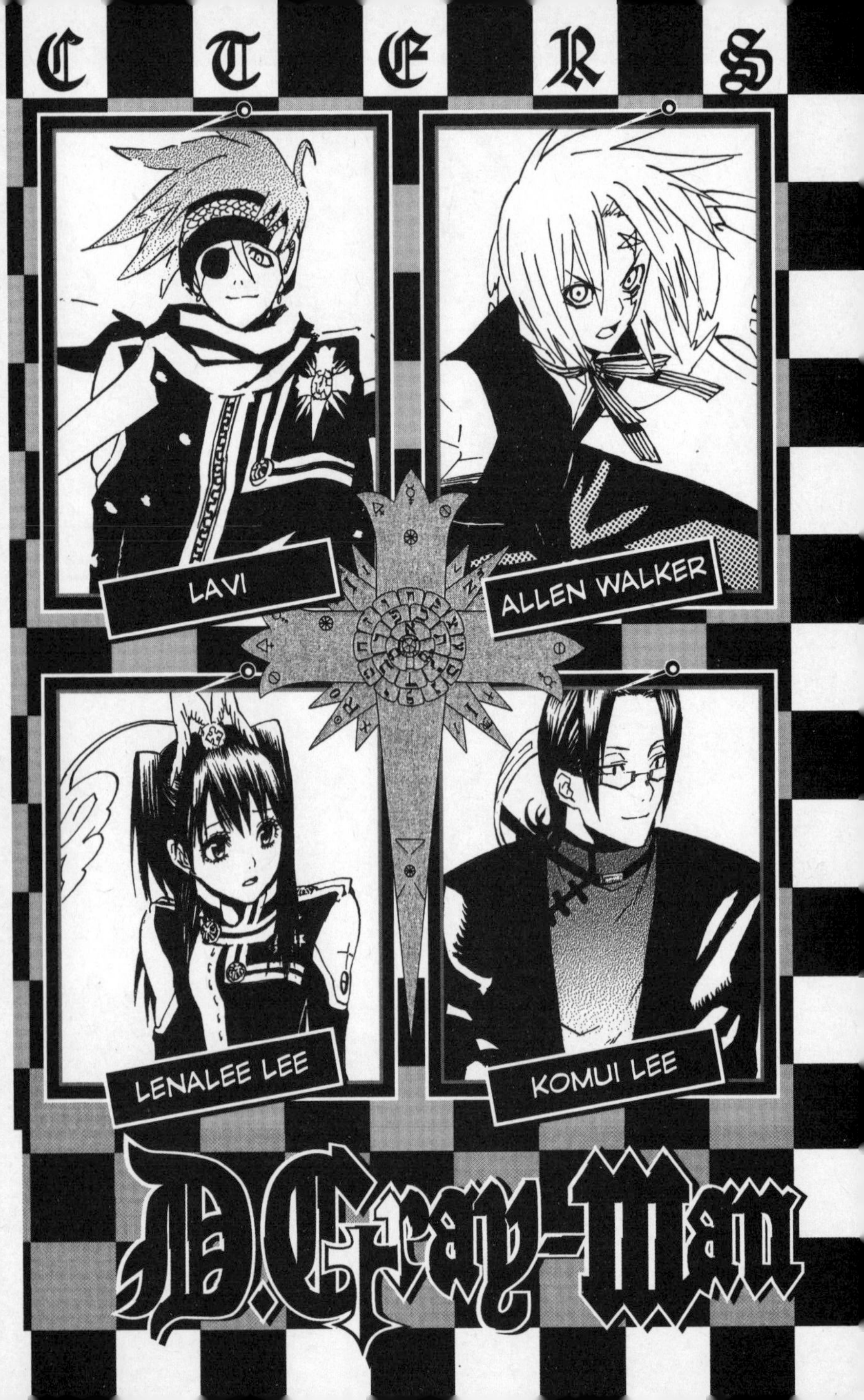
C T E R S
LAVI
ALLEN WALKER
LENALEE LEE
KOMUI LEE
D.Gray-man

CHARA

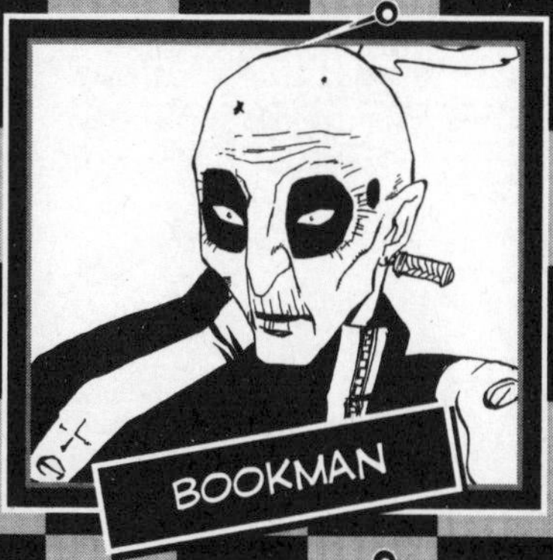
BOOKMAN

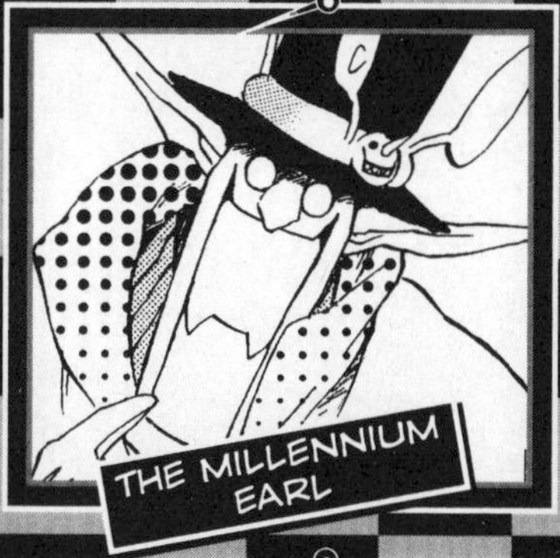
THE MILLENNIUM EARL

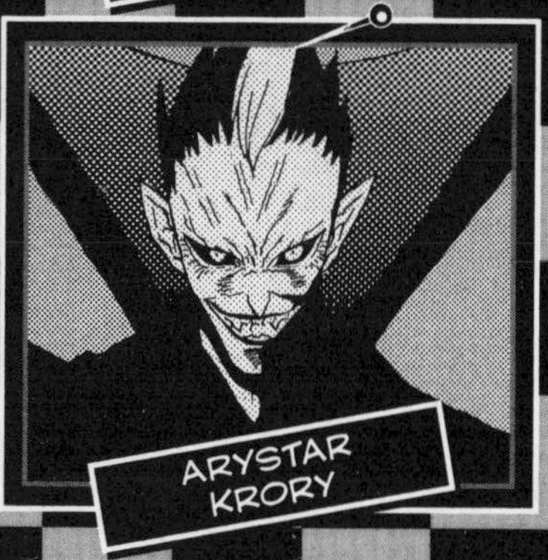
ARYSTAR KRORY

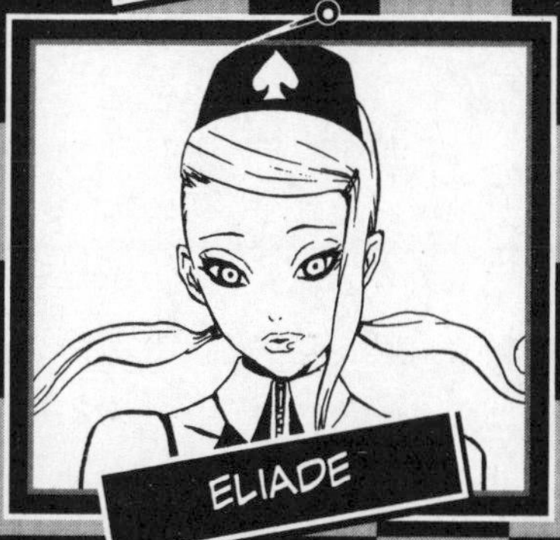
ELIADE

STORY

IT ALL BEGAN CENTURIES AGO WITH THE DISCOVERY OF A CUBE CONTAINING AN APOCALYPTIC PROPHECY FROM AN ANCIENT CIVILIZATION, AND INSTRUCTIONS IN THE USE OF INNOCENCE, A CRYSTALLINE SUBSTANCE OF WONDROUS SUPERNATURAL POWER. THE CREATORS OF THE CUBE CLAIMED TO HAVE DEFEATED AN EVIL KNOWN AS THE MILLENNIUM EARL USING THE INNOCENCE. NEVERTHELESS, THE WORLD WAS DESTROYED BY THE GREAT FLOOD OF THE OLD TESTAMENT. NOW TO AVERT A SECOND END OF THE WORLD, A GROUP OF EXORCISTS WIELDING WEAPONS MADE OF INNOCENCE MUST BATTLE THE MILLENNIUM EARL AND HIS TERRIBLE MINIONS, THE AKUMA.

IN THE MYSTERIOUS REWINDING CITY, WHERE EVERY DAY IS OCTOBER 9, ALLEN MEETS ROAD KAMELOT, A GIRL FROM THE CLAN OF NOAH, HUMAN DISCIPLES OF THE MILLENNIUM EARL. THE BATTLE THAT FOLLOWS LEAVES LENALEE IN A COMA, AND ALLEN'S SPECIAL AKUMA-SEEING EYE BADLY DAMAGED. BUT THERE IS LITTLE TIME TO RECOVER. THE AGENTS OF THE EARL ARE ON THE MOVE, AND ALLEN IS SOON THRUST INTO A STILL DARKER MYSTERY.

D.GRAY-MAN
Vol. 4

CONTENTS

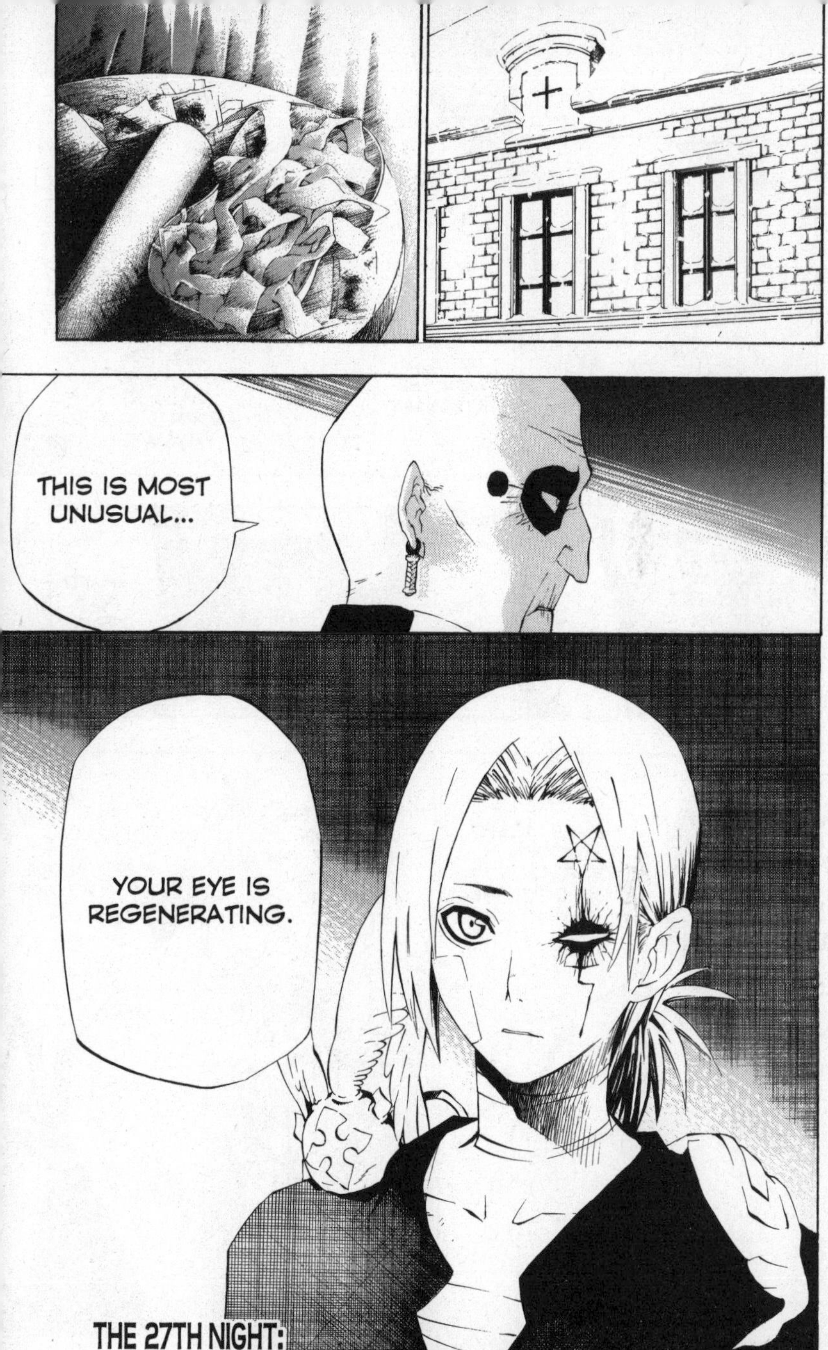
THIS IS MOST UNUSUAL...
YOUR EYE IS REGENERATING.
THE 27TH NIGHT: SLUMP

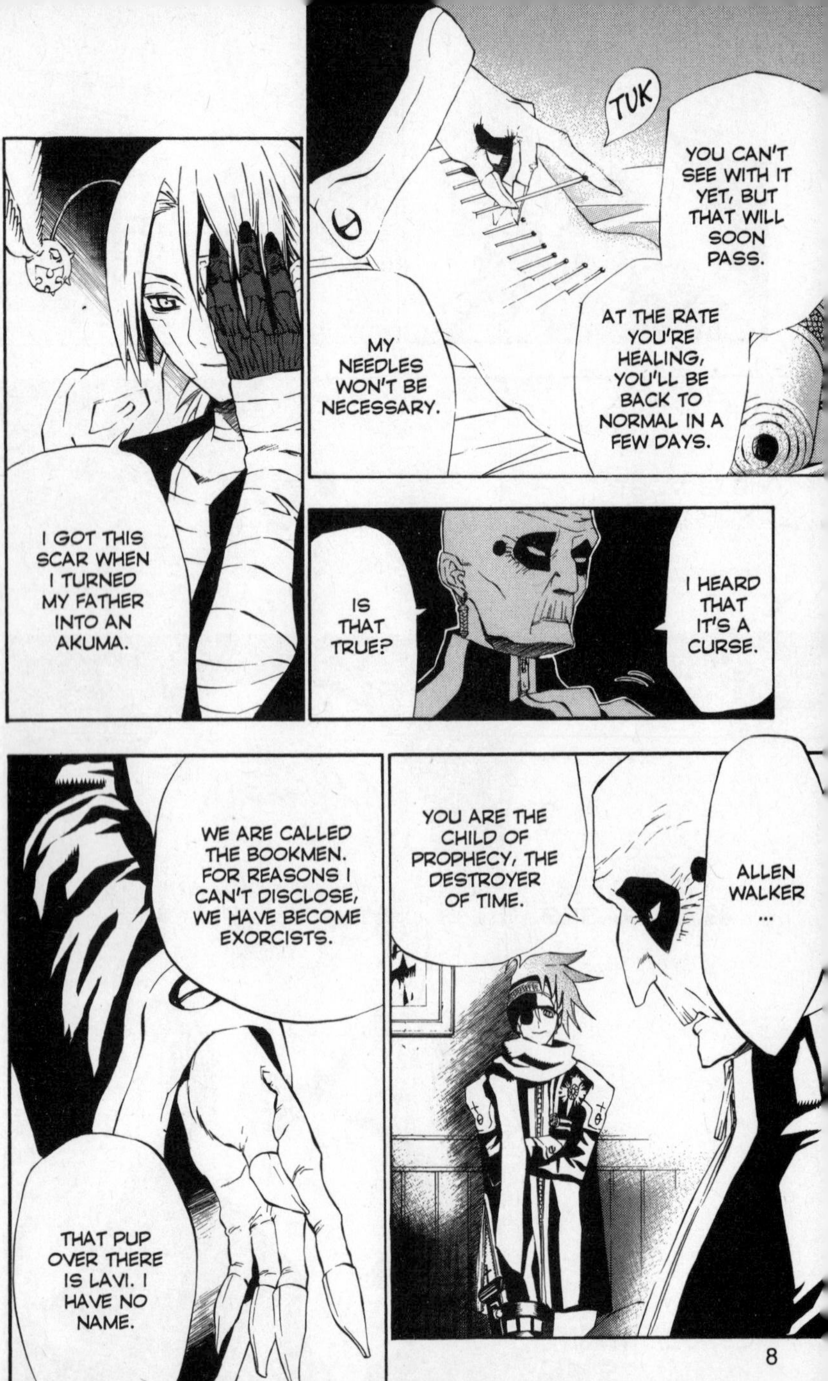
TUK
YOU CAN'T SEE WITH IT YET, BUT THAT WILL SOON PASS.
AT THE RATE YOU'RE HEALING, YOU'LL BE BACK TO NORMAL IN A FEW DAYS.
MY NEEDLES WON'T BE NECESSARY.
I HEARD THAT IT'S A CURSE.
IS THAT TRUE?
I GOT THIS SCAR WHEN I TURNED MY FATHER INTO AN AKUMA.
ALLEN WALKER ...
YOU ARE THE CHILD OF PROPHECY, THE DESTROYER OF TIME.
WE ARE CALLED THE BOOKMEN. FOR REASONS I CAN'T DISCLOSE, WE HAVE BECOME EXORCISTS.
THAT PUP OVER THERE IS LAVI. I HAVE NO NAME.

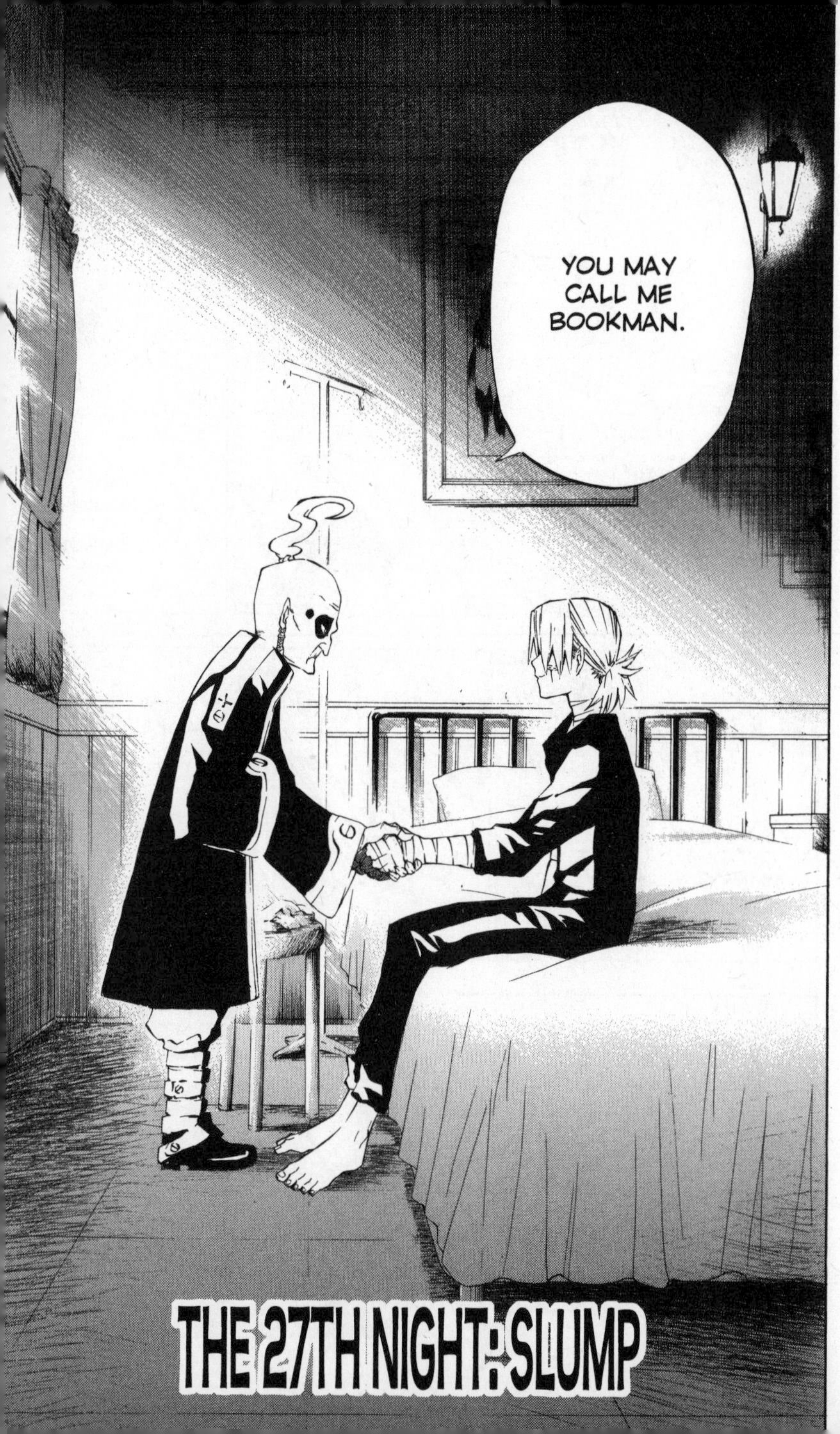
YOU MAY CALL ME BOOKMAN.
THE 27TH NIGHT: SLUMP

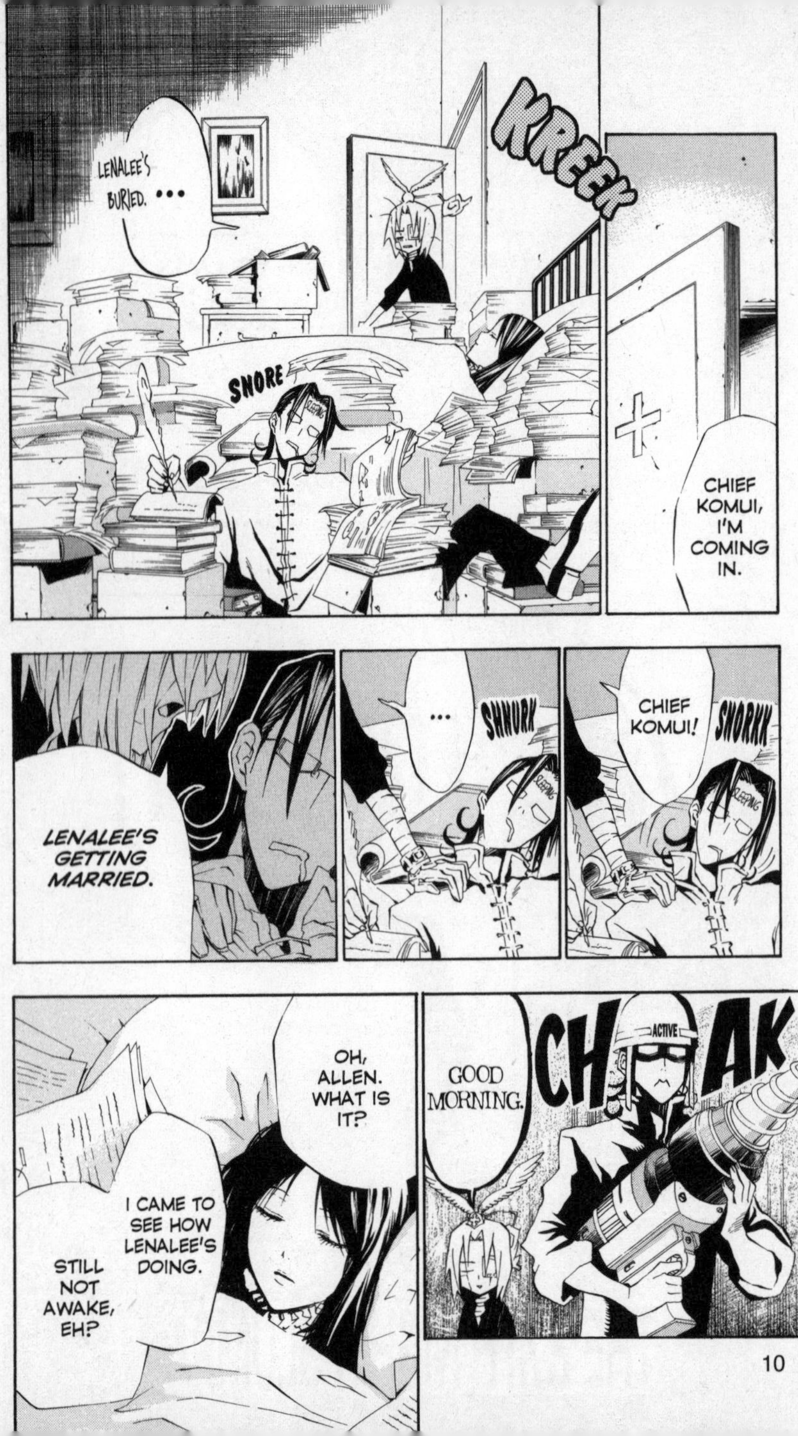
CHIEF KOMUI, I'M COMING IN.
KREEK
LENALEE'S BURIED. ...
SNORE
SLEEPING
CHIEF KOMUI!
SNORKK
SLEEPING
...
SHNURK
SLEEPING
LENALEE'S GETTING MARRIED.
CH AK
ACTIVE
GOOD MORNING.
OH, ALLEN. WHAT IS IT?
I CAME TO SEE HOW LENALEE'S DOING.
STILL NOT AWAKE, EH?

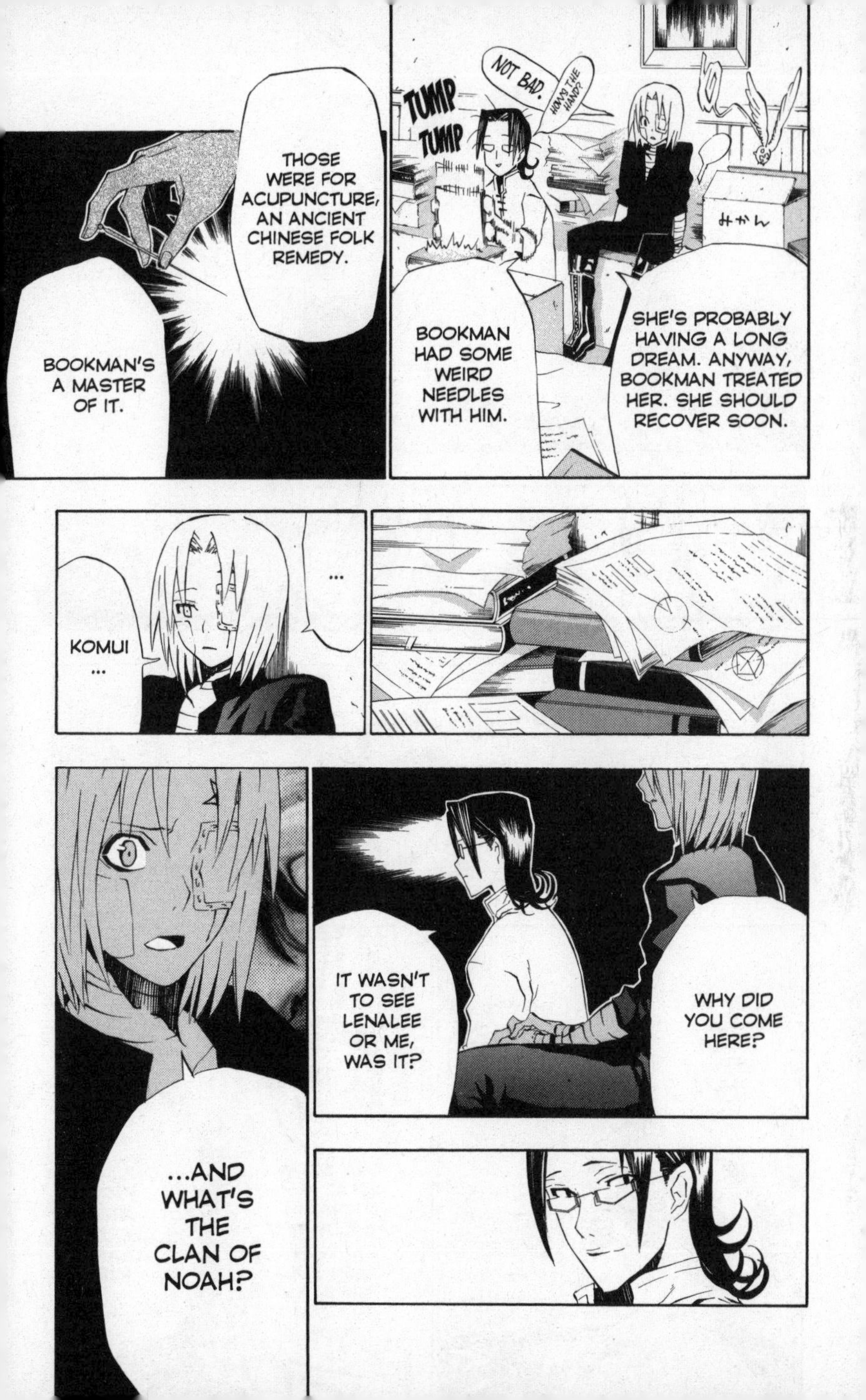
HOW'S THE HAND?
NOT BAD.
TUMP TUMP
みかん
SHE'S PROBABLY HAVING A LONG DREAM. ANYWAY, BOOKMAN TREATED HER. SHE SHOULD RECOVER SOON.
BOOKMAN HAD SOME WEIRD NEEDLES WITH HIM.
THOSE WERE FOR ACUPUNCTURE, AN ANCIENT CHINESE FOLK REMEDY.
BOOKMAN'S A MASTER OF IT.
...
KOMUI ...
WHY DID YOU COME HERE?
IT WASN'T TO SEE LENALEE OR ME, WAS IT?
...AND WHAT'S THE CLAN OF NOAH?

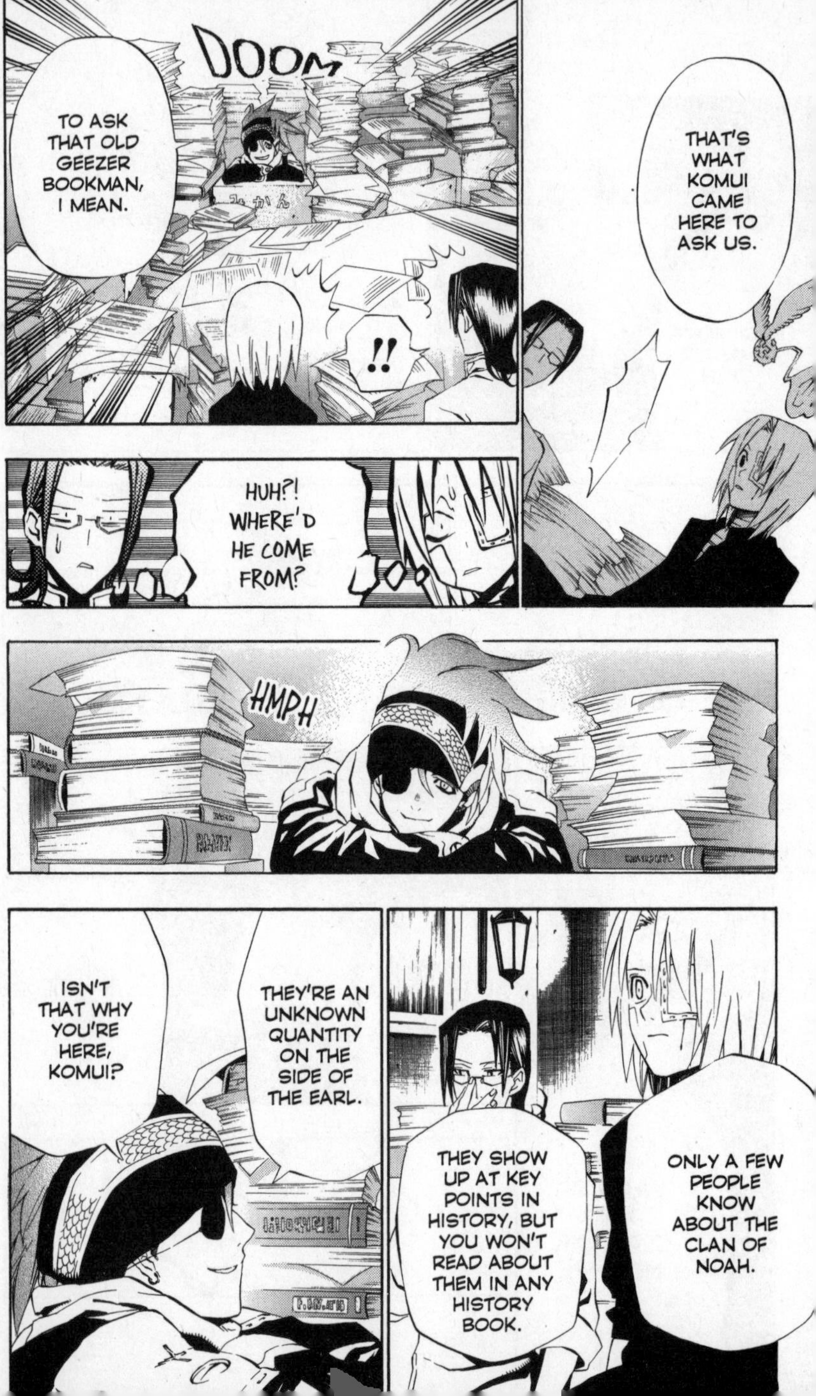
THAT'S WHAT KOMUI CAME HERE TO ASK US.
DOOM
TO ASK THAT OLD GEEZER BOOKMAN, I MEAN.
!!
HUH?! WHERE'D HE COME FROM?
HMPH
ONLY A FEW PEOPLE KNOW ABOUT THE CLAN OF NOAH.
THEY SHOW UP AT KEY POINTS IN HISTORY, BUT YOU WON'T READ ABOUT THEM IN ANY HISTORY BOOK.
THEY'RE AN UNKNOWN QUANTITY ON THE SIDE OF THE EARL.
ISN'T THAT WHY YOU'RE HERE, KOMUI?

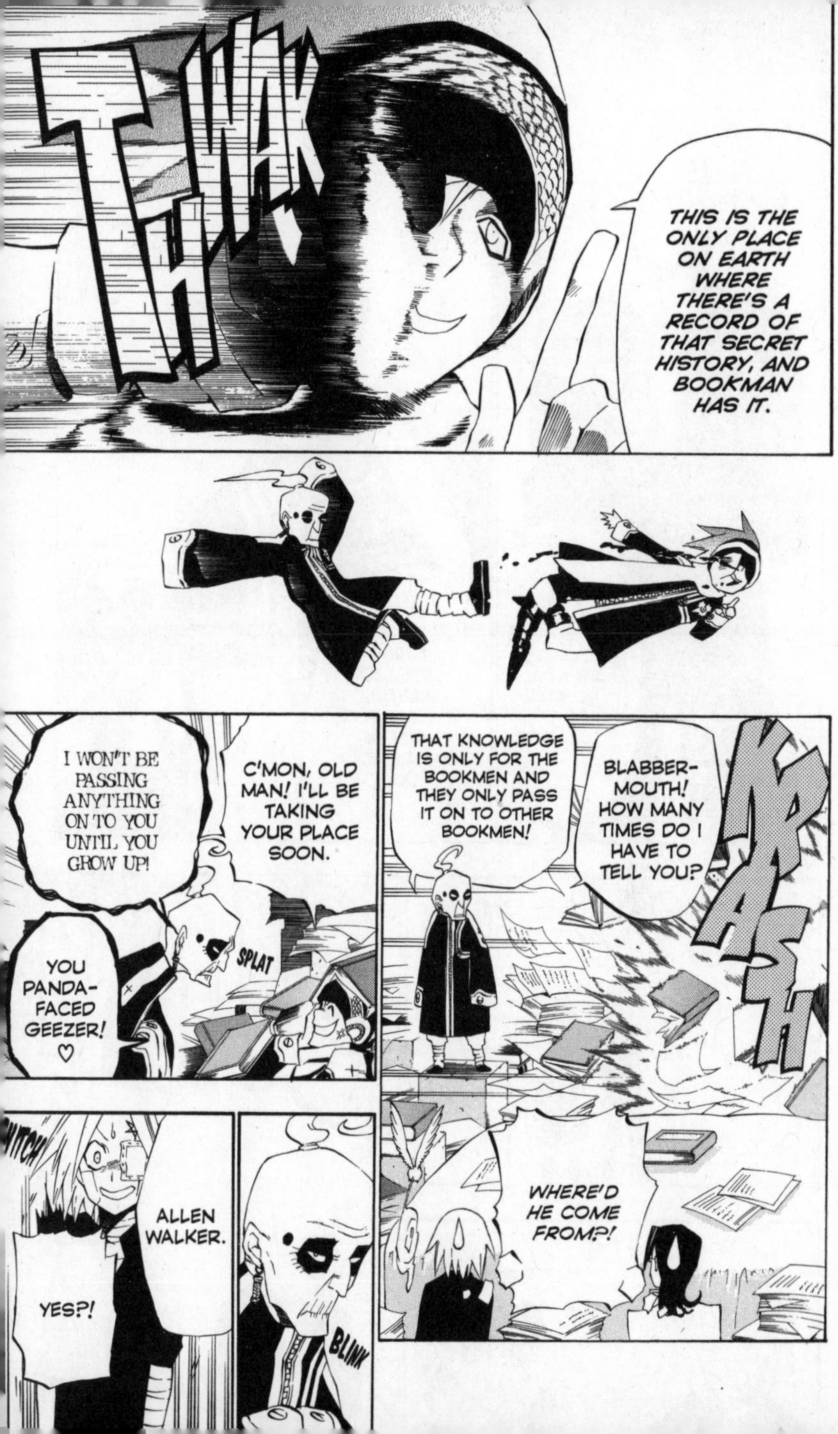

THIS IS THE ONLY PLACE ON EARTH WHERE THERE'S A RECORD OF THAT SECRET HISTORY, AND BOOKMAN HAS IT.
THWAK
KRASH
BLABBER-MOUTH! HOW MANY TIMES DO I HAVE TO TELL YOU?
THAT KNOWLEDGE IS ONLY FOR THE BOOKMEN AND THEY ONLY PASS IT ON TO OTHER BOOKMEN!
C'MON, OLD MAN! I'LL BE TAKING YOUR PLACE SOON.
I WON'T BE PASSING ANYTHING ON TO YOU UNTIL YOU GROW UP!
SPLAT
YOU PANDA-FACED GEEZER! ♡
WHERE'D HE COME FROM?!
ALLEN WALKER.
BLINK
YES?!

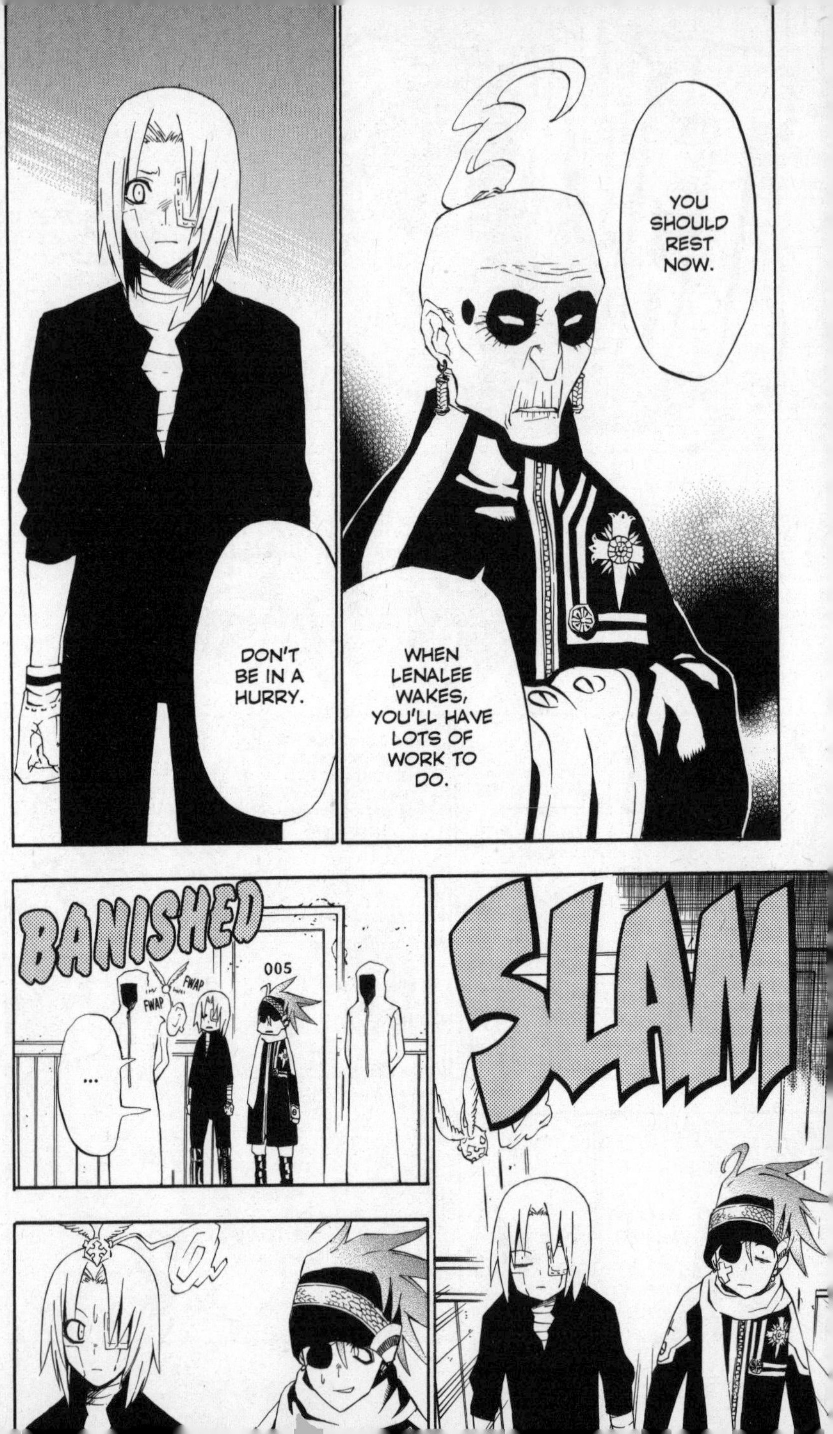
YOU SHOULD REST NOW.
WHEN LENALEE WAKES, YOU'LL HAVE LOTS OF WORK TO DO.
DON'T BE IN A HURRY.
SLAM
BANISHED
005
FWAP
FWAP
...

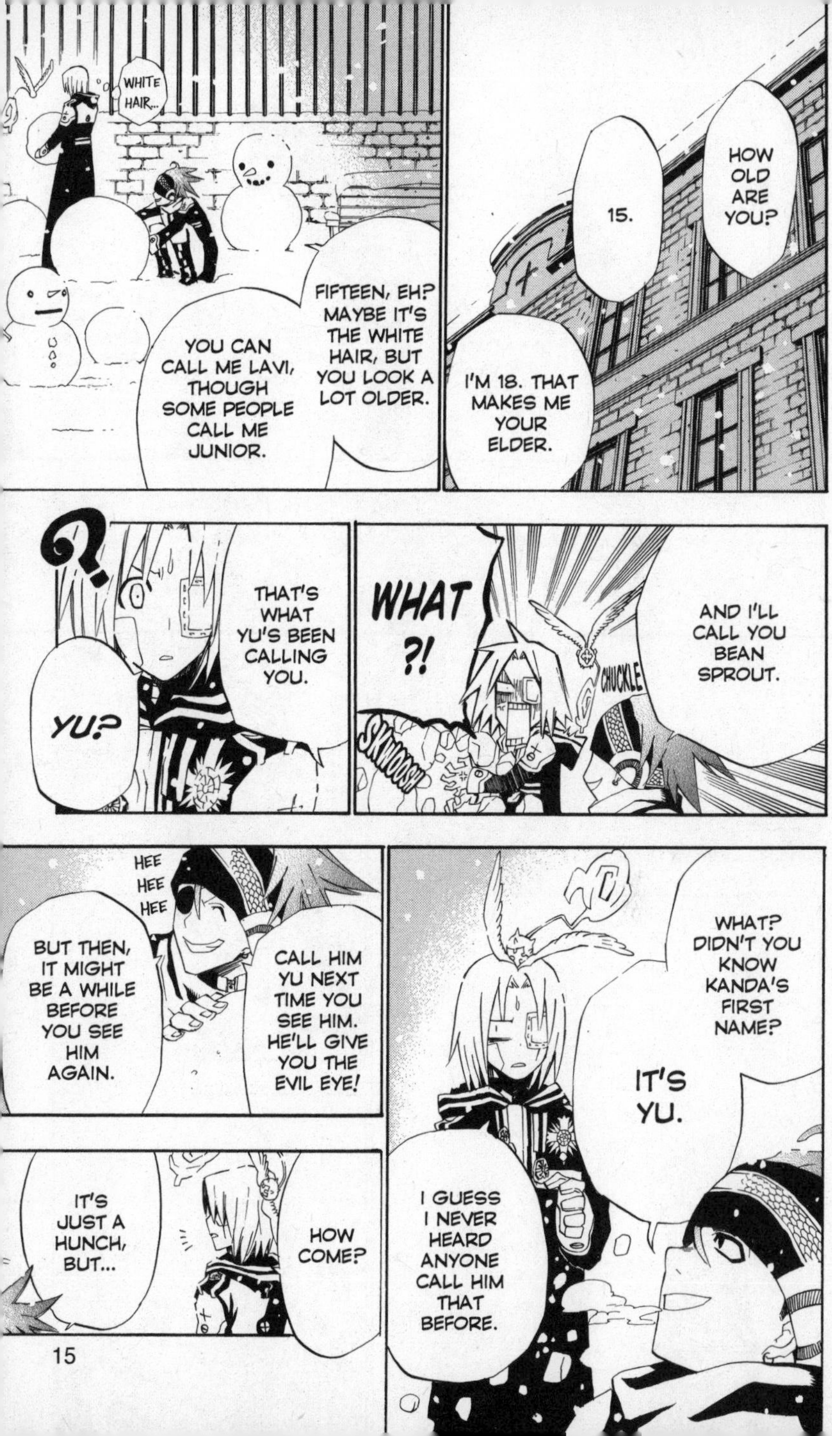
HOW OLD ARE YOU?
15.
I'M 18. THAT MAKES ME YOUR ELDER.
WHITE HAIR...
FIFTEEN, EH? MAYBE IT'S THE WHITE HAIR, BUT YOU LOOK A LOT OLDER.
YOU CAN CALL ME LAVI, THOUGH SOME PEOPLE CALL ME JUNIOR.
AND I'LL CALL YOU BEAN SPROUT.
CHUCKLE
WHAT?!
SKWOOSH
THAT'S WHAT YU'S BEEN CALLING YOU.
YU?
WHAT? DIDN'T YOU KNOW KANDA'S FIRST NAME?
IT'S YU.
I GUESS I NEVER HEARD ANYONE CALL HIM THAT BEFORE.
HEE HEE HEE
CALL HIM YU NEXT TIME YOU SEE HIM. HE'LL GIVE YOU THE EVIL EYE!
BUT THEN, IT MIGHT BE A WHILE BEFORE YOU SEE HIM AGAIN.
HOW COME?
IT'S JUST A HUNCH, BUT...

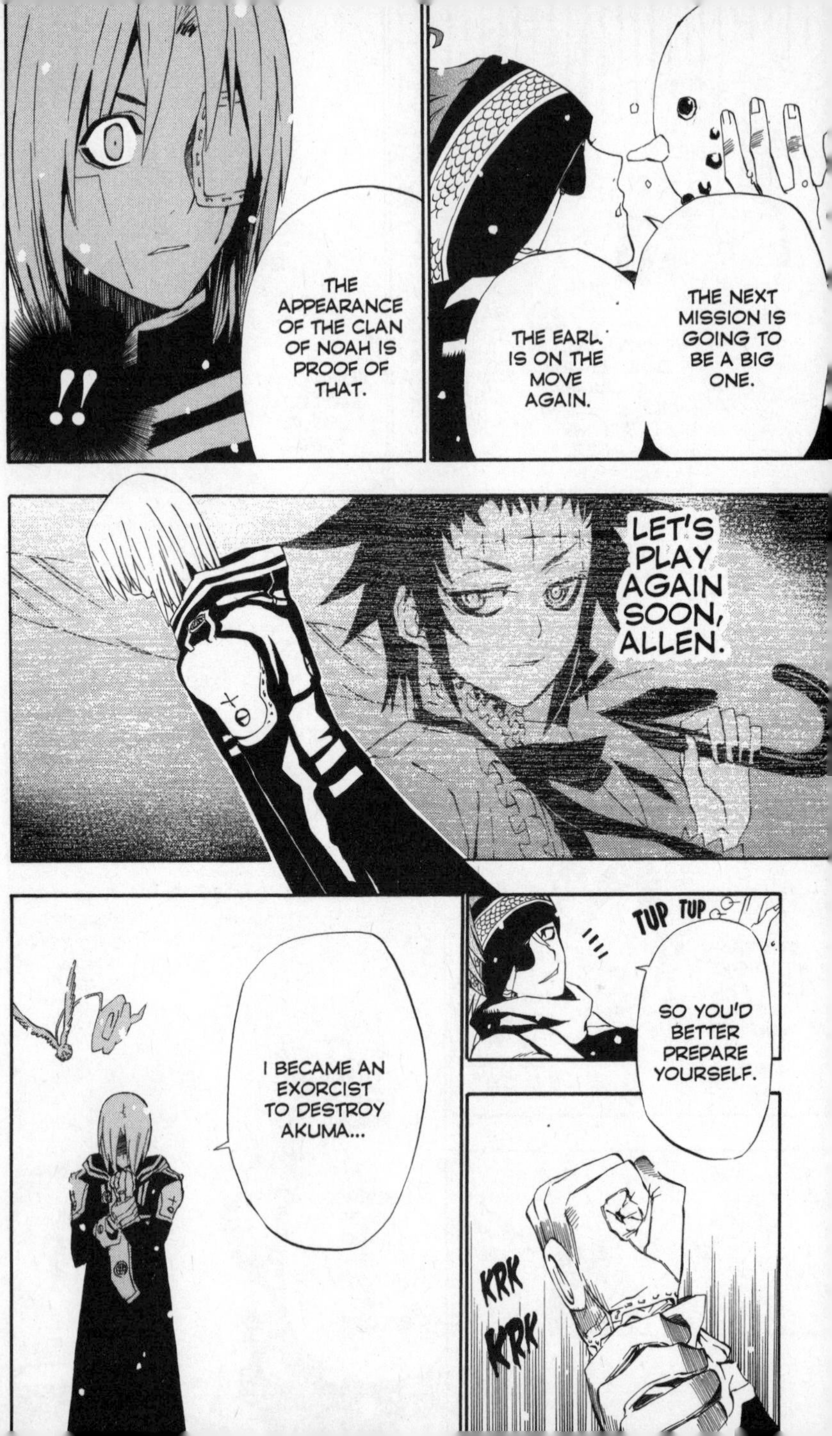
THE NEXT MISSION IS GOING TO BE A BIG ONE.
THE EARL IS ON THE MOVE AGAIN.
THE APPEARANCE OF THE CLAN OF NOAH IS PROOF OF THAT.
!!
LET'S PLAY AGAIN SOON, ALLEN.
TUP TUP
SO YOU'D BETTER PREPARE YOURSELF.
KRK KRK
I BECAME AN EXORCIST TO DESTROY AKUMA...

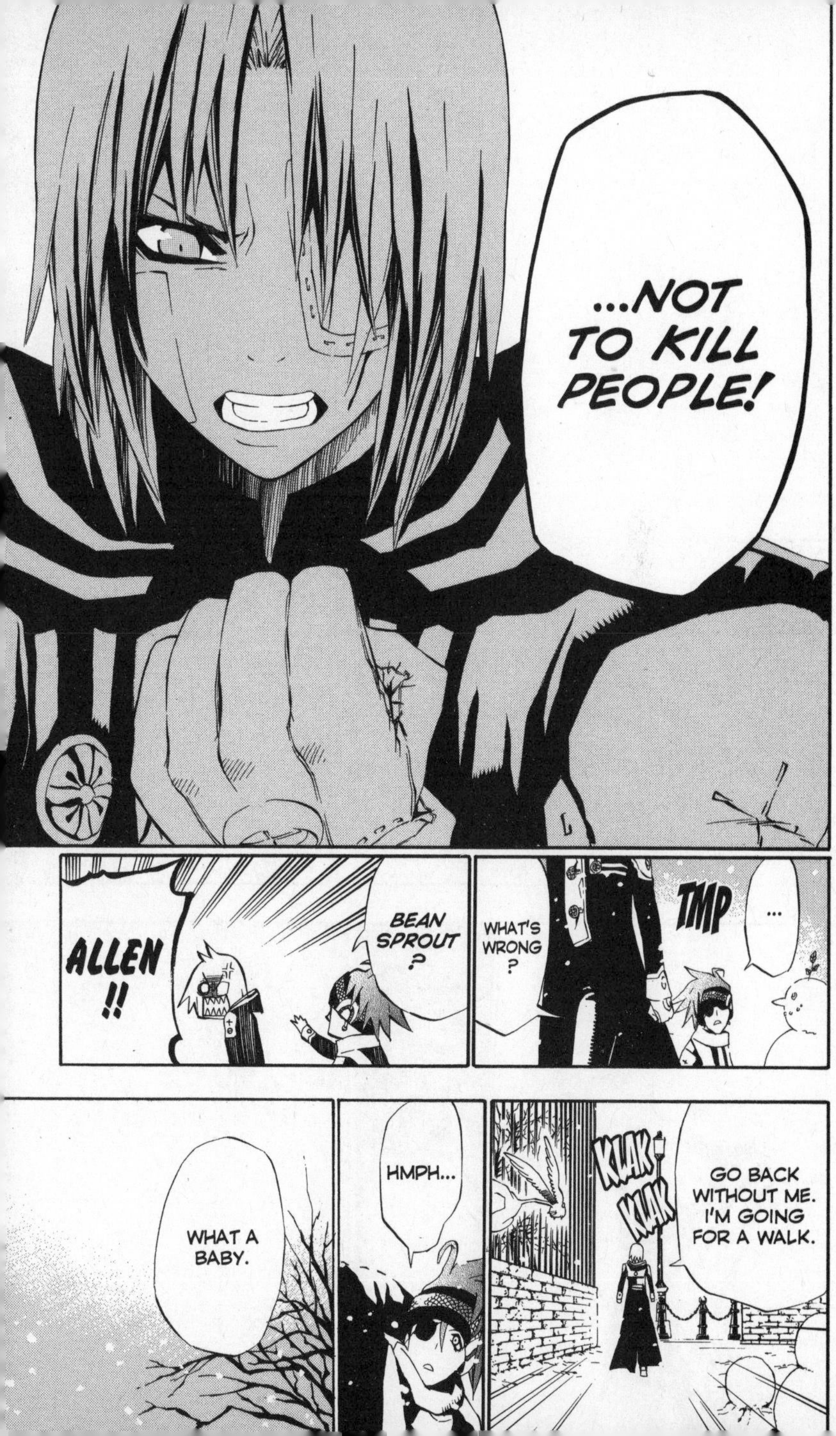
...NOT TO KILL PEOPLE!
...
TMP
WHAT'S WRONG?
BEAN SPROUT?
ALLEN!!
GO BACK WITHOUT ME. I'M GOING FOR A WALK.
KLAK KLAK
HMPH...
WHAT A BABY.

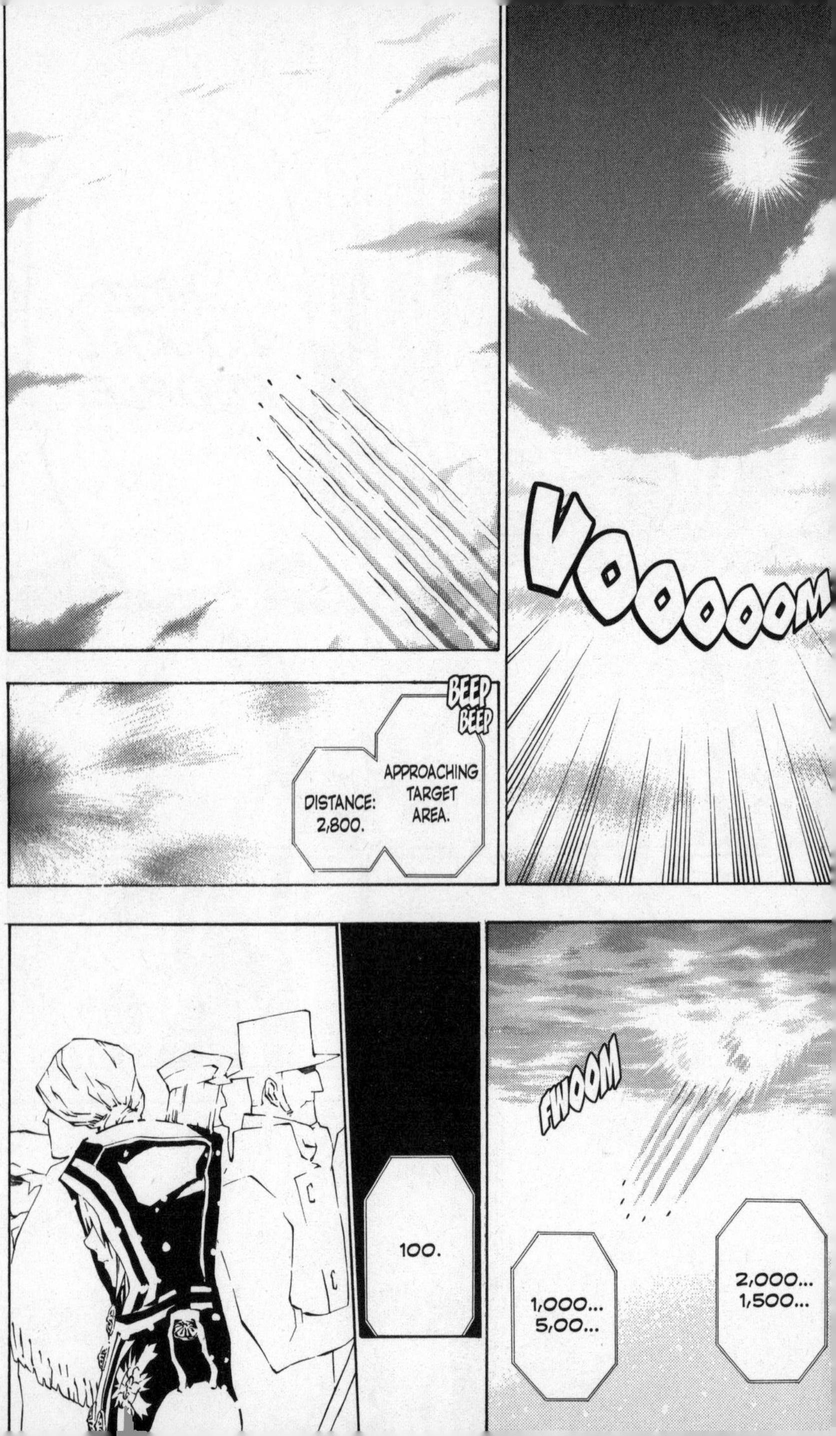
VOOOOOM
BEEP BEEP
APPROACHING TARGET AREA.
DISTANCE: 2,800.
FWOOM
2,000... 1,500...
1,000... 5,00...
100.

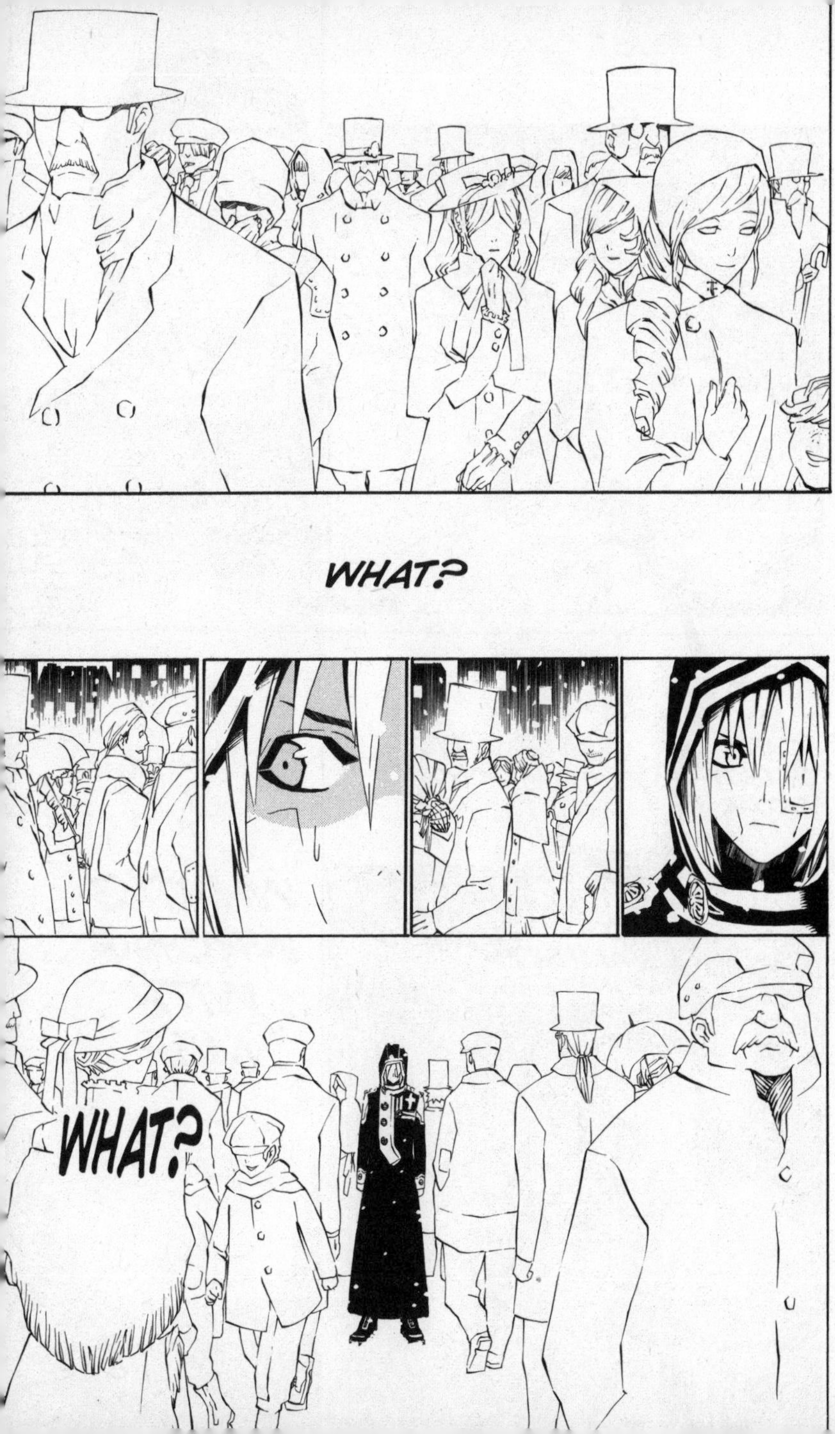
WHAT?
WHAT?

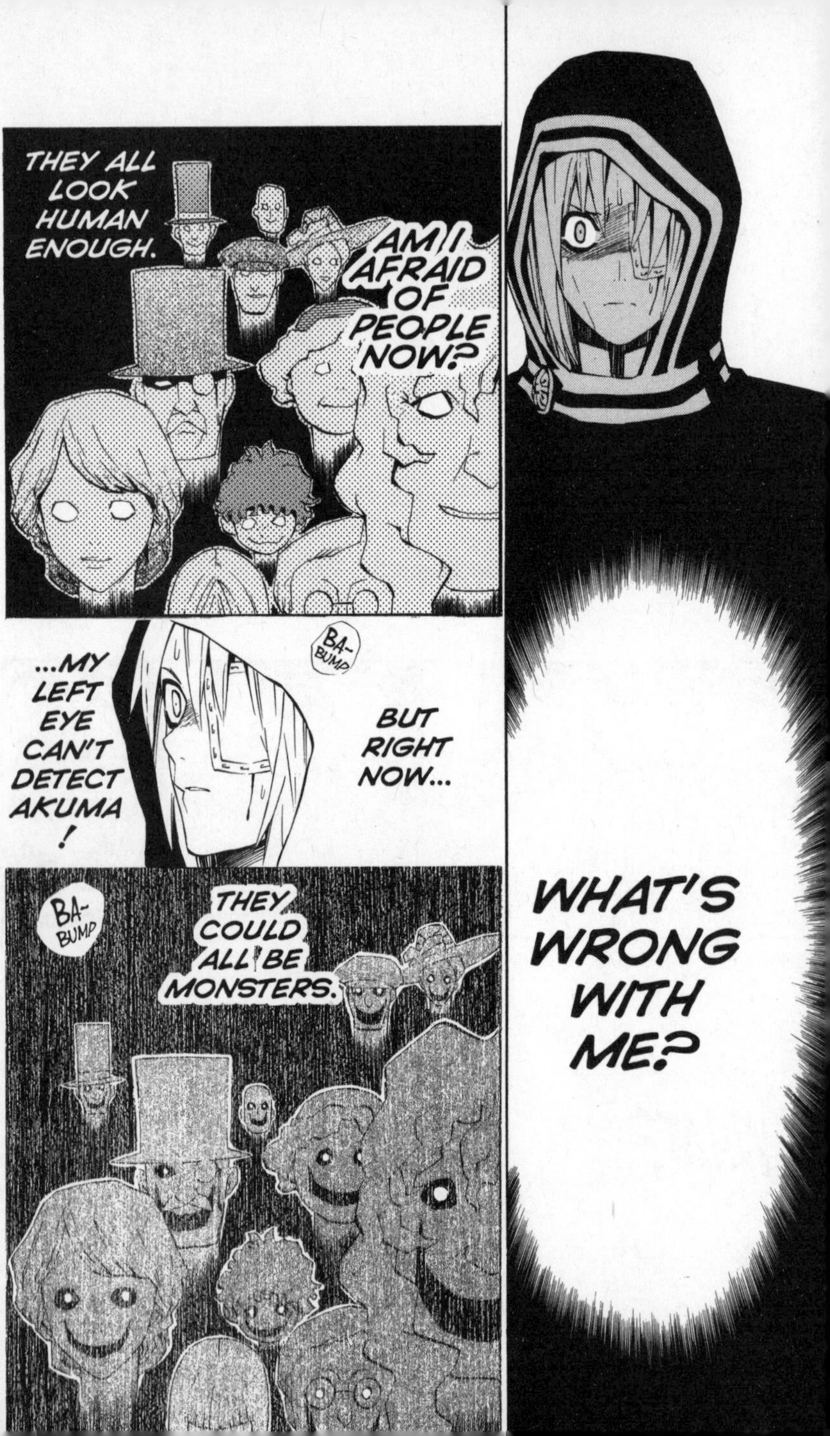
WHAT'S WRONG WITH ME?
THEY ALL LOOK HUMAN ENOUGH.
AM I AFRAID OF PEOPLE NOW?
BA-BUMP
BUT RIGHT NOW...
...MY LEFT EYE CAN'T DETECT AKUMA!
THEY COULD ALL BE MONSTERS.
BA-BUMP

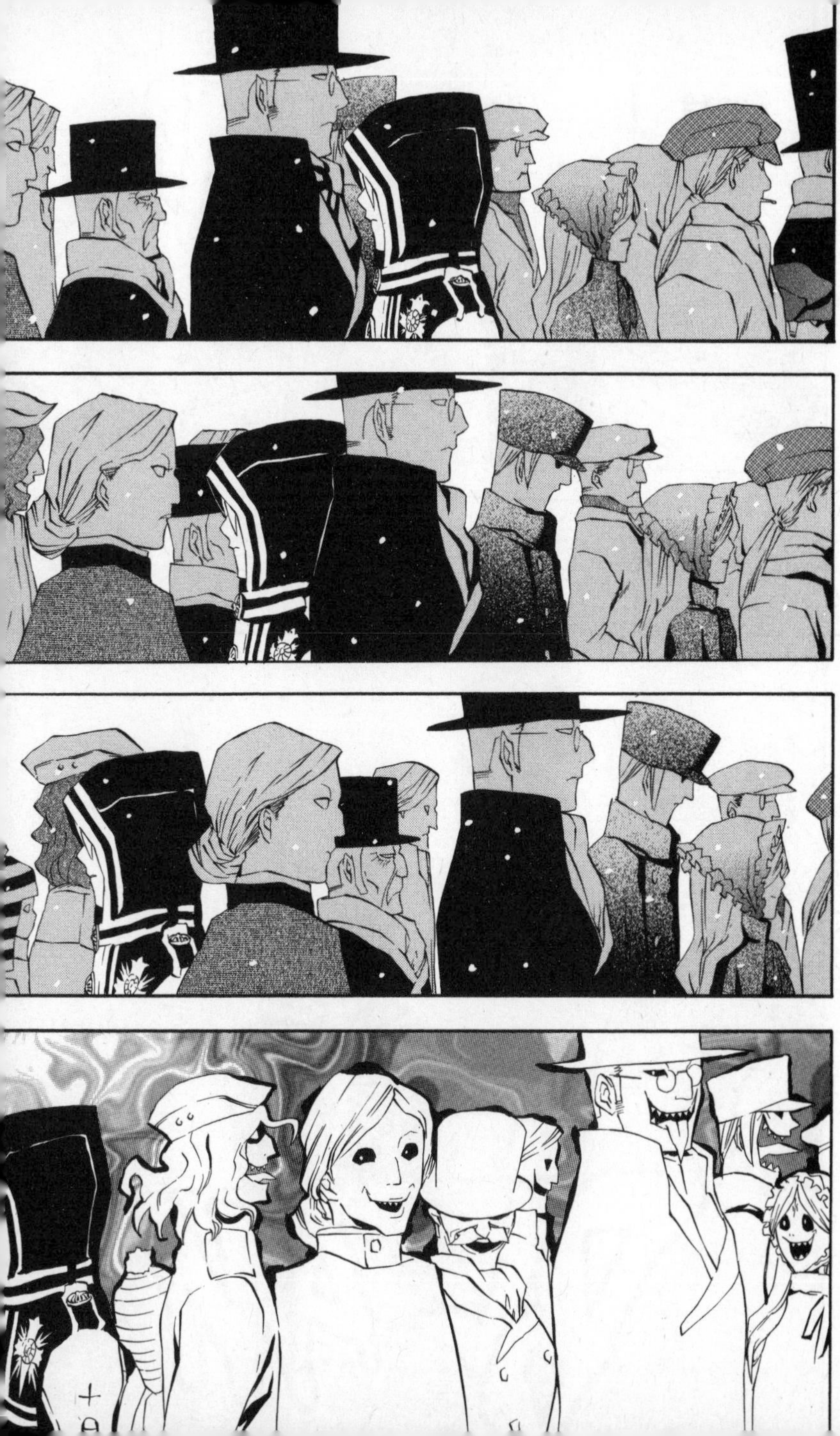

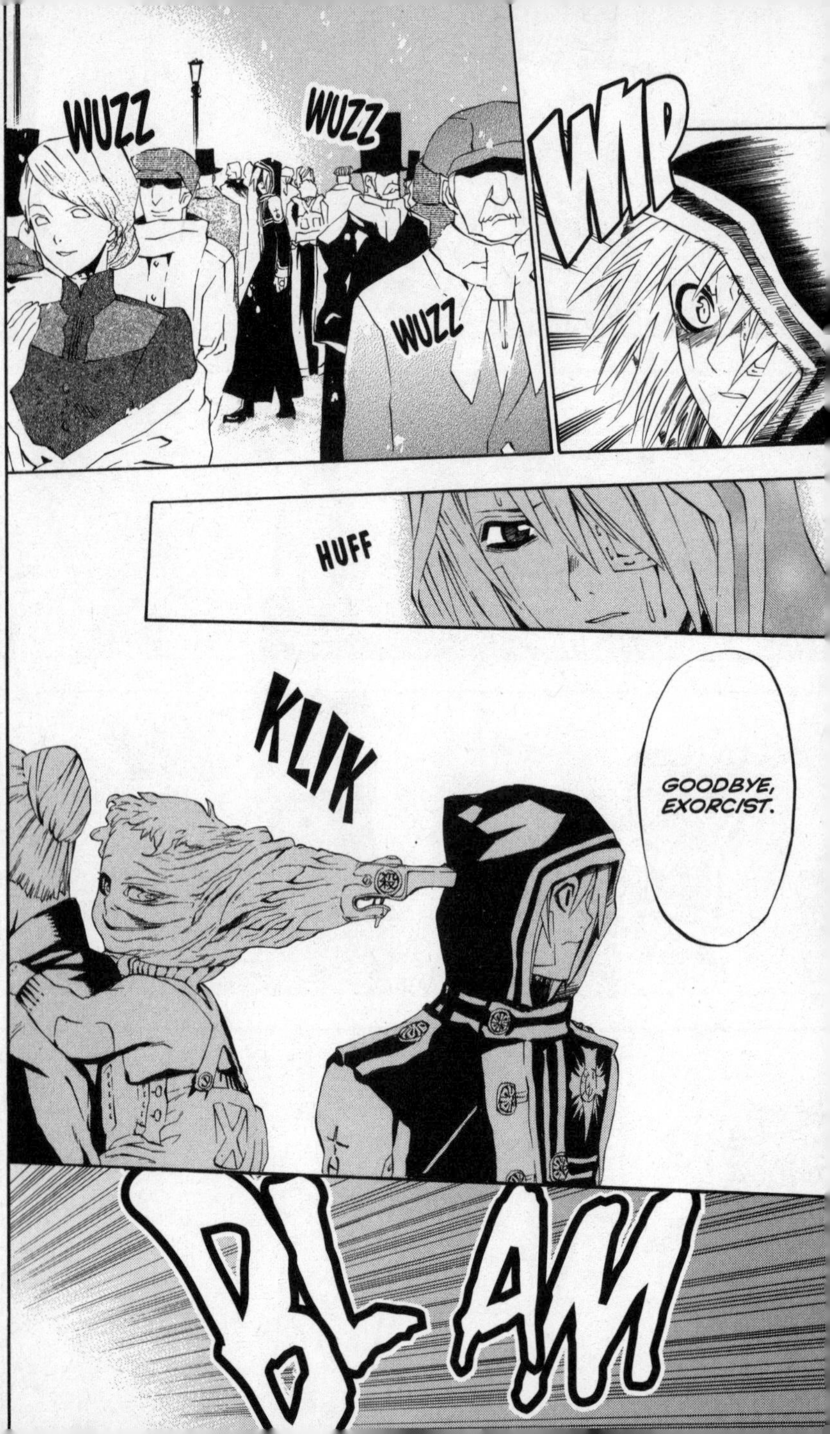
WMP
WUZZ
WUZZ
WUZZ
HUFF
GOODBYE, EXORCIST.
KLIK
BLAM

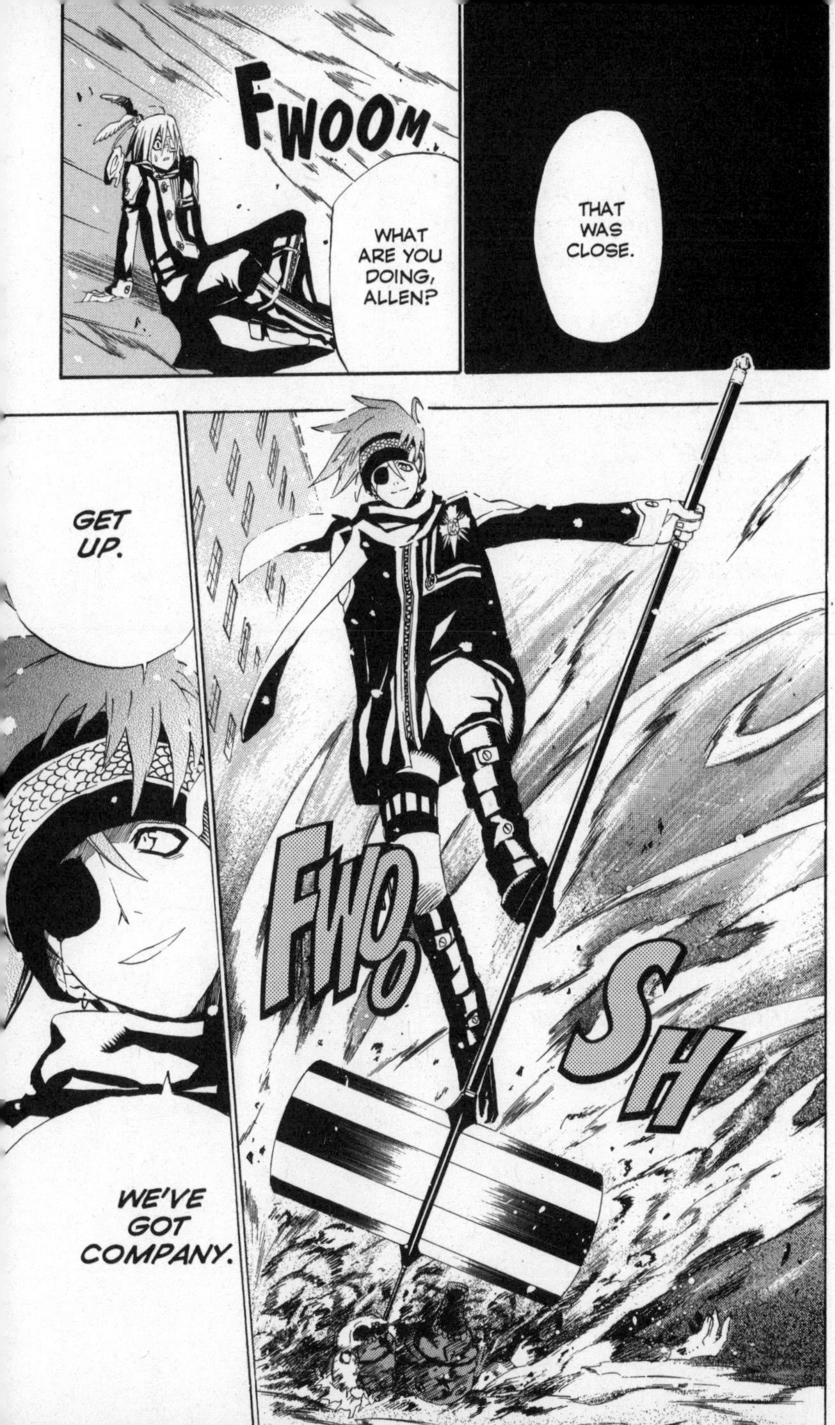
THAT WAS CLOSE.
FWOOM
WHAT ARE YOU DOING, ALLEN?
FWOOSH
GET UP.
WE'VE GOT COMPANY.

LAVI

HE GAVE UP HIS REAL NAME
WHEN HE DECIDED TO BECOME
BOOKMAN'S SUCCESSOR.
RACE MONGREL
NATIONALITY UNKNOWN
AGE 18
HEIGHT 177CM
WEIGHT 68KG
BIRTHDAY AUGUST 10
SIGN LEO
BLOOD TYPE O

ORIGINALLY LAVI WAS
GOING TO BE THE MAIN
CHARACTER OF A SERIES
CALLED BOOK-MAN, WHICH
DIDN'T HAPPEN. BUT I
REALLY LIKED HIM SO I'M
GLAD I FINALLY GOT TO USE
HIM. THE SECRET HISTORY
OF THE WORLD AND THE
ROLE OF THE BOOKMAN ARE
KEY POINTS IN THE STORY
OF D.GRAY-MAN. THE
REASON LAVI WEARS A
PATCH OVER HIS RIGHT
EYE WILL BE REVEALED
EVENTUALLY (IF THE
SERIES LASTS.) PLEASE
BE PATIENT.

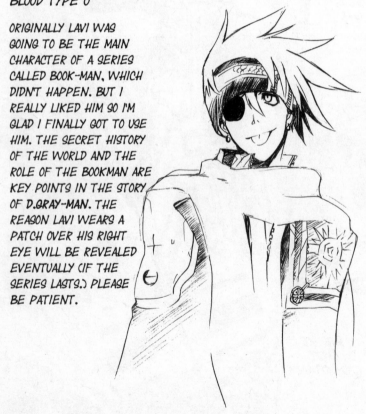

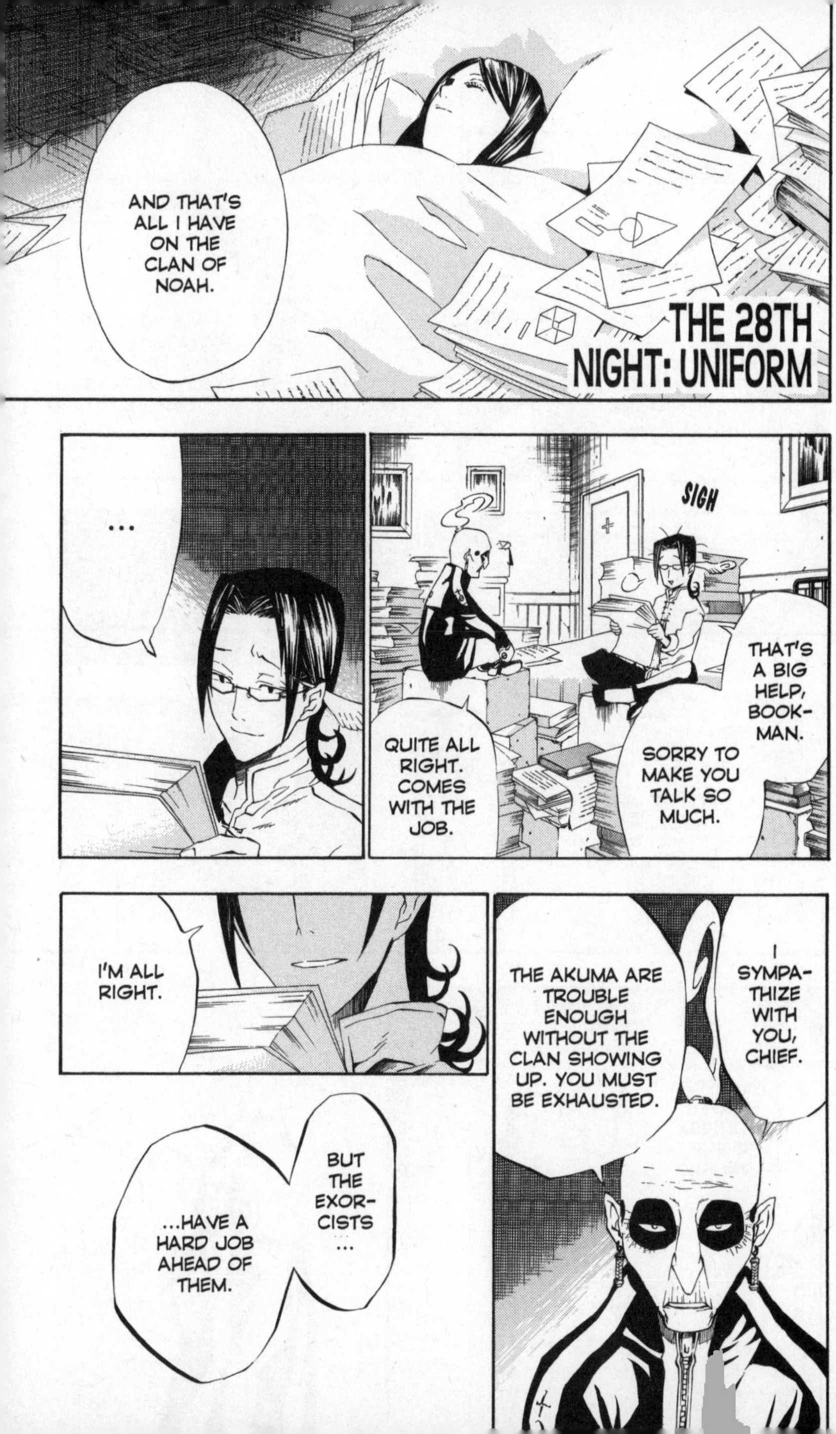
AND THAT'S ALL I HAVE ON THE CLAN OF NOAH.
THE 28TH NIGHT: UNIFORM
SIGH
THAT'S A BIG HELP, BOOKMAN.
SORRY TO MAKE YOU TALK SO MUCH.
QUITE ALL RIGHT. COMES WITH THE JOB.
...
I SYMPATHIZE WITH YOU, CHIEF.
THE AKUMA ARE TROUBLE ENOUGH WITHOUT THE CLAN SHOWING UP. YOU MUST BE EXHAUSTED.
I'M ALL RIGHT.
BUT THE EXORCISTS...
...HAVE A HARD JOB AHEAD OF THEM.

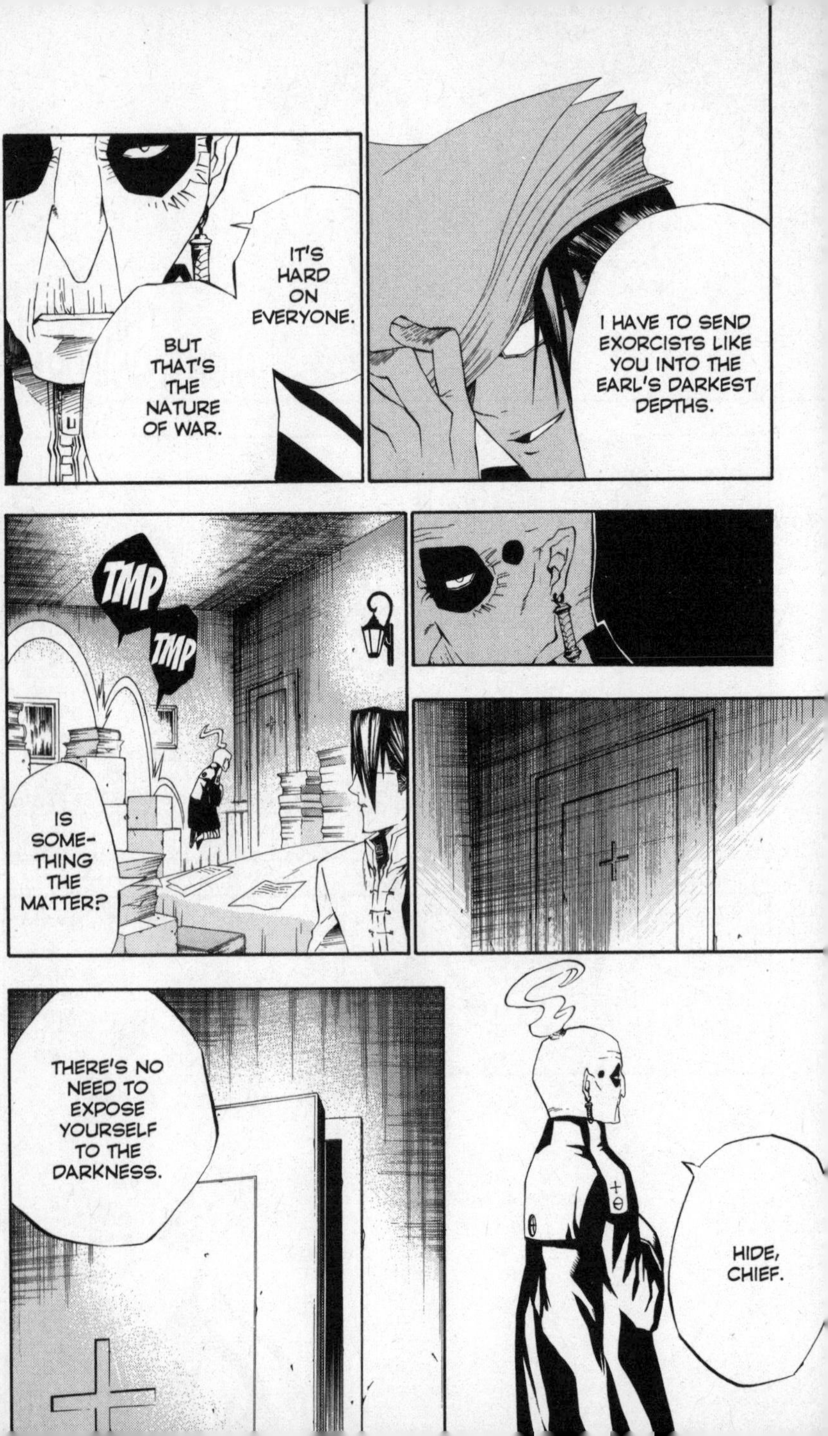
I HAVE TO SEND EXORCISTS LIKE YOU INTO THE EARL'S DARKEST DEPTHS.
IT'S HARD ON EVERYONE.
BUT THAT'S THE NATURE OF WAR.
TMP
TMP
IS SOME-THING THE MATTER?
HIDE, CHIEF.
THERE'S NO NEED TO EXPOSE YOURSELF TO THE DARKNESS.

THE 28TH NIGHT: UNIFORM

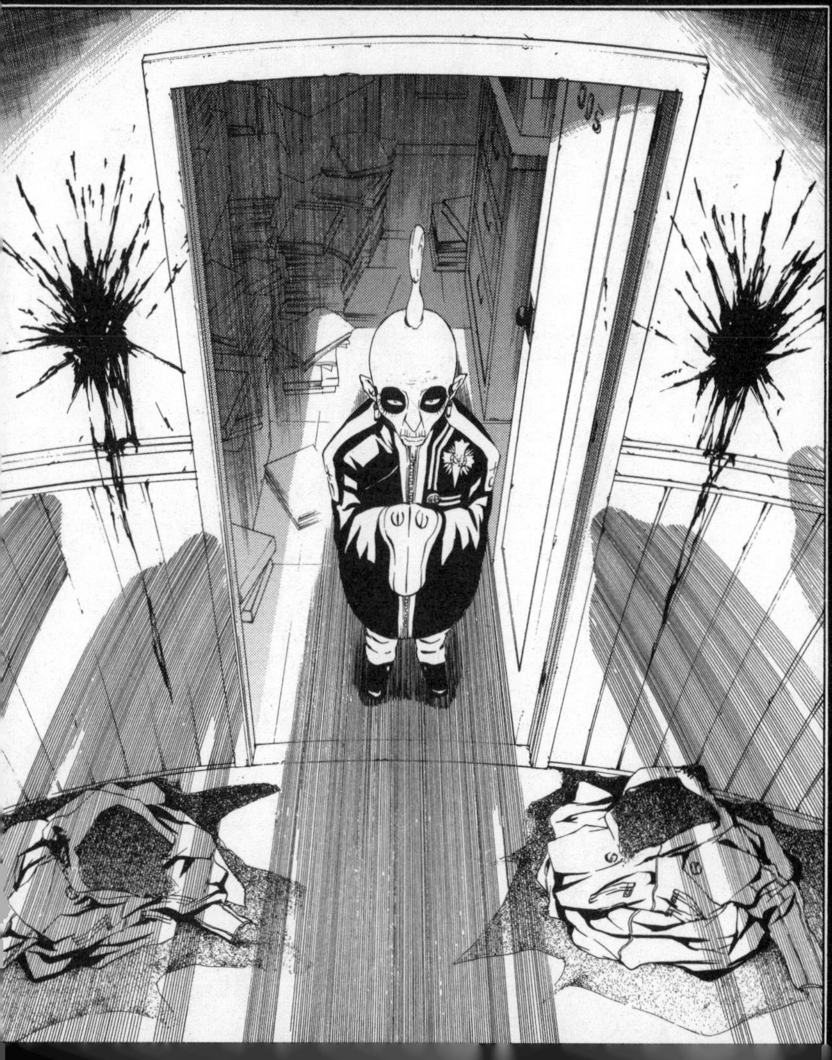

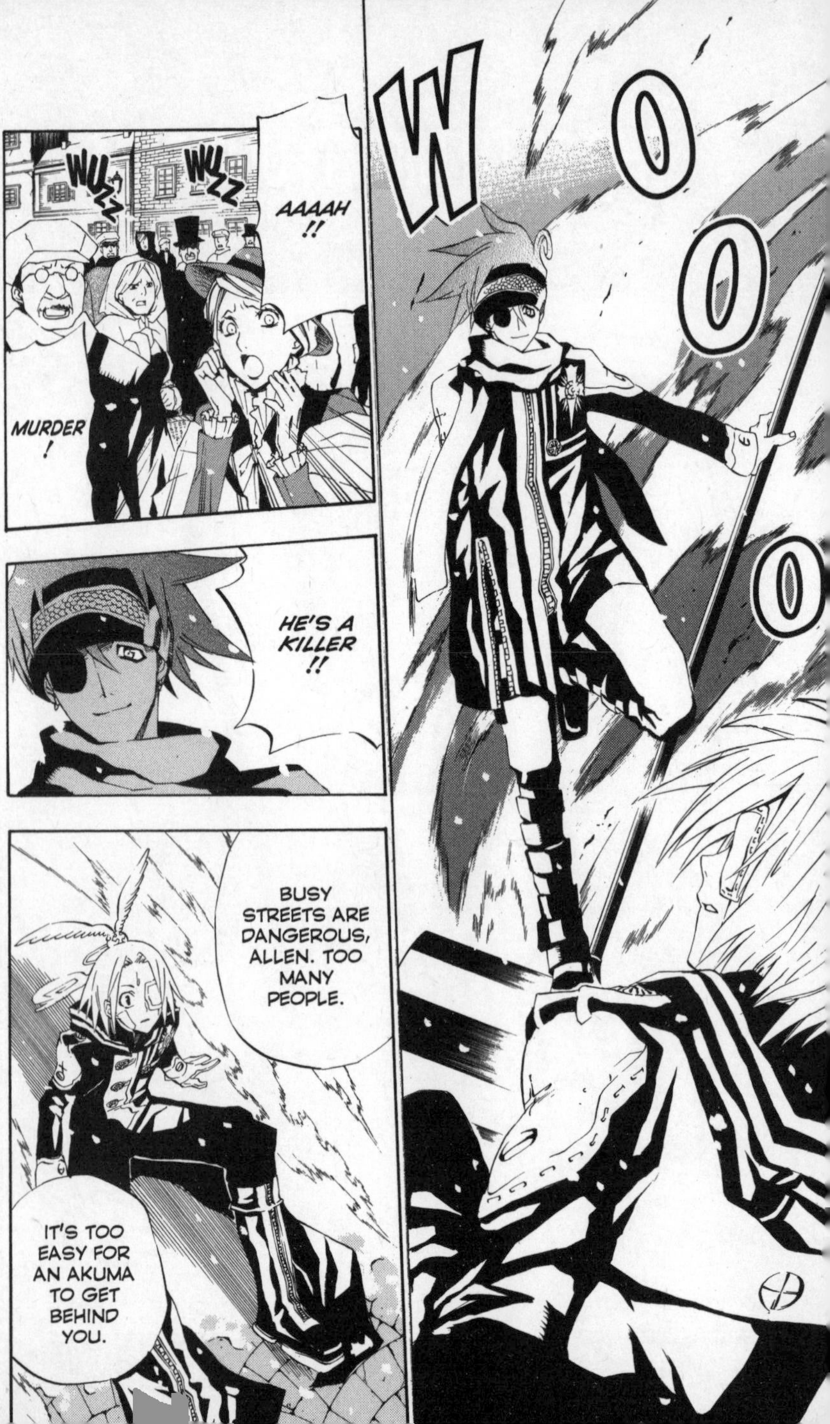
WOOO
AAAAH!!
WUZZ
WUZZ
MURDER!
HE'S A KILLER!!
BUSY STREETS ARE DANGEROUS, ALLEN. TOO MANY PEOPLE.
IT'S TOO EASY FOR AN AKUMA TO GET BEHIND YOU.

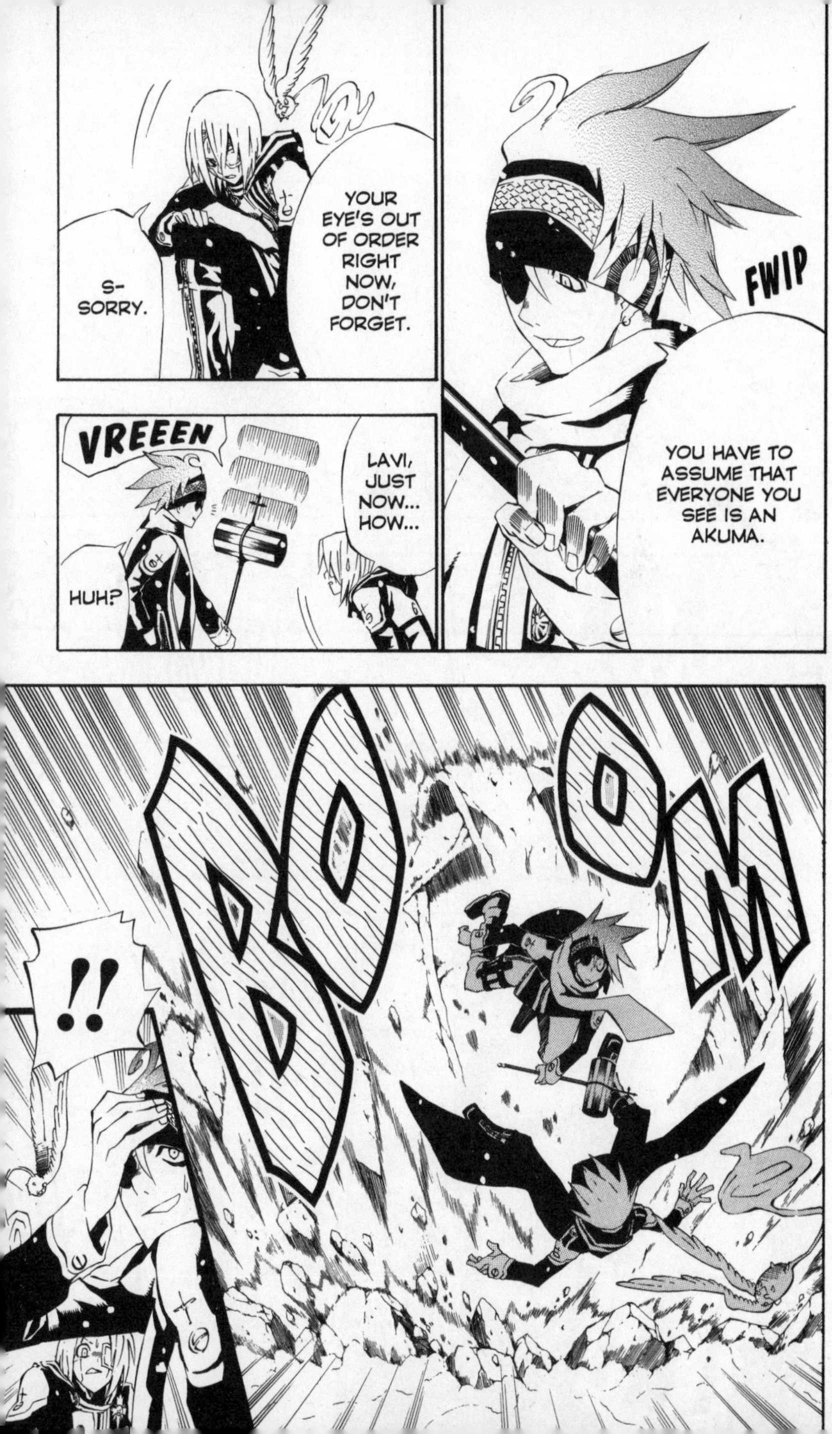
FWIP
YOU HAVE TO ASSUME THAT EVERYONE YOU SEE IS AN AKUMA.
YOUR EYE'S OUT OF ORDER RIGHT NOW, DON'T FORGET.
S-SORRY.
LAVI, JUST NOW... HOW...
VREEEN
HUH?
BOOM
!!

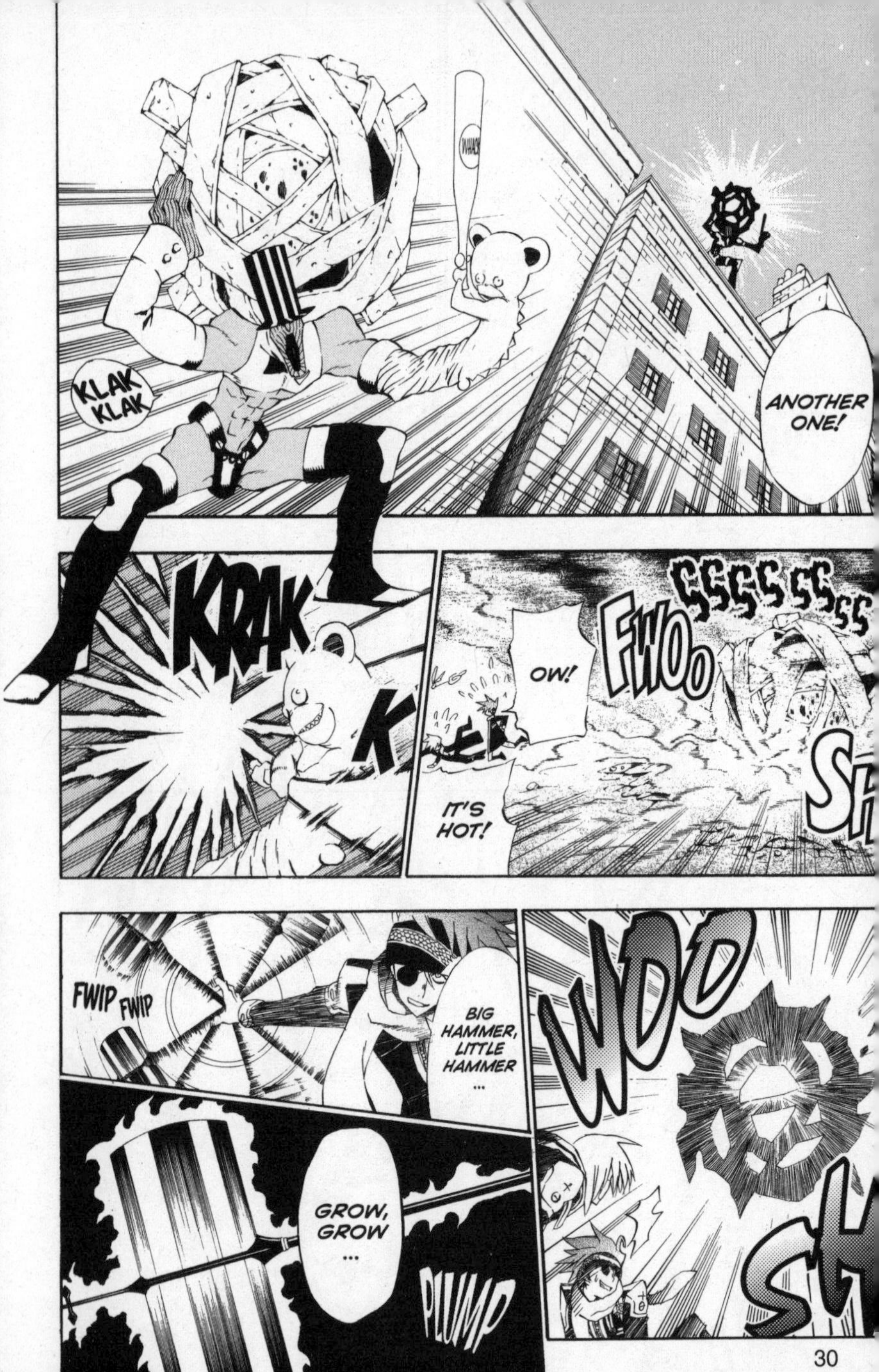
ANOTHER ONE!
WHACK
KLAK KLAK
SSSSSSSS
FWOO
OW!
IT'S HOT!
KRAK
K
WOO
FWIP FWIP
BIG HAMMER, LITTLE HAMMER ...
GROW, GROW ...
PLUMP

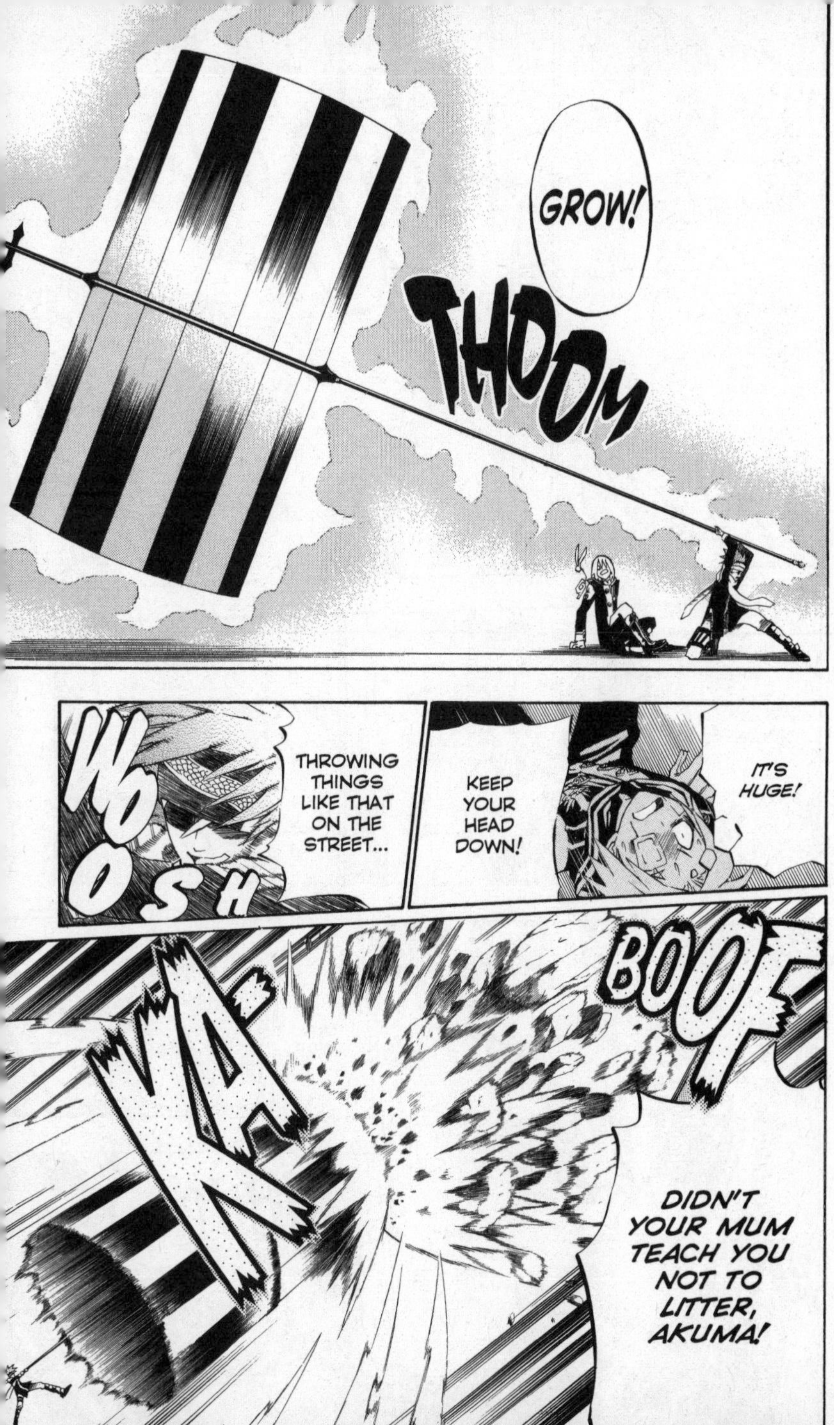
GROW!
THOOM
IT'S HUGE!
KEEP YOUR HEAD DOWN!
THROWING THINGS LIKE THAT ON THE STREET...
WOOSH
BOOF
KA-
DIDN'T YOUR MUM TEACH YOU NOT TO LITTER, AKUMA!

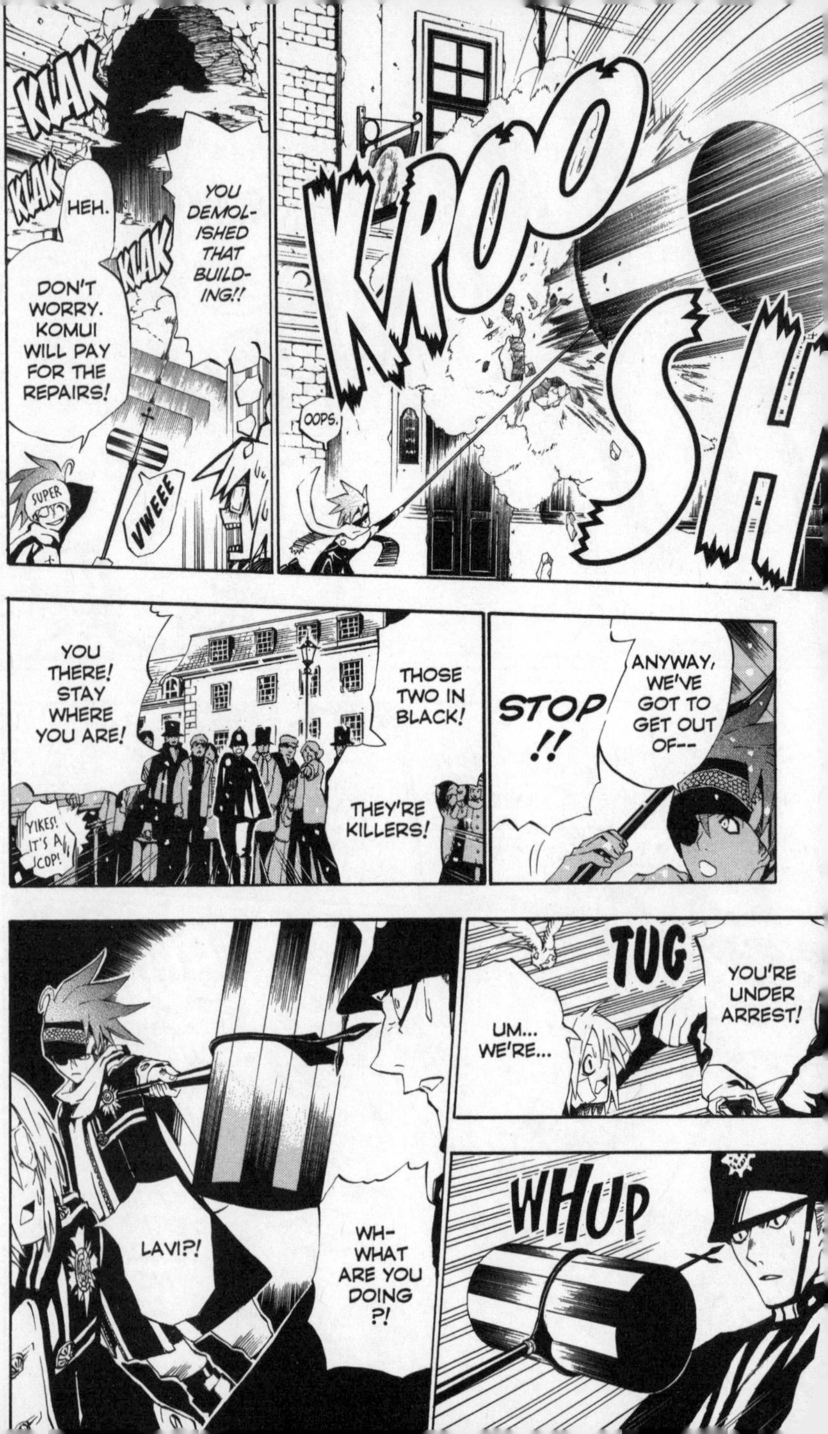
KROOSH
OOPS.
YOU DEMOLISHED THAT BUILDING!!
HEH.
KLAK
KLAK
KLAK
DON'T WORRY. KOMUI WILL PAY FOR THE REPAIRS!
VWEEE
SUPER
ANYWAY, WE'VE GOT TO GET OUT OF--
STOP!!
THOSE TWO IN BLACK!
YOU THERE! STAY WHERE YOU ARE!
THEY'RE KILLERS!
YIKES! IT'S A COP!
YOU'RE UNDER ARREST!
TUG
UM... WE'RE...
WHUP
WH-WHAT ARE YOU DOING?!
LAVI?!

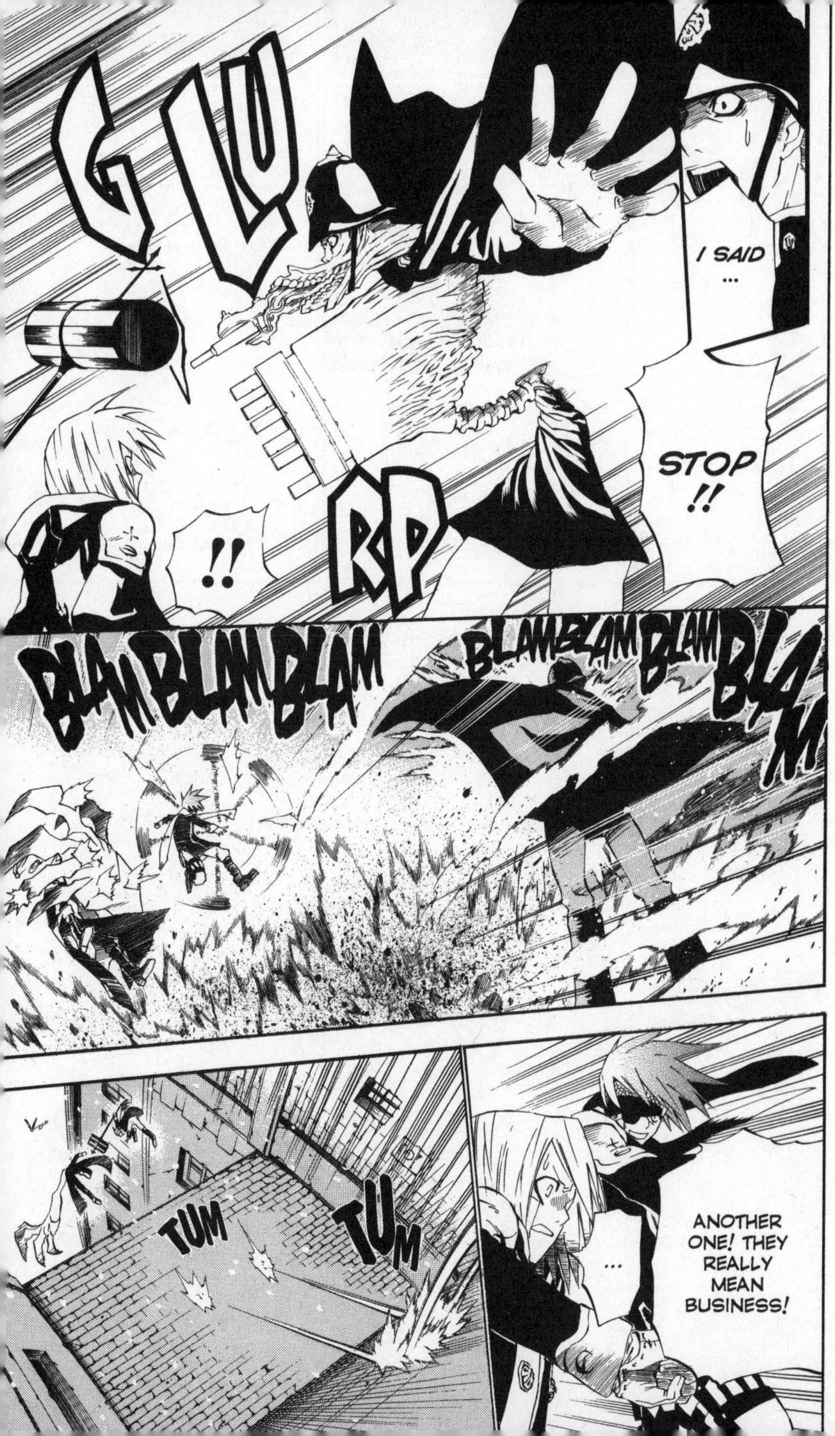
I SAID ...
STOP !!
G LU
RIP
!!
BLAMBLAM BLAM BLAM
BLAM
BLAM BLAM BLAM
ANOTHER ONE! THEY REALLY MEAN BUSINESS!
...
TUM
TUM

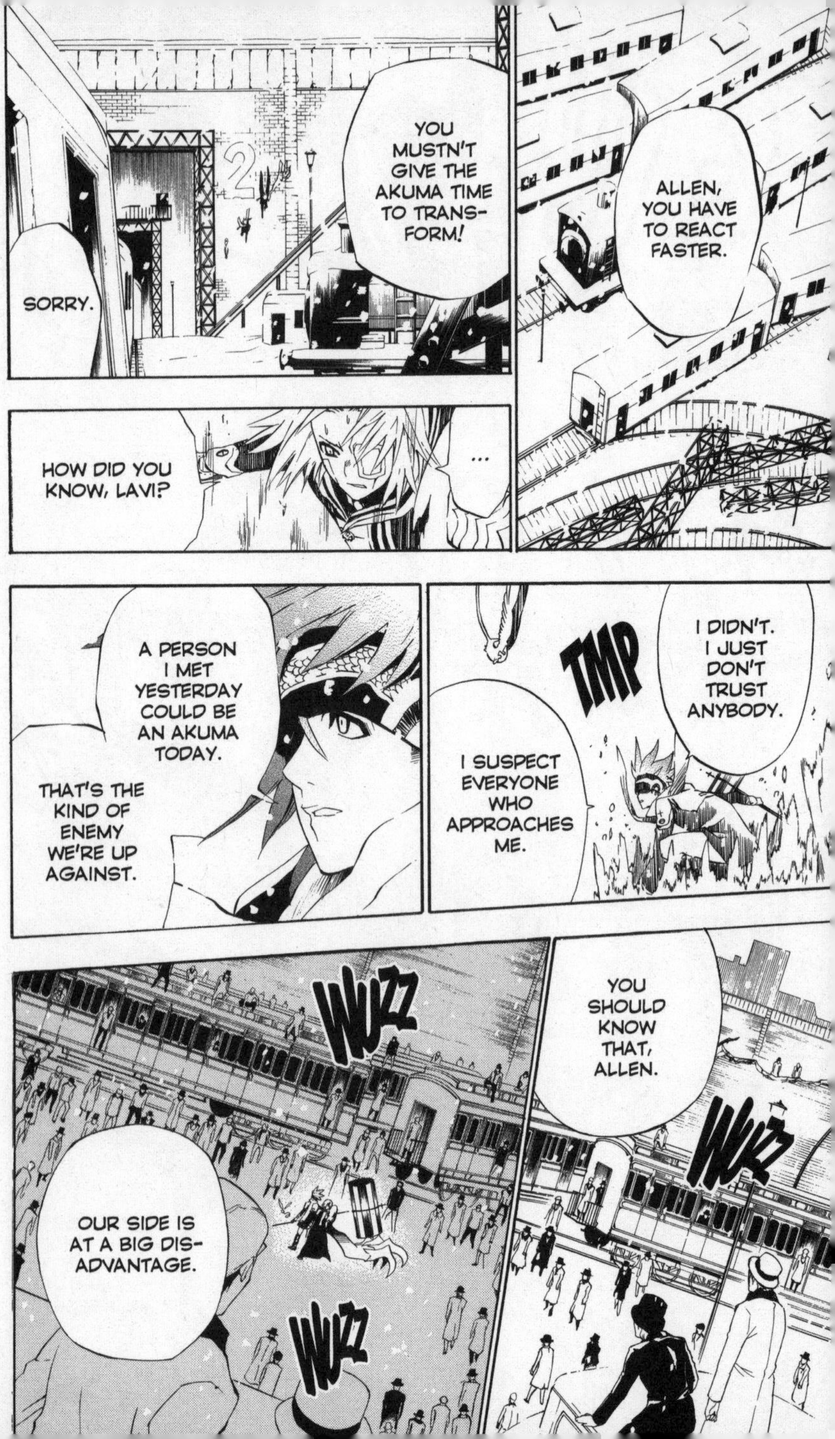

ALLEN, YOU HAVE TO REACT FASTER.
YOU MUSTN'T GIVE THE AKUMA TIME TO TRANS-FORM!
SORRY.
...
HOW DID YOU KNOW, LAVI?
I DIDN'T. I JUST DON'T TRUST ANYBODY.
TMP
I SUSPECT EVERYONE WHO APPROACHES ME.
A PERSON I MET YESTERDAY COULD BE AN AKUMA TODAY.
THAT'S THE KIND OF ENEMY WE'RE UP AGAINST.
YOU SHOULD KNOW THAT, ALLEN.
WUZZ
WUZZ
OUR SIDE IS AT A BIG DIS-ADVANTAGE.
WUZZ

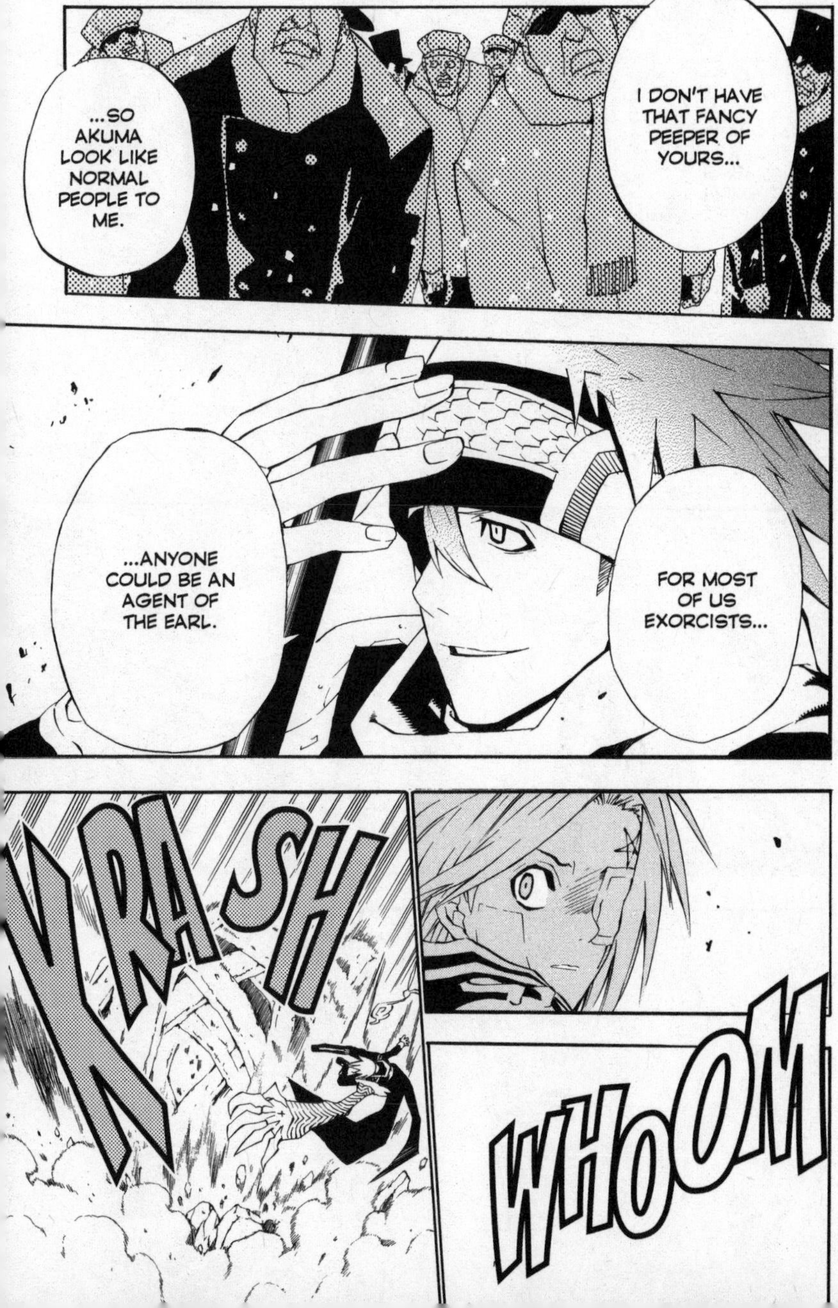
I DON'T HAVE THAT FANCY PEEPER OF YOURS...
...SO AKUMA LOOK LIKE NORMAL PEOPLE TO ME.
FOR MOST OF US EXORCISTS...
...ANYONE COULD BE AN AGENT OF THE EARL.
KRASH
WHOOM

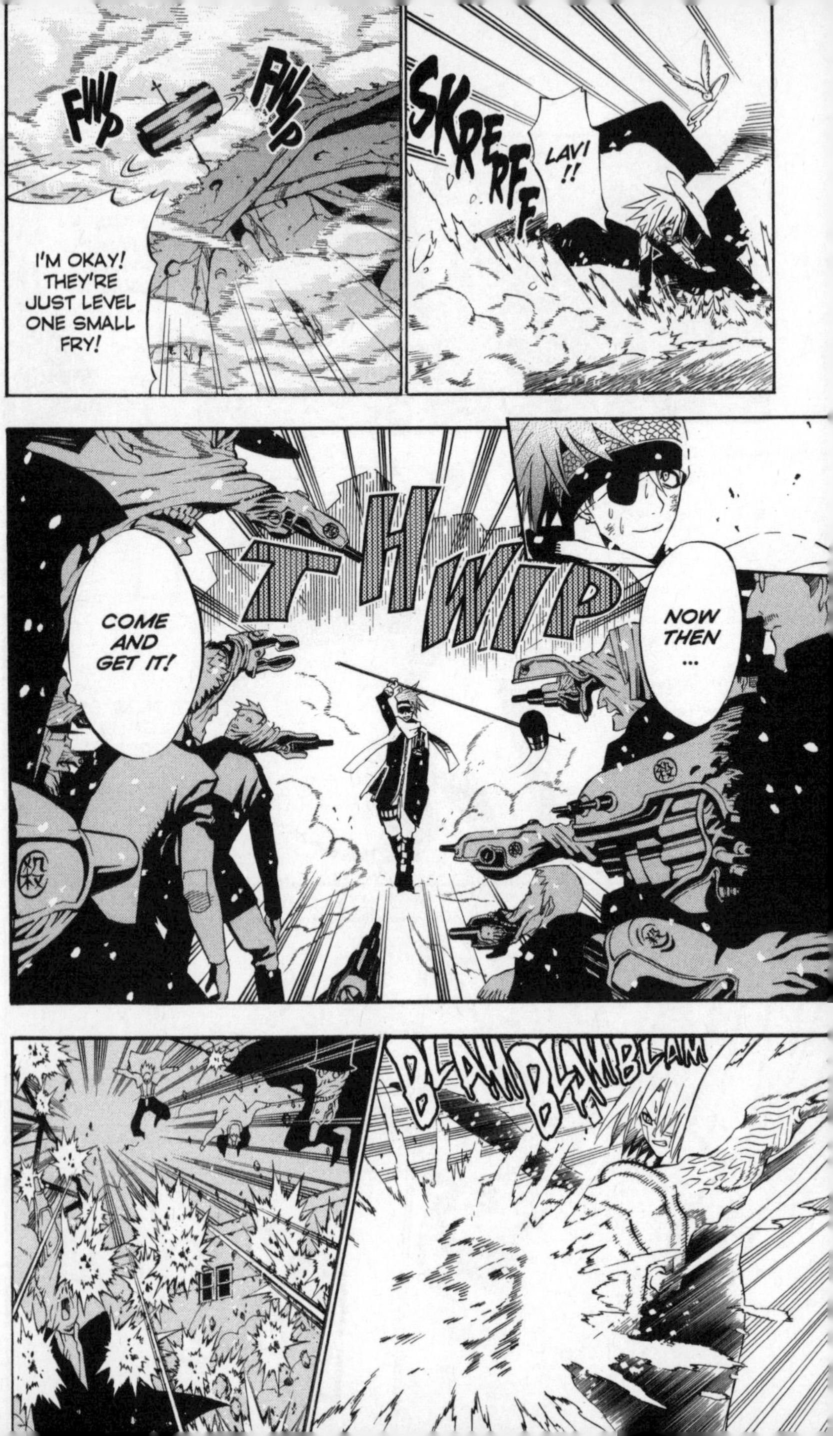
SKRERFF
LAVI !!
FWIP
FWIP
I'M OKAY! THEY'RE JUST LEVEL ONE SMALL FRY!
NOW THEN ...
THWIP
COME AND GET IT!
BLAM BLAM BLAM

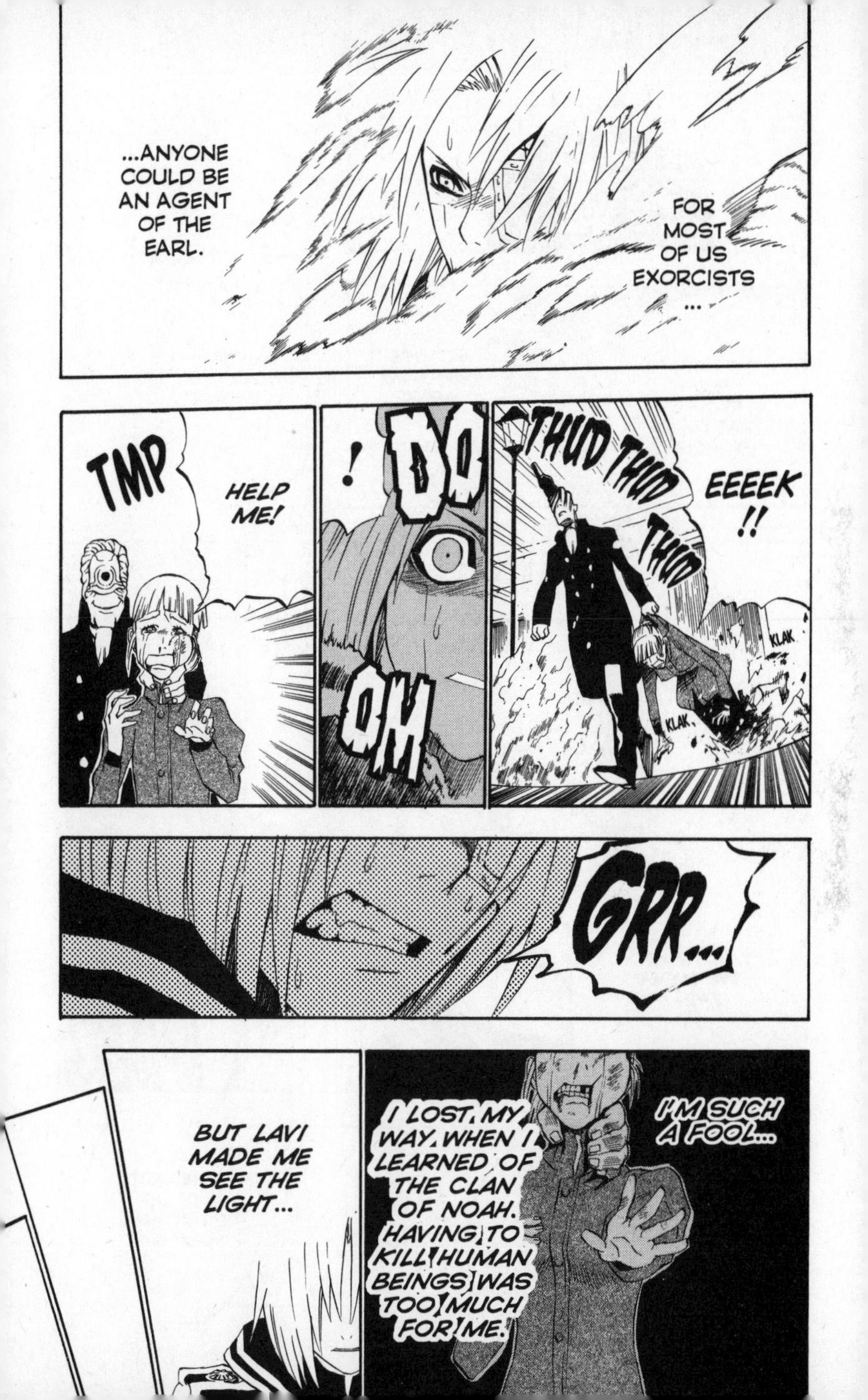
FOR MOST OF US EXORCISTS ...
...ANYONE COULD BE AN AGENT OF THE EARL.
THUD THUD THUD
EEEEK !!
KLAK
KLAK
!
DOOM
TMP
HELP ME!
GRR...
I'M SUCH A FOOL...
I LOST MY WAY WHEN I LEARNED OF THE CLAN OF NOAH. HAVING TO KILL HUMAN BEINGS WAS TOO MUCH FOR ME.
BUT LAVI MADE ME SEE THE LIGHT...

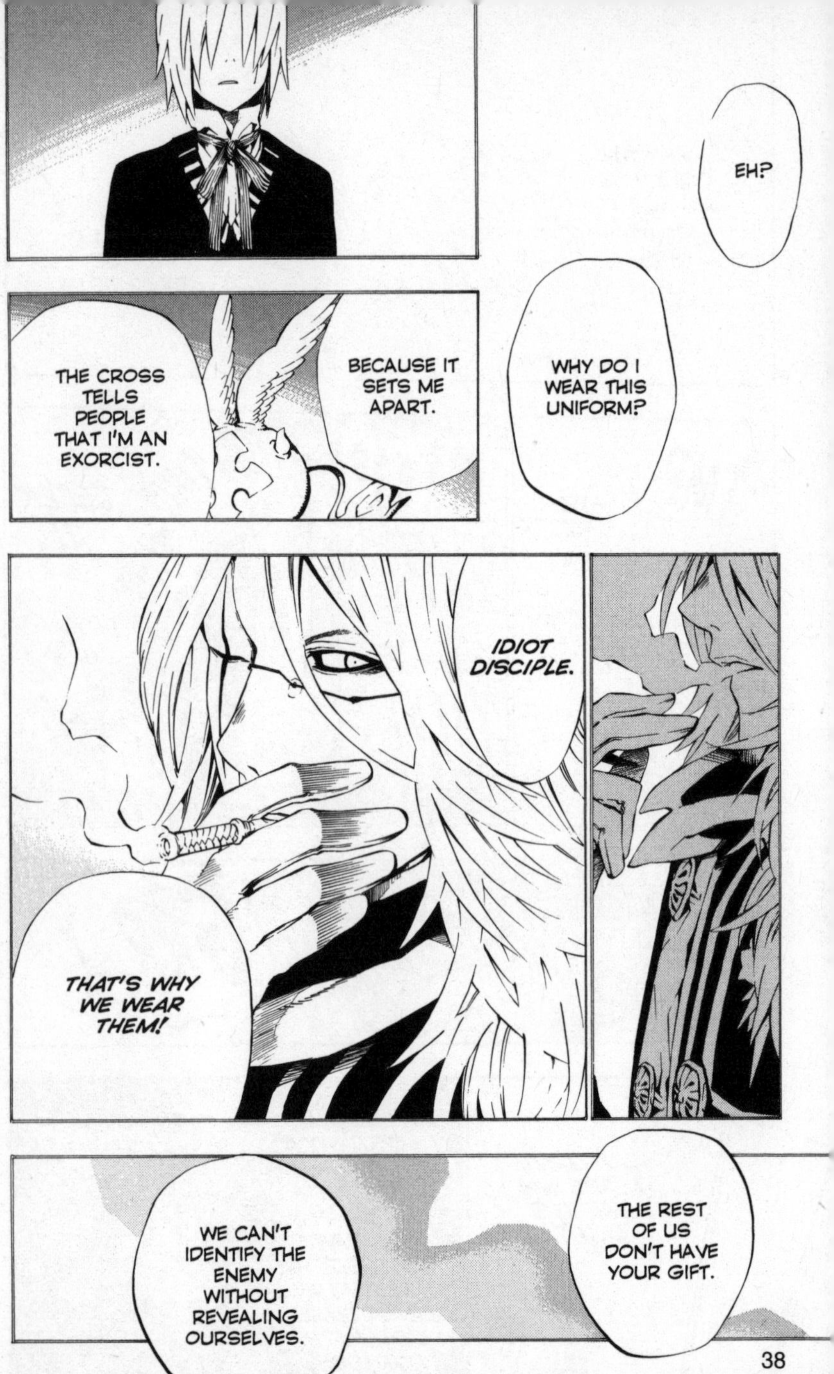
EH?
WHY DO I WEAR THIS UNIFORM?
BECAUSE IT SETS ME APART.
THE CROSS TELLS PEOPLE THAT I'M AN EXORCIST.
IDIOT DISCIPLE.
THAT'S WHY WE WEAR THEM!
THE REST OF US DON'T HAVE YOUR GIFT.
WE CAN'T IDENTIFY THE ENEMY WITHOUT REVEALING OURSELVES.

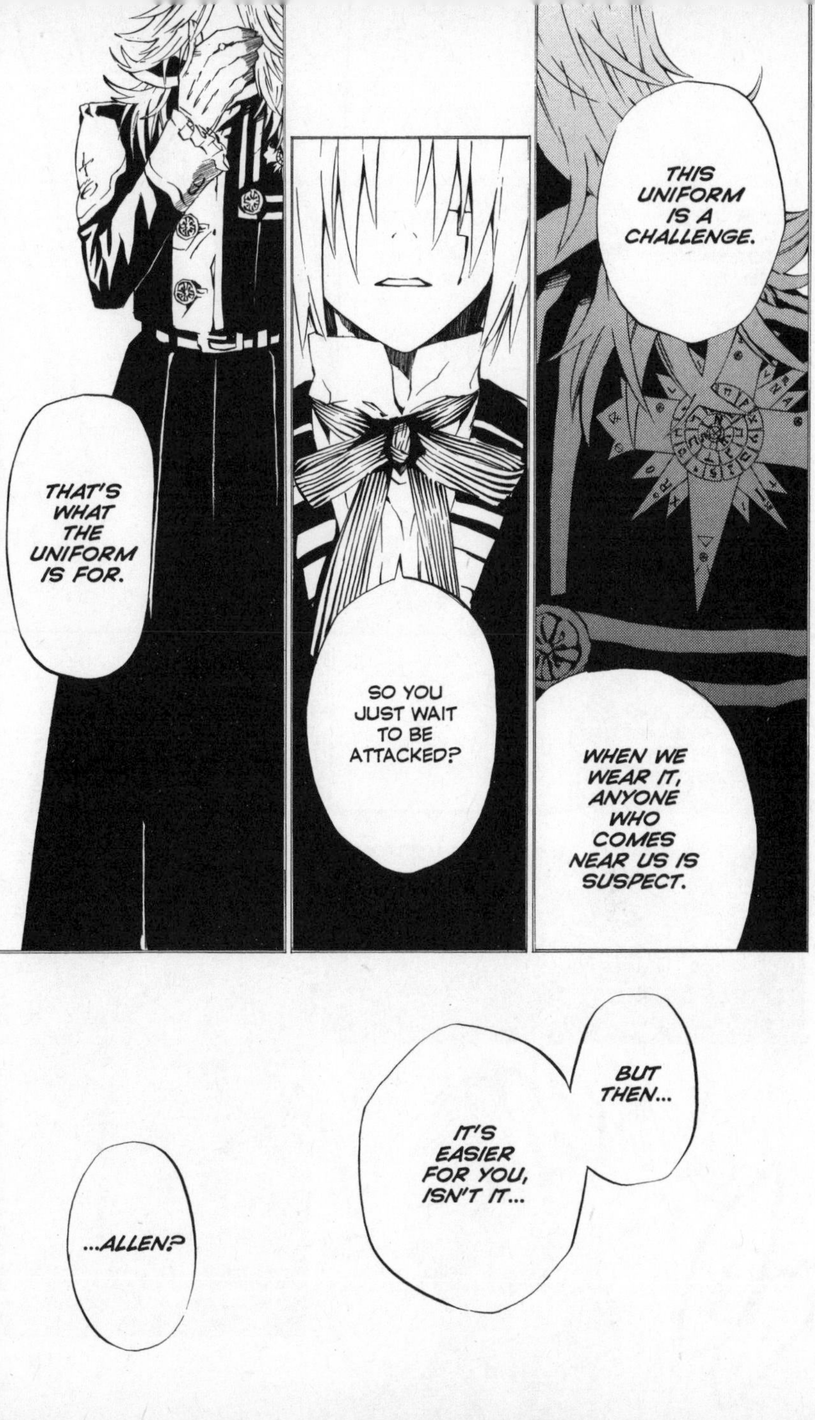
THIS UNIFORM IS A CHALLENGE.
WHEN WE WEAR IT, ANYONE WHO COMES NEAR US IS SUSPECT.
SO YOU JUST WAIT TO BE ATTACKED?
THAT'S WHAT THE UNIFORM IS FOR.
BUT THEN...
IT'S EASIER FOR YOU, ISN'T IT...
...ALLEN?

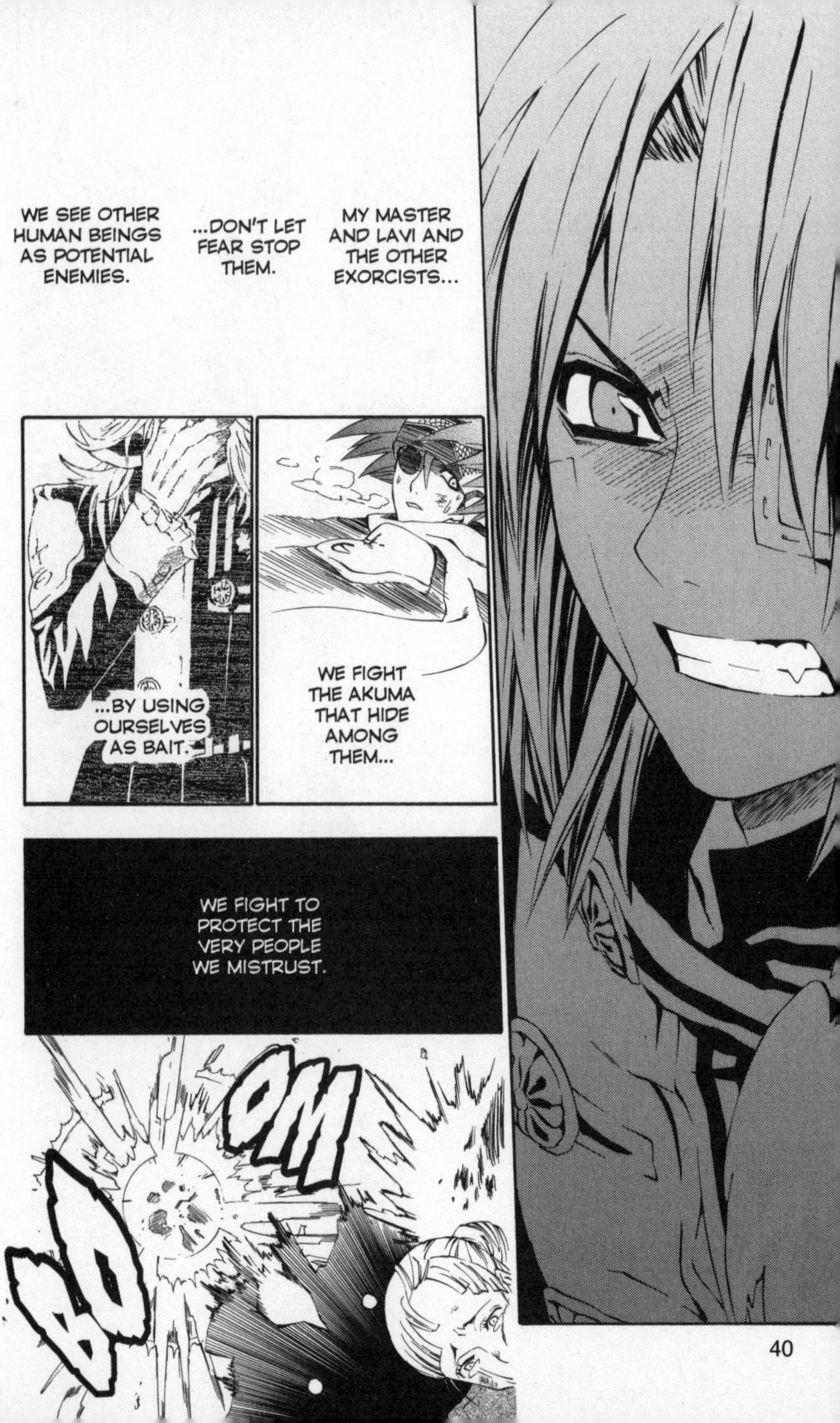
MY MASTER AND LAVI AND THE OTHER EXORCISTS...
...DON'T LET FEAR STOP THEM.
WE SEE OTHER HUMAN BEINGS AS POTENTIAL ENEMIES.
WE FIGHT THE AKUMA THAT HIDE AMONG THEM...
...BY USING OURSELVES AS BAIT.
WE FIGHT TO PROTECT THE VERY PEOPLE WE MISTRUST.
BOOM

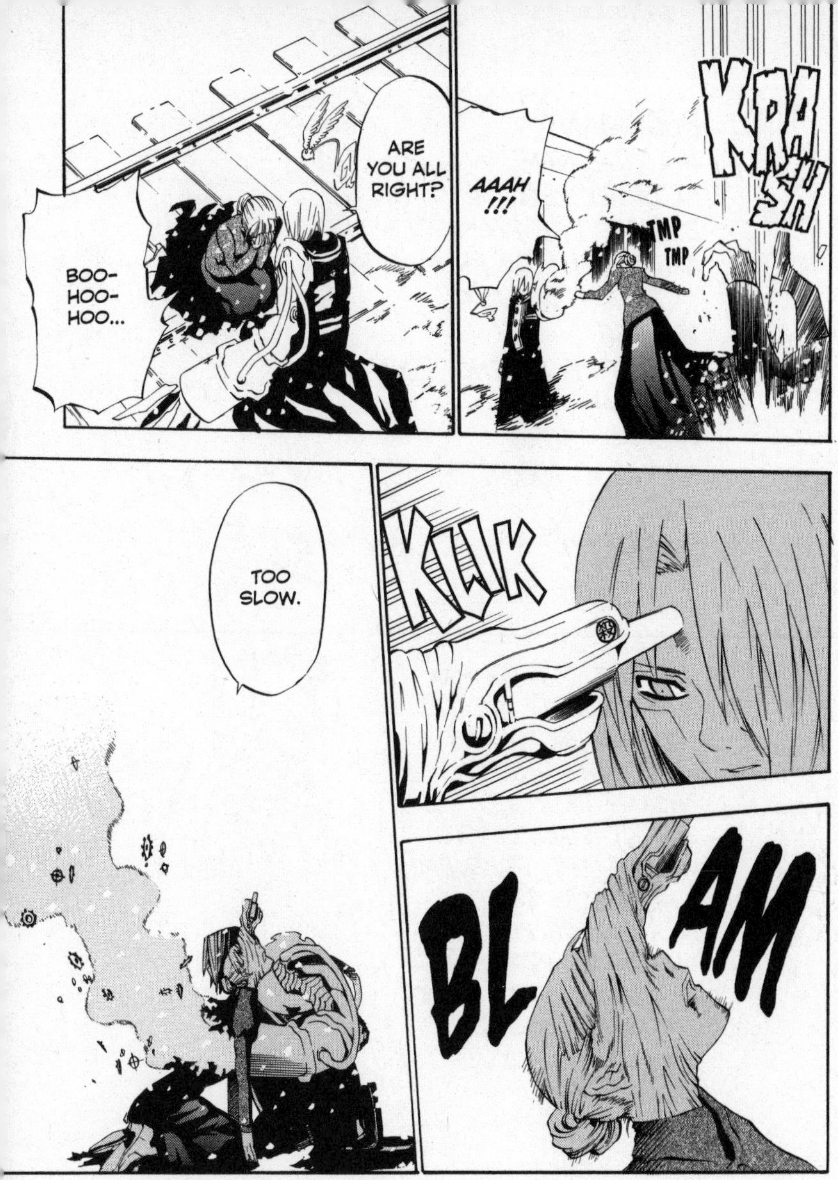
KRASH
TMP
TMP
AAAH !!!
ARE YOU ALL RIGHT?
BOO-HOO-HOO...
KLIK
BLAM
TOO SLOW.

I'M GOING TO KEEP FOLLOWING THE PATH.

BUT IF I'M GOING TO WEAR THIS UNIFORM, I'LL HAVE TO BE ON MY GUARD.

BOOKMAN

HIS REAL NAME WAS DELETED FROM ALL RECORDS WHEN HE BECAME THE BOOKMAN.

NATIONALITY UNKNOWN, BUT THE SAME AS LAVI'S.

AGE 88

HEIGHT 140CM (NOT COUNTING THE HAIR)

WEIGHT 38KG

BIRTHDAY AUGUST 5

SIGN LEO

BLOOD TYPE A

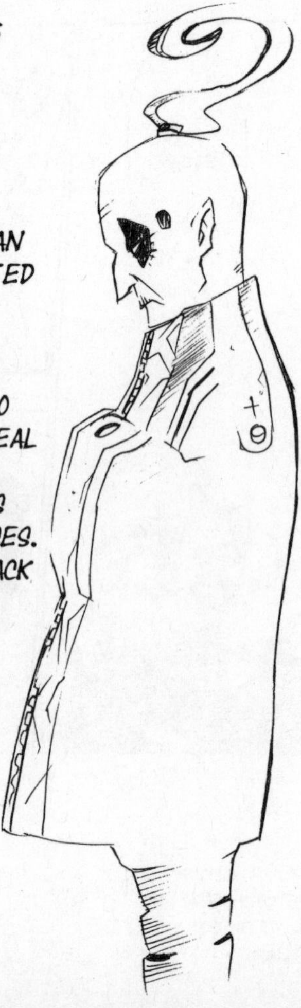

LIKE LAVI, THIS OLD MAN WAS ORIGINALLY CREATED FOR ANOTHER MANGA. I LIKE HIM MAINLY BECAUSE HE'S THE EASIEST CHARACTER TO DRAW. I HOPE TO REVEAL A NUMBER OF THE BOOKMAN'S SECRETS AS THE SERIES PROGRESSES. BY THE WAY, THE BLACK AROUND HIS EYES IS MAKEUP.

THE 29TH NIGHT: CRISIS OF THE GENERALS

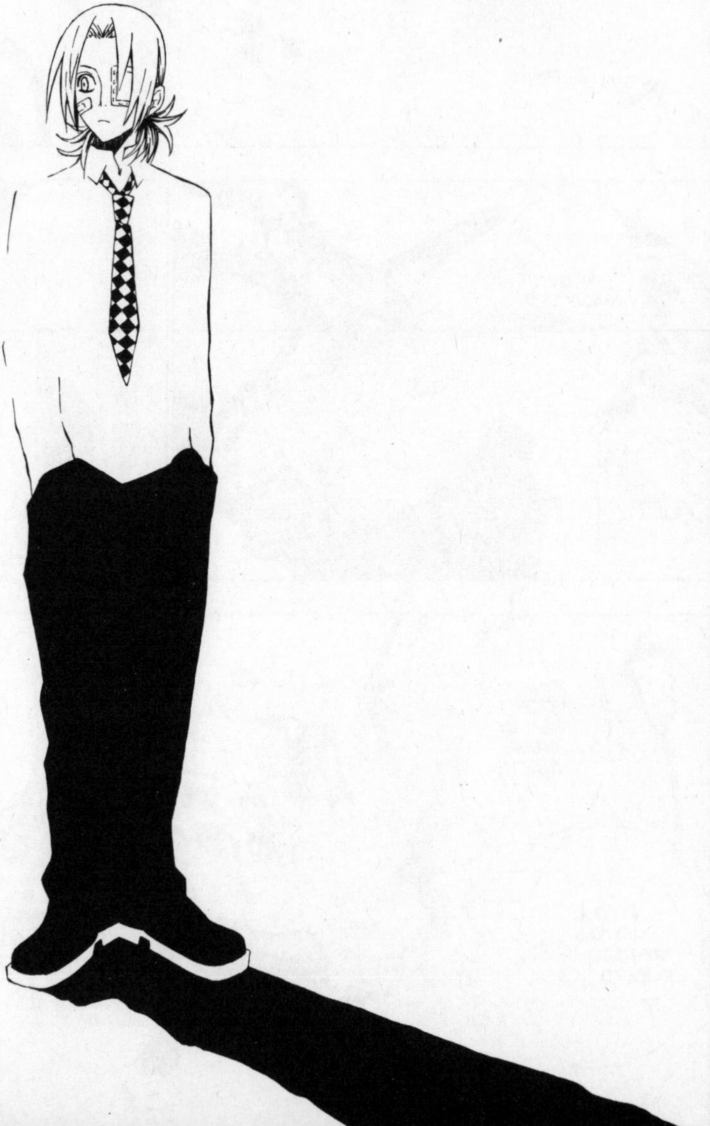

HOW MANY DID YOU GET?

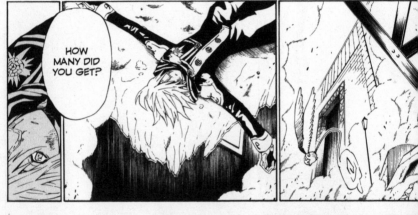

... I DON'T REALLY KEEP TRACK.

THIRTY OR SO.

I KEEP A MENTAL RECORD OF EVERYTHING.

I GOT 37. I WIN.

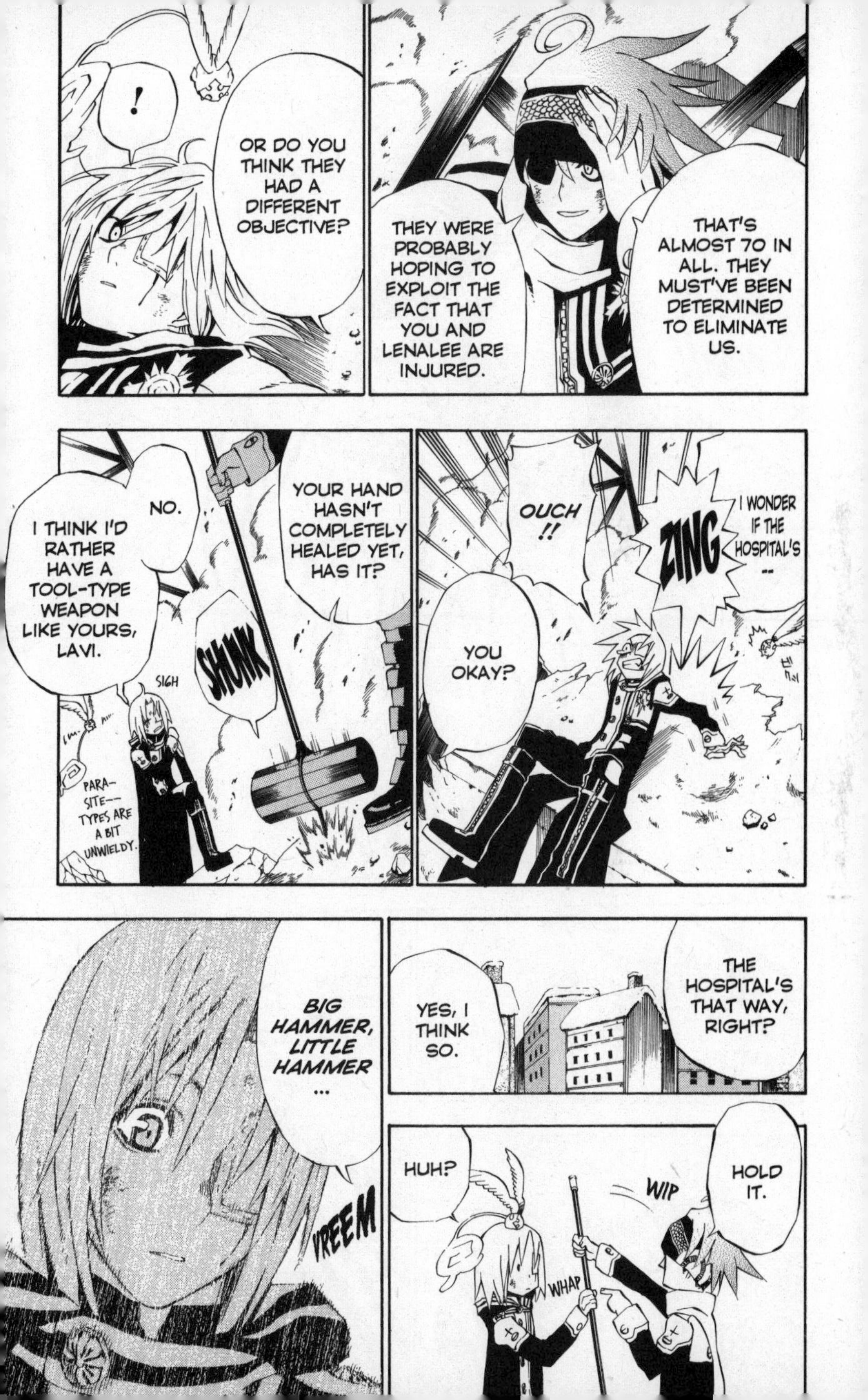
THAT'S ALMOST 70 IN ALL. THEY MUST'VE BEEN DETERMINED TO ELIMINATE US.
THEY WERE PROBABLY HOPING TO EXPLOIT THE FACT THAT YOU AND LENALEE ARE INJURED.
!
OR DO YOU THINK THEY HAD A DIFFERENT OBJECTIVE?
I WONDER IF THE HOSPITAL'S --
ZING
OUCH !!
YOU OKAY?
YOUR HAND HASN'T COMPLETELY HEALED YET, HAS IT?
NO.
I THINK I'D RATHER HAVE A TOOL-TYPE WEAPON LIKE YOURS, LAVI.
SHUNK
SIGH
PARA-SITE--TYPES ARE A BIT UNWIELDY.
THE HOSPITAL'S THAT WAY, RIGHT?
YES, I THINK SO.
HOLD IT.
WIP
HUH?
WHAP
BIG HAMMER, LITTLE HAMMER ...
VREEM

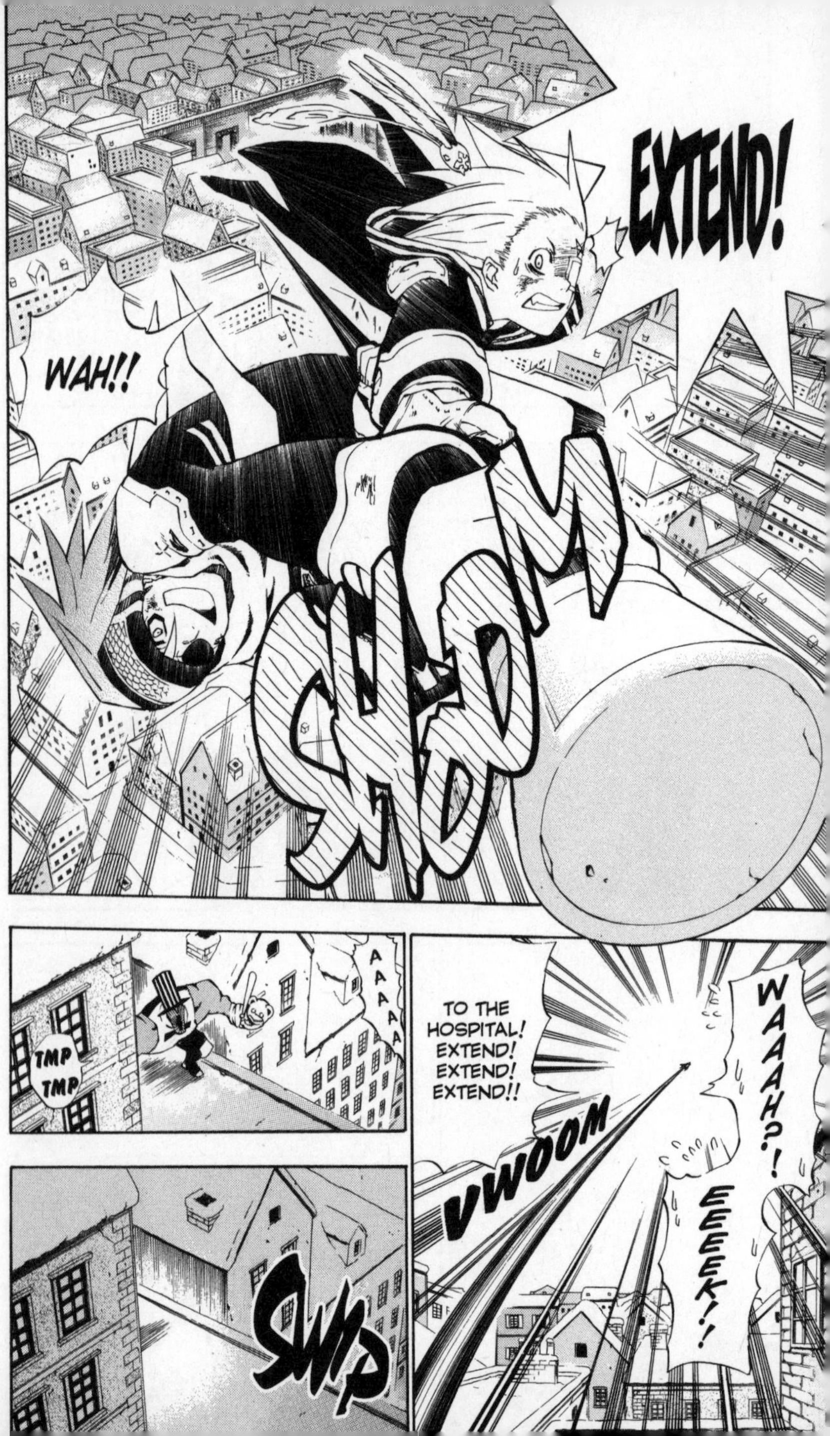
EXTEND!
WAH!!
SHOOM
TO THE HOSPITAL! EXTEND! EXTEND! EXTEND!!
WAAAH?!
VWOOM
EEEEK!!
AAAAA
TMP TMP
SWP

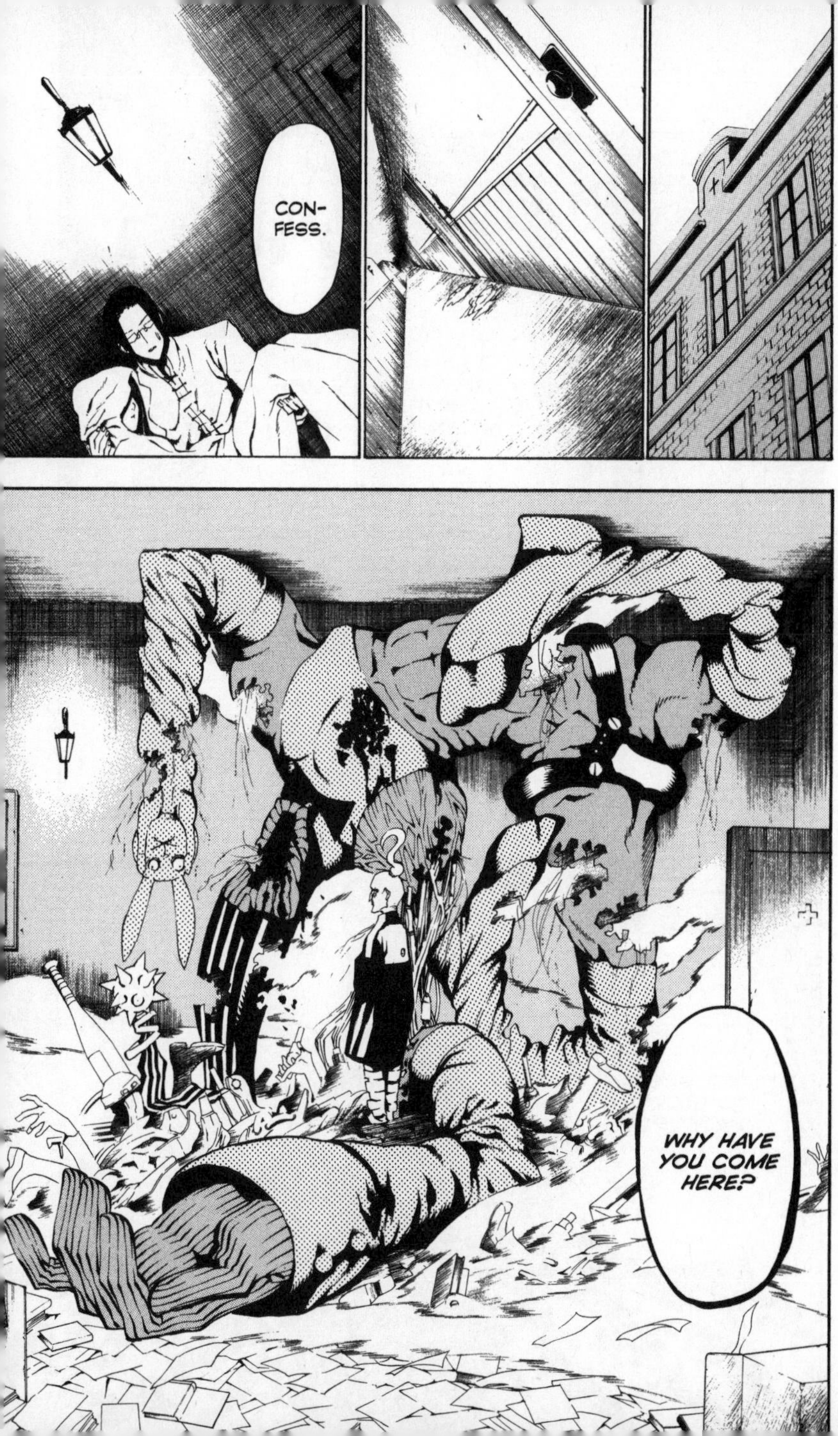
CON-FESS.
WHY HAVE YOU COME HERE?

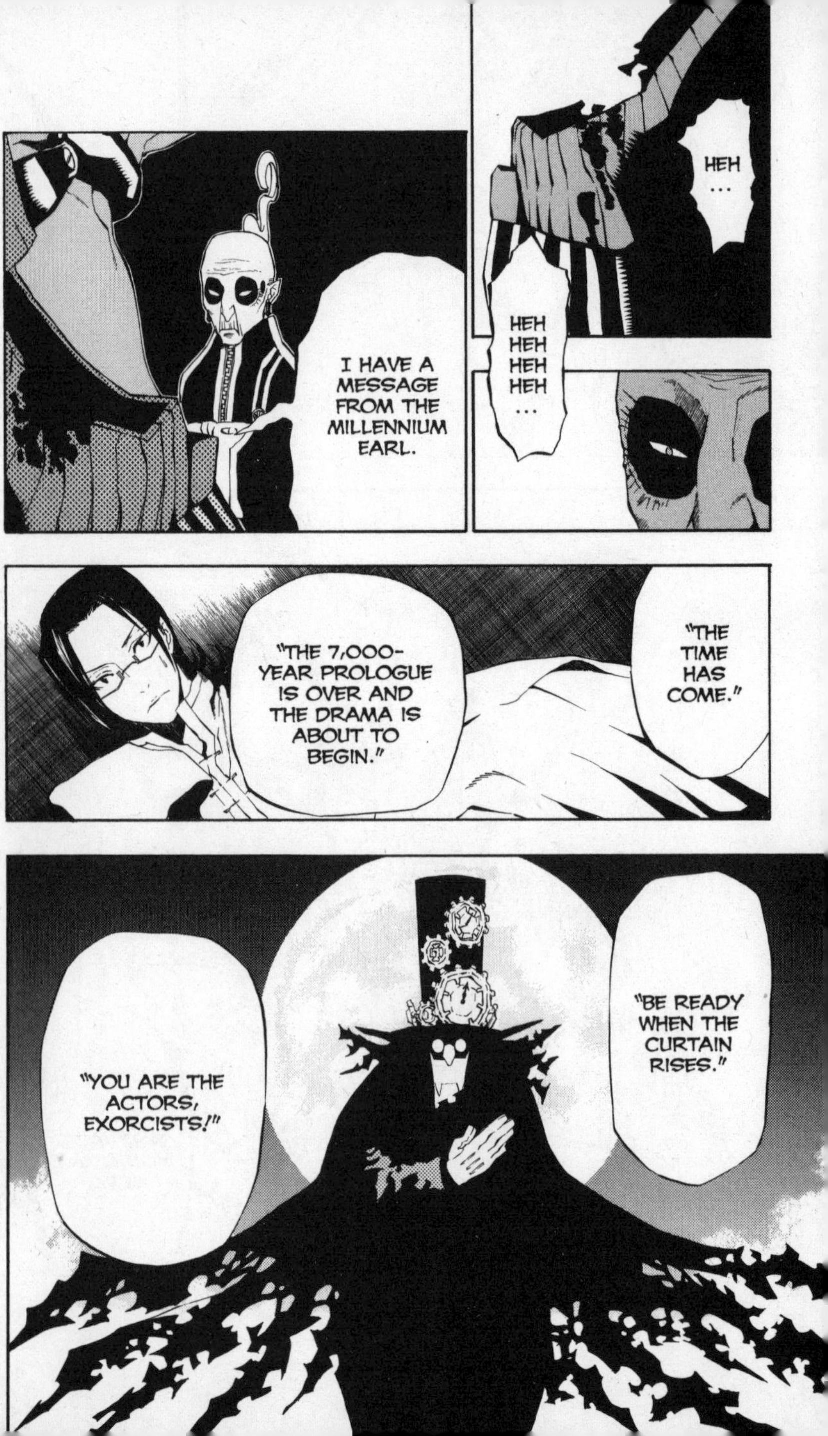
HEH ...
HEH HEH HEH HEH ...
I HAVE A MESSAGE FROM THE MILLENNIUM EARL.
"THE TIME HAS COME."
"THE 7,000-YEAR PROLOGUE IS OVER AND THE DRAMA IS ABOUT TO BEGIN."
"BE READY WHEN THE CURTAIN RISES."
"YOU ARE THE ACTORS, EXORCISTS!"

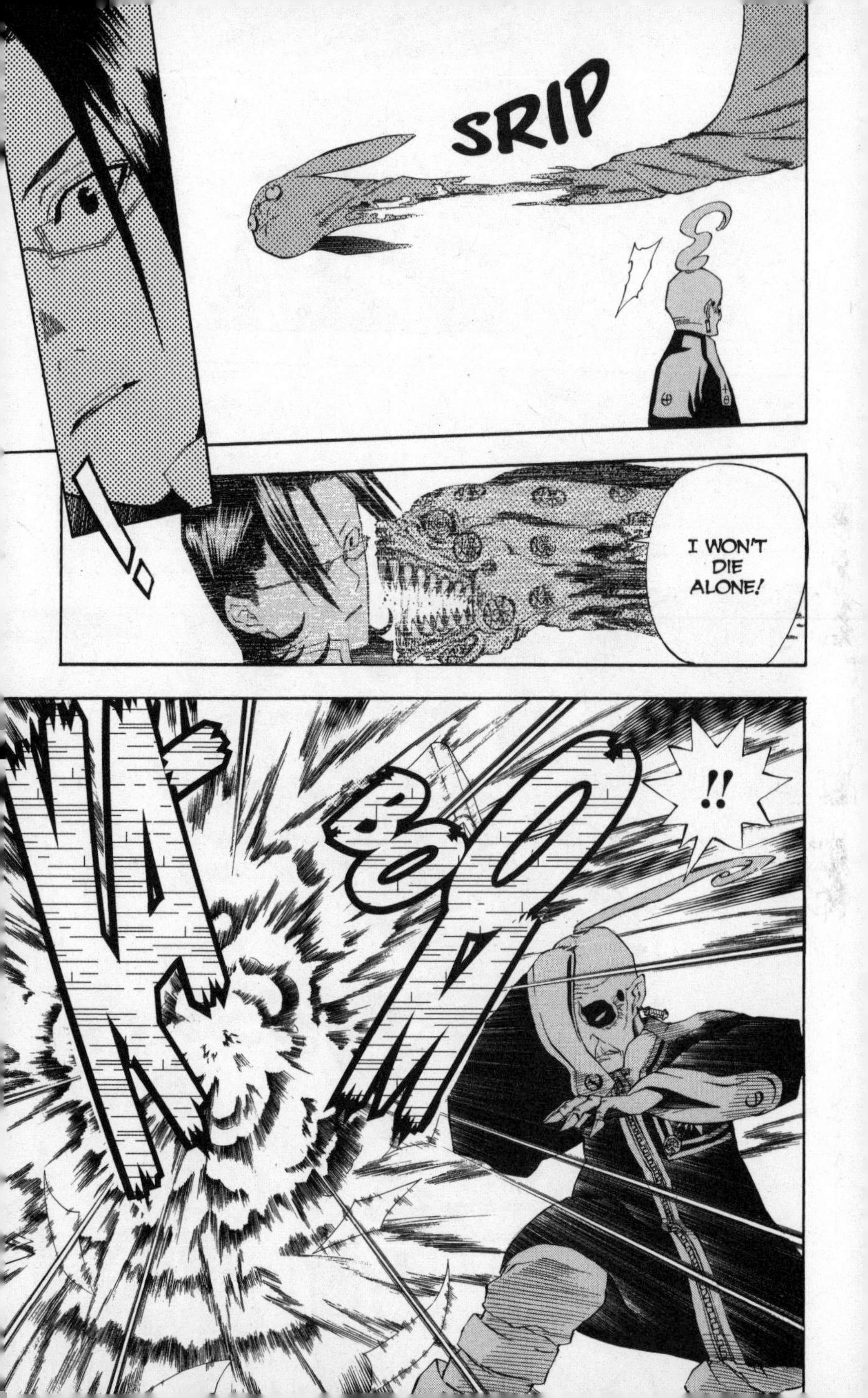
SRIP
I WON'T DIE ALONE!
!!
BOOM

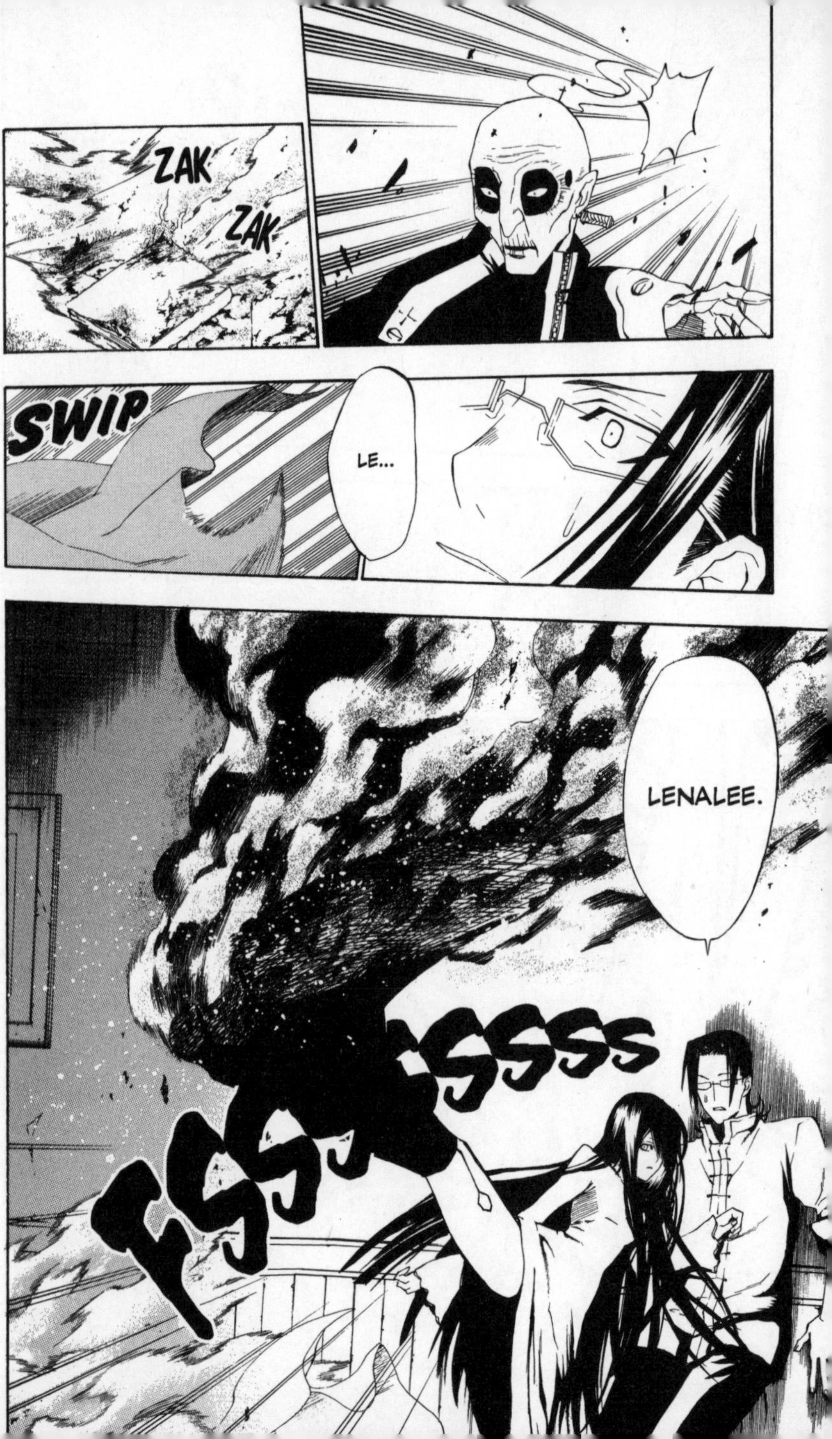
ZAK
ZAK
LE...
SWIP
LENALEE.
FSSSSSSSS

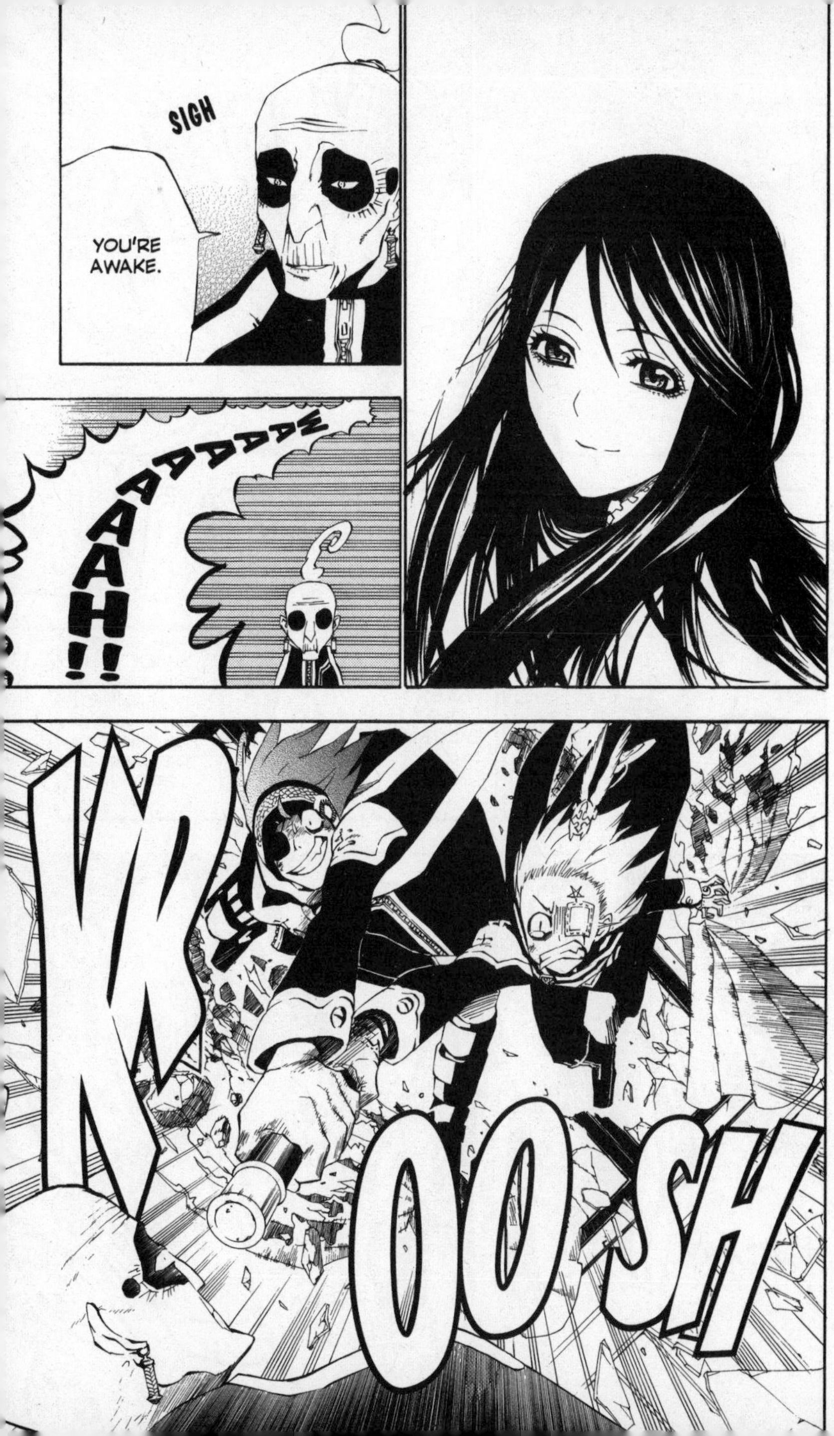
SIGH
YOU'RE AWAKE.
WAAAAAAH!!
KROOOSH

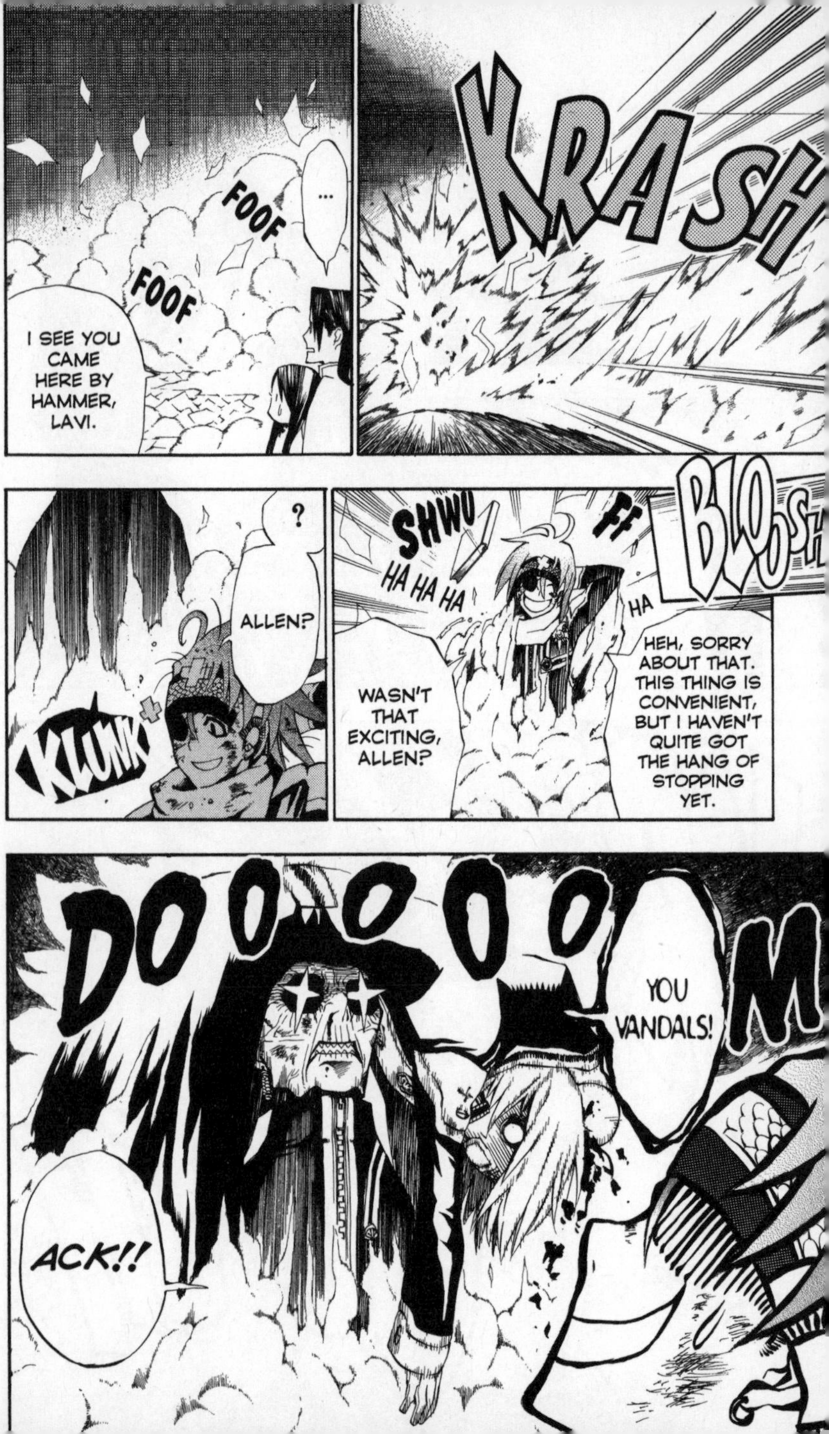
KRASH
...
FOOF
FOOF
I SEE YOU CAME HERE BY HAMMER, LAVI.
BLOOSH
SHWU
FF
HA
HA HA HA
HEH, SORRY ABOUT THAT. THIS THING IS CONVENIENT, BUT I HAVEN'T QUITE GOT THE HANG OF STOPPING YET.
WASN'T THAT EXCITING, ALLEN?
?
ALLEN?
KLUNK
DOOOOOOM
YOU VANDALS!
ACK!!

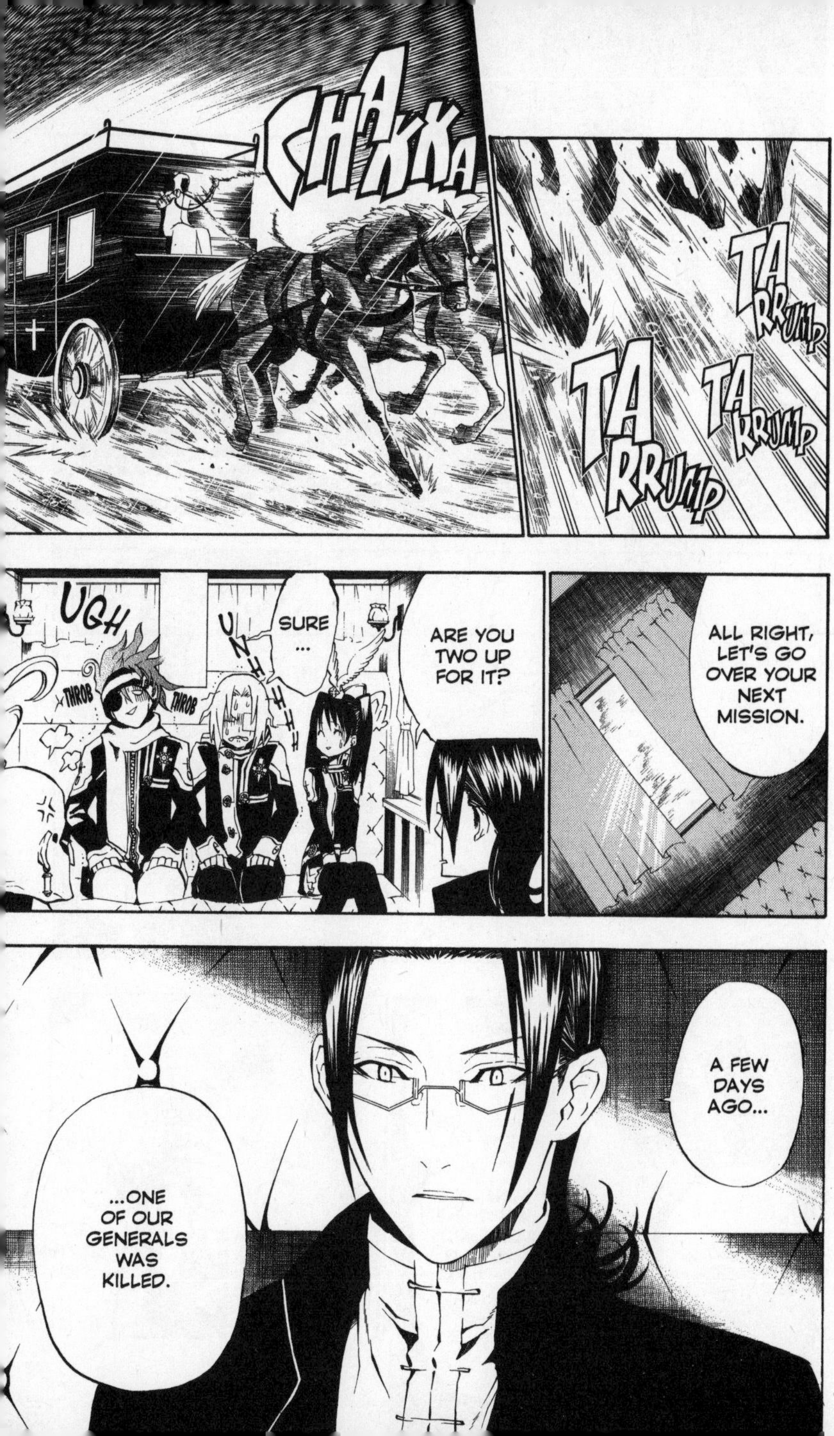
TA RRUMP
TA RRUMP
TA RRUMP
CHAKKA
ALL RIGHT, LET'S GO OVER YOUR NEXT MISSION.
ARE YOU TWO UP FOR IT?
SURE ...
UNHHHHHH
THROB
THROB
UGH
A FEW DAYS AGO...
...ONE OF OUR GENERALS WAS KILLED.

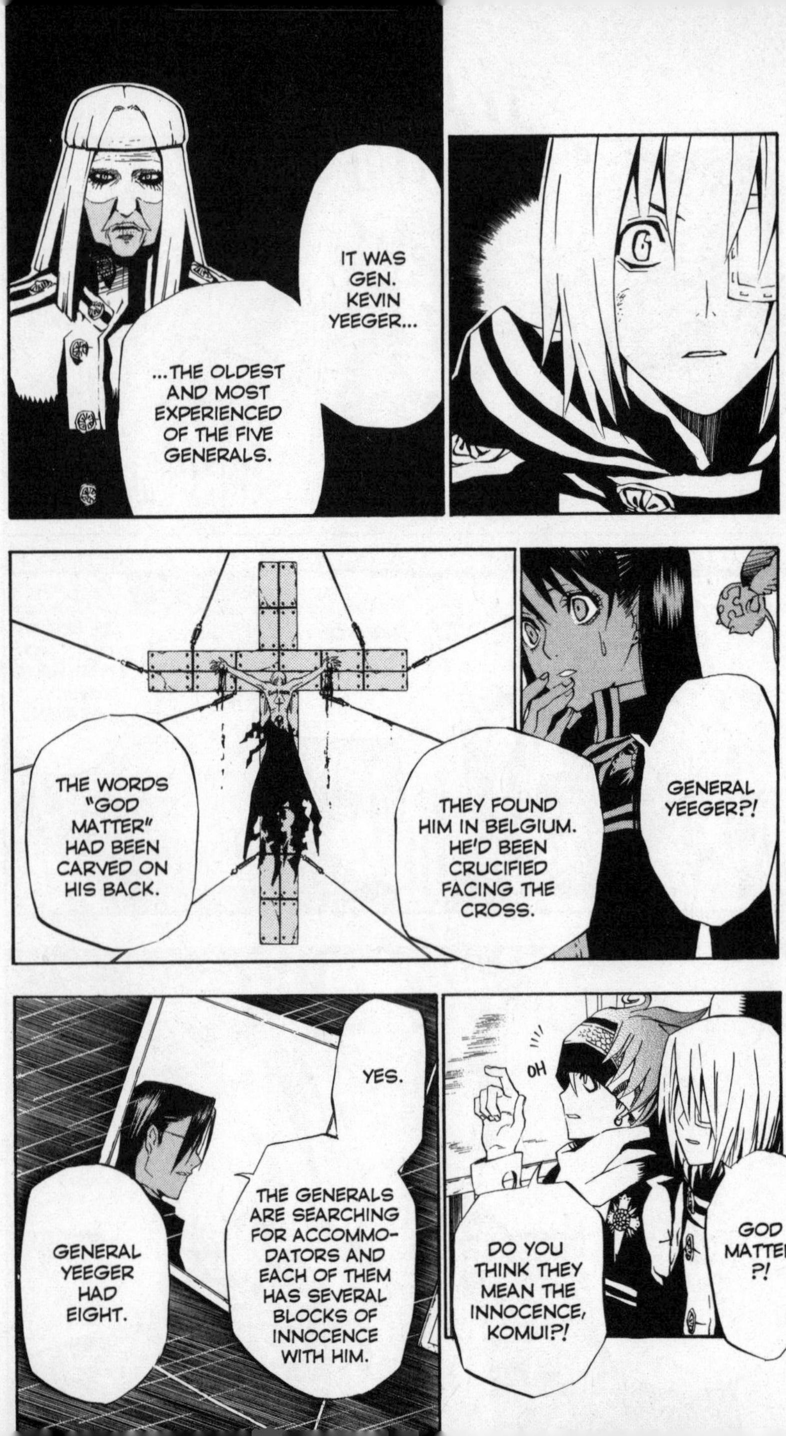
IT WAS GEN. KEVIN YEEGER...
...THE OLDEST AND MOST EXPERIENCED OF THE FIVE GENERALS.
GENERAL YEEGER?!
THEY FOUND HIM IN BELGIUM. HE'D BEEN CRUCIFIED FACING THE CROSS.
THE WORDS "GOD MATTER" HAD BEEN CARVED ON HIS BACK.
GOD MATTER?!
OH
DO YOU THINK THEY MEAN THE INNOCENCE, KOMUI?!
YES.
THE GENERALS ARE SEARCHING FOR ACCOMMODATORS AND EACH OF THEM HAS SEVERAL BLOCKS OF INNOCENCE WITH HIM.
GENERAL YEEGER HAD EIGHT.

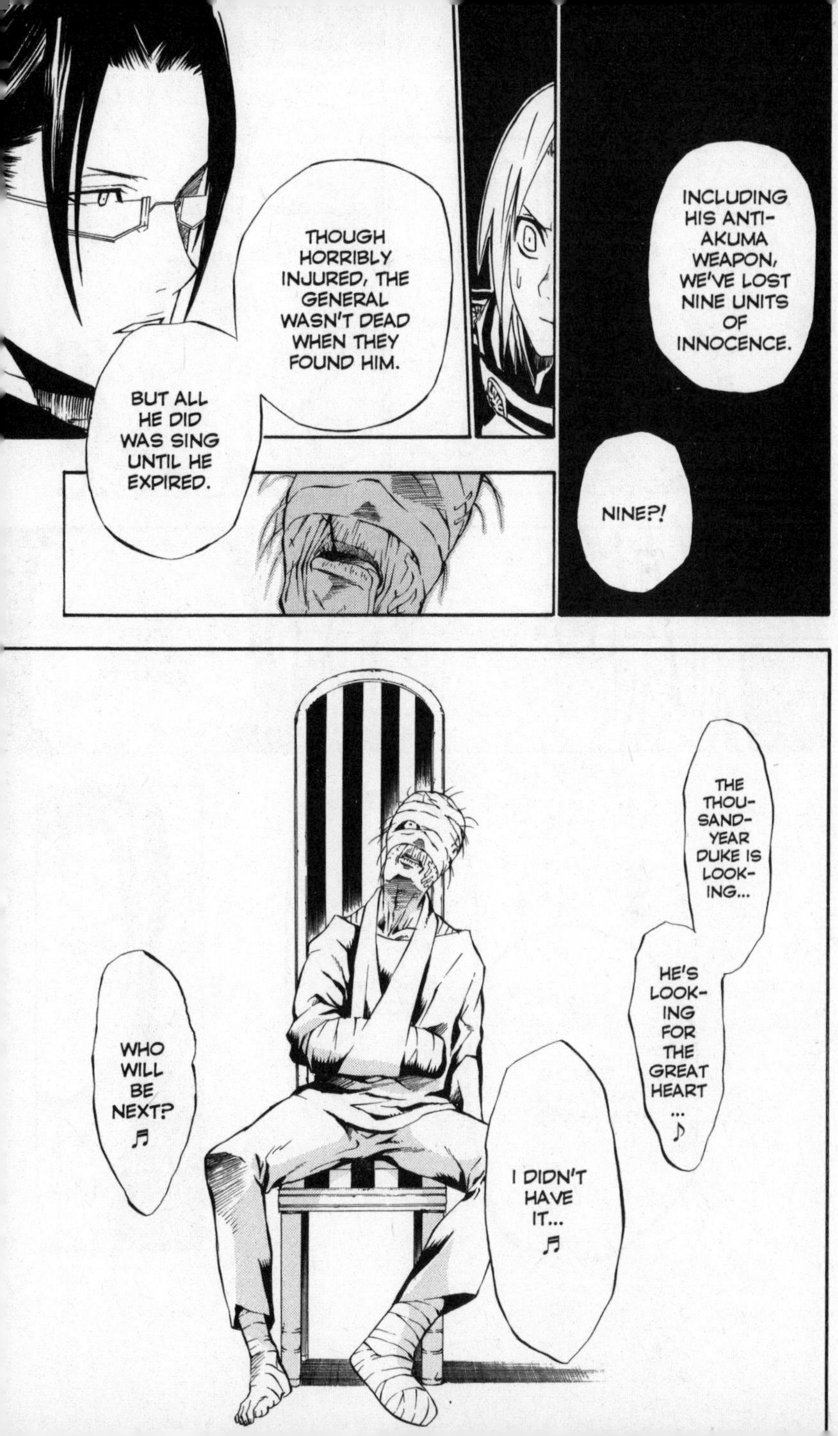

INCLUDING HIS ANTI-AKUMA WEAPON, WE'VE LOST NINE UNITS OF INNOCENCE.
NINE?!
THOUGH HORRIBLY INJURED, THE GENERAL WASN'T DEAD WHEN THEY FOUND HIM.
BUT ALL HE DID WAS SING UNTIL HE EXPIRED.
THE THOUSAND-YEAR DUKE IS LOOKING...
HE'S LOOKING FOR THE GREAT HEART... ♪
I DIDN'T HAVE IT... ♬
WHO WILL BE NEXT? ♬

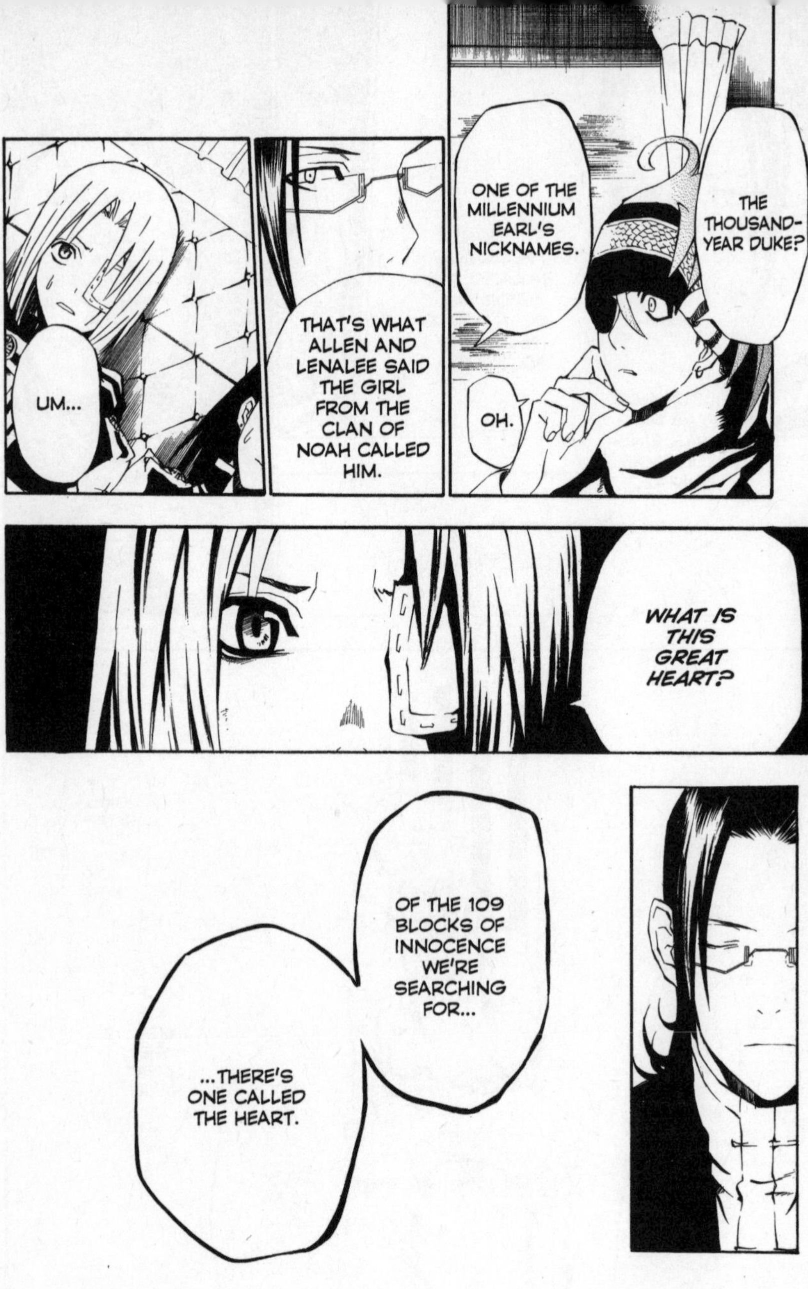
THE THOUSAND-YEAR DUKE?
ONE OF THE MILLENNIUM EARL'S NICKNAMES.
OH.
THAT'S WHAT ALLEN AND LENALEE SAID THE GIRL FROM THE CLAN OF NOAH CALLED HIM.
UM...
WHAT IS THIS GREAT HEART?
OF THE 109 BLOCKS OF INNOCENCE WE'RE SEARCHING FOR...
...THERE'S ONE CALLED THE HEART.

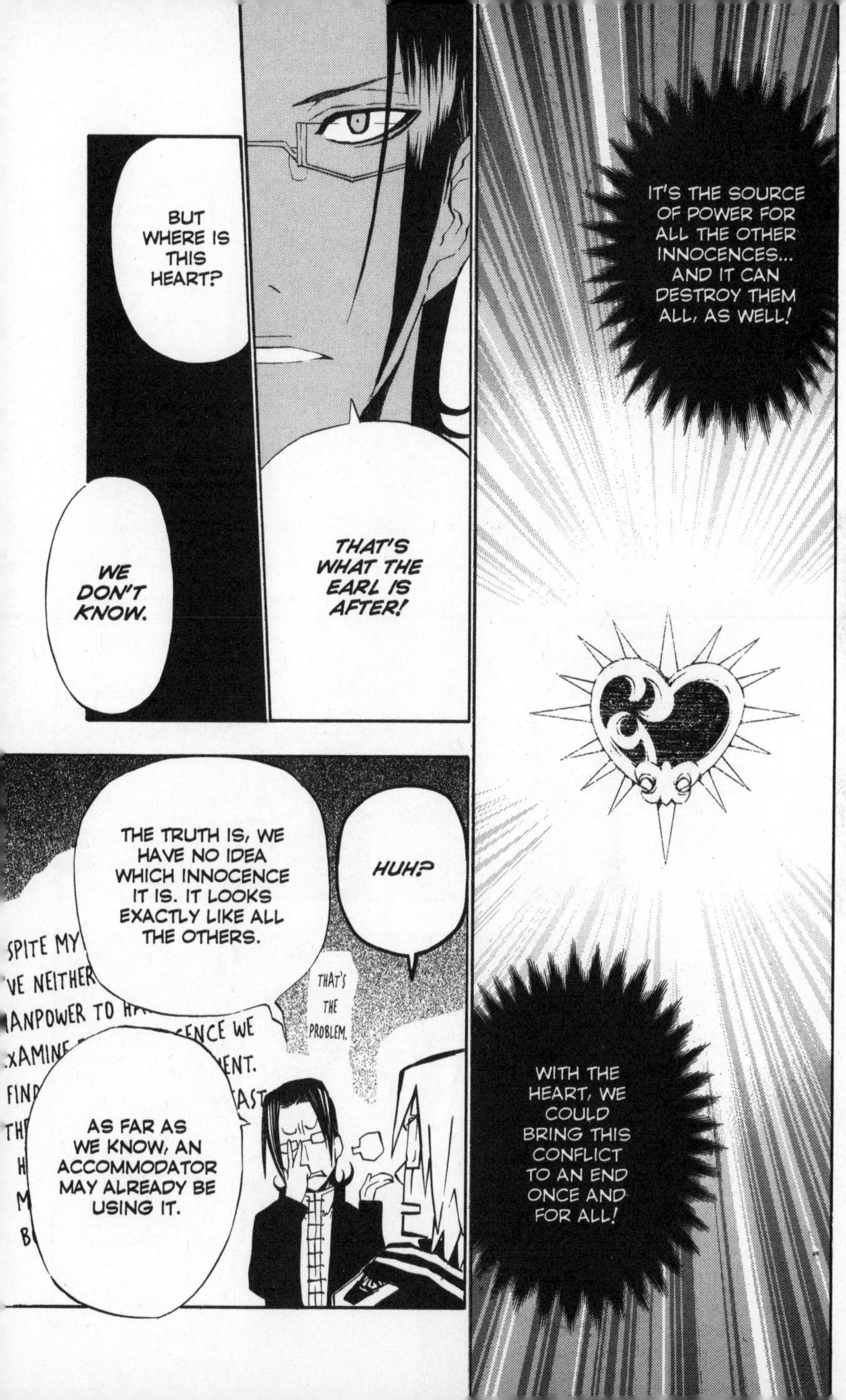

IT'S THE SOURCE OF POWER FOR ALL THE OTHER INNOCENCES... AND IT CAN DESTROY THEM ALL, AS WELL!
WITH THE HEART, WE COULD BRING THIS CONFLICT TO AN END ONCE AND FOR ALL!
THAT'S WHAT THE EARL IS AFTER!
BUT WHERE IS THIS HEART?
WE DON'T KNOW.
HUH?
THE TRUTH IS, WE HAVE NO IDEA WHICH INNOCENCE IT IS. IT LOOKS EXACTLY LIKE ALL THE OTHERS.
THAT'S THE PROBLEM.
AS FAR AS WE KNOW, AN ACCOMMODATOR MAY ALREADY BE USING IT.

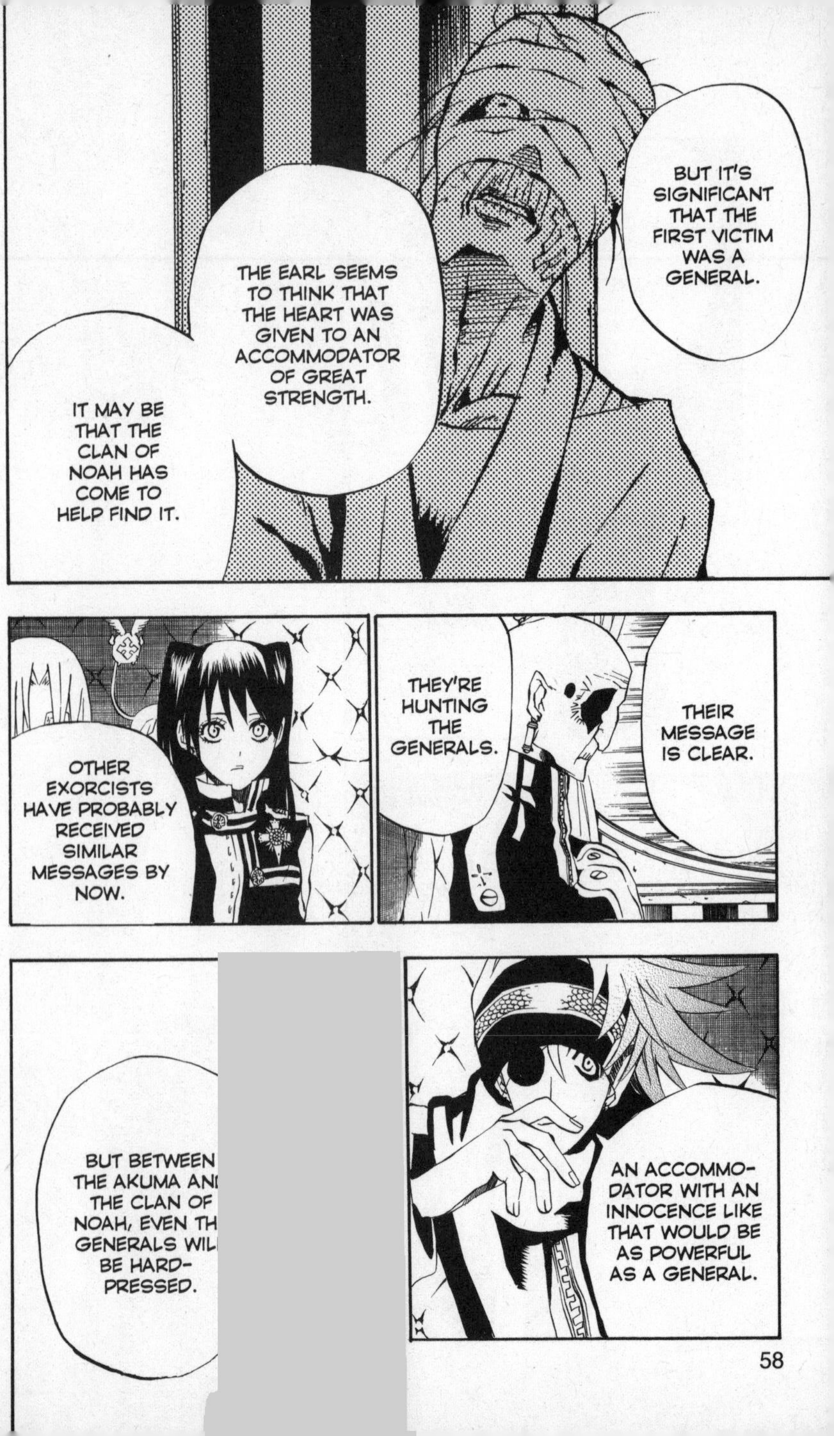
BUT IT'S SIGNIFICANT THAT THE FIRST VICTIM WAS A GENERAL.
THE EARL SEEMS TO THINK THAT THE HEART WAS GIVEN TO AN ACCOMMODATOR OF GREAT STRENGTH.
IT MAY BE THAT THE CLAN OF NOAH HAS COME TO HELP FIND IT.
THEIR MESSAGE IS CLEAR.
THEY'RE HUNTING THE GENERALS.
OTHER EXORCISTS HAVE PROBABLY RECEIVED SIMILAR MESSAGES BY NOW.
AN ACCOMMODATOR WITH AN INNOCENCE LIKE THAT WOULD BE AS POWERFUL AS A GENERAL.
BUT BETWEEN THE AKUMA AN THE CLAN OF NOAH, EVEN TH GENERALS WIL BE HARD-PRESSED.

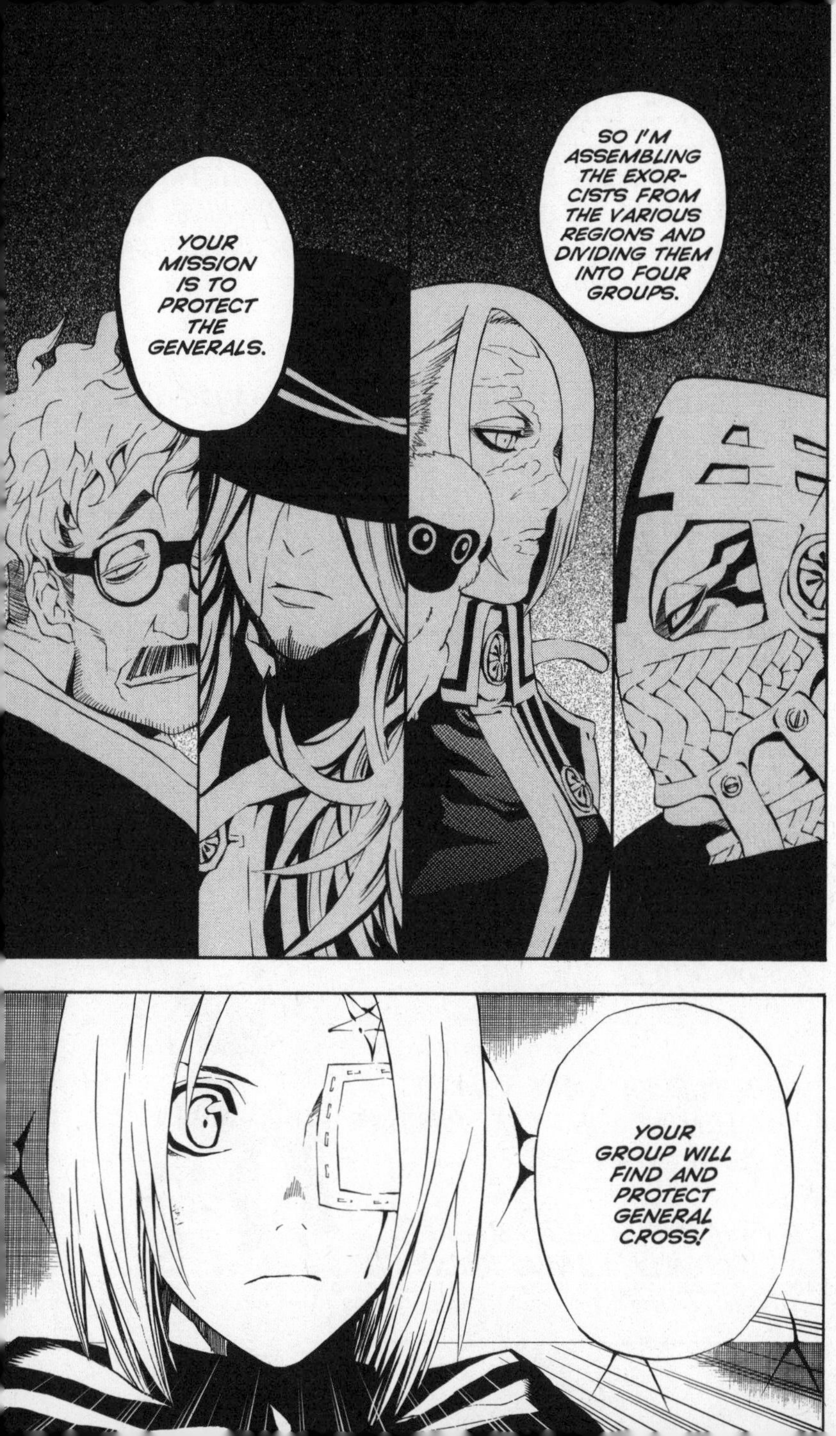
SO I'M ASSEMBLING THE EXOR-CISTS FROM THE VARIOUS REGIONS AND DIVIDING THEM INTO FOUR GROUPS.
YOUR MISSION IS TO PROTECT THE GENERALS.
YOUR GROUP WILL FIND AND PROTECT GENERAL CROSS!

KOMUI'S DISCUSSION ROOM VOL. 1

★ HOW DO YOU DO? I'M ALLEN WALKER. DUE TO THE SUDDEN ILLNESS OF CREATOR KATSURA HOSHINO, I'LL BE HANDLING THE DISCUSSION ROOM FOR THIS VOLUME. THANK YOU. NOW LET'S BEGIN.

Q. IF ALLEN, LALA, KANDA, LENALEE, LAVI, AND BOOKMAN WERE TO ARM-WRESTLE, WHO WOULD WIN?

A. CAN WE USE OUR INNOCENCES? IF SO, I THINK I MIGHT WIN. :) OH, BUT I COULDN'T USE MY FULL STRENGTH AGAINST THE GIRLS, SO EITHER LENALEE OR LALA WOULD WIN AND I'D COME IN SECOND. EVERYONE ELSE WOULD BE BELOW ME. :)

Q. WHY DOES GENERAL CROSS DISLIKE THE BLACK ORDER?

A. I REALLY DON'T WANT TO TALK ABOUT MY MASTER. I THINK I'M GOING TO BE SICK.

Q. IN THE 1ST NIGHT, WHY IS ALLEN WEARING THAT PIECE OF CLOTH ON HIS HEAD?

A. I WAS WEARING IT AS A HAT. (ACTUALLY, HE WAS HIDING HIS WHITE HAIR.)

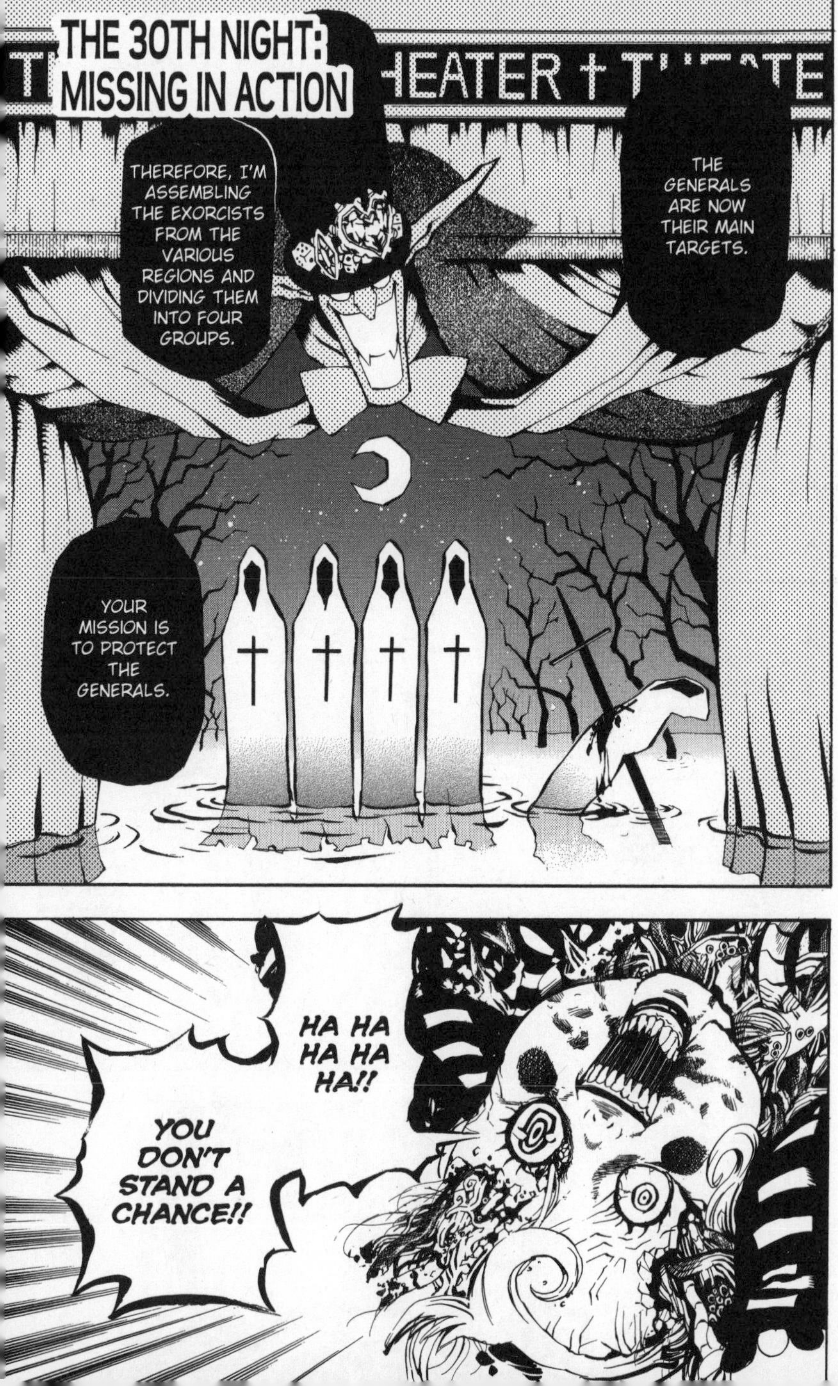
THE 30TH NIGHT: MISSING IN ACTION
THE GENERALS ARE NOW THEIR MAIN TARGETS.
THEREFORE, I'M ASSEMBLING THE EXORCISTS FROM THE VARIOUS REGIONS AND DIVIDING THEM INTO FOUR GROUPS.
YOUR MISSION IS TO PROTECT THE GENERALS.
HA HA HA HA HA!!
YOU DON'T STAND A CHANCE!!

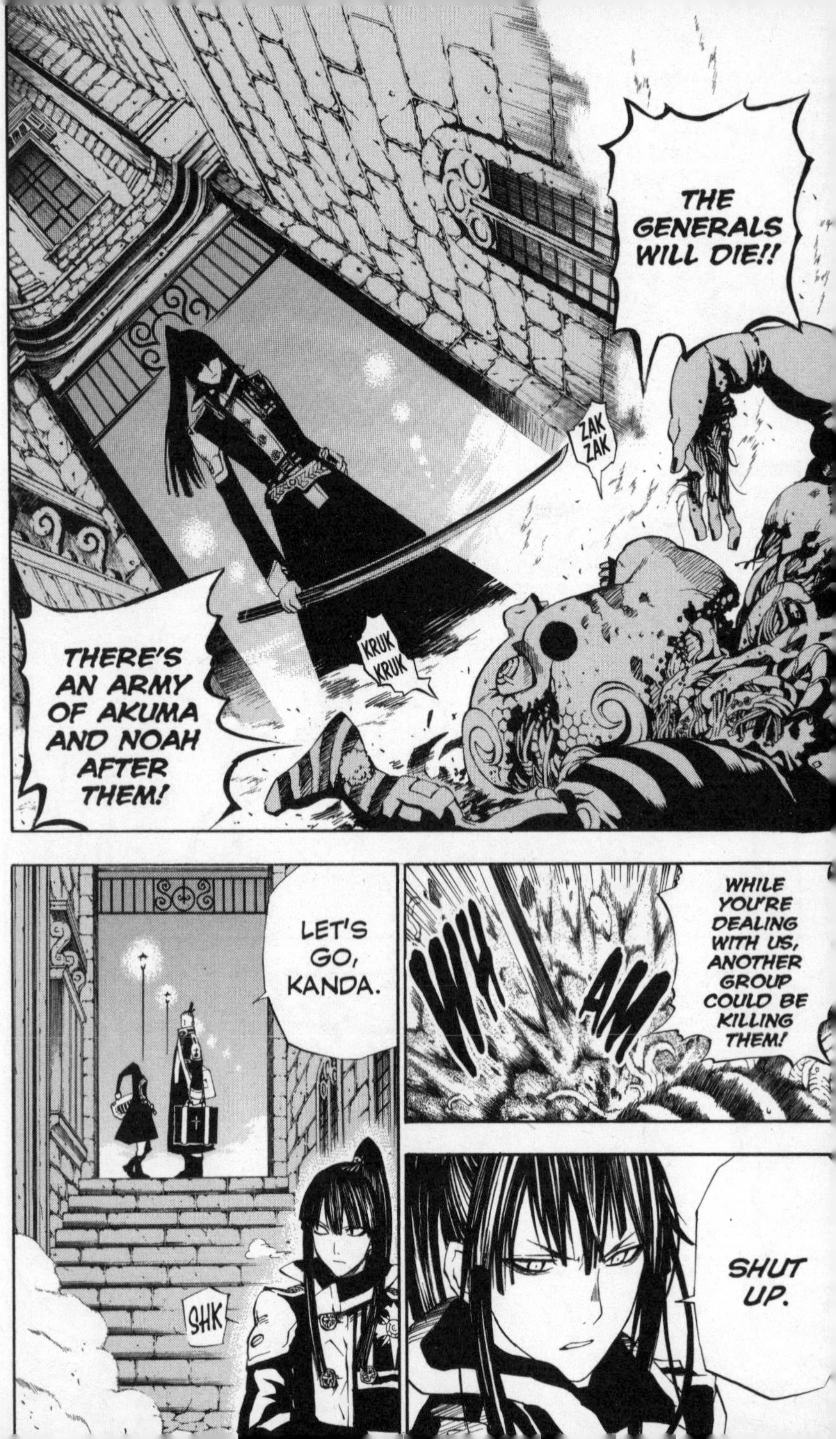
THE GENERALS WILL DIE!!
ZAK ZAK
THERE'S AN ARMY OF AKUMA AND NOAH AFTER THEM!
KRUK KRUK
WHILE YOU'RE DEALING WITH US, ANOTHER GROUP COULD BE KILLING THEM!
WHAM
LET'S GO, KANDA.
SHUT UP.
SHK

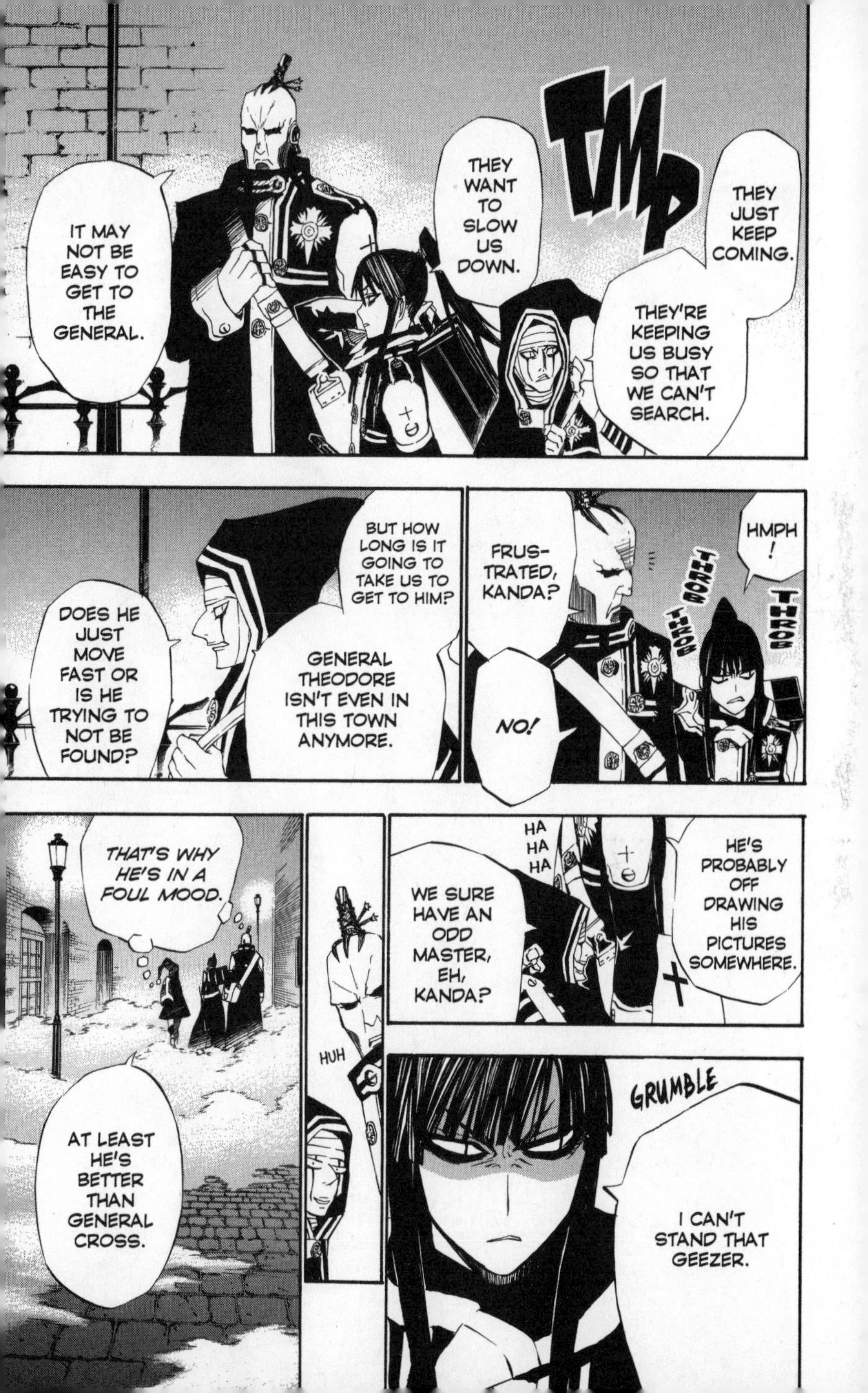
THEY JUST KEEP COMING.
TMP
THEY'RE KEEPING US BUSY SO THAT WE CAN'T SEARCH.
THEY WANT TO SLOW US DOWN.
IT MAY NOT BE EASY TO GET TO THE GENERAL.
HMPH!
THROB THROB
THROB
FRUS-TRATED, KANDA?
NO!
BUT HOW LONG IS IT GOING TO TAKE US TO GET TO HIM?
GENERAL THEODORE ISN'T EVEN IN THIS TOWN ANYMORE.
DOES HE JUST MOVE FAST OR IS HE TRYING TO NOT BE FOUND?
HE'S PROBABLY OFF DRAWING HIS PICTURES SOMEWHERE.
HA HA HA
WE SURE HAVE AN ODD MASTER, EH, KANDA?
GRUMBLE
I CAN'T STAND THAT GEEZER.
HUH
THAT'S WHY HE'S IN A FOUL MOOD.
AT LEAST HE'S BETTER THAN GENERAL CROSS.

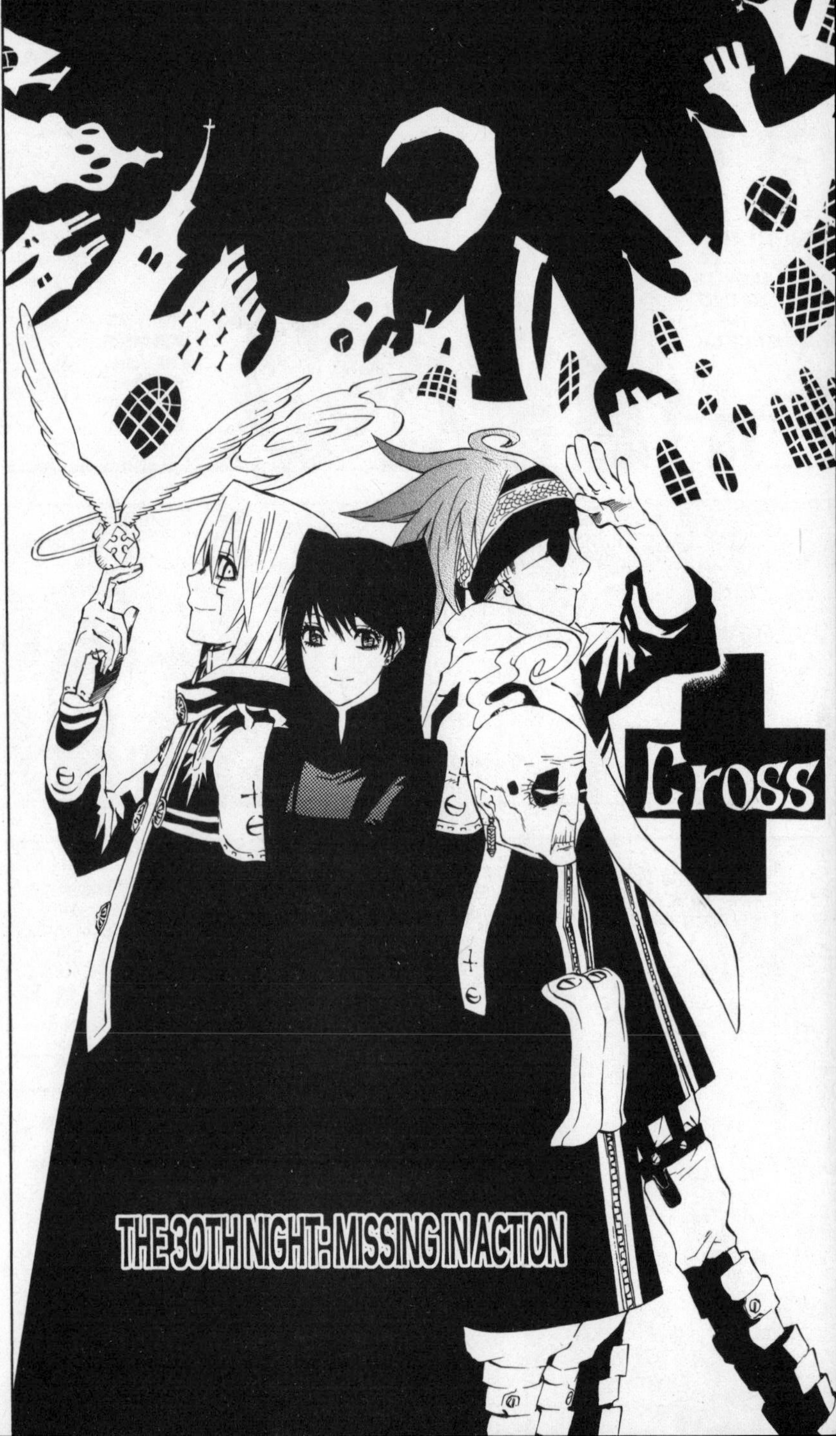
Cross
THE 30TH NIGHT: MISSING IN ACTION

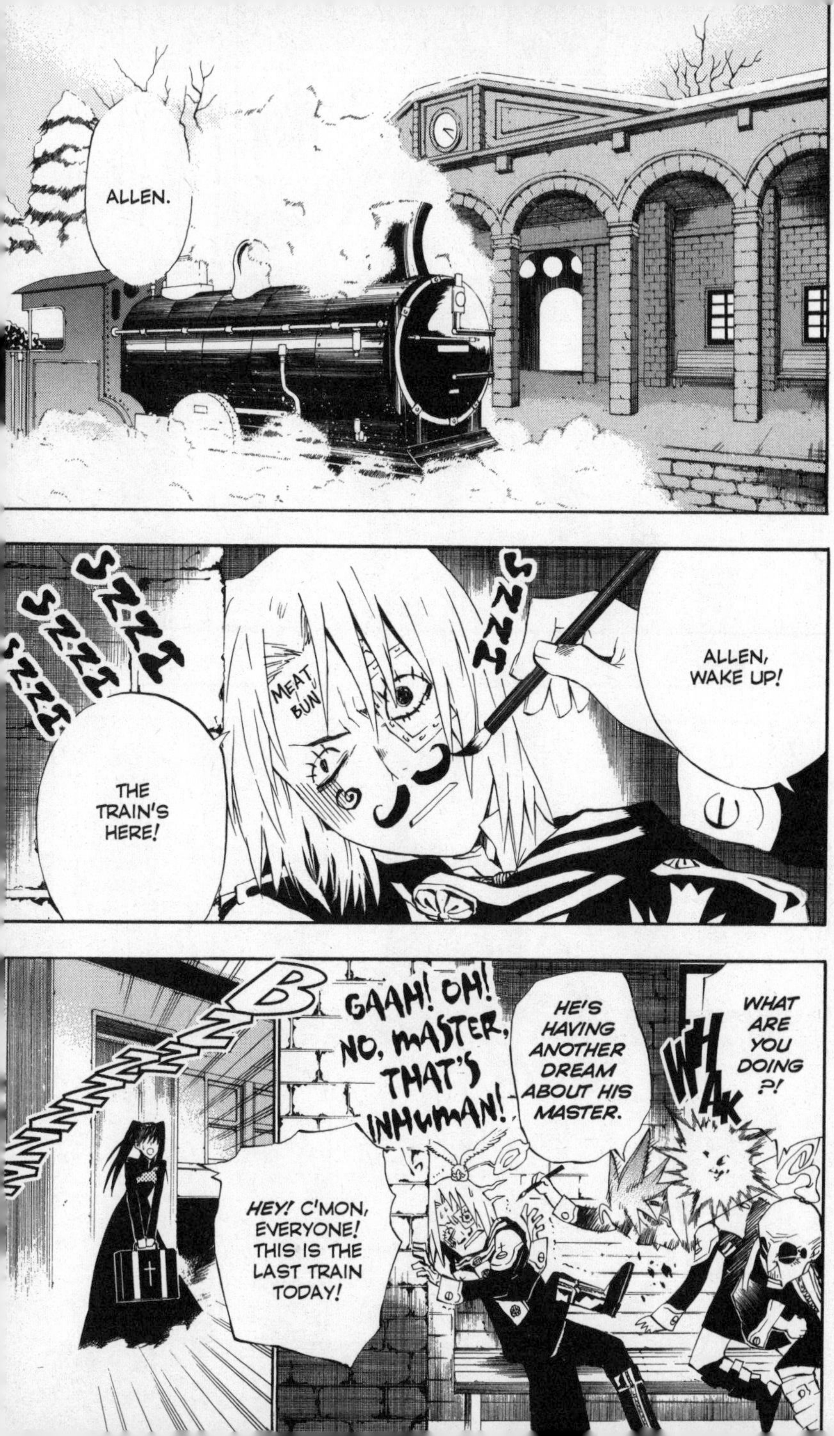
ALLEN.
ALLEN, WAKE UP!
MEAT BUN
THE TRAIN'S HERE!
WHAT ARE YOU DOING?!
WHAK
HE'S HAVING ANOTHER DREAM ABOUT HIS MASTER.
GAAH! OH! NO, MASTER, THAT'S INHUMAN!
HEY! C'MON, EVERYONE! THIS IS THE LAST TRAIN TODAY!

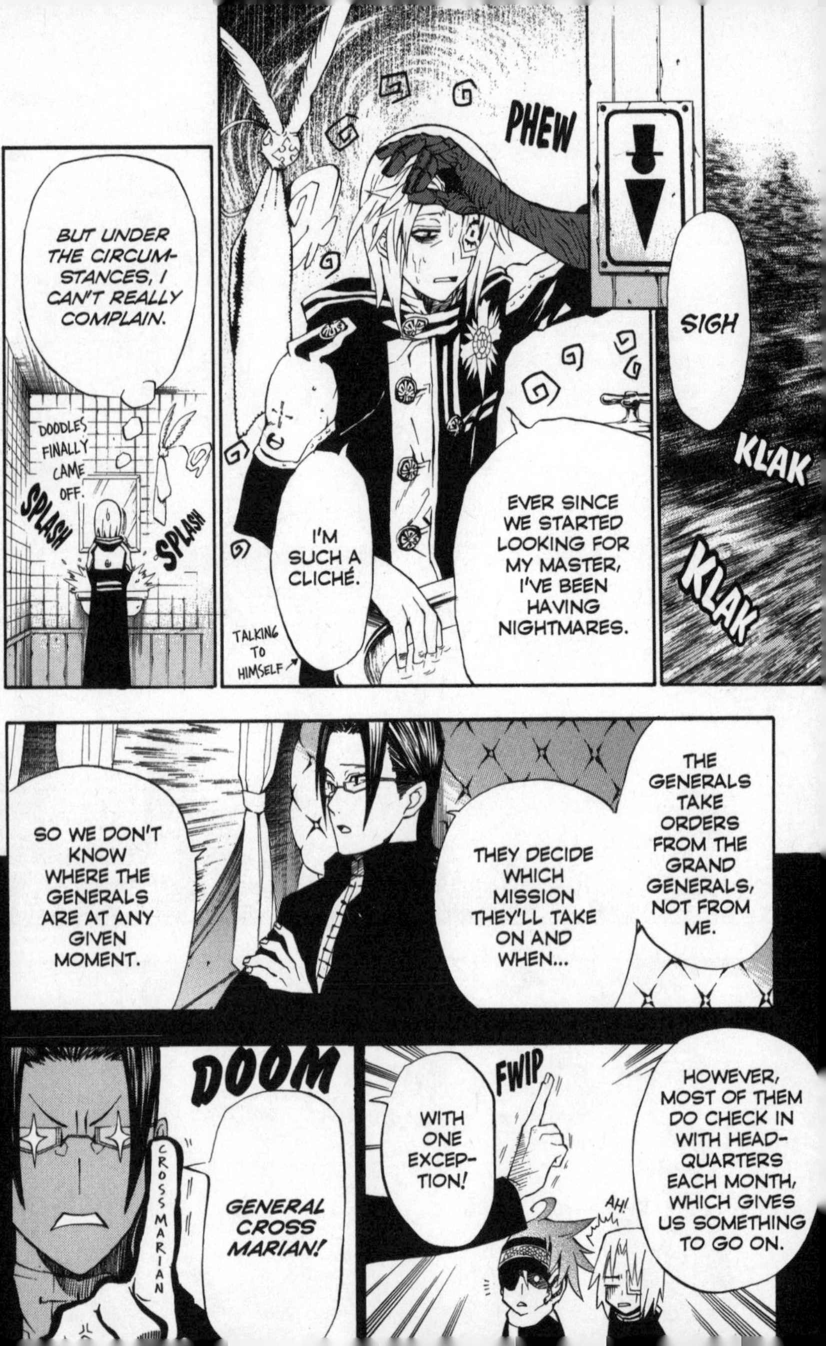
SIGH
KLAK
KLAK
PHEW
EVER SINCE WE STARTED LOOKING FOR MY MASTER, I'VE BEEN HAVING NIGHTMARES.
I'M SUCH A CLICHÉ.
TALKING TO HIMSELF
BUT UNDER THE CIRCUM-STANCES, I CAN'T REALLY COMPLAIN.
DOODLES FINALLY CAME OFF.
SPLASH
SPLASH
THE GENERALS TAKE ORDERS FROM THE GRAND GENERALS, NOT FROM ME.
THEY DECIDE WHICH MISSION THEY'LL TAKE ON AND WHEN...
SO WE DON'T KNOW WHERE THE GENERALS ARE AT ANY GIVEN MOMENT.
HOWEVER, MOST OF THEM DO CHECK IN WITH HEAD-QUARTERS EACH MONTH, WHICH GIVES US SOMETHING TO GO ON.
FWIP
WITH ONE EXCEP-TION!
AH!
DOOM
GENERAL CROSS MARIAN!
CROSS MARIAN

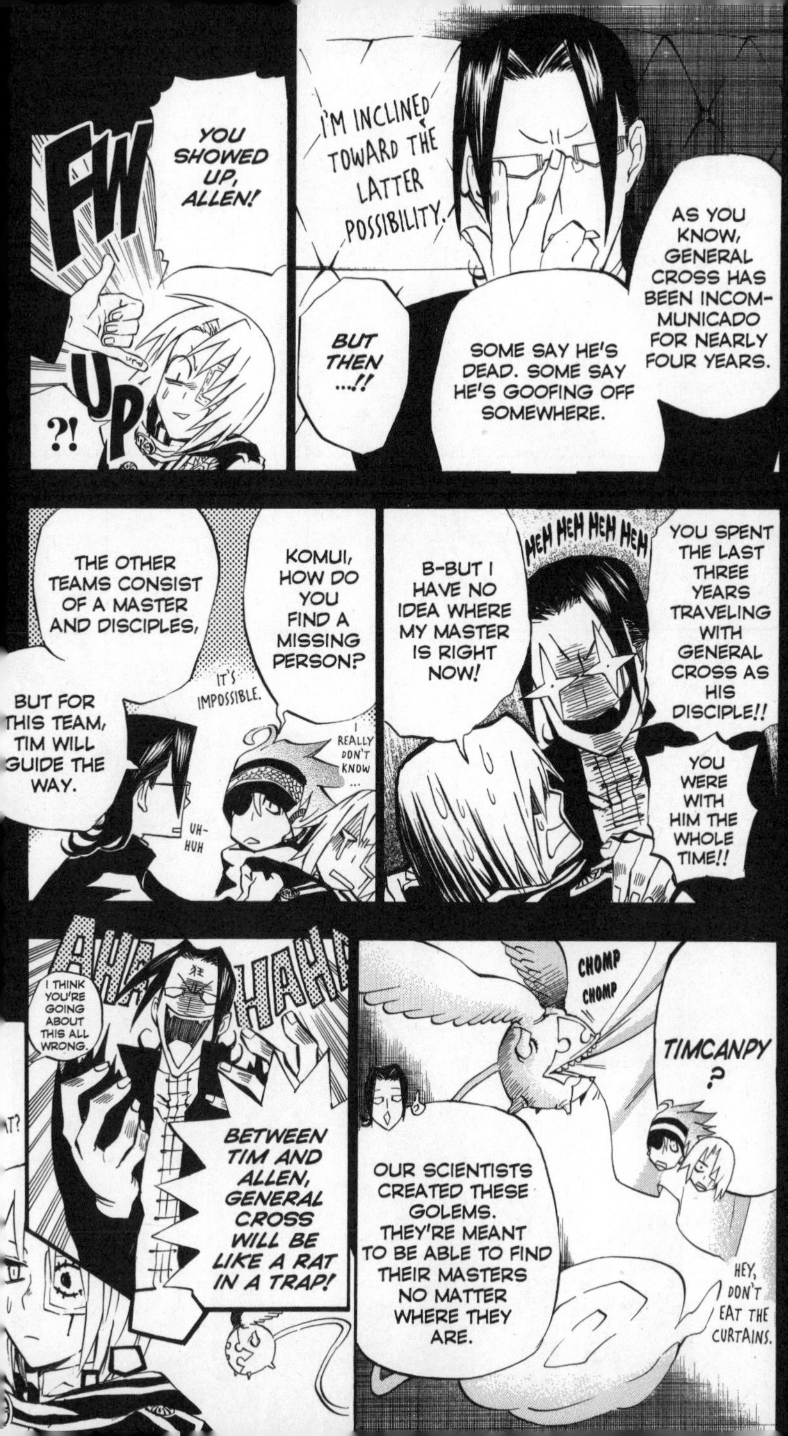
AS YOU KNOW, GENERAL CROSS HAS BEEN INCOMMUNICADO FOR NEARLY FOUR YEARS.
SOME SAY HE'S DEAD. SOME SAY HE'S GOOFING OFF SOMEWHERE.
I'M INCLINED TOWARD THE LATTER POSSIBILITY.
BUT THEN ...!!
FWUP
YOU SHOWED UP, ALLEN!
?!
YOU SPENT THE LAST THREE YEARS TRAVELING WITH GENERAL CROSS AS HIS DISCIPLE!!
HEH HEH HEH HEH
B-BUT I HAVE NO IDEA WHERE MY MASTER IS RIGHT NOW!
YOU WERE WITH HIM THE WHOLE TIME!!
KOMUI, HOW DO YOU FIND A MISSING PERSON?
THE OTHER TEAMS CONSIST OF A MASTER AND DISCIPLES,
IT'S IMPOSSIBLE.
I REALLY DON'T KNOW ...
BUT FOR THIS TEAM, TIM WILL GUIDE THE WAY.
UH-HUH
TIMCANPY?
CHOMP CHOMP
OUR SCIENTISTS CREATED THESE GOLEMS. THEY'RE MEANT TO BE ABLE TO FIND THEIR MASTERS NO MATTER WHERE THEY ARE.
HEY, DON'T EAT THE CURTAINS.
I THINK YOU'RE GOING ABOUT THIS ALL WRONG.
BETWEEN TIM AND ALLEN, GENERAL CROSS WILL BE LIKE A RAT IN A TRAP!

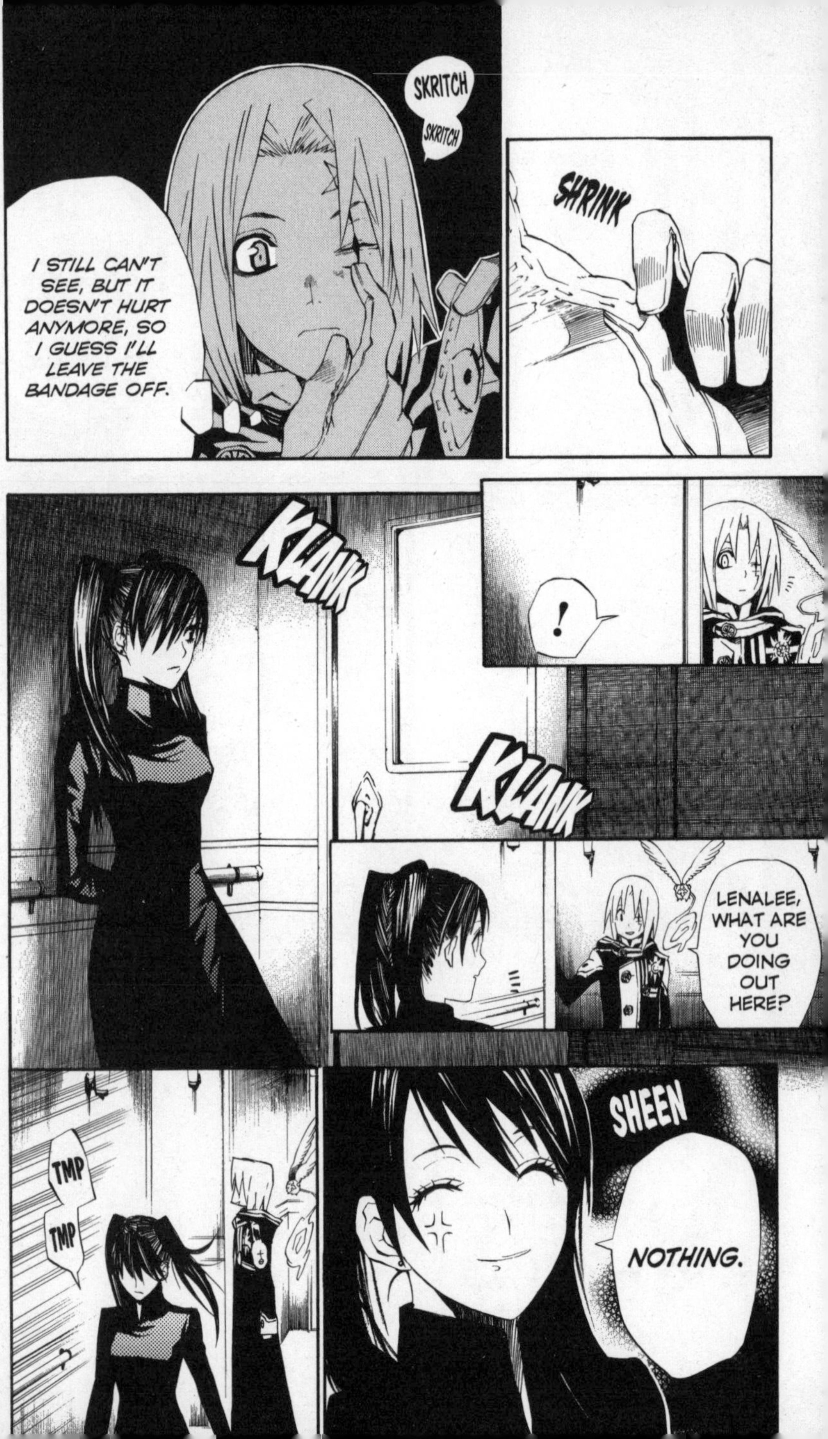
SHRINK
SKRITCH
SKRITCH
I STILL CAN'T SEE, BUT IT DOESN'T HURT ANYMORE, SO I GUESS I'LL LEAVE THE BANDAGE OFF.
!
LENALEE, WHAT ARE YOU DOING OUT HERE?
KLANK
KLANK
SHEEN
NOTHING.
TMP
TMP

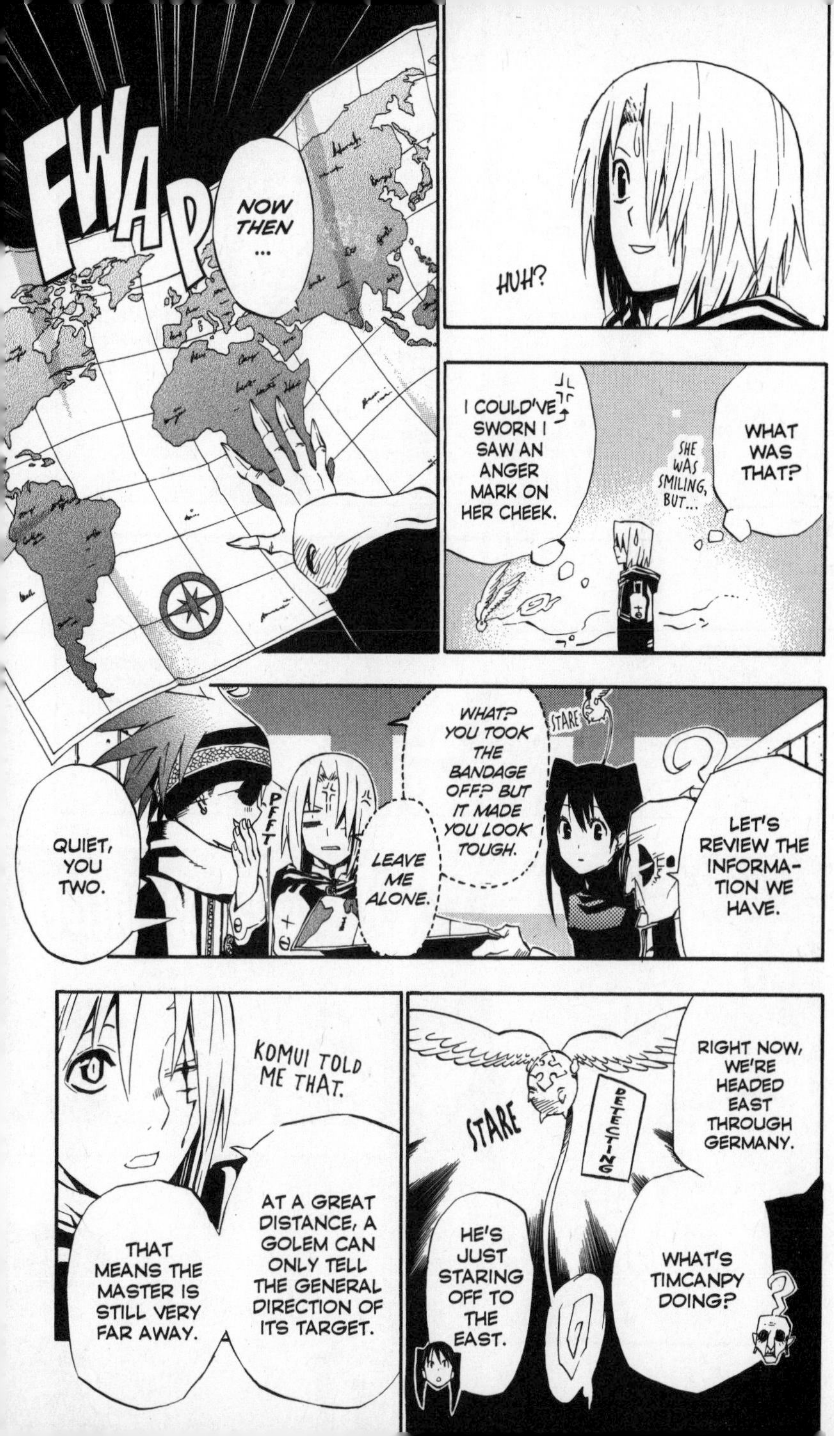
HUH?
WHAT WAS THAT?
SHE WAS SMILING, BUT...
I COULD'VE SWORN I SAW AN ANGER MARK ON HER CHEEK.
FWAP
NOW THEN ...
LET'S REVIEW THE INFORMATION WE HAVE.
STARE
WHAT? YOU TOOK THE BANDAGE OFF? BUT IT MADE YOU LOOK TOUGH.
LEAVE ME ALONE.
PFFT
QUIET, YOU TWO.
RIGHT NOW, WE'RE HEADED EAST THROUGH GERMANY.
DETECTING
STARE
WHAT'S TIMCANPY DOING?
HE'S JUST STARING OFF TO THE EAST.
AT A GREAT DISTANCE, A GOLEM CAN ONLY TELL THE GENERAL DIRECTION OF ITS TARGET.
KOMUI TOLD ME THAT.
THAT MEANS THE MASTER IS STILL VERY FAR AWAY.

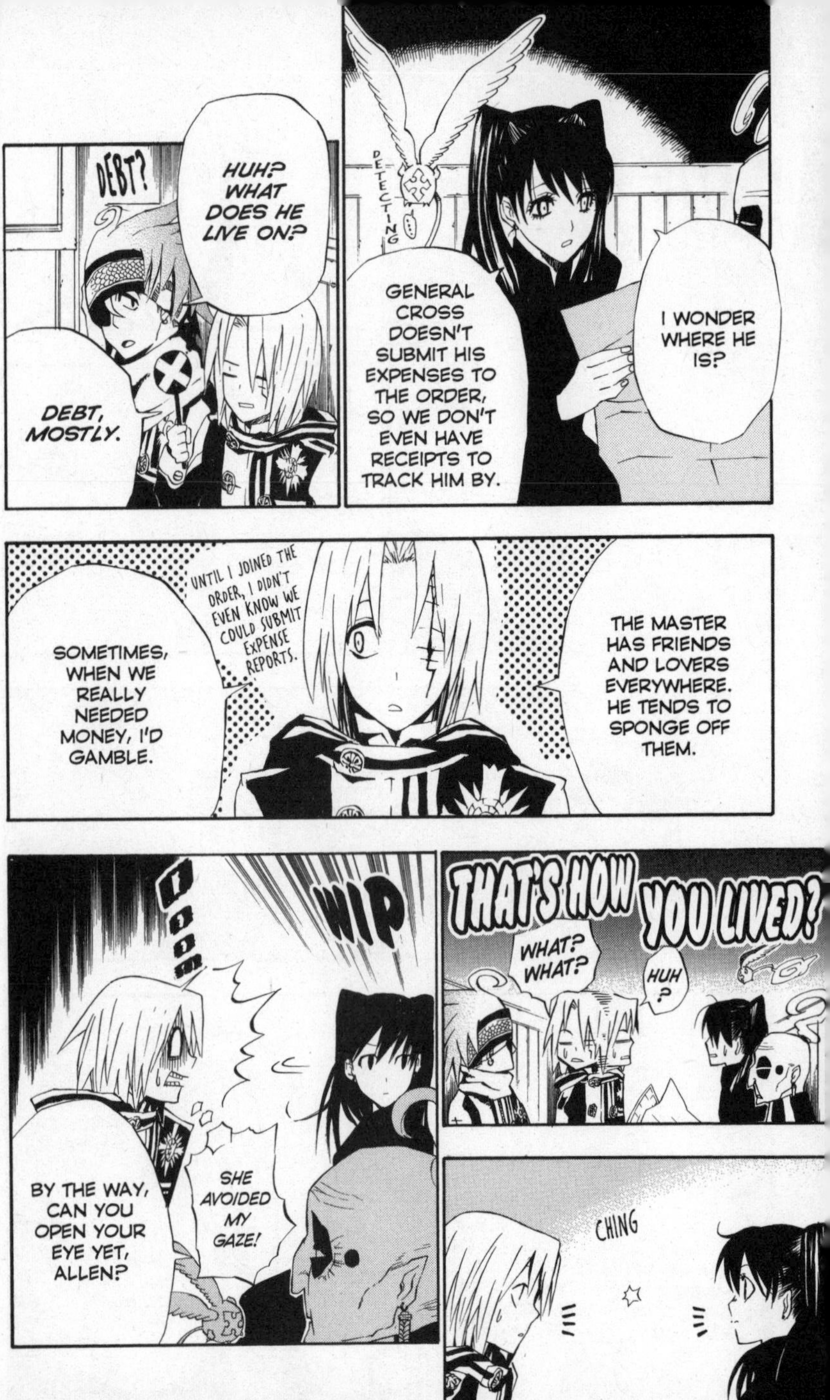
I WONDER WHERE HE IS?
DETECTING
GENERAL CROSS DOESN'T SUBMIT HIS EXPENSES TO THE ORDER, SO WE DON'T EVEN HAVE RECEIPTS TO TRACK HIM BY.
HUH? WHAT DOES HE LIVE ON?
DEBT?
DEBT, MOSTLY.
THE MASTER HAS FRIENDS AND LOVERS EVERYWHERE. HE TENDS TO SPONGE OFF THEM.
UNTIL I JOINED THE ORDER, I DIDN'T EVEN KNOW WE COULD SUBMIT EXPENSE REPORTS.
SOMETIMES, WHEN WE REALLY NEEDED MONEY, I'D GAMBLE.
THAT'S HOW YOU LIVED?
WHAT? WHAT?
HUH?
CHING
WHIP
SHE AVOIDED MY GAZE!
BY THE WAY, CAN YOU OPEN YOUR EYE YET, ALLEN?

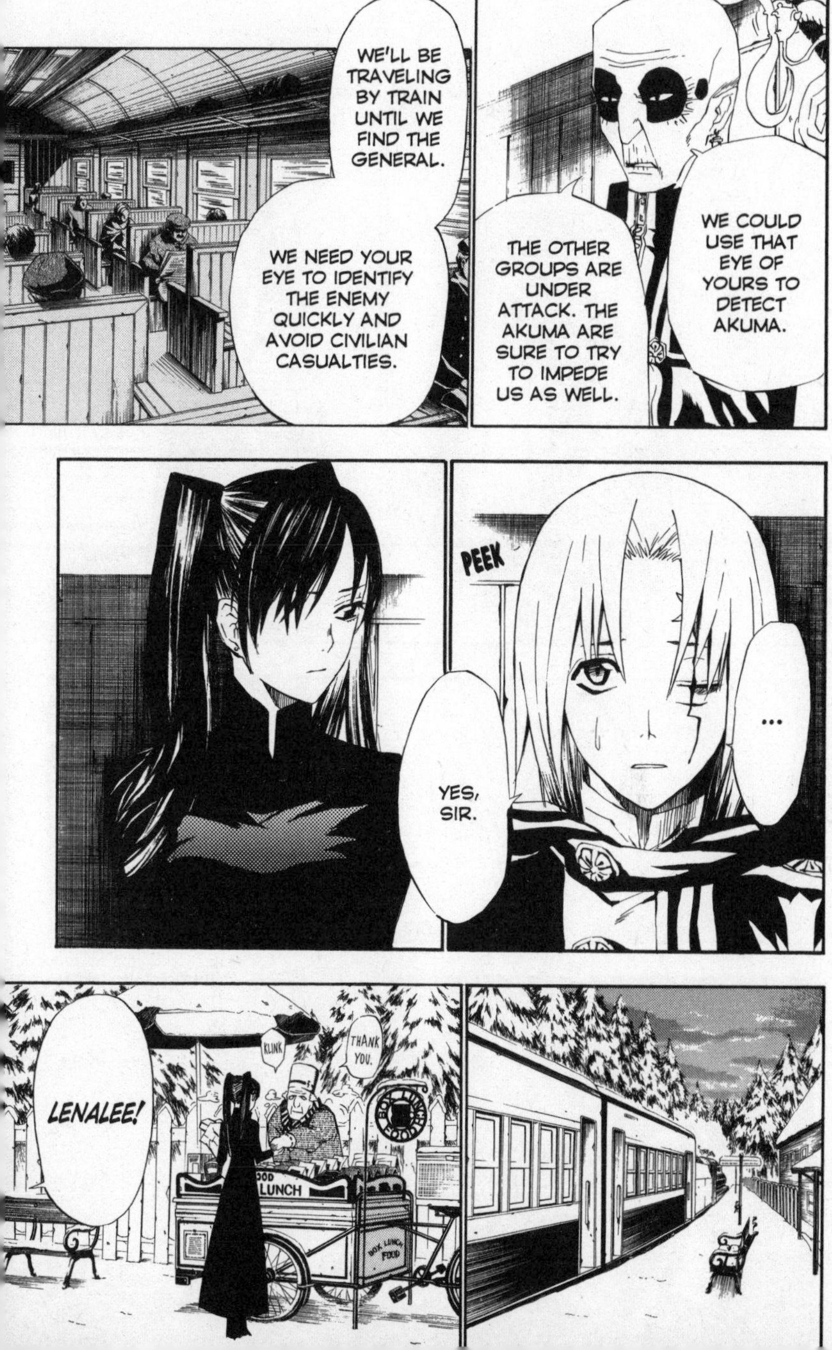
WE COULD USE THAT EYE OF YOURS TO DETECT AKUMA.
THE OTHER GROUPS ARE UNDER ATTACK. THE AKUMA ARE SURE TO TRY TO IMPEDE US AS WELL.
WE'LL BE TRAVELING BY TRAIN UNTIL WE FIND THE GENERAL.
WE NEED YOUR EYE TO IDENTIFY THE ENEMY QUICKLY AND AVOID CIVILIAN CASUALTIES.
...
PEEK
YES, SIR.
THANK YOU.
KLINK
BOX LUNCH FOOD
FOOD LUNCH
LENALEE!

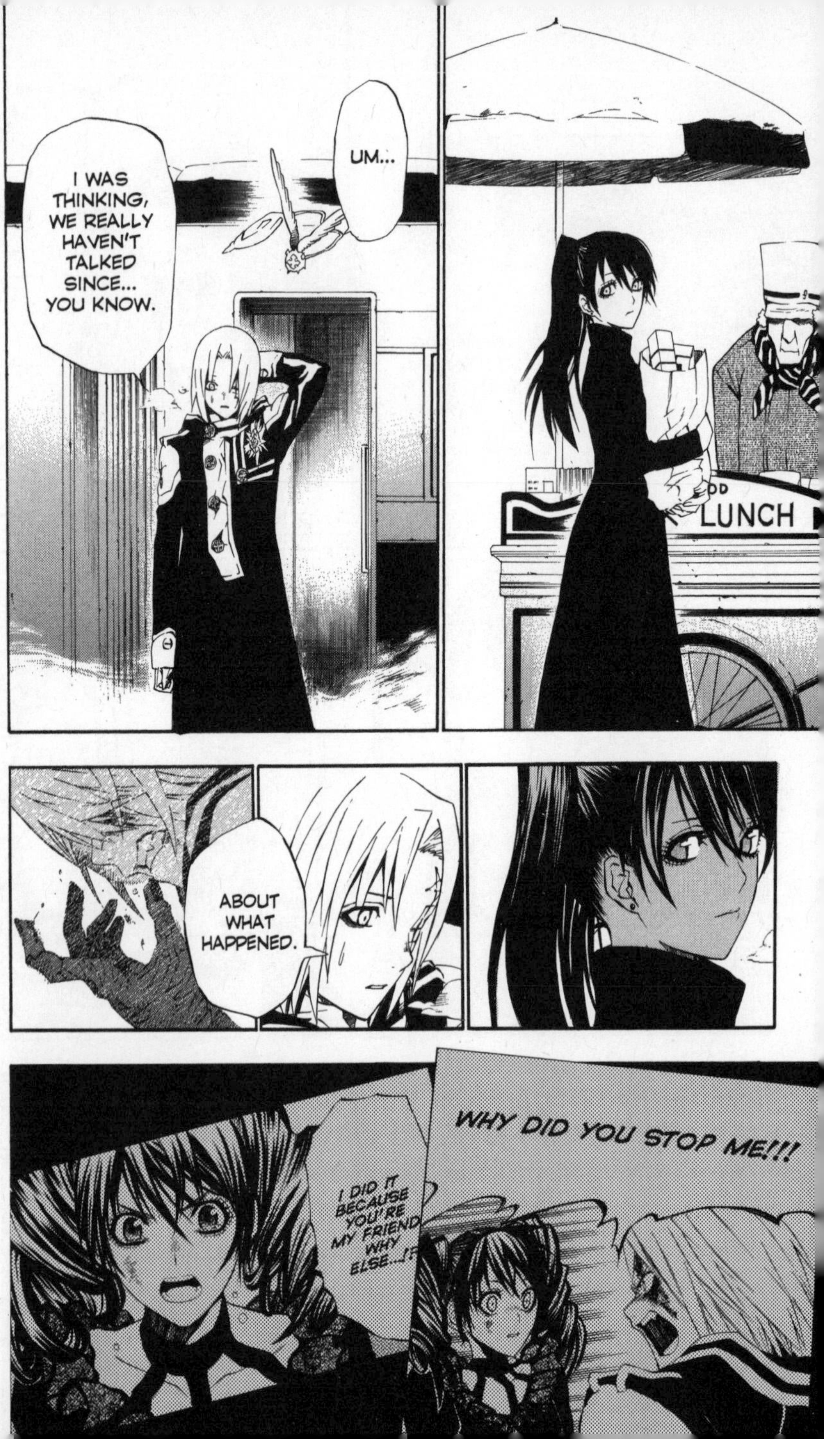
UM...
I WAS THINKING, WE REALLY HAVEN'T TALKED SINCE... YOU KNOW.
ABOUT WHAT HAPPENED.
LUNCH
WHY DID YOU STOP ME!!!
I DID IT BECAUSE YOU'RE MY FRIEND WHY ELSE...!?

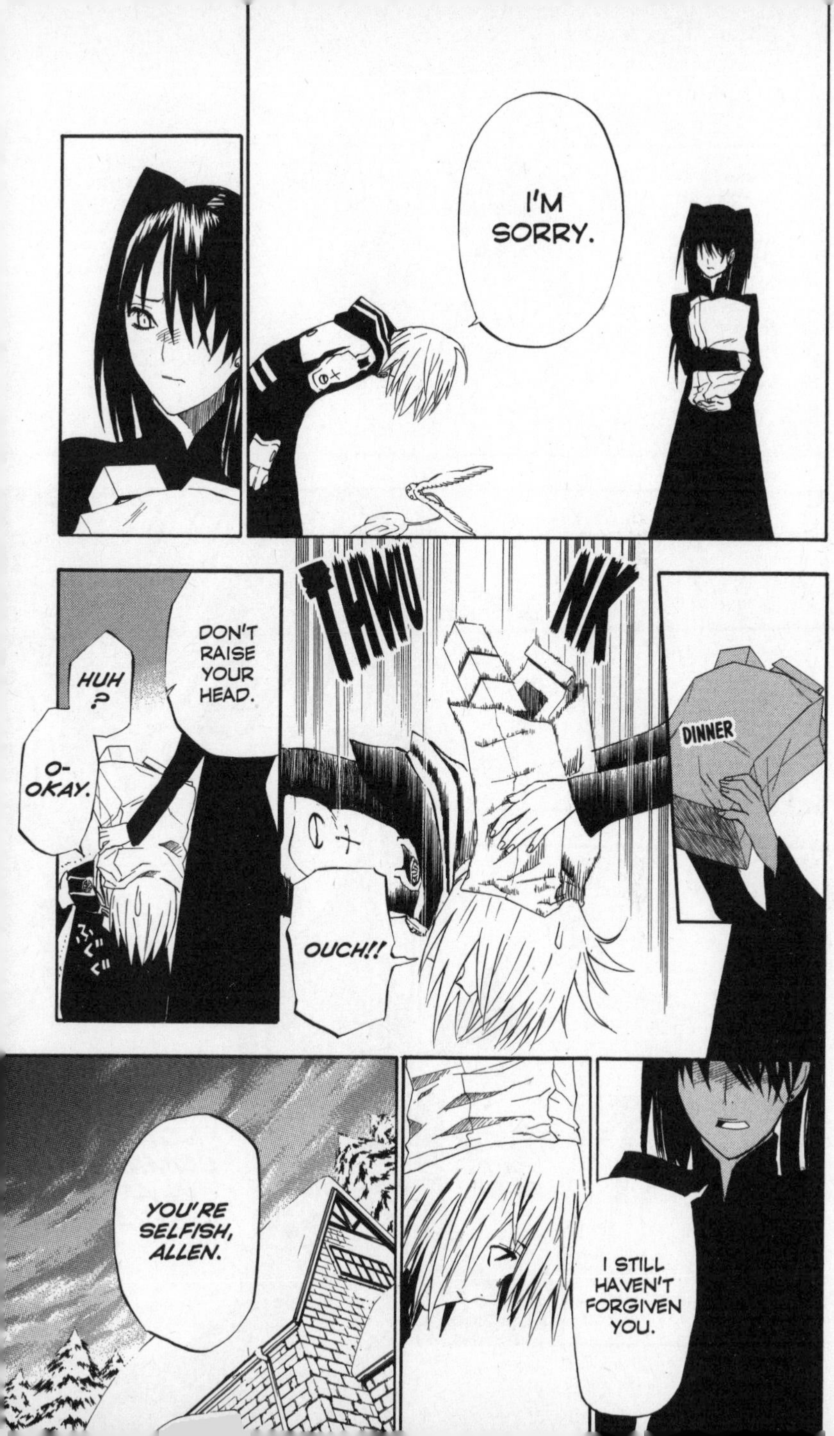
I'M SORRY.
DINNER
THWUNK
OUCH!!
DON'T RAISE YOUR HEAD.
HUH?
O-OKAY.
I STILL HAVEN'T FORGIVEN YOU.
YOU'RE SELFISH, ALLEN.

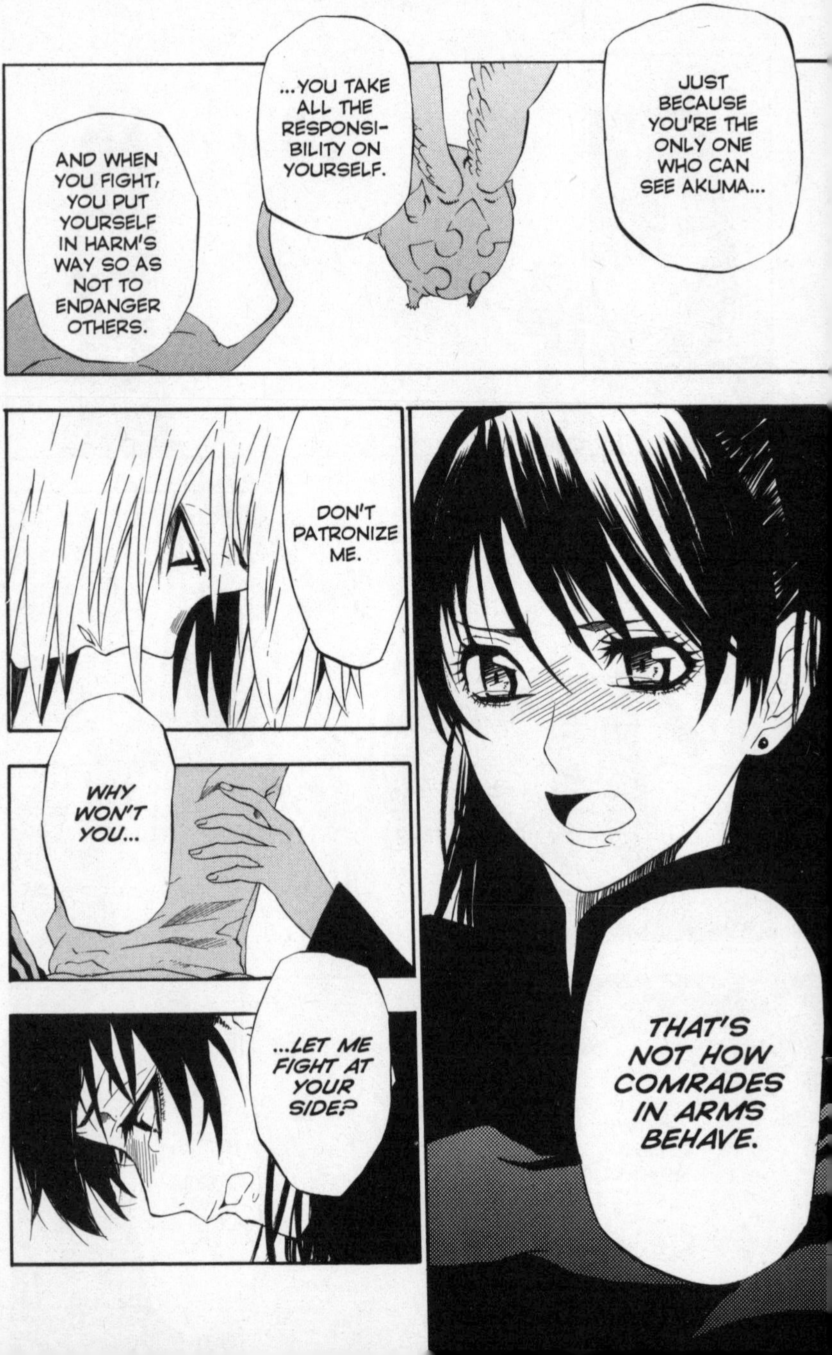
JUST BECAUSE YOU'RE THE ONLY ONE WHO CAN SEE AKUMA...
...YOU TAKE ALL THE RESPONSI-BILITY ON YOURSELF.
AND WHEN YOU FIGHT, YOU PUT YOURSELF IN HARM'S WAY SO AS NOT TO ENDANGER OTHERS.
THAT'S NOT HOW COMRADES IN ARMS BEHAVE.
DON'T PATRONIZE ME.
WHY WON'T YOU...
...LET ME FIGHT AT YOUR SIDE?

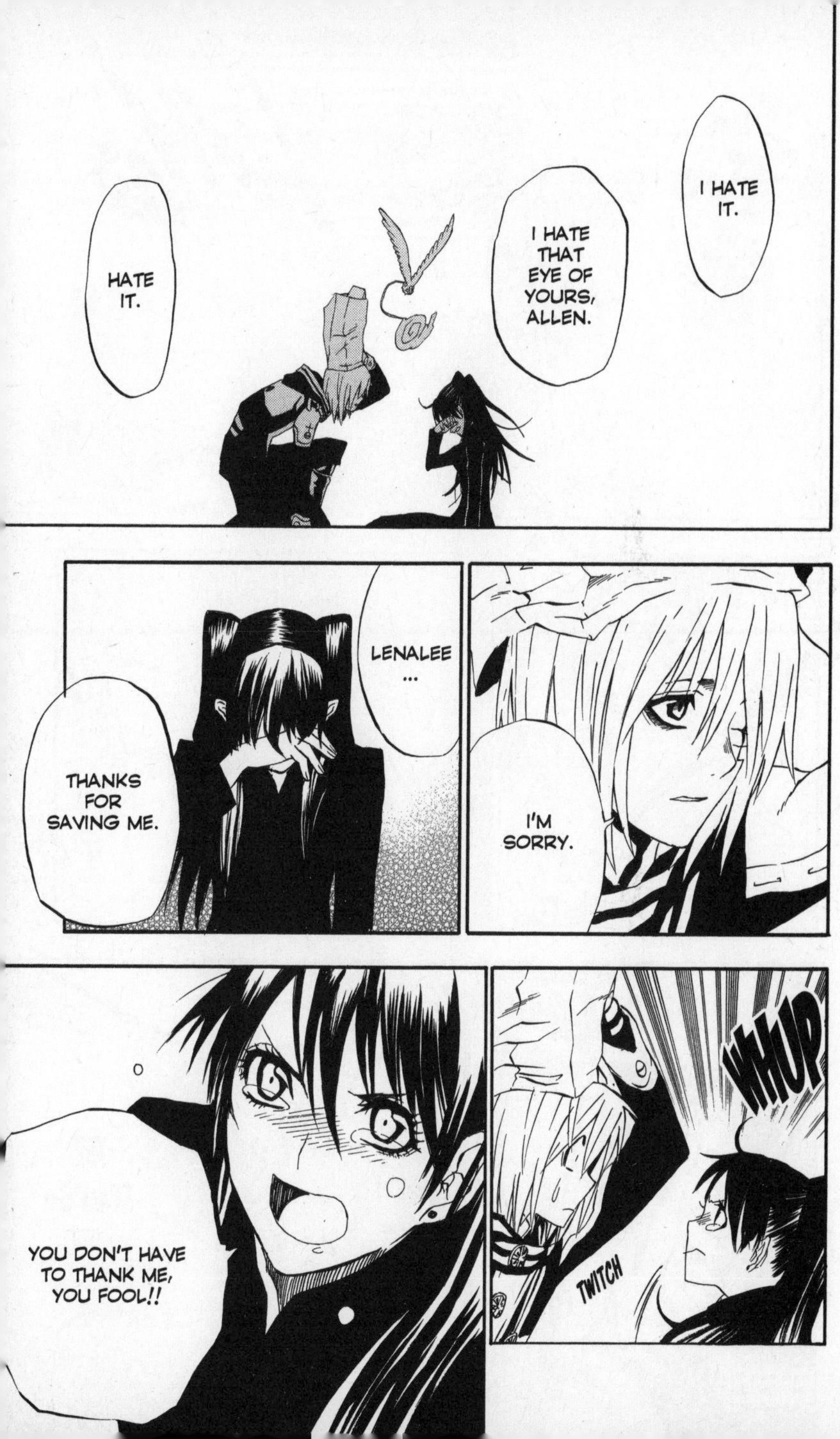
I HATE IT.
I HATE THAT EYE OF YOURS, ALLEN.
HATE IT.
I'M SORRY.
LENALEE ...
THANKS FOR SAVING ME.
WHUP
TWITCH
YOU DON'T HAVE TO THANK ME, YOU FOOL!!

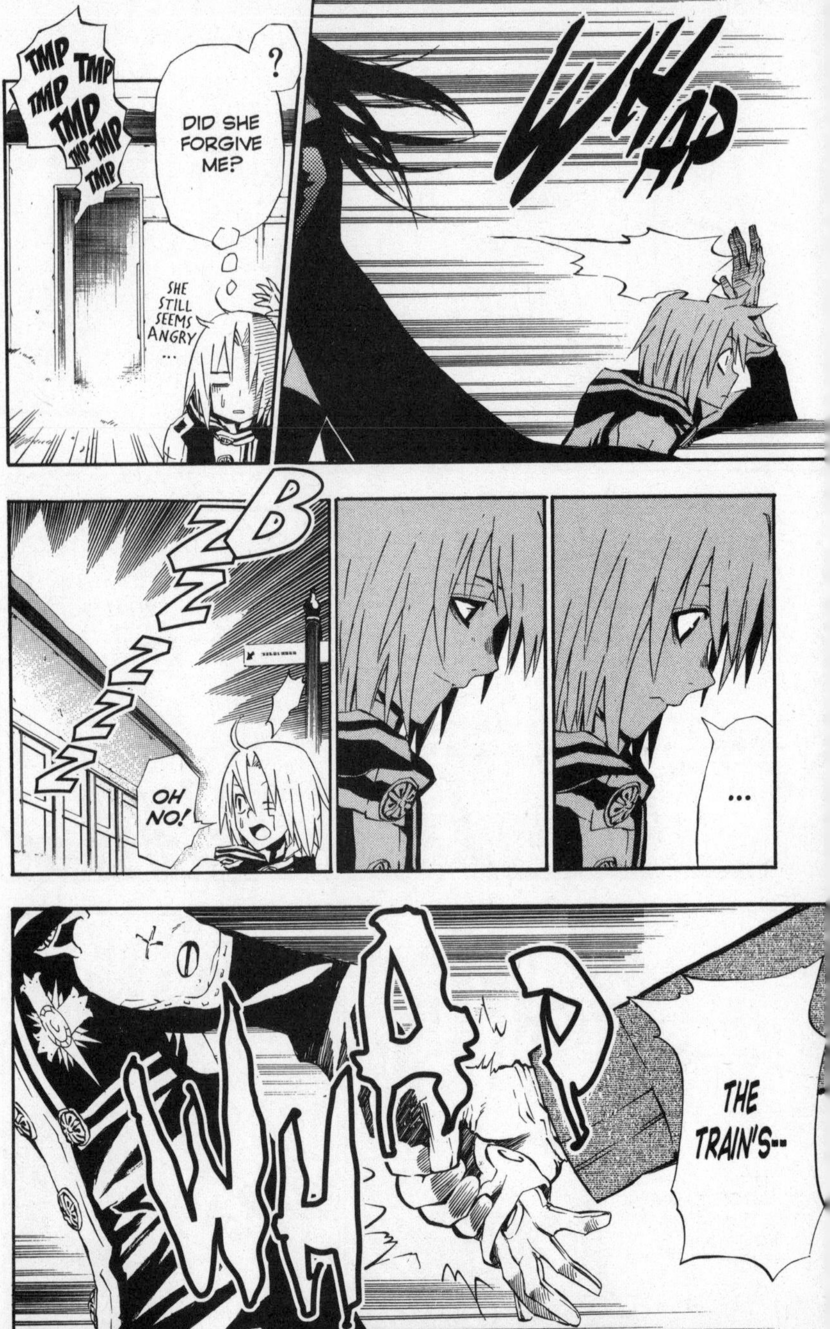
WHAP
TMP TMP TMP TMP TMP TMP TMP
?
DID SHE FORGIVE ME?
SHE STILL SEEMS ANGRY...
...
ZZZZZB
OH NO!
WHAP
THE TRAIN'S--

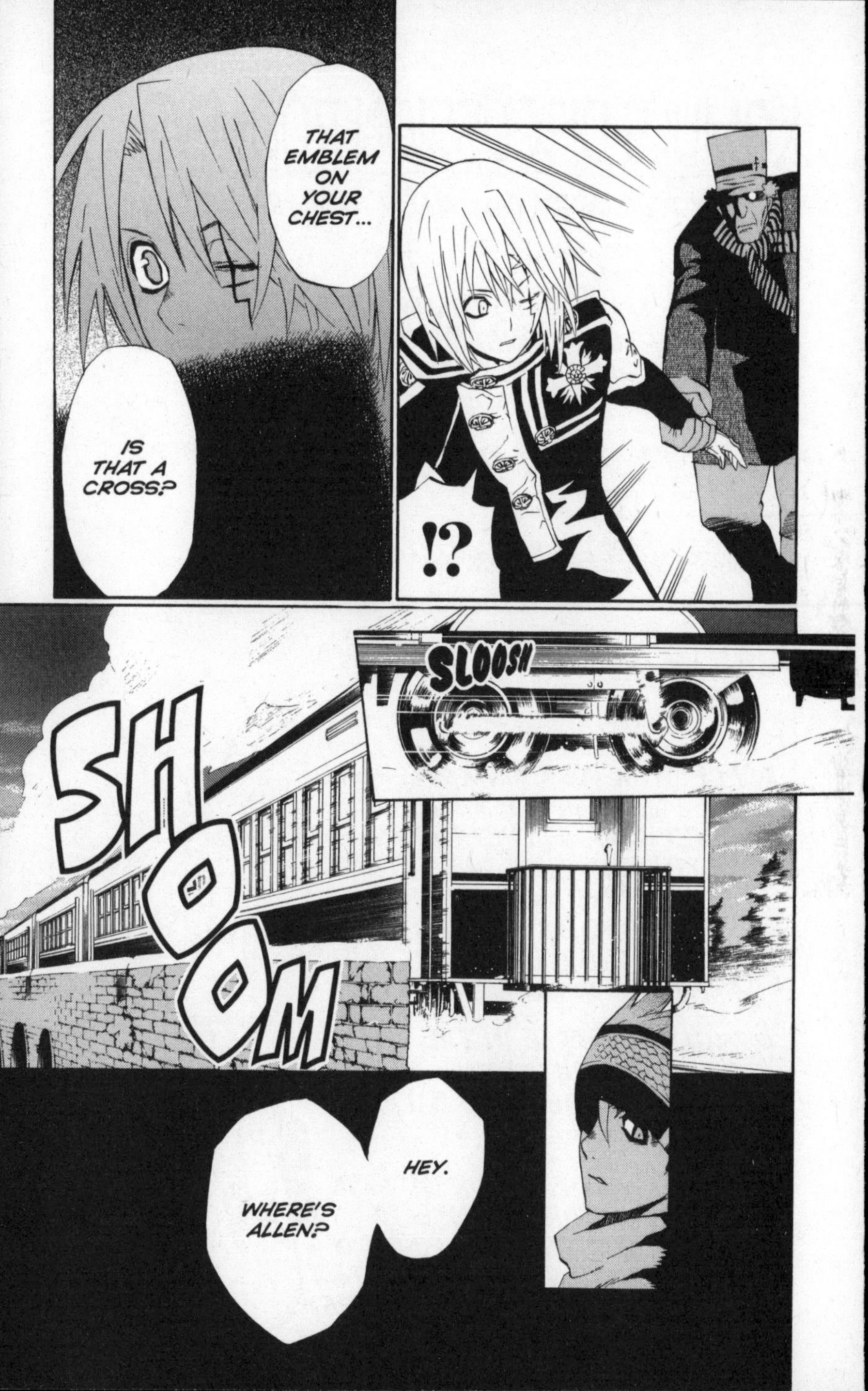

!?
THAT EMBLEM ON YOUR CHEST...
IS THAT A CROSS?
SLOOSH
SHOOM
HEY.
WHERE'S ALLEN?

KOMUI'S DISCUSSION ROOM VOL. 2

Q. WHY DOES KANDA CALL ALLEN "BEAN SPROUT"?

A. I HAVE NO IDEA! IT'S REALLY RUDE, DON'T YOU THINK? THAT DARNED PONYTAIL! WHAT PART OF ME LOOKS LIKE A BEAN SPROUT?! (HMPH!)

Q. JUST HOW DEEPLY IS GENERAL CROSS IN DEBT?

A. UGH? I'M FEELING SICK AGAIN...

Q. WHAT COLOR ARE ALLEN'S EYES REALLY?

A. I GET THIS QUESTION A LOT. WELL, LET'S SEE. THEY'RE REALLY SILVER-GRAY. IF THEY LOOK BLUE OR RED IN SOME COLOR PAGES, THAT'S JUST HOSHINO AND HIS EDITOR HAVING FUN. BUT I HEAR THAT MY OFFICIAL EYE COLOR WAS RECENTLY FINALIZED AS SILVER-GRAY.

Q. WHAT DO PEOPLE IN THE ORDER DO ABOUT BATHS? DO ALL THE LIVING QUARTERS HAVE BATHS?

A. BATHS? WE DON'T HAVE BATHS IN OUR ROOMS. WOULD YOU LIKE TO HAVE A LOOK? (GETTING UP OUT OF CHAIR) WHY DON'T YOU COME WITH ME NOW. LET'S GO! (GO TO PAGE 96)

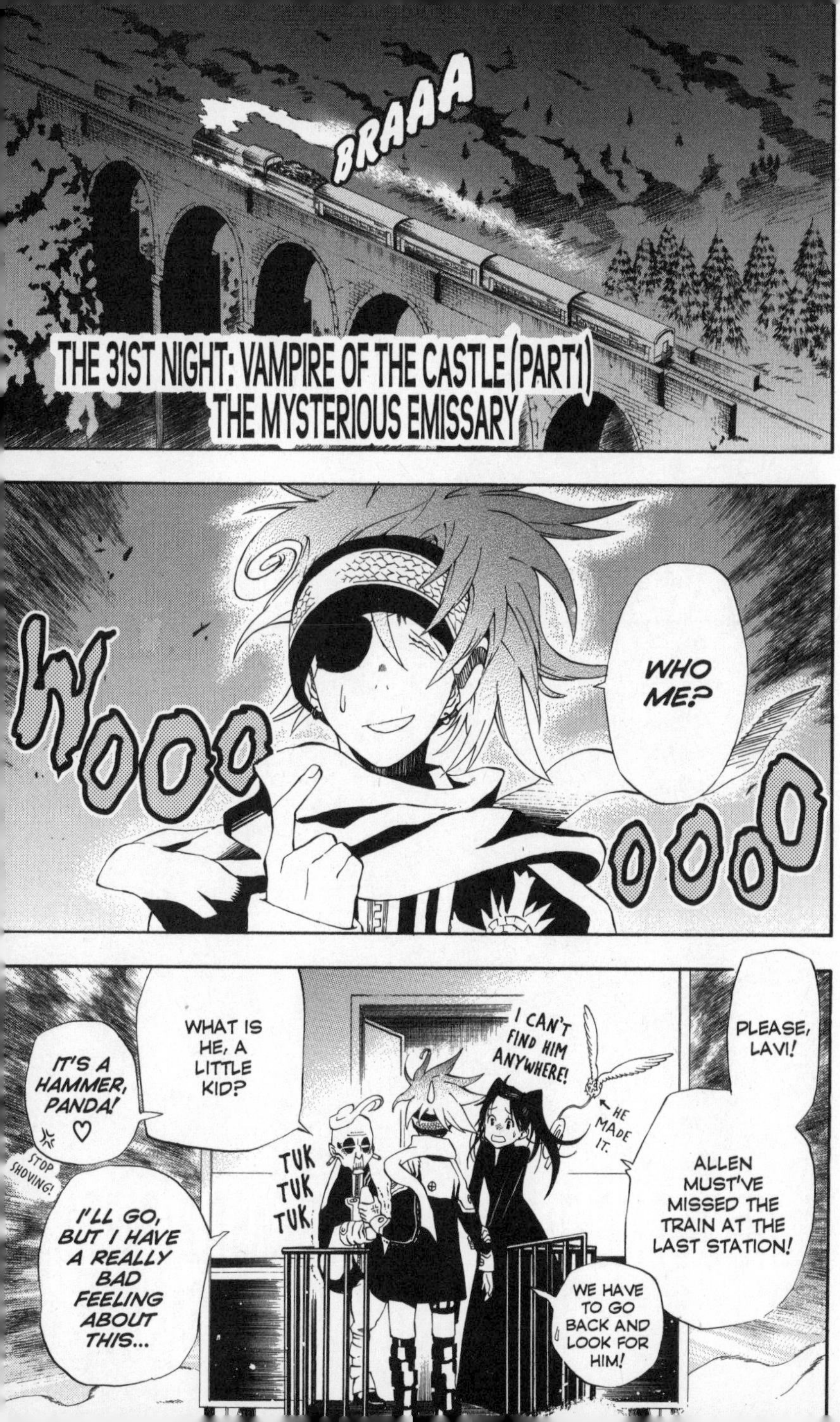
BRAAA
THE 31ST NIGHT: VAMPIRE OF THE CASTLE (PART1)
THE MYSTERIOUS EMISSARY
WHO ME?
WOOOOOOOO
PLEASE, LAVI!
ALLEN MUST'VE MISSED THE TRAIN AT THE LAST STATION!
WE HAVE TO GO BACK AND LOOK FOR HIM!
I CAN'T FIND HIM ANYWHERE!
HE MADE IT.
WHAT IS HE, A LITTLE KID?
TUK TUK TUK
IT'S A HAMMER, PANDA! ♡
STOP SHOVING!
I'LL GO, BUT I HAVE A REALLY BAD FEELING ABOUT THIS...

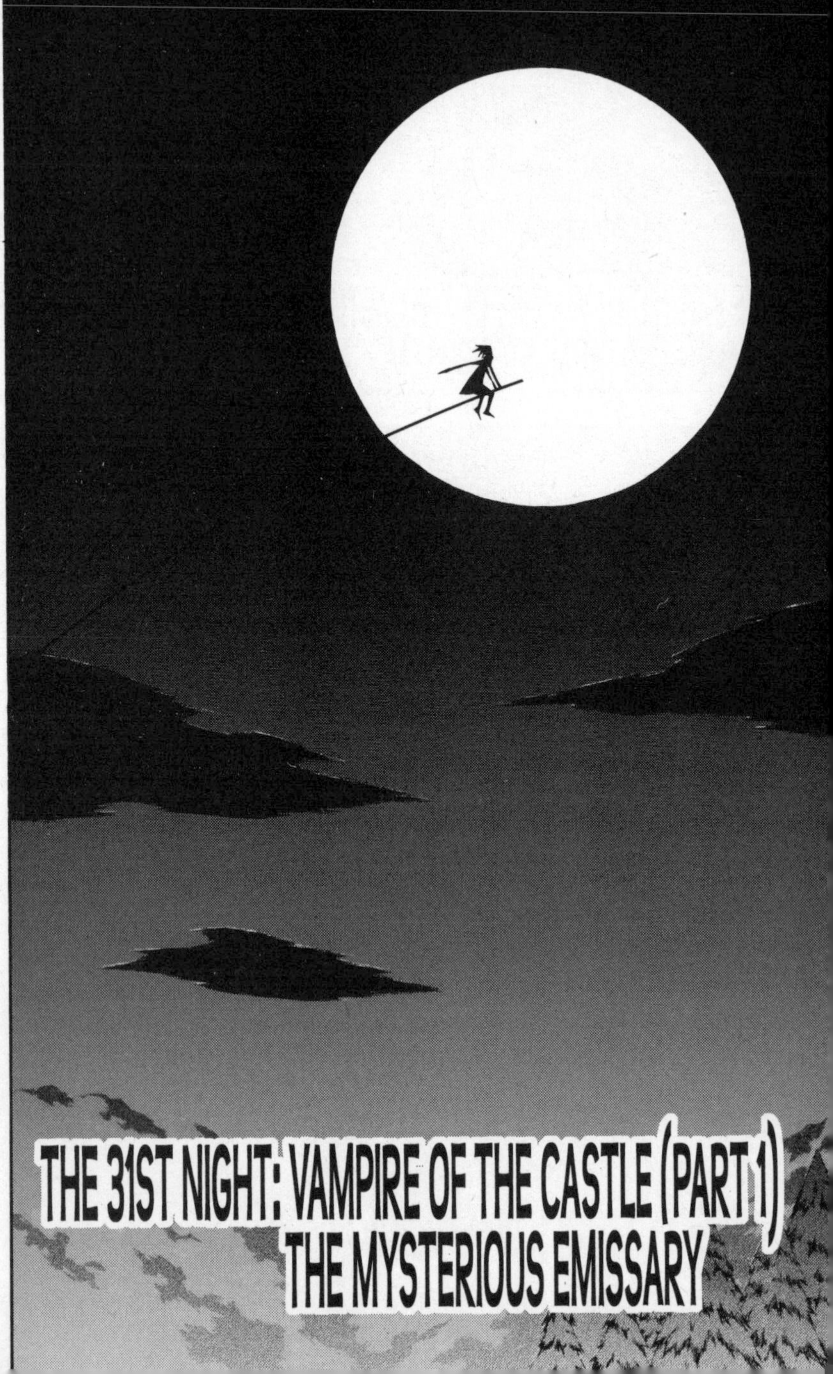
THE 31ST NIGHT: VAMPIRE OF THE CASTLE (PART 1)
THE MYSTERIOUS EMISSARY

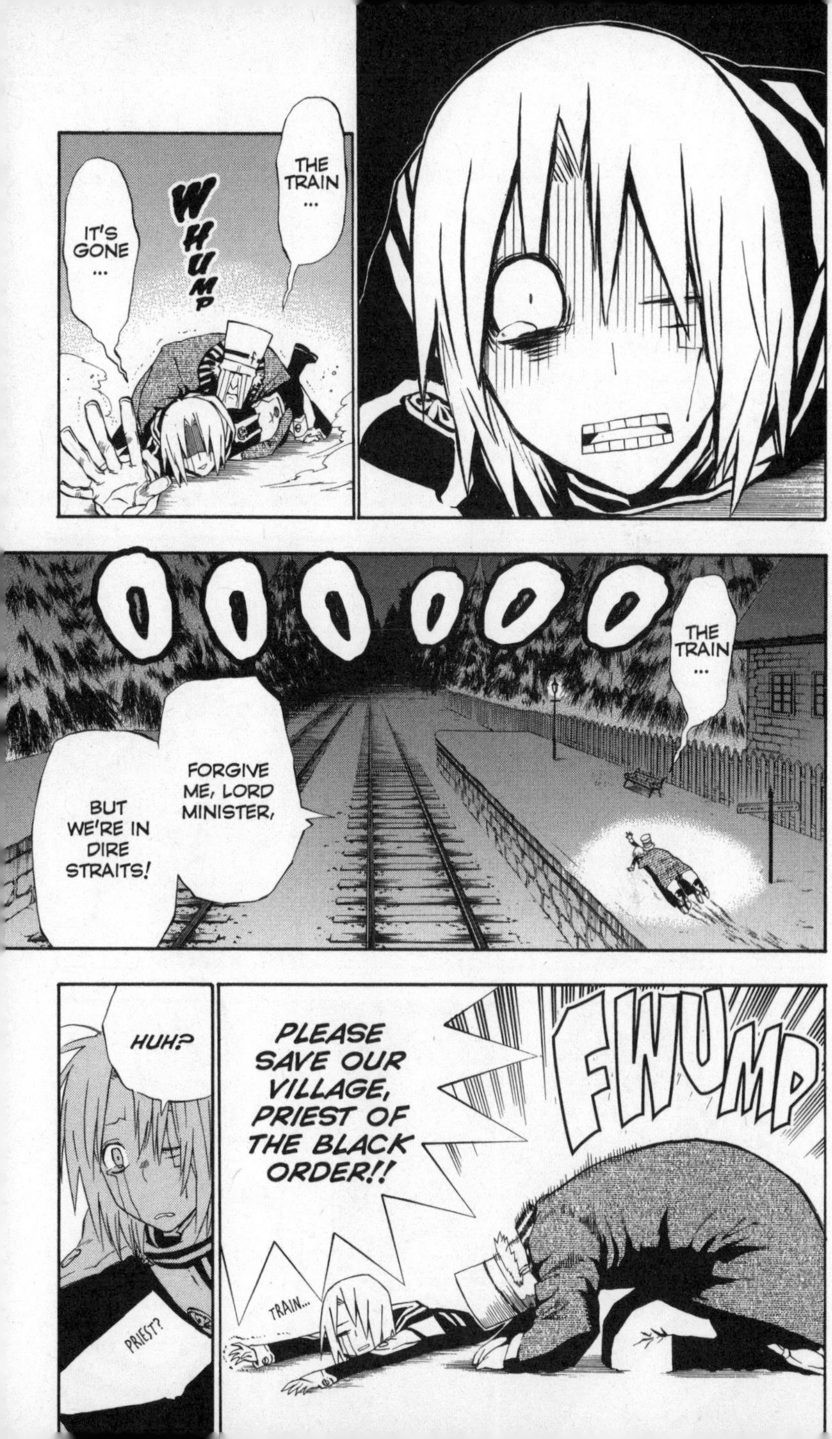
THE TRAIN ...
WHUMP
IT'S GONE ...
OOOOOO
THE TRAIN ...
FORGIVE ME, LORD MINISTER,
BUT WE'RE IN DIRE STRAITS!
FWUMP
PLEASE SAVE OUR VILLAGE, PRIEST OF THE BLACK ORDER!!
TRAIN...
HUH?
PRIEST?

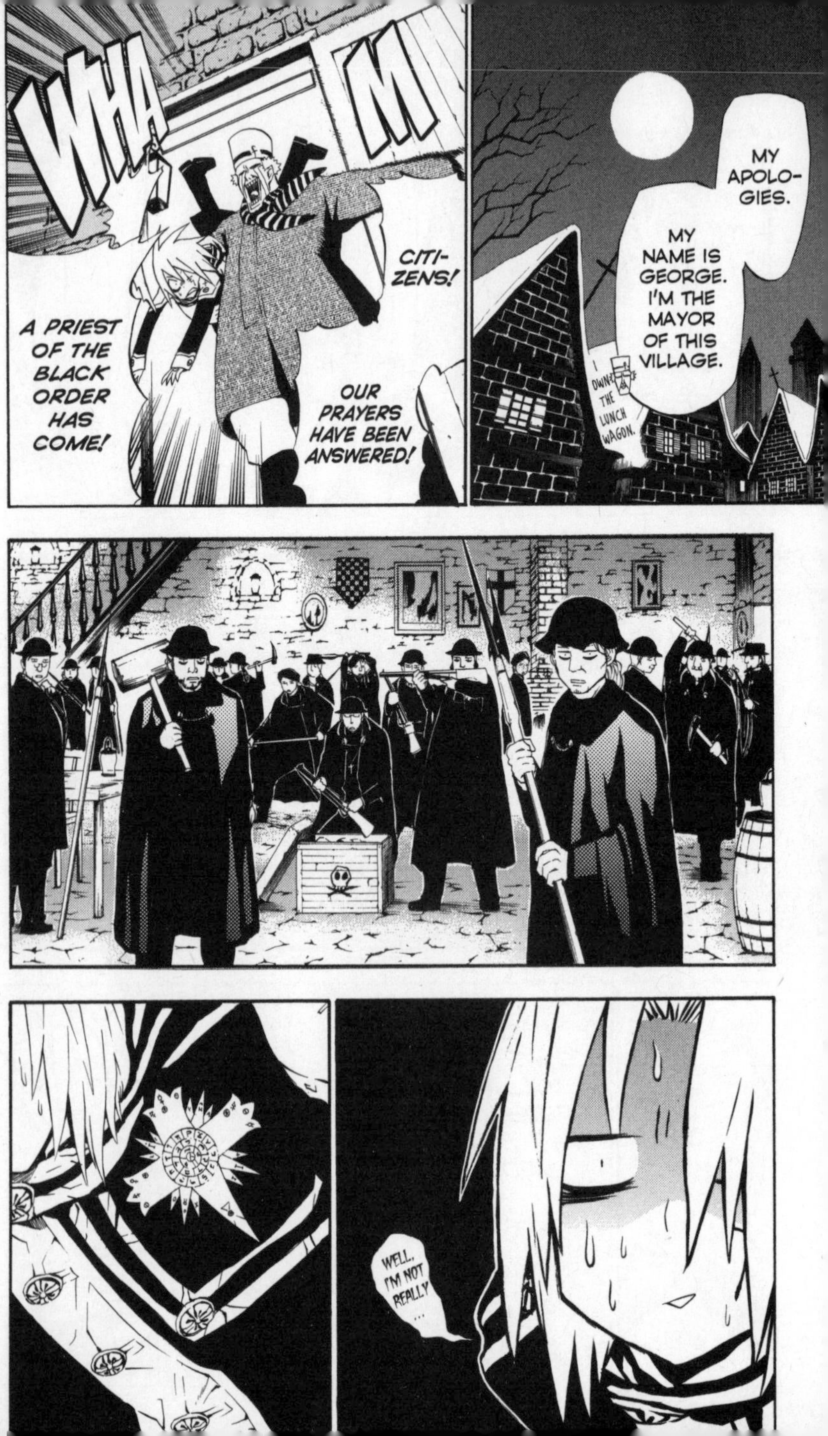
MY APOLOGIES.
MY NAME IS GEORGE. I'M THE MAYOR OF THIS VILLAGE.
I OWN THE LUNCH WAGON.
WHAM
CITIZENS!
OUR PRAYERS HAVE BEEN ANSWERED!
A PRIEST OF THE BLACK ORDER HAS COME!
WELL, I'M NOT REALLY...

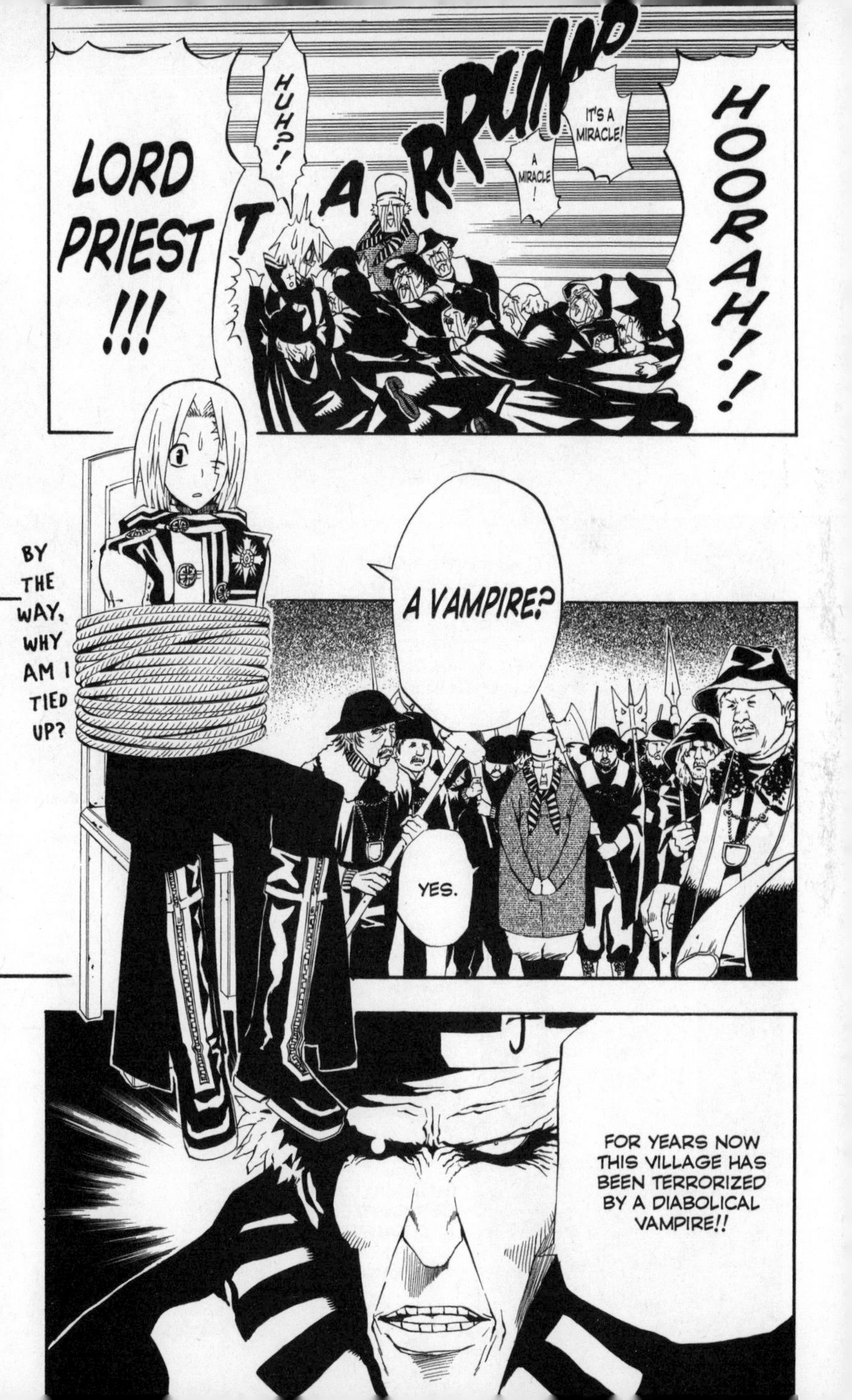
HOORAH!!
IT'S A MIRACLE!
A MIRACLE!
TARRUMP
HUH?!
LORD PRIEST!!!
A VAMPIRE?
YES.
BY THE WAY, WHY AM I TIED UP?
FOR YEARS NOW THIS VILLAGE HAS BEEN TERRORIZED BY A DIABOLICAL VAMPIRE!!

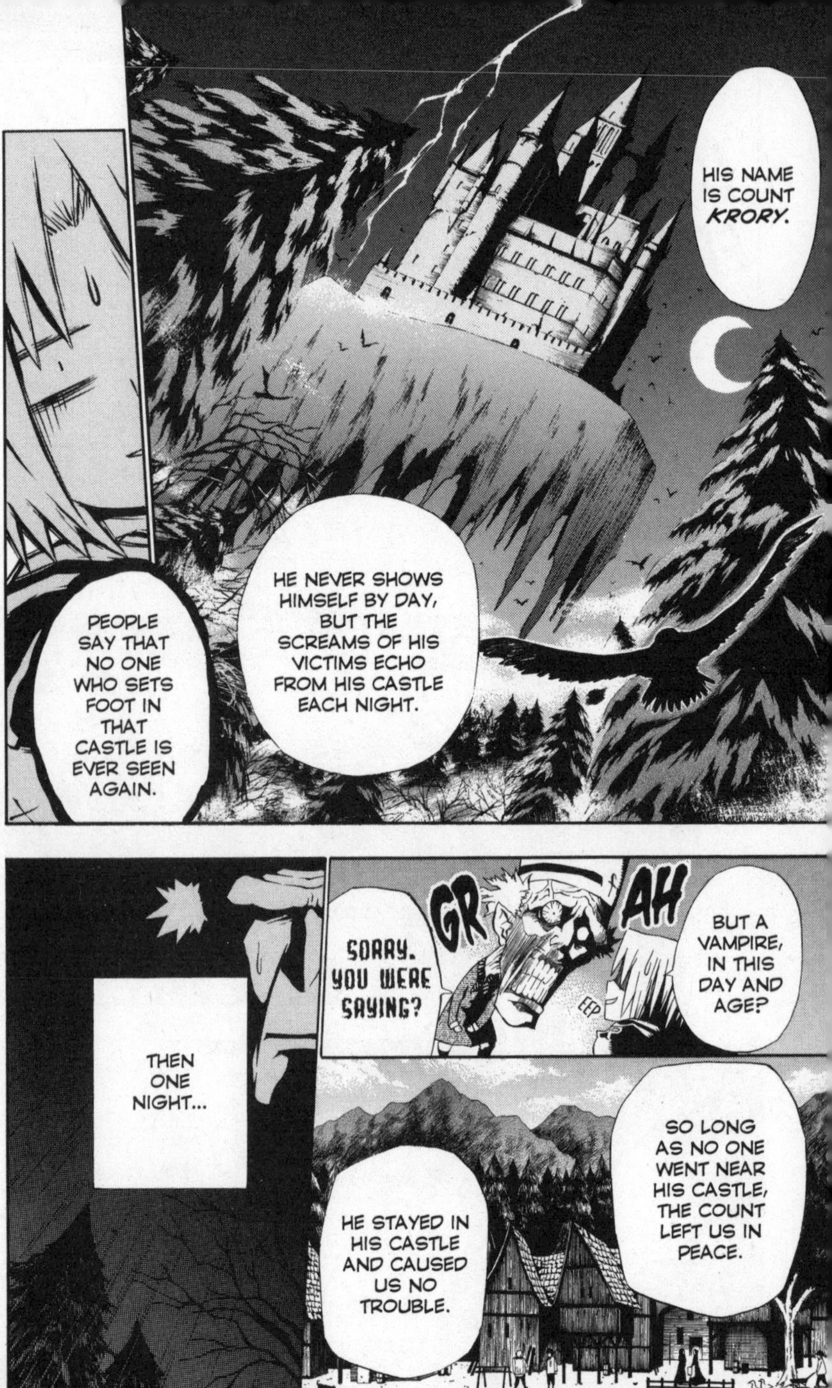
HIS NAME IS COUNT *KRORY*.
HE NEVER SHOWS HIMSELF BY DAY, BUT THE SCREAMS OF HIS VICTIMS ECHO FROM HIS CASTLE EACH NIGHT.
PEOPLE SAY THAT NO ONE WHO SETS FOOT IN THAT CASTLE IS EVER SEEN AGAIN.
BUT A VAMPIRE, IN THIS DAY AND AGE?
GR
AH
EEP
SORRY. YOU WERE SAYING?
SO LONG AS NO ONE WENT NEAR HIS CASTLE, THE COUNT LEFT US IN PEACE.
HE STAYED IN HIS CASTLE AND CAUSED US NO TROUBLE.
THEN ONE NIGHT...

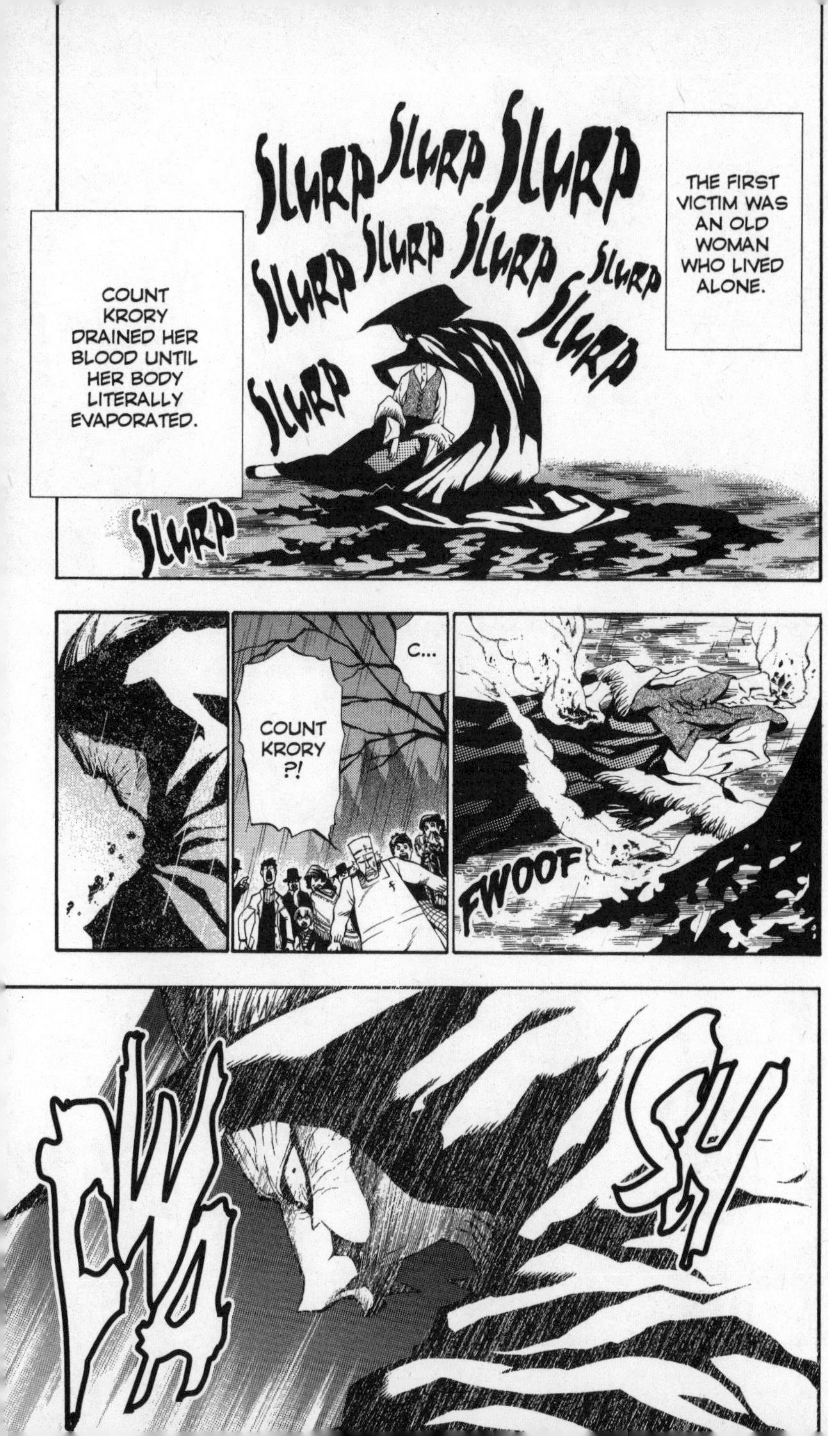
THE FIRST VICTIM WAS AN OLD WOMAN WHO LIVED ALONE.
SLURP SLURP SLURP
SLURP SLURP SLURP SLURP
SLURP
SLURP
COUNT KRORY DRAINED HER BLOOD UNTIL HER BODY LITERALLY EVAPORATED.
SLURP
FWOOF
C...
COUNT KRORY ?!
?..

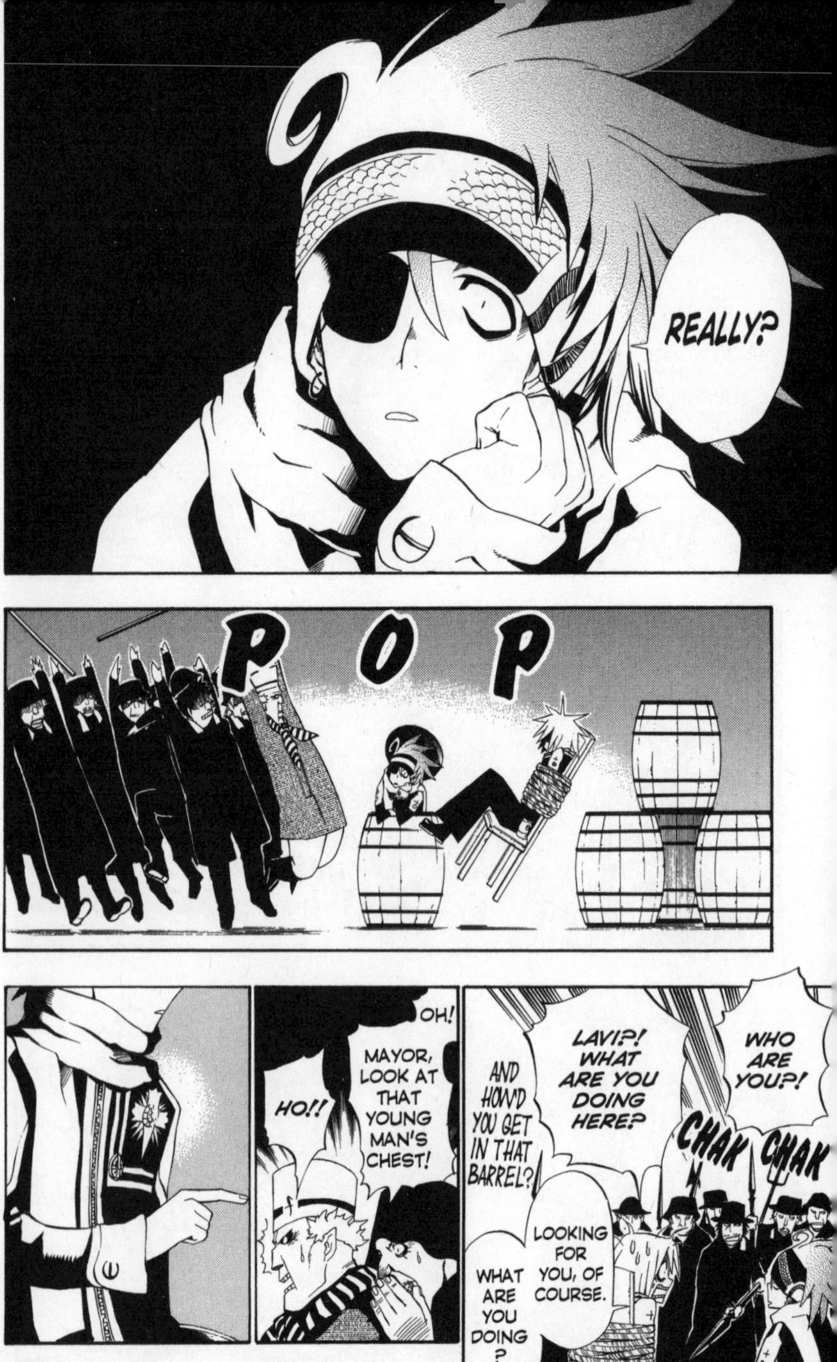
REALLY?
POP
WHO ARE YOU?!
CHAK CHAK
LAVI?! WHAT ARE YOU DOING HERE?
AND HOW'D YOU GET IN THAT BARREL?
LOOKING FOR YOU, OF COURSE.
WHAT ARE YOU DOING?
OH!
MAYOR, LOOK AT THAT YOUNG MAN'S CHEST!
HO!!

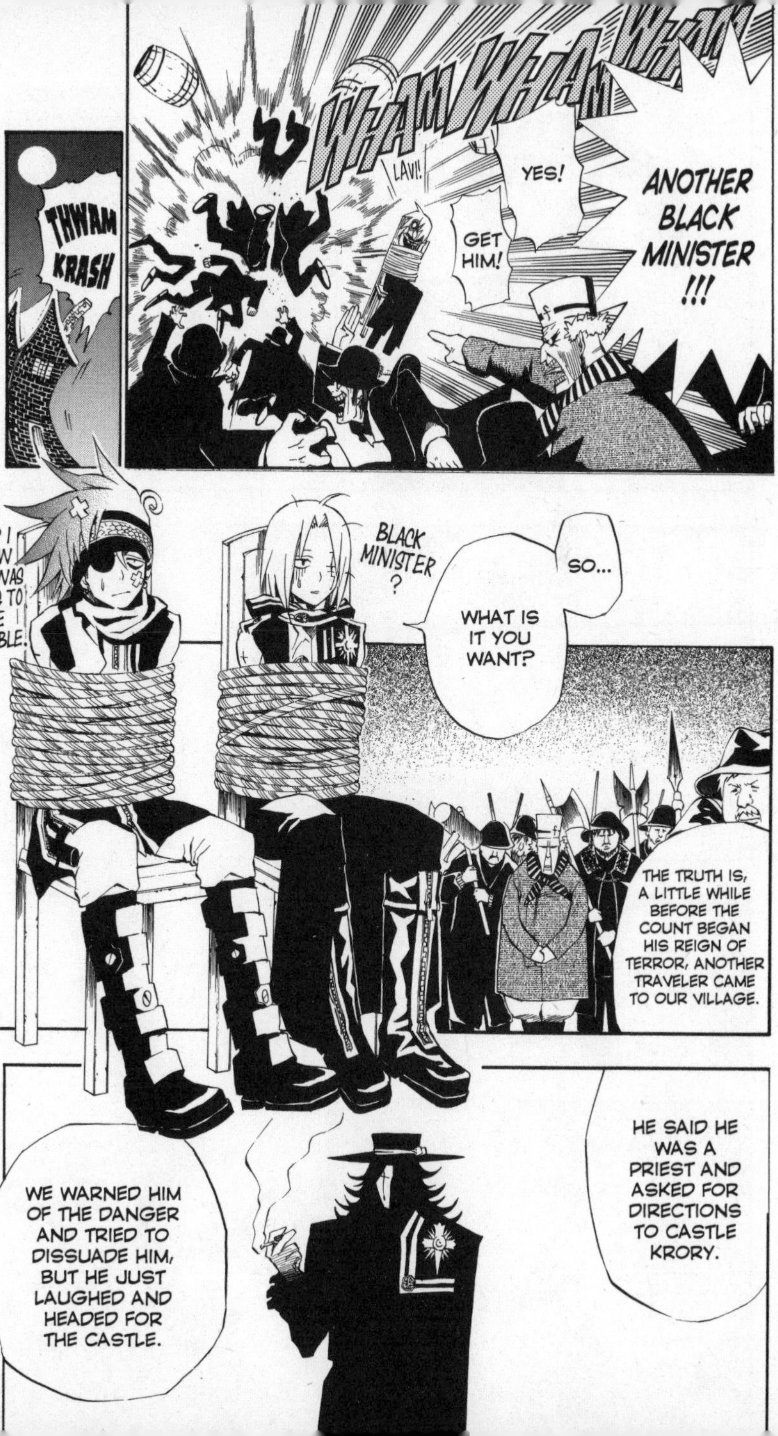
WHAM WHAM WHAM
ANOTHER BLACK MINISTER!!!
YES!
GET HIM!
LAVI!
THWAM KRASH
SO...
WHAT IS IT YOU WANT?
BLACK MINISTER?
SEE? I KNEW THIS WAS GOING TO BE TROUBLE.
THE TRUTH IS, A LITTLE WHILE BEFORE THE COUNT BEGAN HIS REIGN OF TERROR, ANOTHER TRAVELER CAME TO OUR VILLAGE.
HE SAID HE WAS A PRIEST AND ASKED FOR DIRECTIONS TO CASTLE KRORY.
WE WARNED HIM OF THE DANGER AND TRIED TO DISSUADE HIM, BUT HE JUST LAUGHED AND HEADED FOR THE CASTLE.

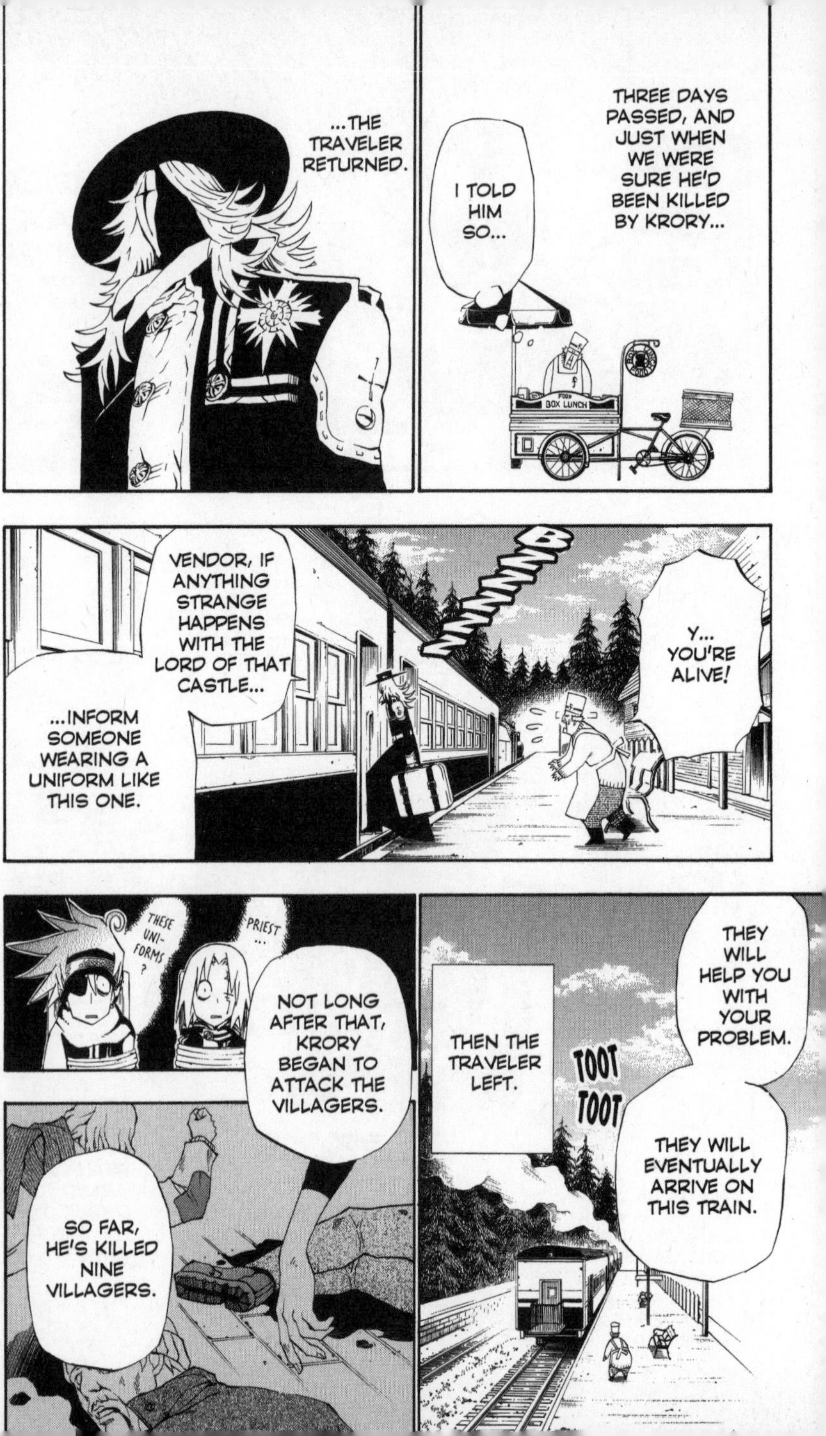
THREE DAYS PASSED, AND JUST WHEN WE WERE SURE HE'D BEEN KILLED BY KRORY...
I TOLD HIM SO...
FOOD
BOX LUNCH
...THE TRAVELER RETURNED.
Y... YOU'RE ALIVE!
VENDOR, IF ANYTHING STRANGE HAPPENS WITH THE LORD OF THAT CASTLE...
...INFORM SOMEONE WEARING A UNIFORM LIKE THIS ONE.
THEY WILL HELP YOU WITH YOUR PROBLEM.
THEN THE TRAVELER LEFT.
TOOT TOOT
THEY WILL EVENTUALLY ARRIVE ON THIS TRAIN.
PRIEST...
THESE UNIFORMS?
NOT LONG AFTER THAT, KRORY BEGAN TO ATTACK THE VILLAGERS.
SO FAR, HE'S KILLED NINE VILLAGERS.

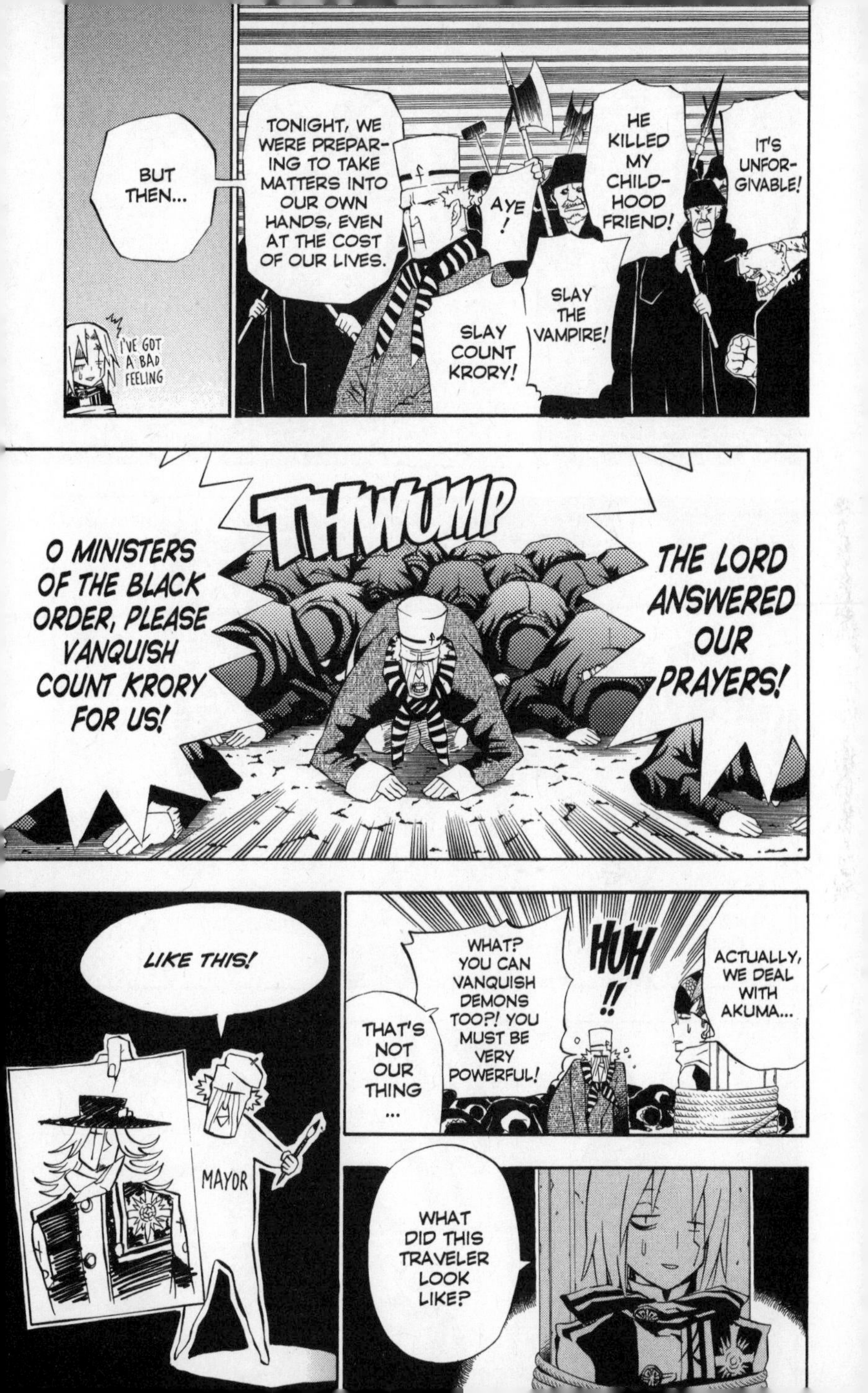
IT'S UNFORGIVABLE!
HE KILLED MY CHILDHOOD FRIEND!
AYE!
TONIGHT, WE WERE PREPARING TO TAKE MATTERS INTO OUR OWN HANDS, EVEN AT THE COST OF OUR LIVES.
SLAY THE VAMPIRE!
SLAY COUNT KRORY!
BUT THEN...
I'VE GOT A BAD FEELING
THWUMP
THE LORD ANSWERED OUR PRAYERS!
O MINISTERS OF THE BLACK ORDER, PLEASE VANQUISH COUNT KRORY FOR US!
ACTUALLY, WE DEAL WITH AKUMA...
HUH!!
WHAT? YOU CAN VANQUISH DEMONS TOO?! YOU MUST BE VERY POWERFUL!
THAT'S NOT OUR THING...
WHAT DID THIS TRAVELER LOOK LIKE?
LIKE THIS!
MAYOR

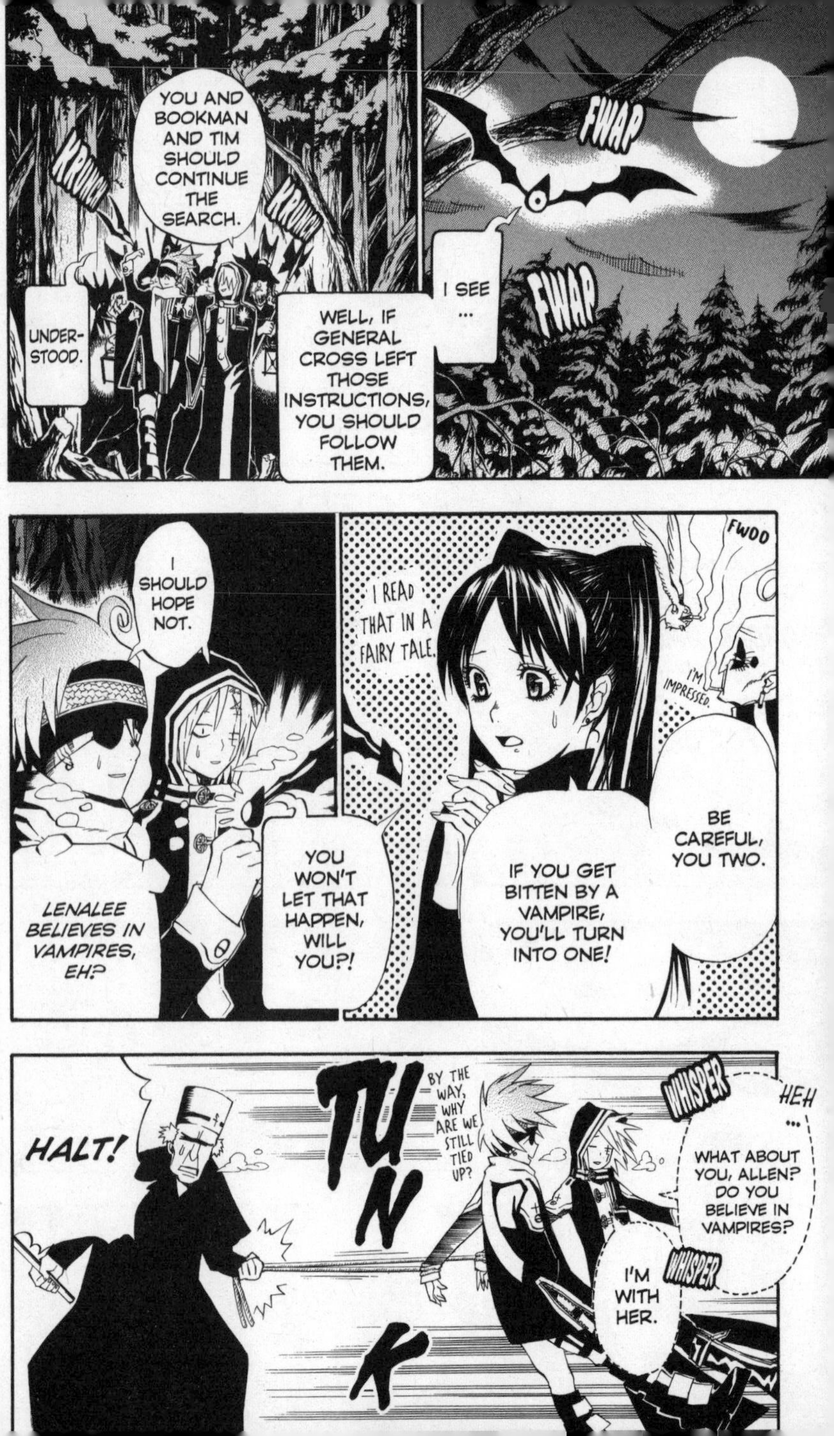
FWAP
I SEE ...
FWAP
WELL, IF GENERAL CROSS LEFT THOSE INSTRUCTIONS, YOU SHOULD FOLLOW THEM.
YOU AND BOOKMAN AND TIM SHOULD CONTINUE THE SEARCH.
UNDER-STOOD.
FWOO
BE CAREFUL, YOU TWO.
IF YOU GET BITTEN BY A VAMPIRE, YOU'LL TURN INTO ONE!
I READ THAT IN A FAIRY TALE.
I'M IMPRESSED.
YOU WON'T LET THAT HAPPEN, WILL YOU?!
I SHOULD HOPE NOT.
LENALEE BELIEVES IN VAMPIRES, EH?
WHISPER
HEH ... WHAT ABOUT YOU, ALLEN? DO YOU BELIEVE IN VAMPIRES?
WHISPER
I'M WITH HER.
BY THE WAY, WHY ARE WE STILL TIED UP?
TUNK
HALT!

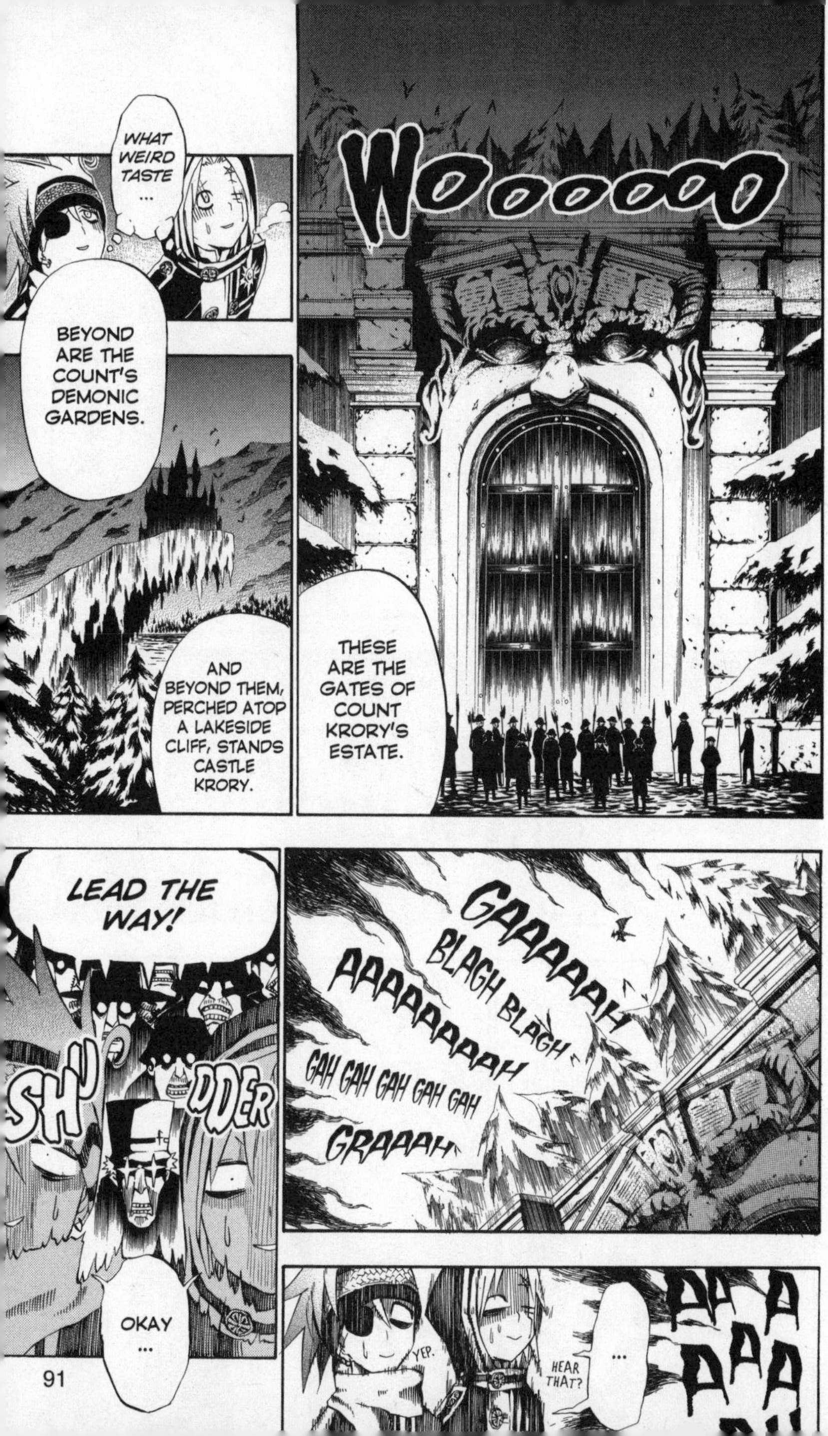
WOOOOOO
THESE ARE THE GATES OF COUNT KRORY'S ESTATE.
WHAT WEIRD TASTE ...
BEYOND ARE THE COUNT'S DEMONIC GARDENS.
AND BEYOND THEM, PERCHED ATOP A LAKESIDE CLIFF, STANDS CASTLE KRORY.
GAAAAAAH
BLAGH BLAGH
AAAAAAAAAH
GAH GAH GAH GAH GAH
GRAAAH
AAA AAA
...
HEAR THAT?
YEP.
LEAD THE WAY!
SHUDDER
OKAY ...

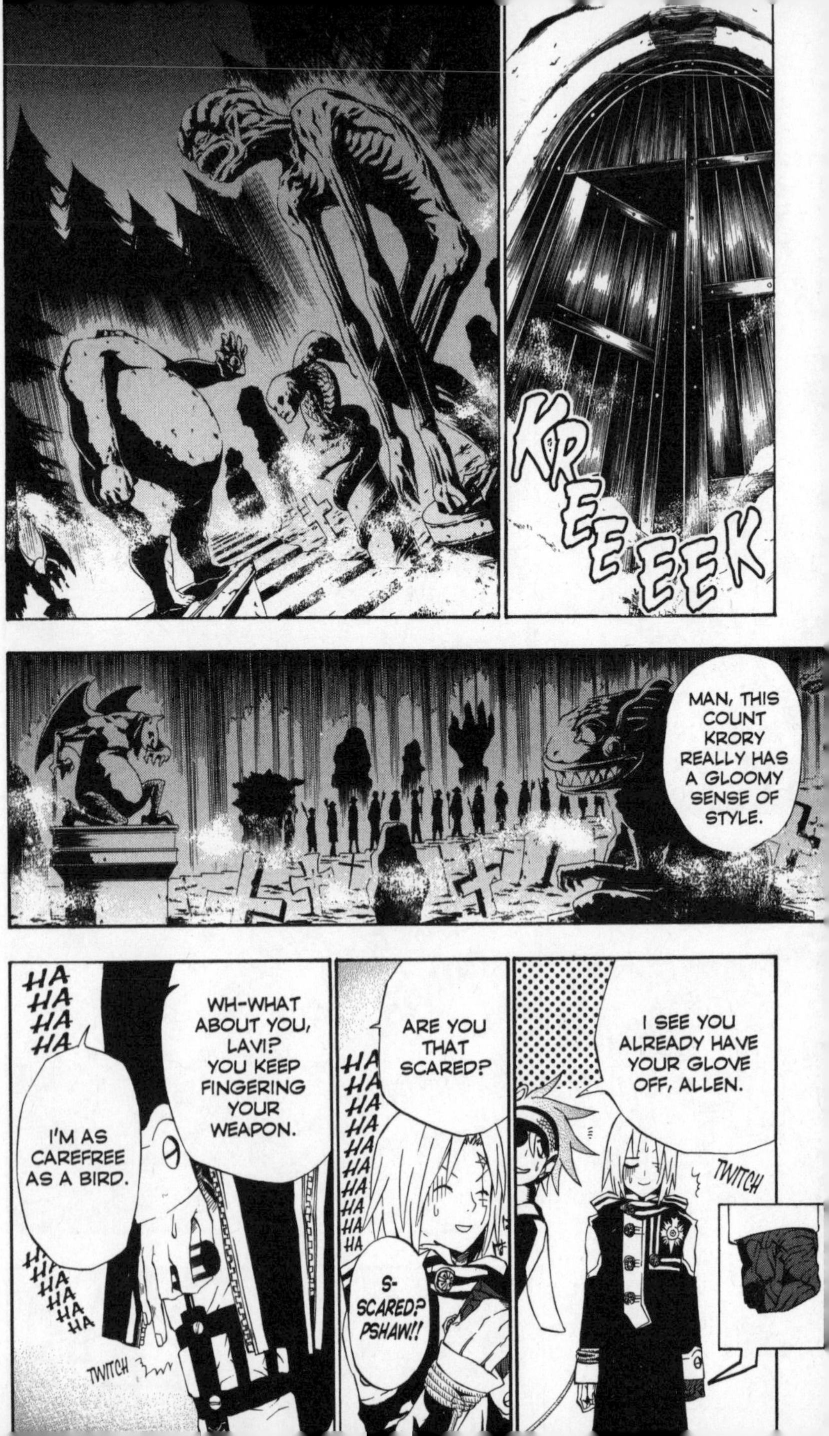
KREEEEEK
MAN, THIS COUNT KRORY REALLY HAS A GLOOMY SENSE OF STYLE.
I SEE YOU ALREADY HAVE YOUR GLOVE OFF, ALLEN.
TWITCH
ARE YOU THAT SCARED?
HA HA HA HA HA HA HA HA HA HA HA HA
S-SCARED? PSHAW!!
WH-WHAT ABOUT YOU, LAVI? YOU KEEP FINGERING YOUR WEAPON.
HA HA HA HA
I'M AS CAREFREE AS A BIRD.
HA HA HA HA HA HA
TWITCH

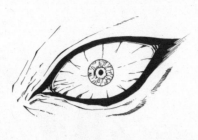

WHAT'S WRONG?

TMP

TH...

THERE'S SOMETHING THERE!

AND IT'S COMING THIS WAY!

TMP TMP TMP TMPTMP TMP TMP TMP

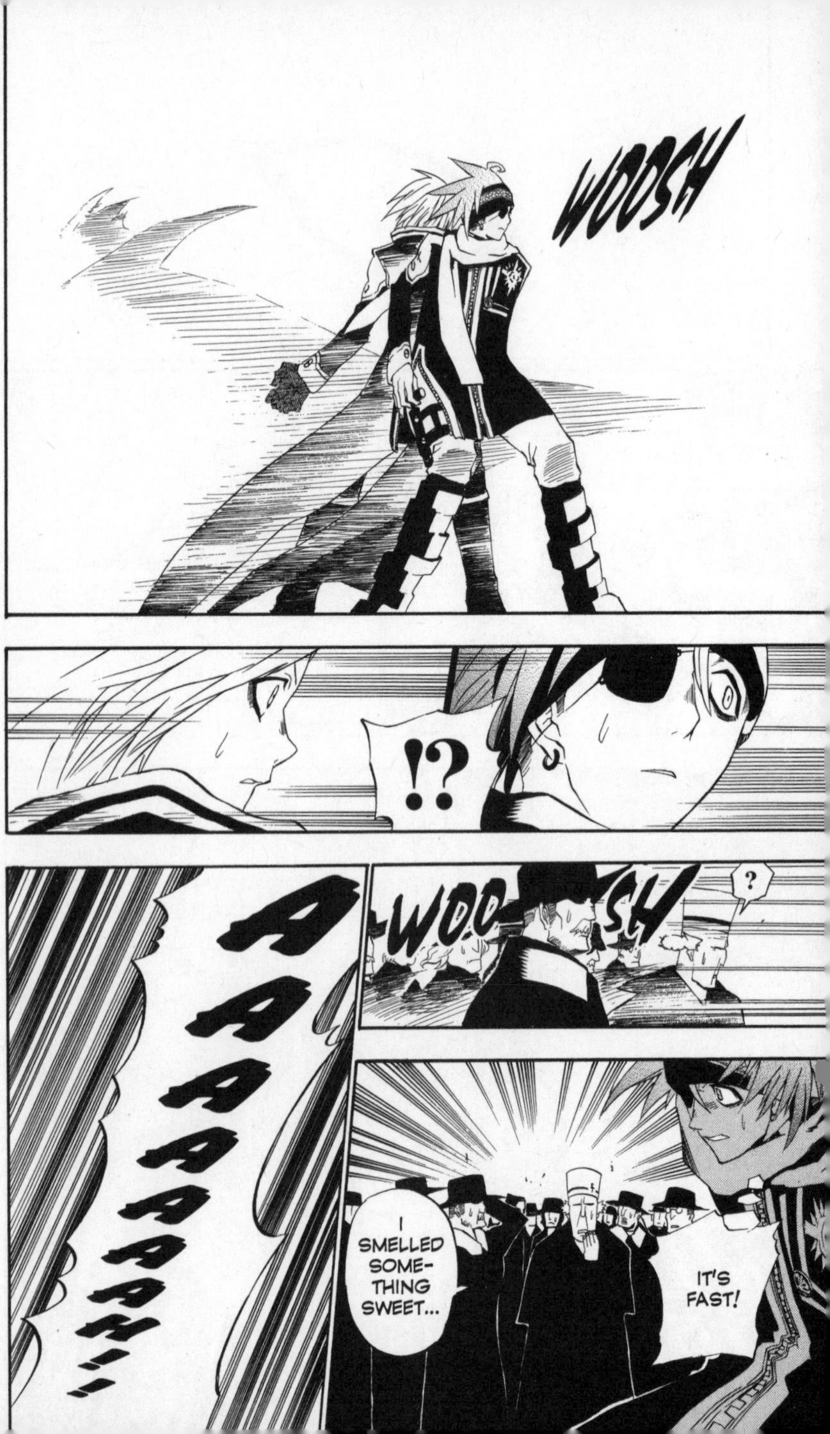
WOOSH
!?
?
WOO-SH
IT'S FAST!
I SMELLED SOME-THING SWEET...
AAAAAAAAAH!!!

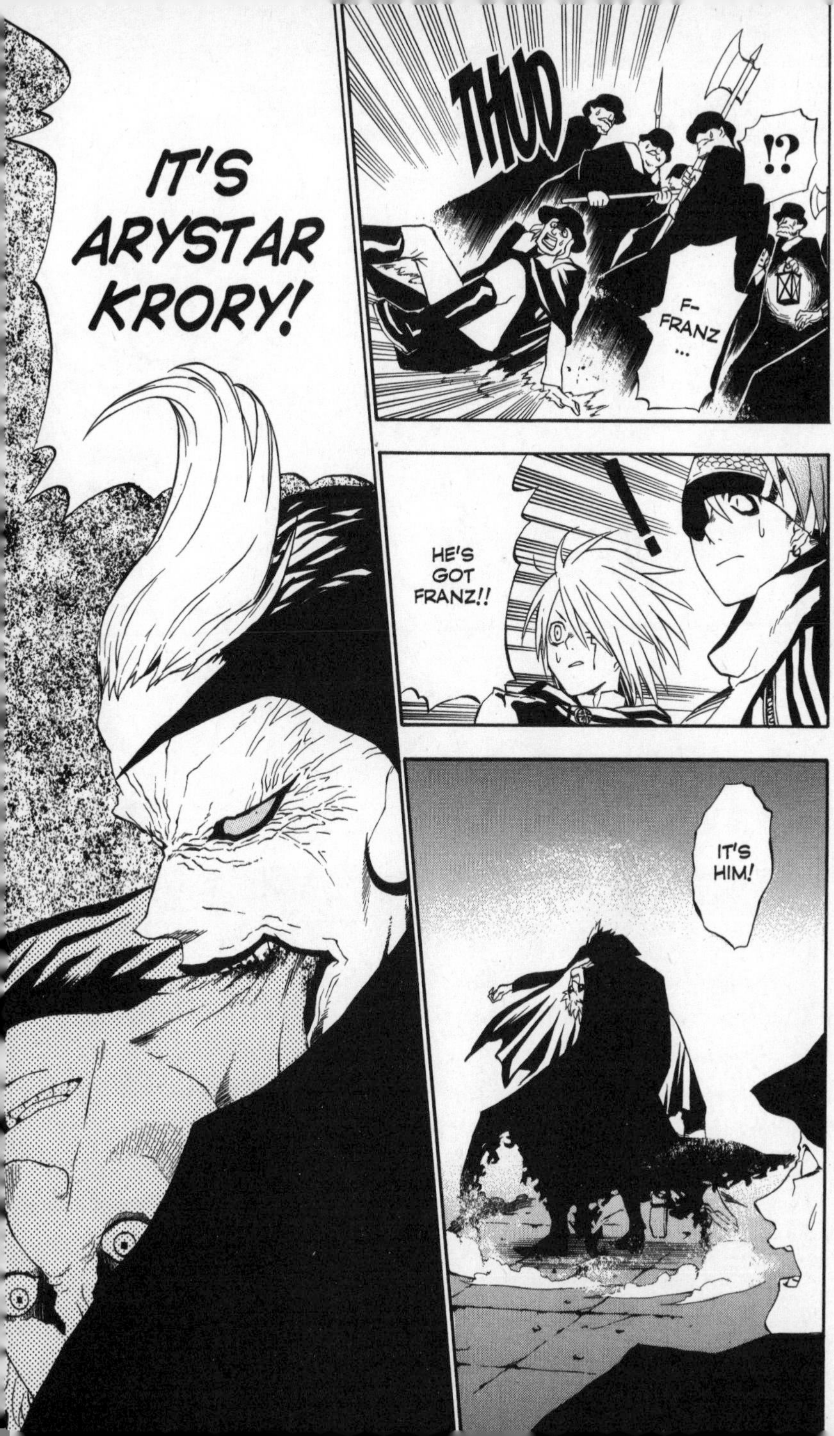
!?
THUD
F-FRANZ...
HE'S GOT FRANZ!!
IT'S HIM!
IT'S ARYSTAR KRORY!

KOMUI'S DISCUSSION ROOM VOL. 3

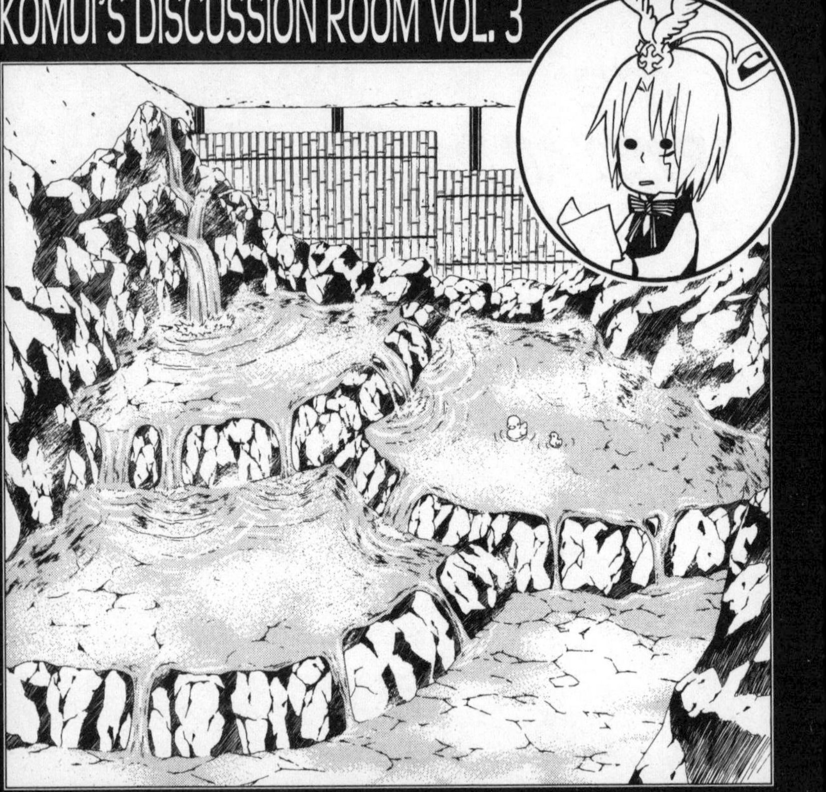

SORRY TO KEEP YOU WAITING. THESE ARE THE BATHS OF THE BLACK ORDER. (MEN'S.) ARENT THEY AMAZING? FROM WHAT I'VE HEARD, THE LIVING QUARTERS USED TO BE EQUIPPED WITH SHOWERS, BUT WHEN KOMUI BECAME THE CHIEF, THERE WAS A MAJOR RENOVATION AND THESE BATHS WERE PUT IN. I GUESS PEOPLE FROM THE THE FAR EAST LIKE TAKING BATHS. THE WATER SEEMS FINE TODAY, BUT OCCASIONALLY KOMUI ADDS UNKNOWN SUBSTANCES TO IT, SO ONE HAS TO BE CAREFUL.

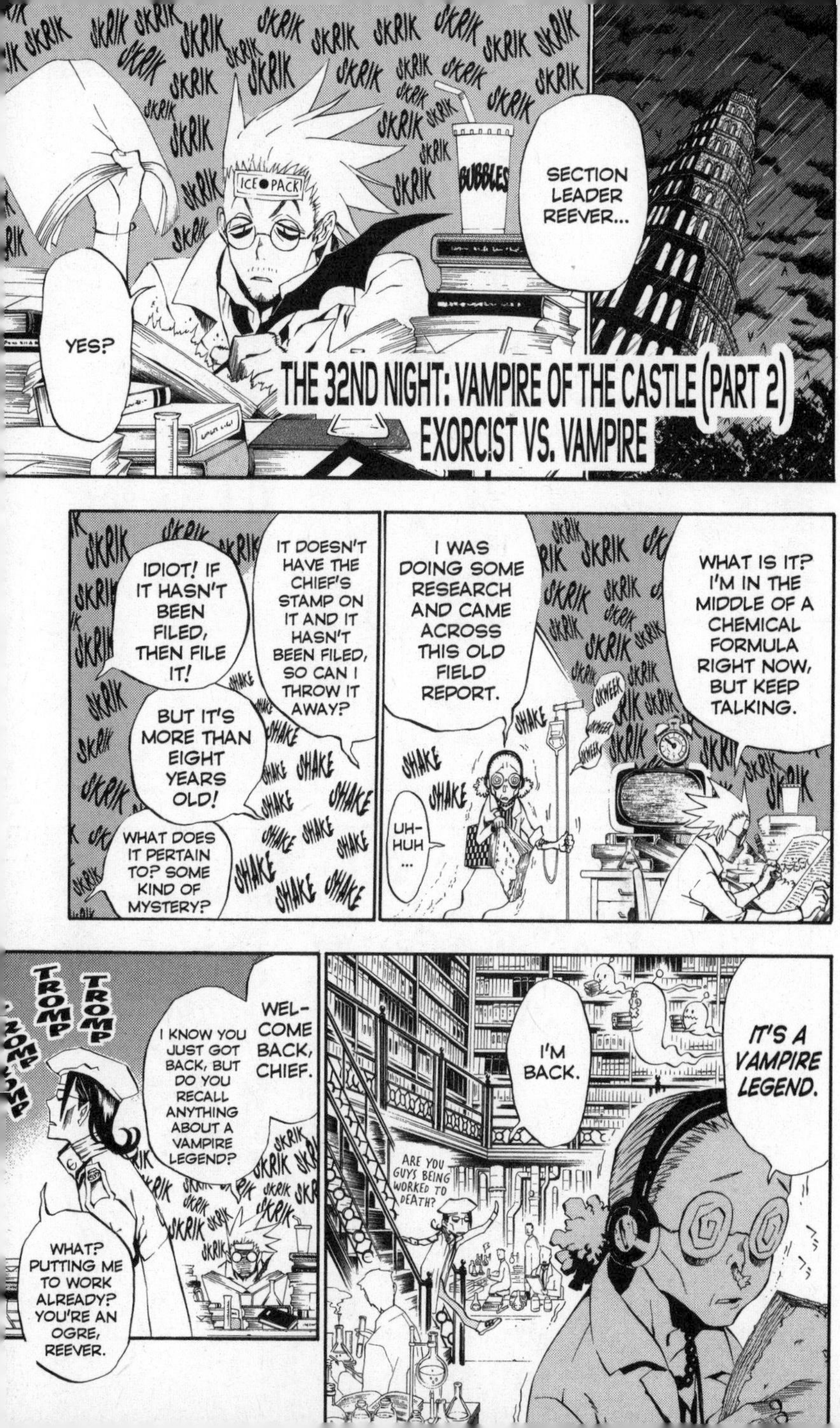
SECTION LEADER REEVER...
SKRIK
ICE PACK
BUBBLES
YES?
THE 32ND NIGHT: VAMPIRE OF THE CASTLE (PART 2)
EXORCIST VS. VAMPIRE
WHAT IS IT? I'M IN THE MIDDLE OF A CHEMICAL FORMULA RIGHT NOW, BUT KEEP TALKING.
SKWEEK
I WAS DOING SOME RESEARCH AND CAME ACROSS THIS OLD FIELD REPORT.
SHAKE
UH-HUH...
IT DOESN'T HAVE THE CHIEF'S STAMP ON IT AND IT HASN'T BEEN FILED, SO CAN I THROW IT AWAY?
IDIOT! IF IT HASN'T BEEN FILED, THEN FILE IT!
BUT IT'S MORE THAN EIGHT YEARS OLD!
WHAT DOES IT PERTAIN TO? SOME KIND OF MYSTERY?
IT'S A VAMPIRE LEGEND.
I'M BACK.
ARE YOU GUYS BEING WORKED TO DEATH?
WELCOME BACK, CHIEF.
I KNOW YOU JUST GOT BACK, BUT DO YOU RECALL ANYTHING ABOUT A VAMPIRE LEGEND?
TROMP TROMP
WHAT? PUTTING ME TO WORK ALREADY? YOU'RE AN OGRE, REEVER.

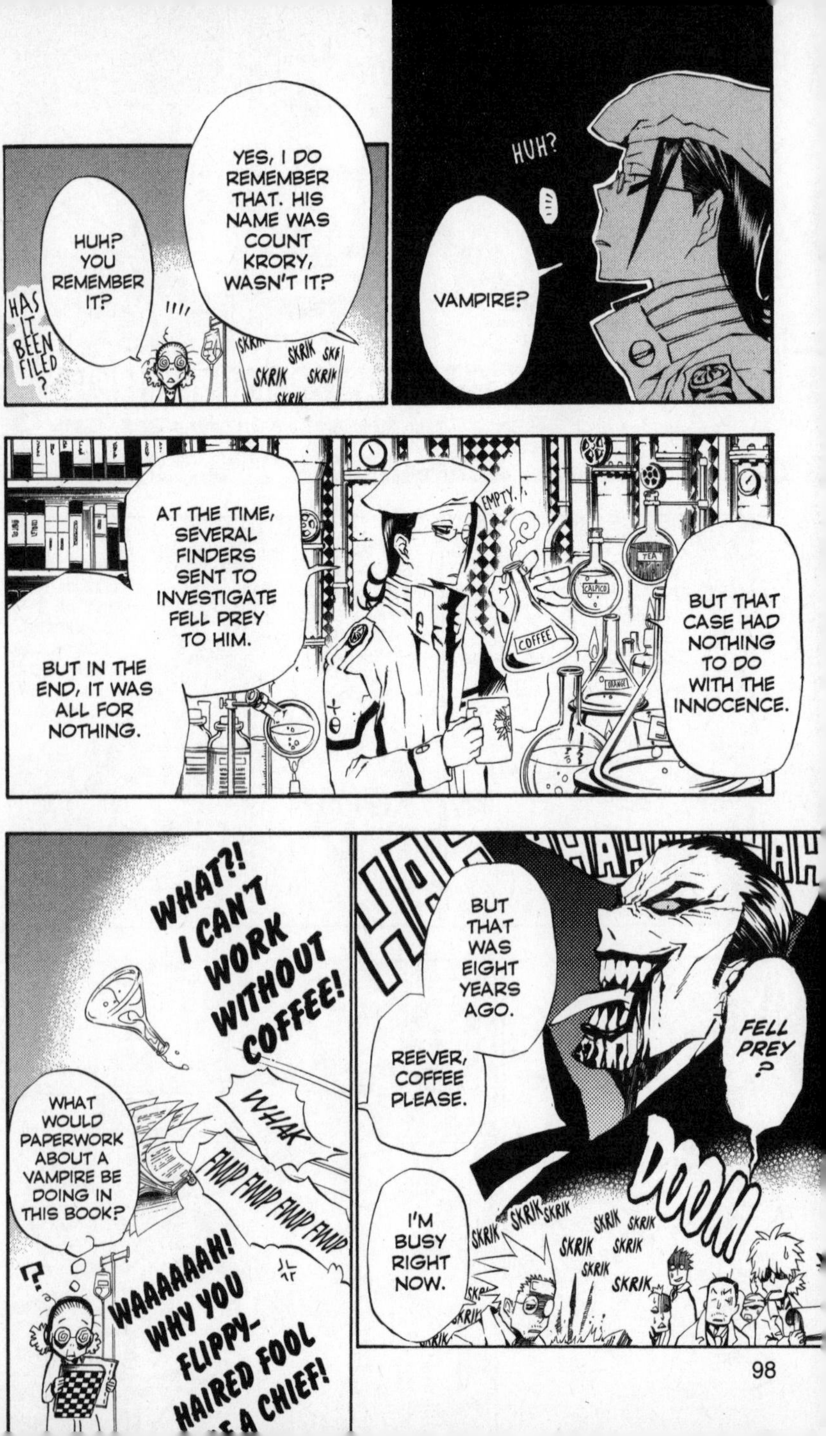
HUH?
...
VAMPIRE?
YES, I DO REMEMBER THAT. HIS NAME WAS COUNT KRORY, WASN'T IT?
HUH? YOU REMEMBER IT?
HAS IT BEEN FILED?
SKRIK SKRIK SKRIK SKRIK
BUT THAT CASE HAD NOTHING TO DO WITH THE INNOCENCE.
EMPTY.
TEA
CALPICO
COFFEE
ORANGE
AT THE TIME, SEVERAL FINDERS SENT TO INVESTIGATE FELL PREY TO HIM.
BUT IN THE END, IT WAS ALL FOR NOTHING.
FELL PREY?
BUT THAT WAS EIGHT YEARS AGO.
REEVER, COFFEE PLEASE.
DOOM
I'M BUSY RIGHT NOW.
SKRIK SKRIK SKRIK SKRIK SKRIK SKRIK SKRIK SKRIK
WHAT?! I CAN'T WORK WITHOUT COFFEE!
WHAK
FWUP FWUP FWUP FWUP
WHAT WOULD PAPERWORK ABOUT A VAMPIRE BE DOING IN THIS BOOK?
WAAAAAAH! WHY YOU FLIPPY-HAIRED FOOL

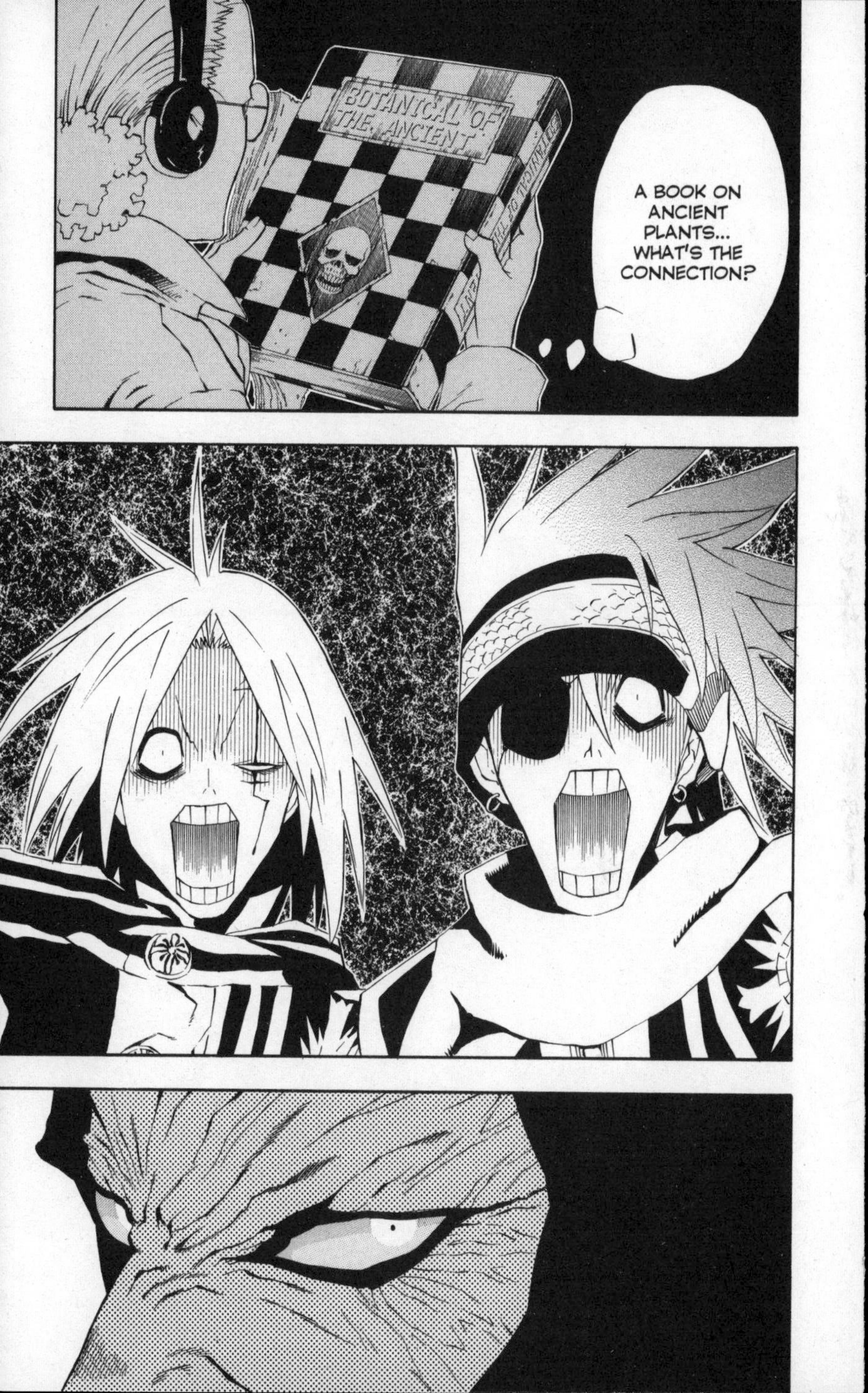
BOTANICAL OF THE ANCIENT
A BOOK ON ANCIENT PLANTS... WHAT'S THE CONNECTION?

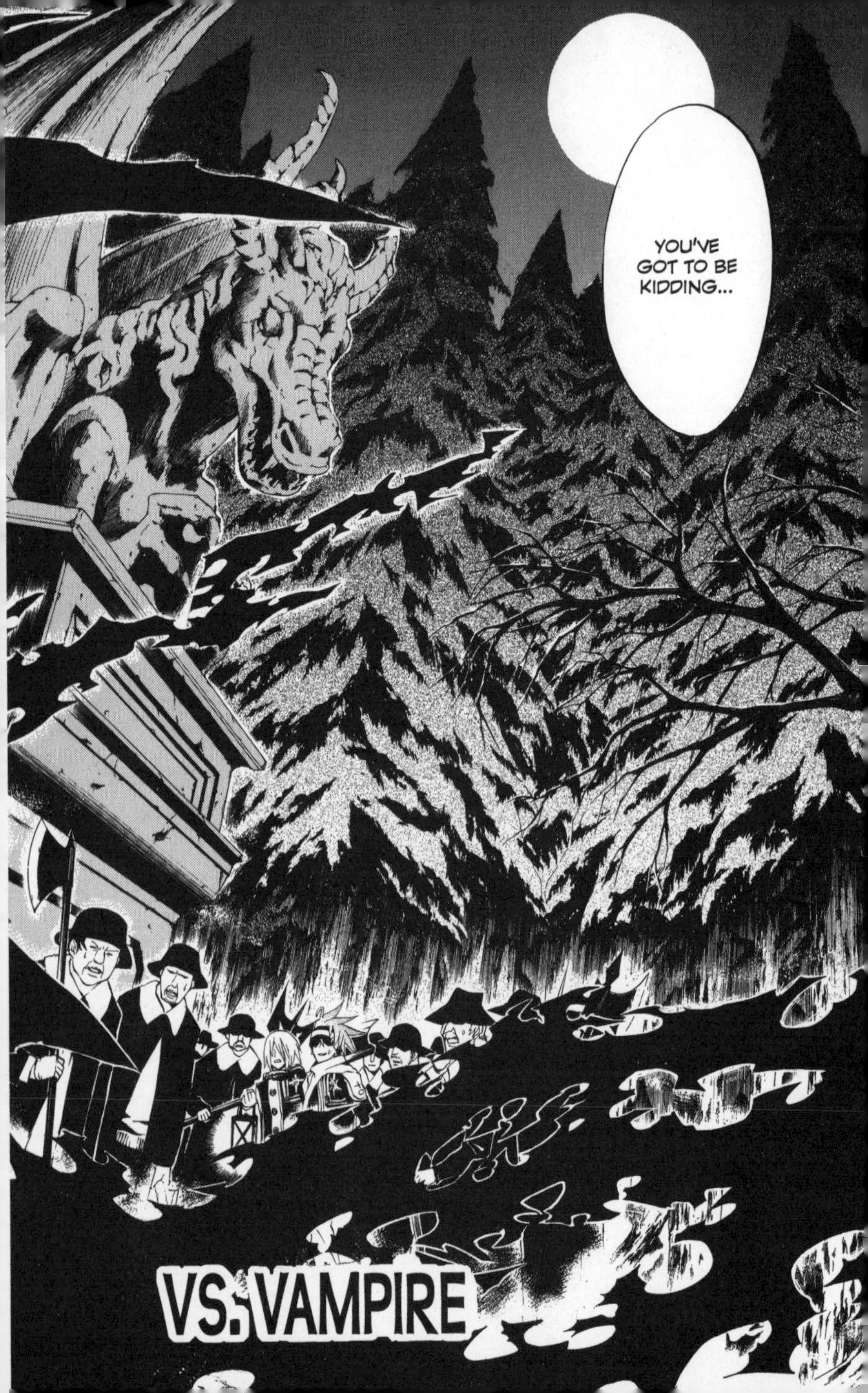
YOU'VE GOT TO BE KIDDING...
VS. VAMPIRE

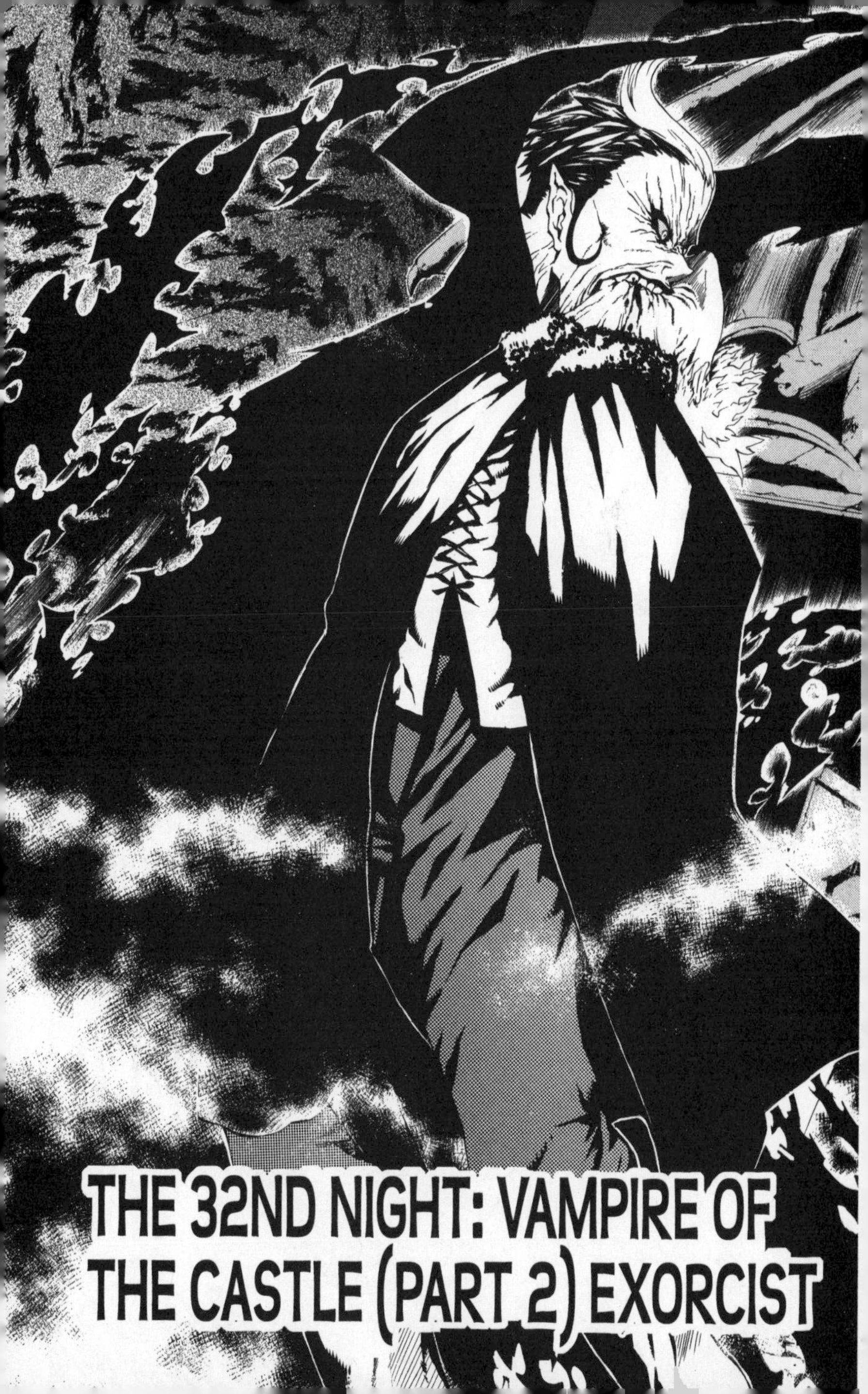
THE 32ND NIGHT: VAMPIRE OF
THE CASTLE (PART 2) EXORCIST

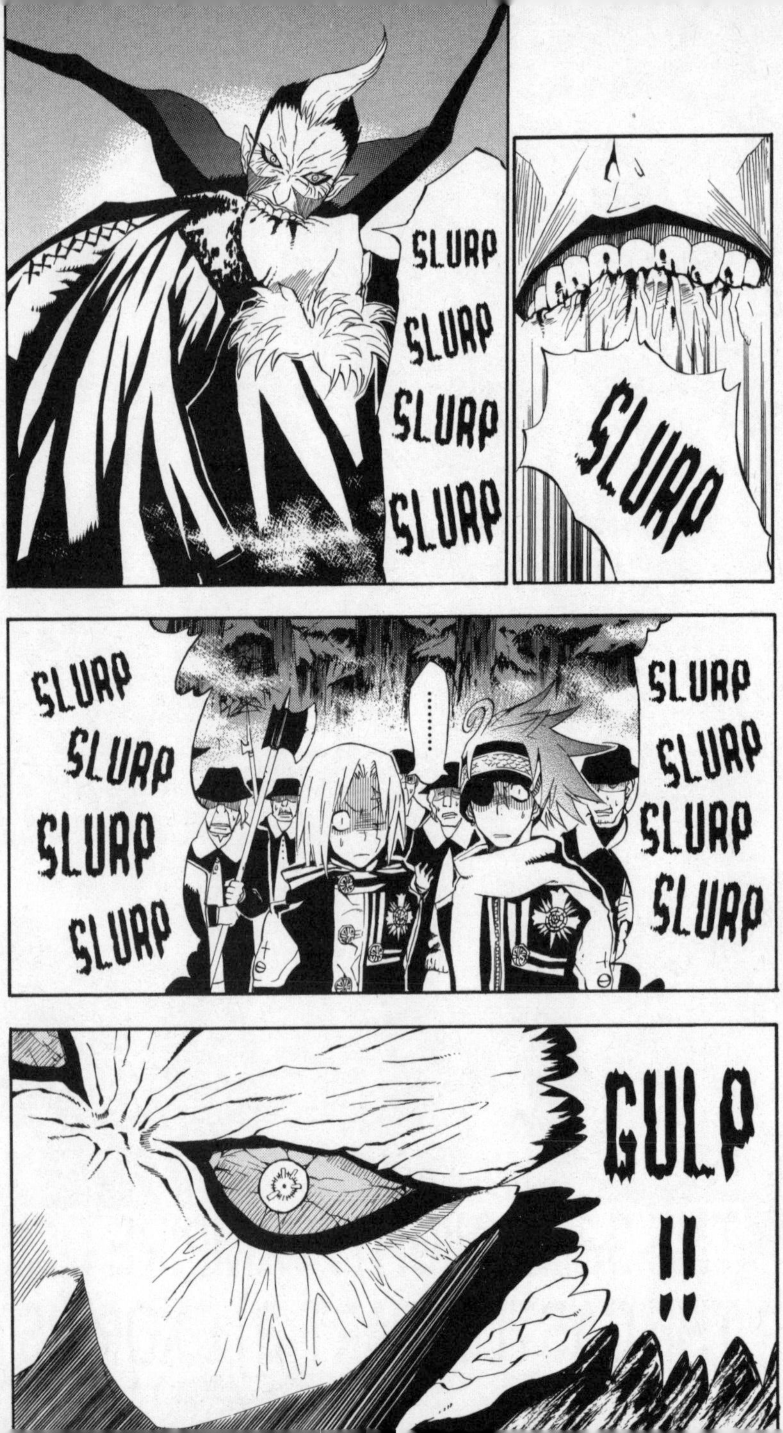
SLURP
SLURP
SLURP
SLURP
SLURP
SLURP
SLURP
SLURP
SLURP
......
SLURP
SLURP
SLURP
SLURP
GULP!!

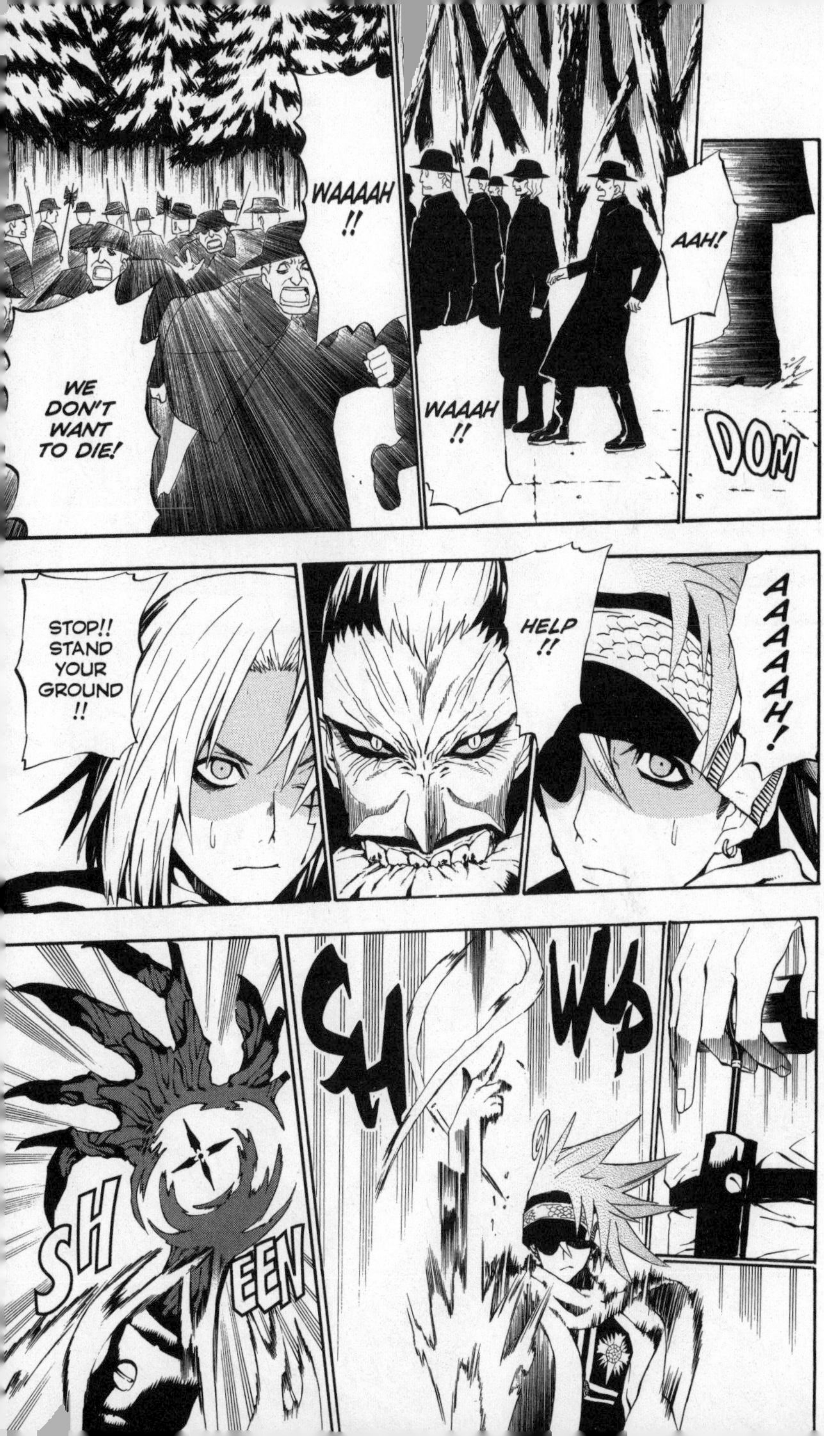
AAH!
DOM
WAAAH !!
WAAAAH !!
WE DON'T WANT TO DIE!
AAAAAAH!
HELP !!
STOP!! STAND YOUR GROUND !!
SH
WS
SH
EEN

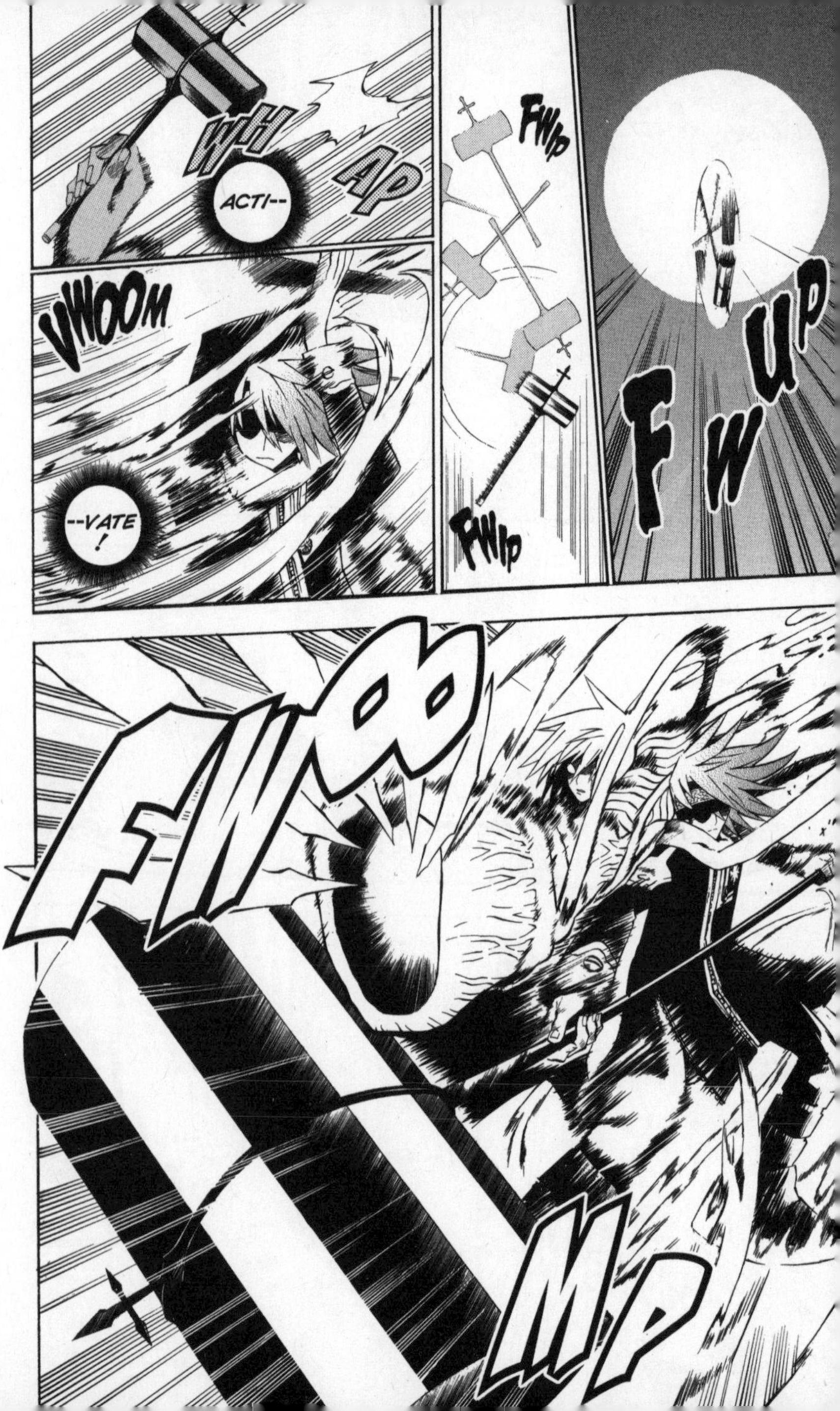
FWUP
FWIP
FWIP
WHAP
ACTI--
VWOOM
--VATE!
FWOOMP

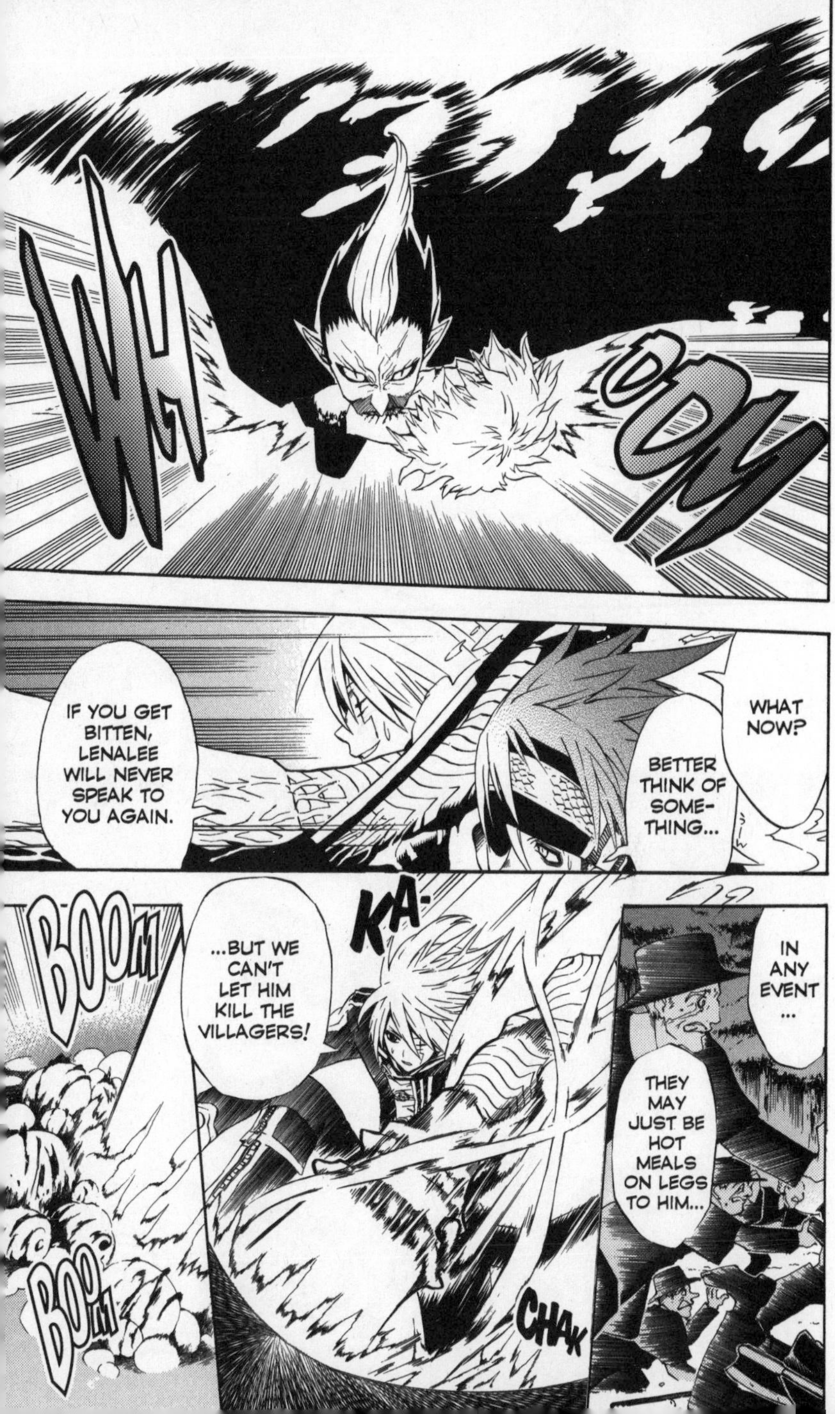
WH
WHAT NOW?
BETTER THINK OF SOME-THING...
IF YOU GET BITTEN, LENALEE WILL NEVER SPEAK TO YOU AGAIN.
IN ANY EVENT ...
THEY MAY JUST BE HOT MEALS ON LEGS TO HIM...
KA-
...BUT WE CAN'T LET HIM KILL THE VILLAGERS!
CHAK
BOOM
BOOM

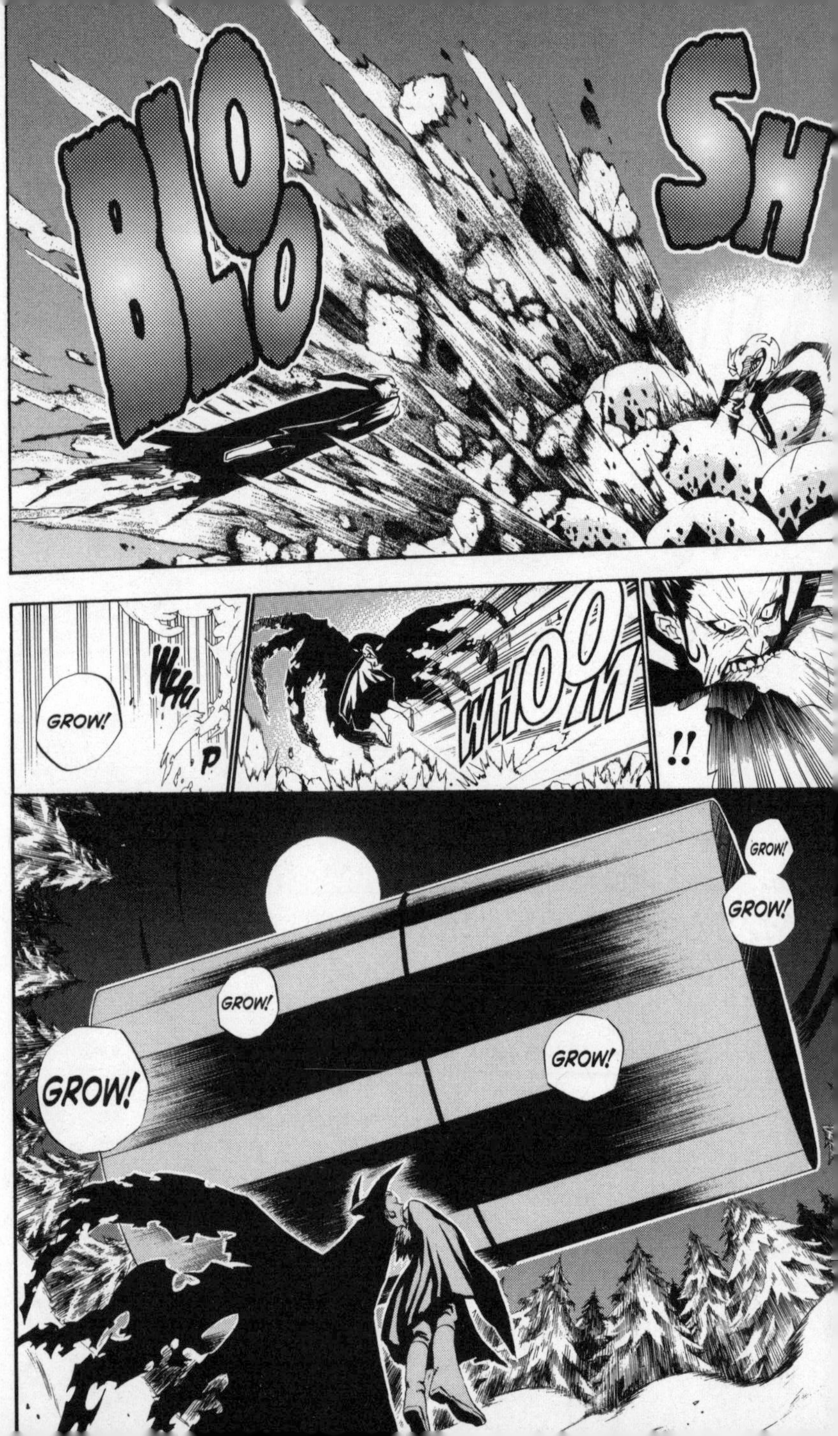
BLOOO
SH
!!
WHOOM
WHUP
GROW!
GROW!
GROW!
GROW!
GROW!
GROW!

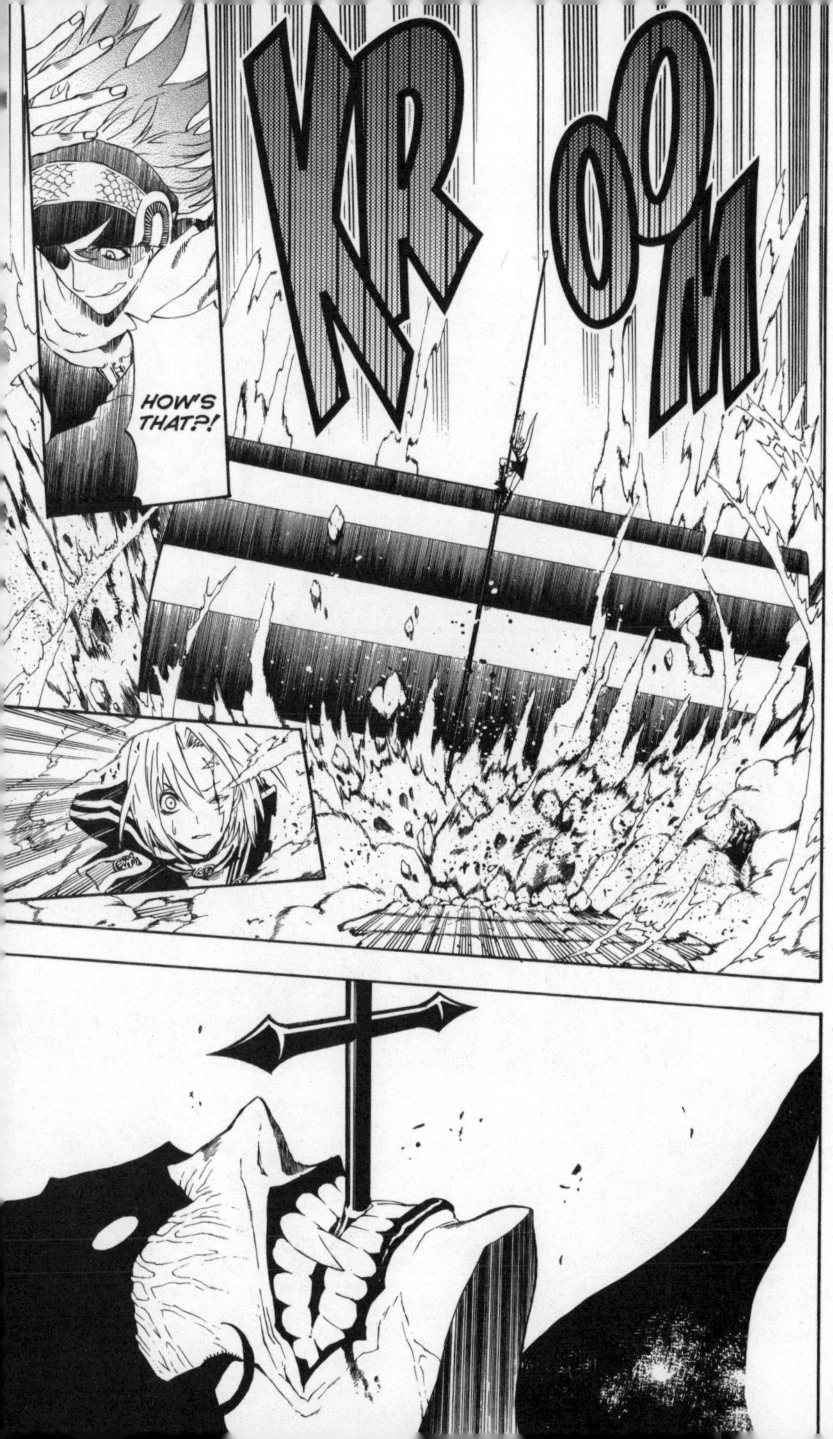
KRA
BOOM
HOW'S THAT?!

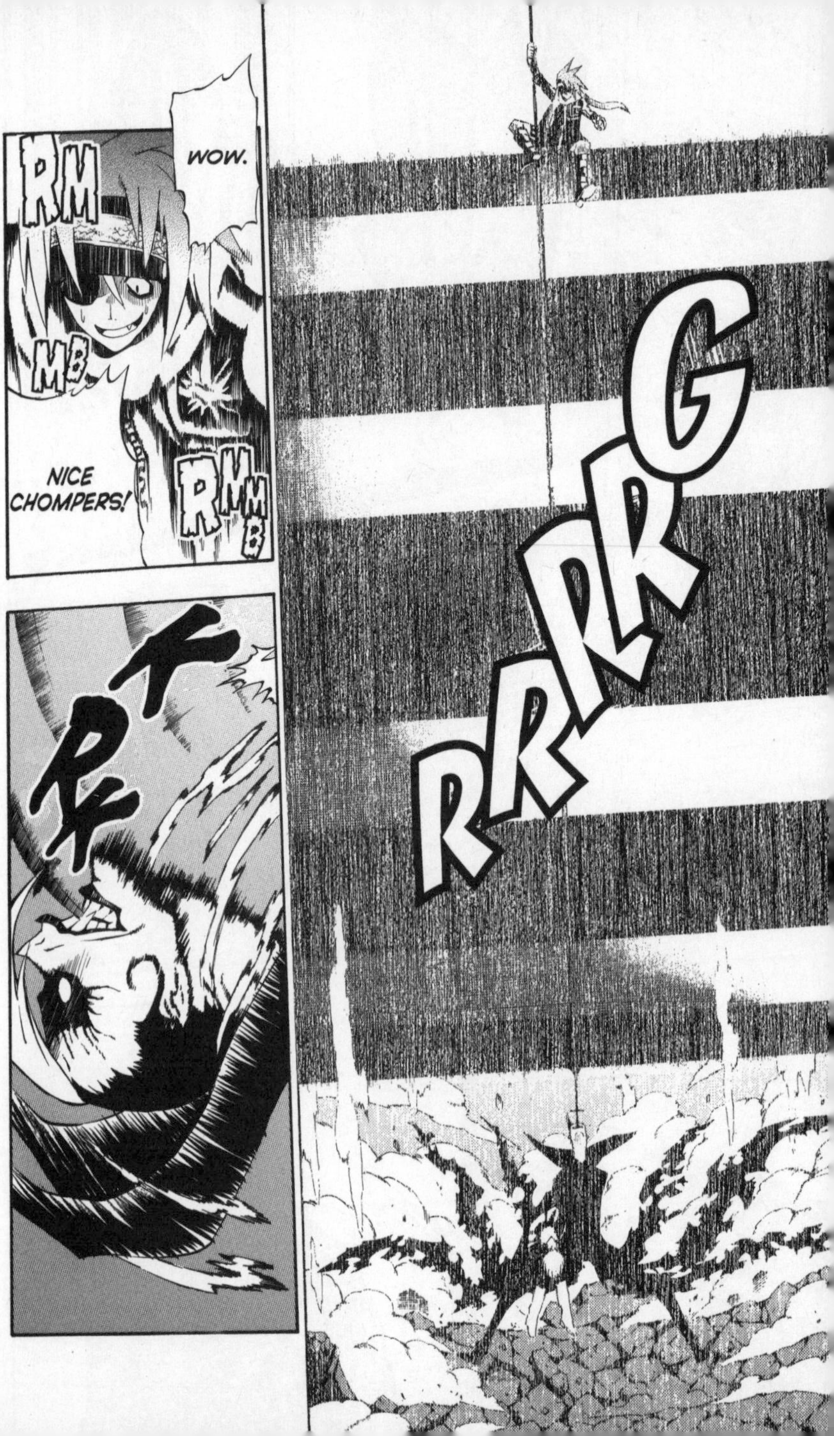
RRRRG
WOW.
RMMB
NICE CHOMPERS!
RMMB

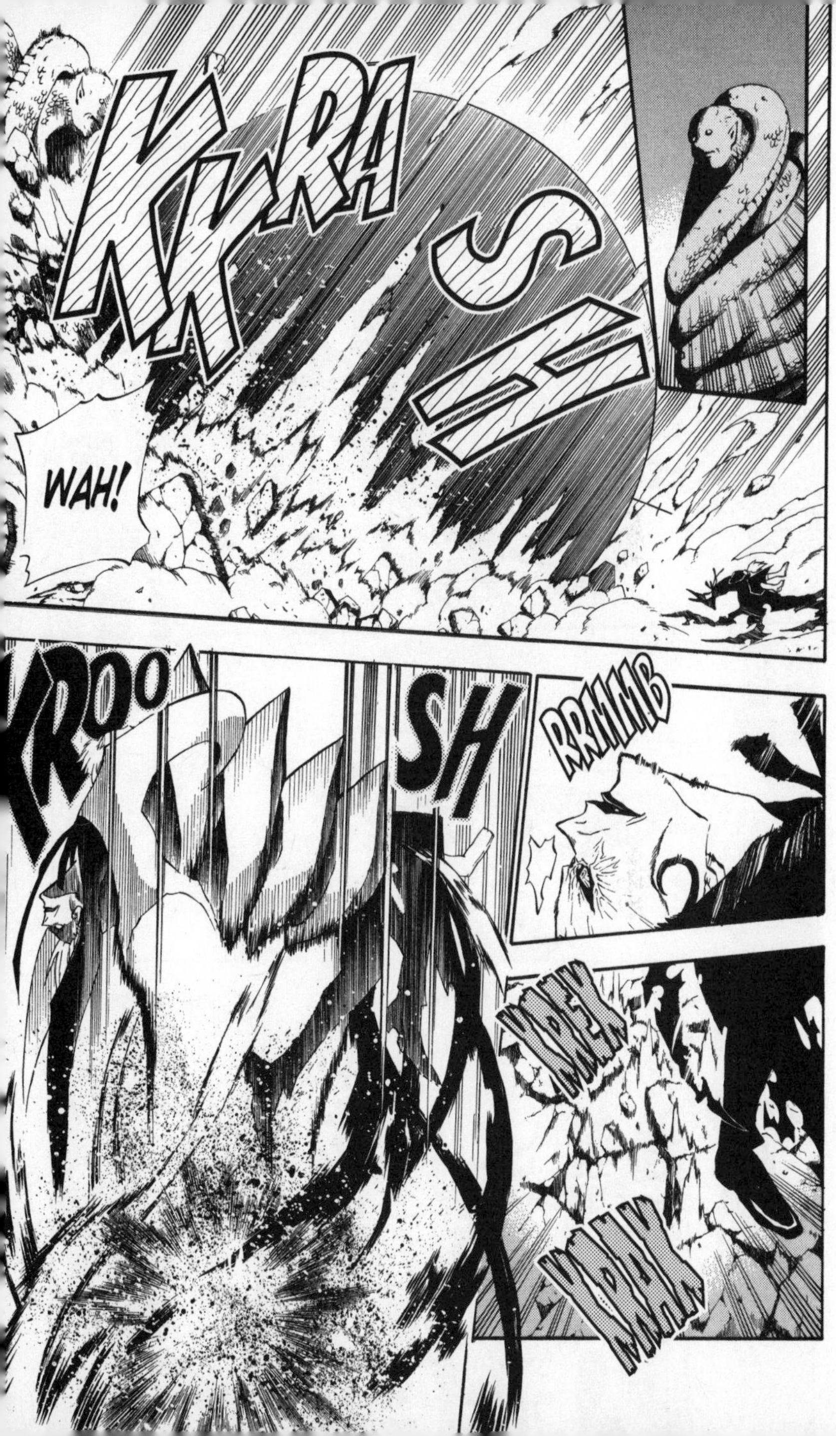
KA-RASH
WAH!
RRMMB
VROOSH

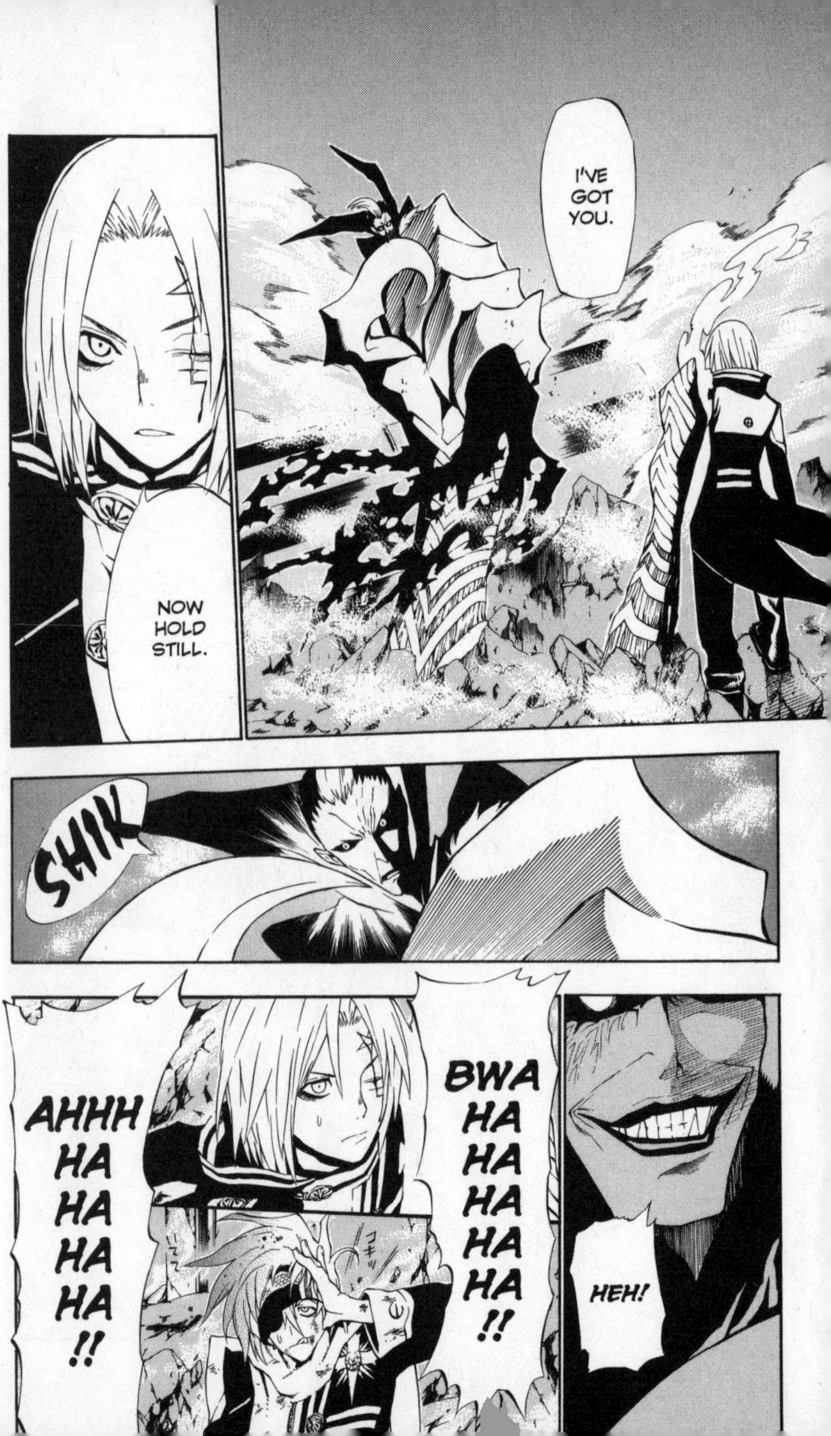
I'VE GOT YOU.
NOW HOLD STILL.
SHIK
HEH!
BWA HA HA HA HA HA HA !!
AHHH HA HA HA HA !!

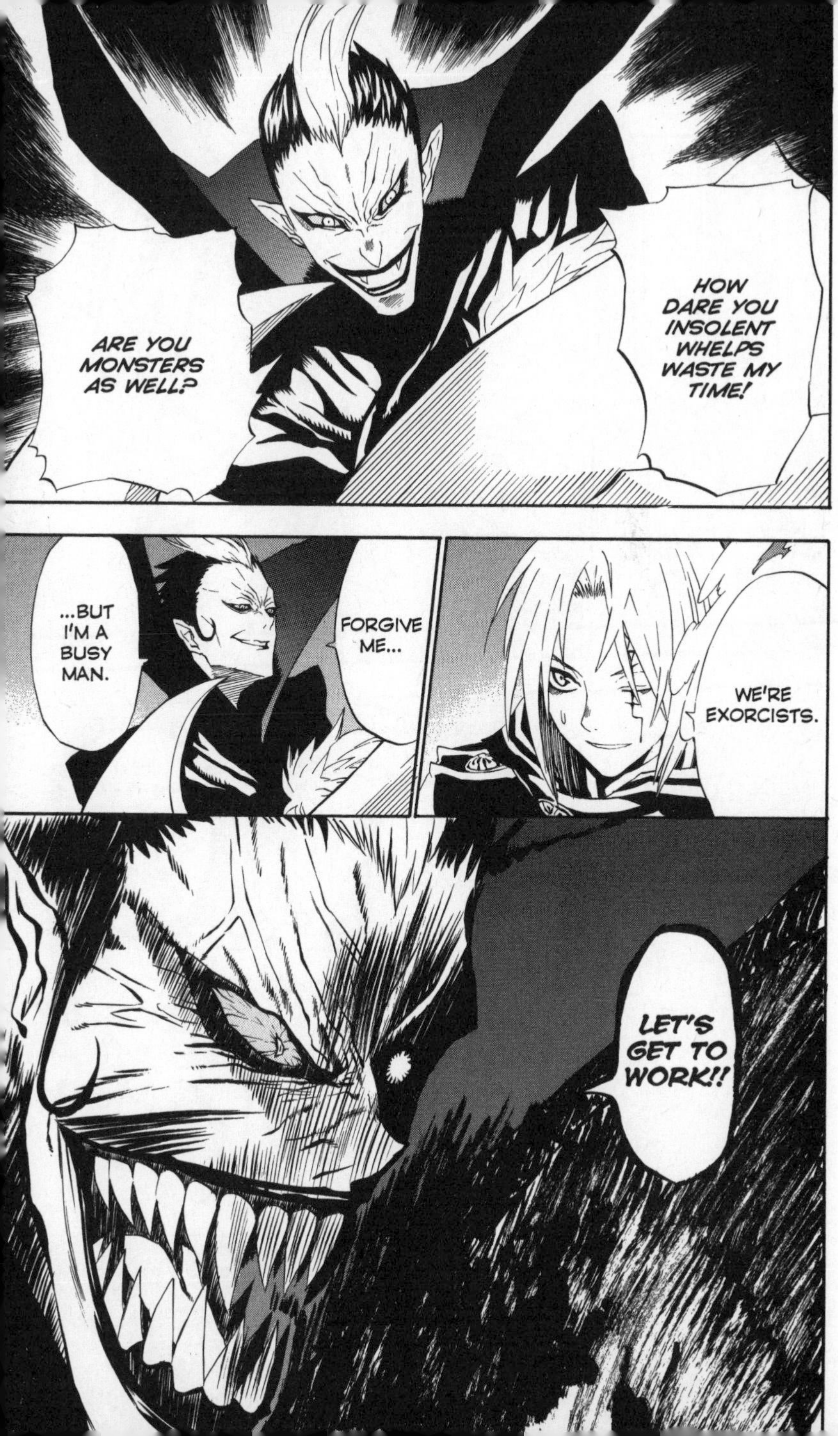
HOW DARE YOU INSOLENT WHELPS WASTE MY TIME!
ARE YOU MONSTERS AS WELL?
WE'RE EXORCISTS.
FORGIVE ME...
...BUT I'M A BUSY MAN.
LET'S GET TO WORK!!

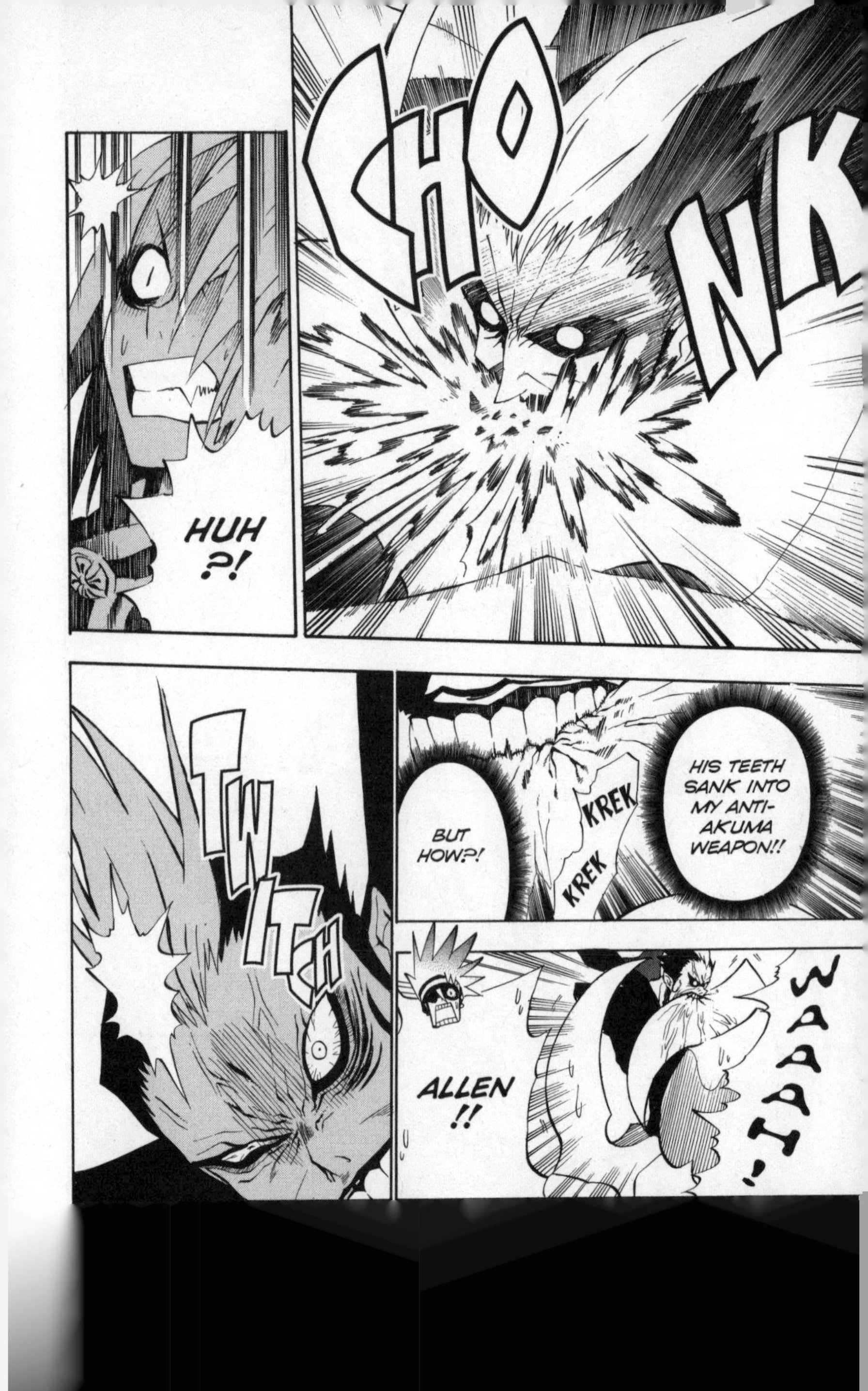
CHONK
HUH ?!
HIS TEETH SANK INTO MY ANTI-AKUMA WEAPON!!
KREK
KREK
BUT HOW?!
WAAAAI!
ALLEN !!
TWITCH

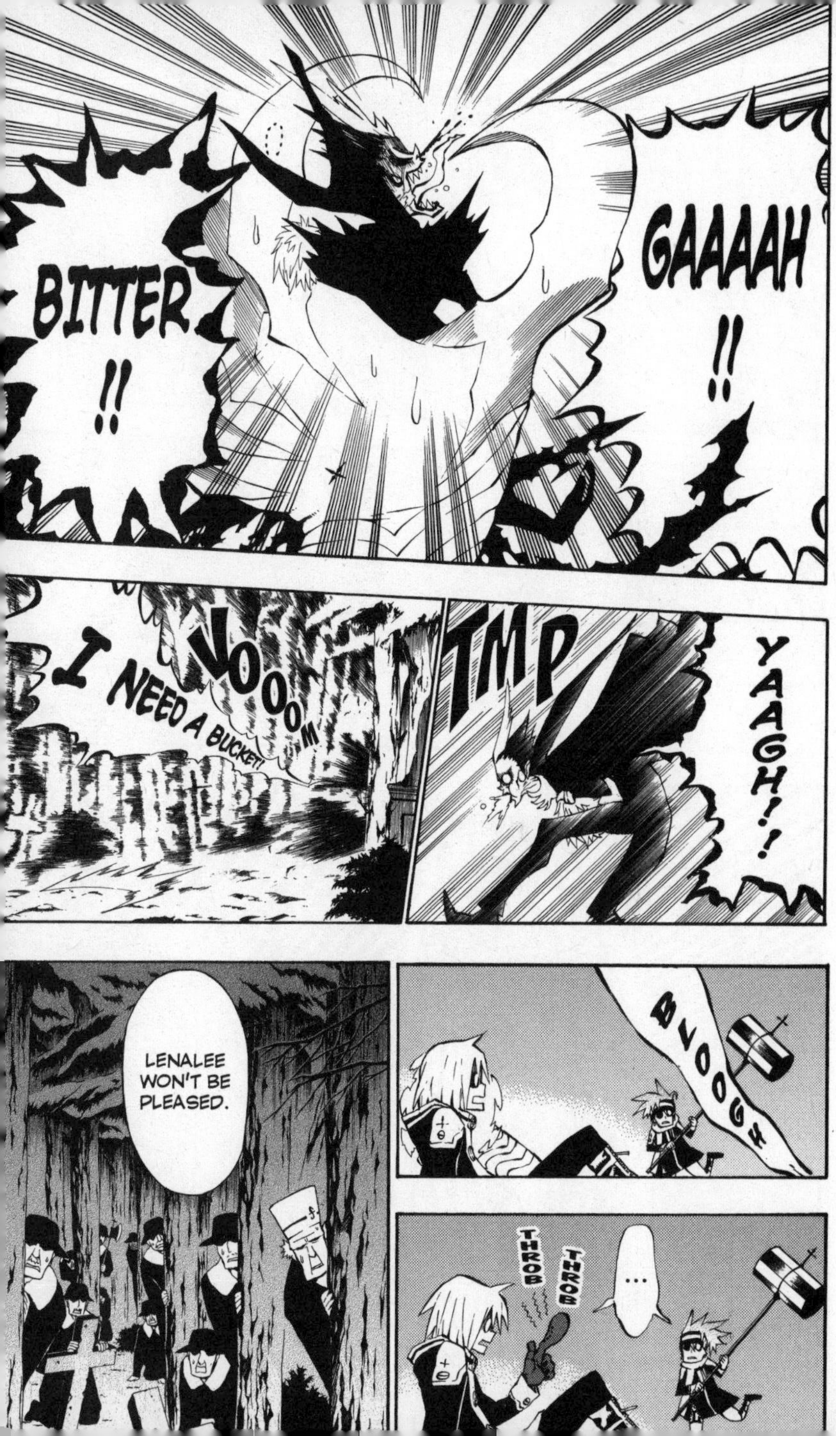
GAAAAH!!
BITTER!!
YAAGH!!!
TMP
VOOOOM
I NEED A BUCKET!!
BLOOGH
THROB
THROB
...
LENALEE WON'T BE PLEASED.

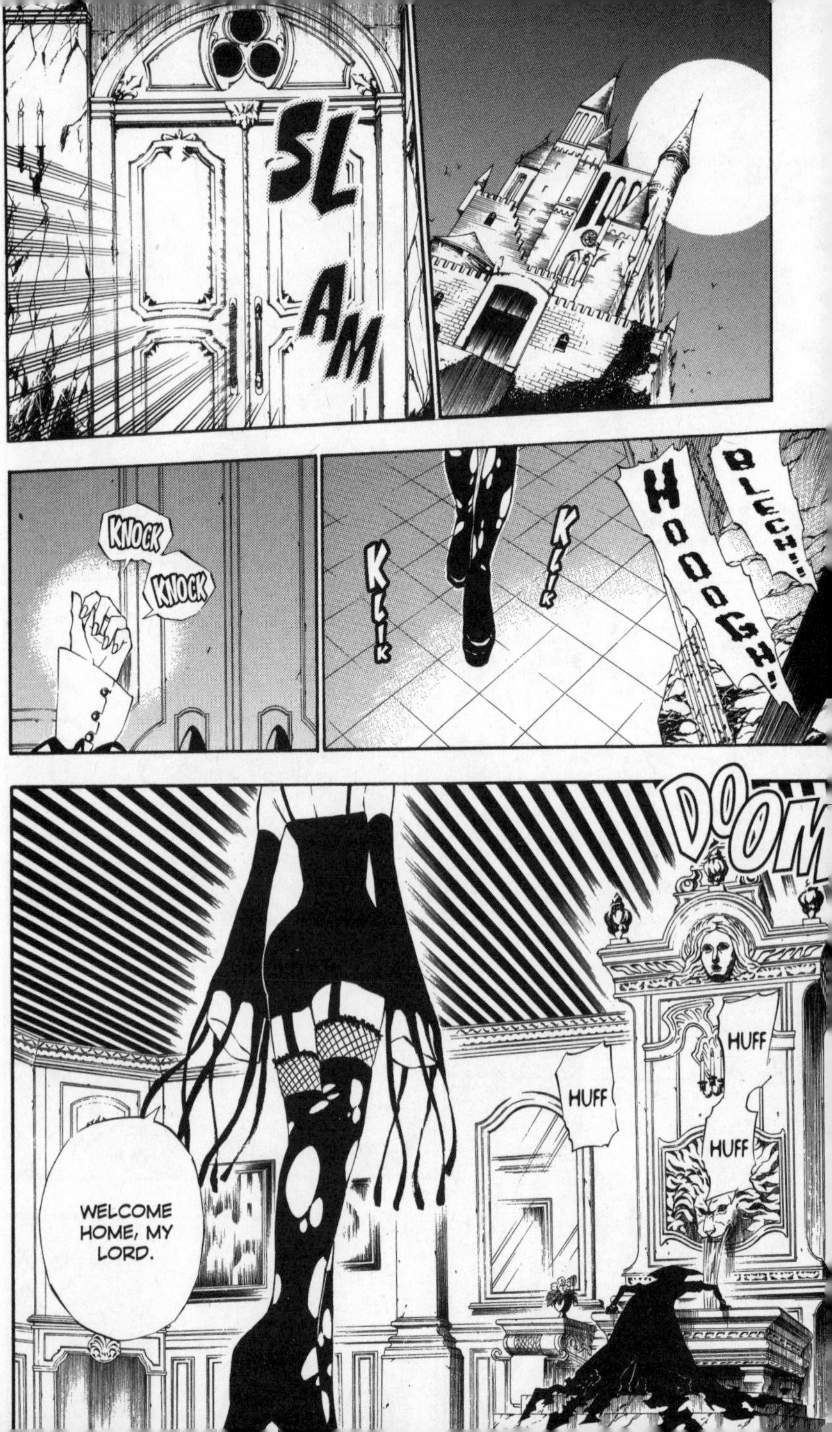
SLAM
BLECH!!
HOOOGH!!
KLIK
KLIK
KNOCK
KNOCK
DOOM
HUFF
HUFF
HUFF
WELCOME HOME, MY LORD.

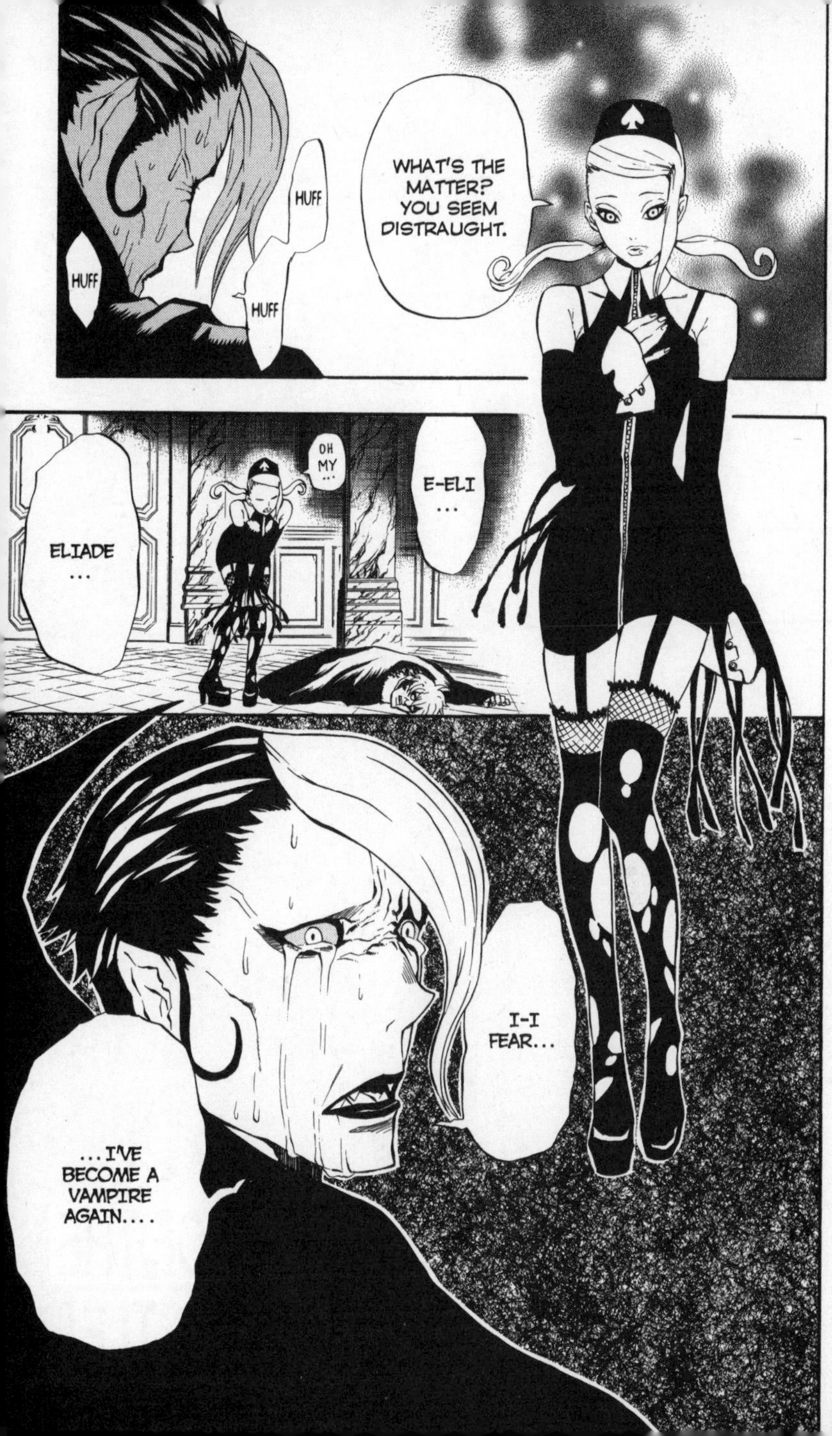

WHAT'S THE MATTER? YOU SEEM DISTRAUGHT.
HUFF
HUFF
HUFF
E-ELI...
OH MY...
ELIADE...
I-I FEAR...
...I'VE BECOME A VAMPIRE AGAIN....

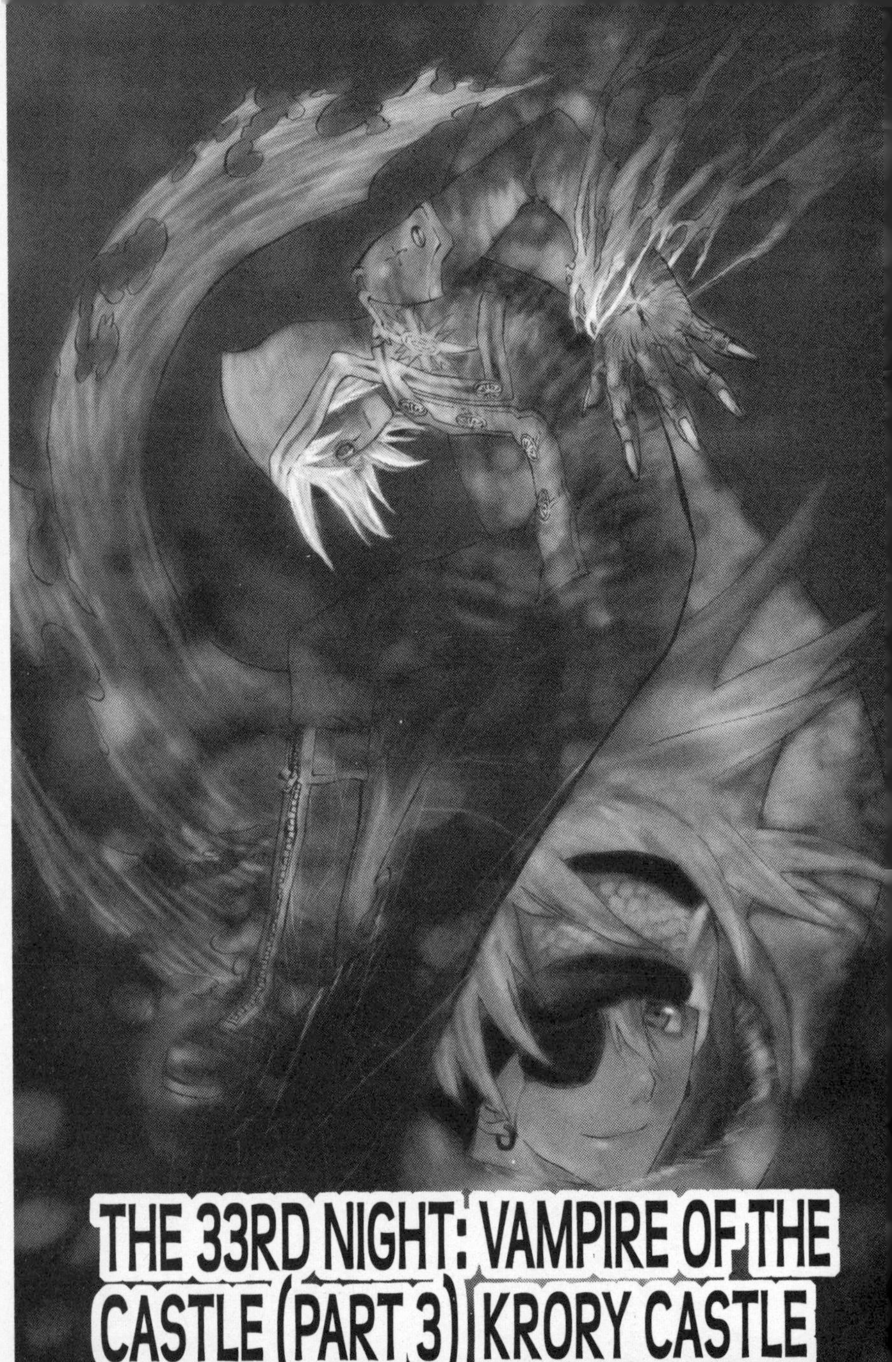

THE 33RD NIGHT: VAMPIRE OF THE CASTLE (PART 3) KRORY CASTLE

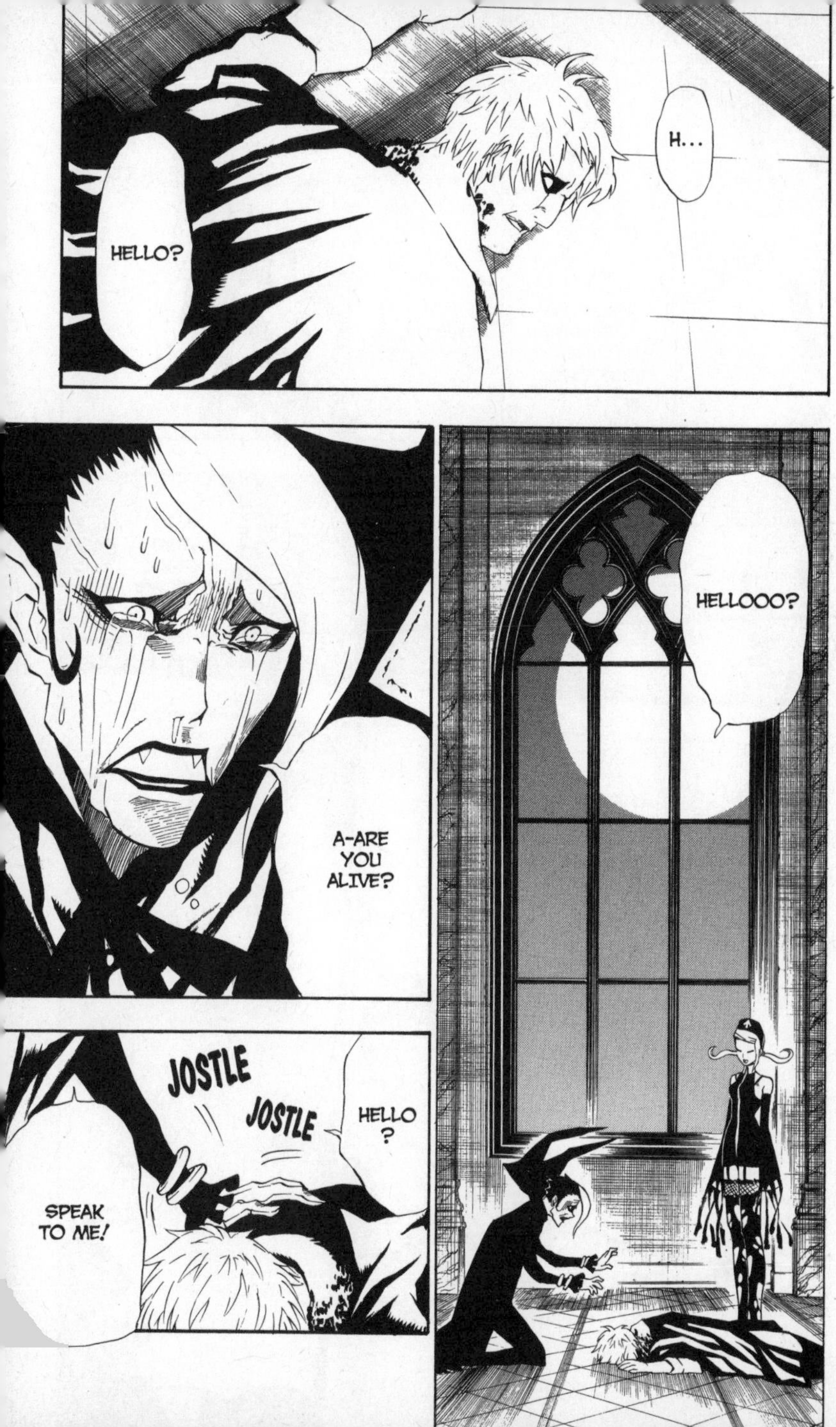
H...
HELLO?
HELLOOO?
A-ARE YOU ALIVE?
HELLO?
JOSTLE JOSTLE
SPEAK TO ME!

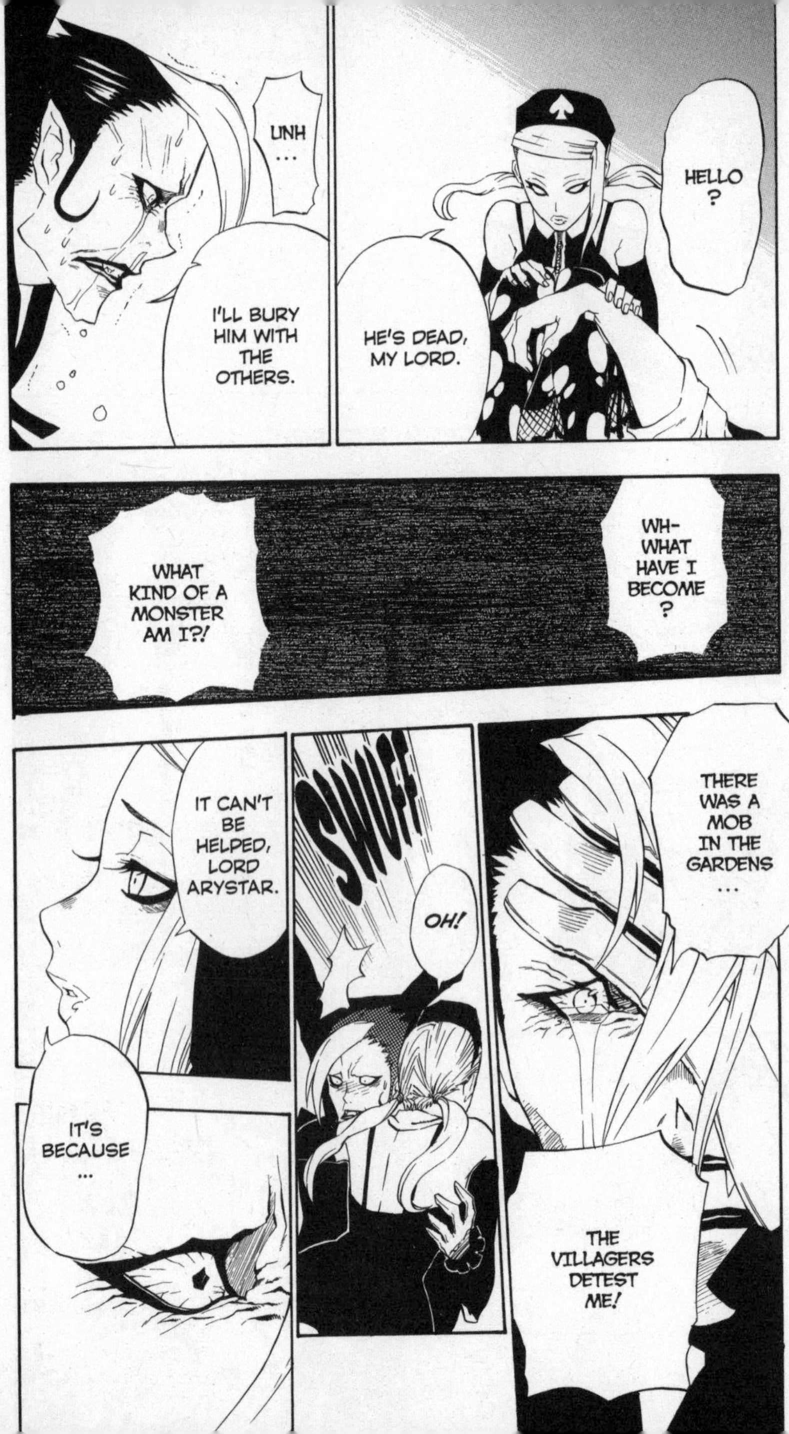
HELLO?
HE'S DEAD, MY LORD.
UNH...
I'LL BURY HIM WITH THE OTHERS.
WH- WHAT HAVE I BECOME?
WHAT KIND OF A MONSTER AM I?!
THERE WAS A MOB IN THE GARDENS...
THE VILLAGERS DETEST ME!
SWUFF
OH!
IT CAN'T BE HELPED, LORD ARYSTAR.
IT'S BECAUSE...

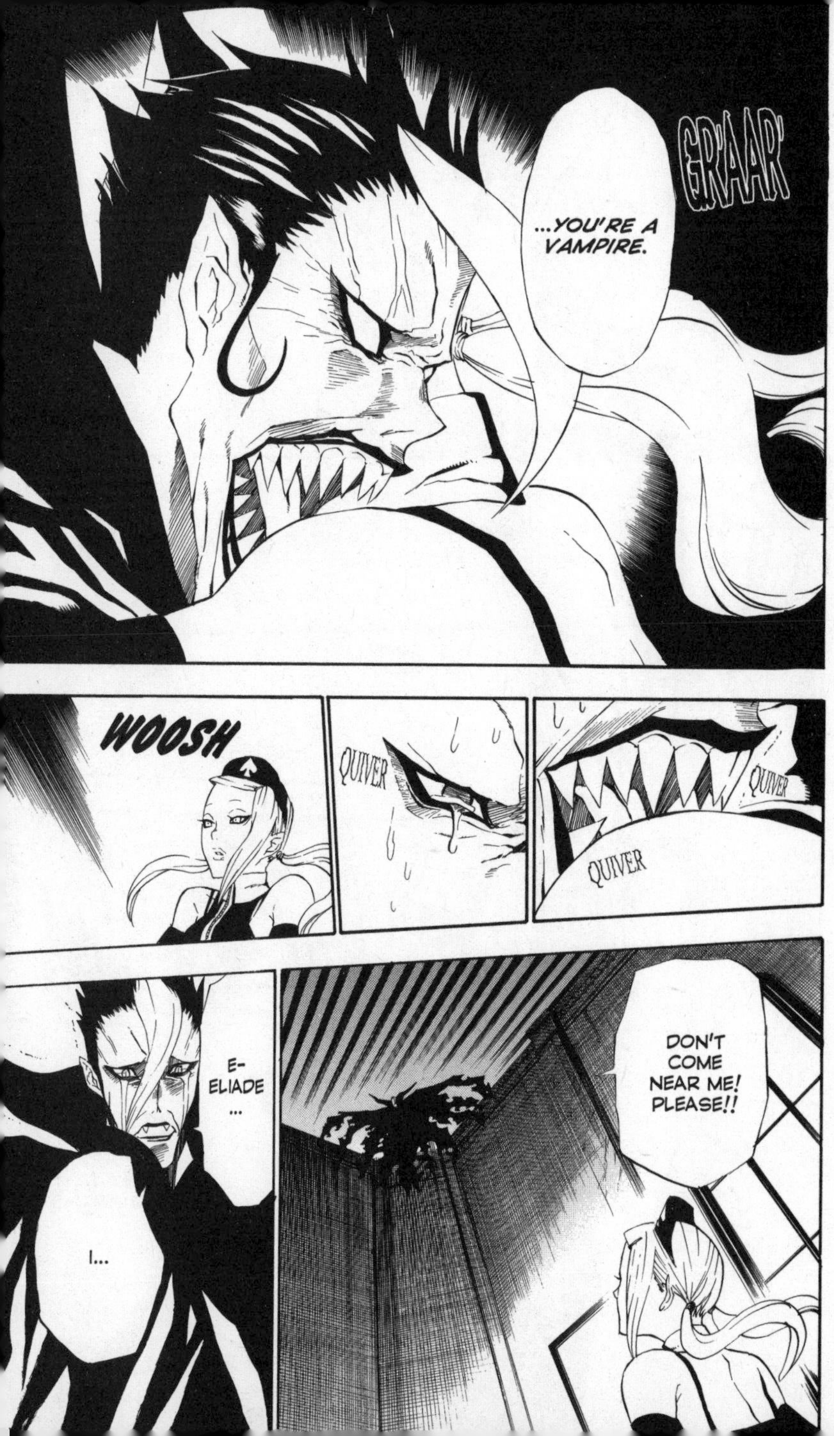
GR'AAR'
...YOU'RE A VAMPIRE.
QUIVER
QUIVER
QUIVER
WOOSH
DON'T COME NEAR ME! PLEASE!!
E-ELIADE...
I...

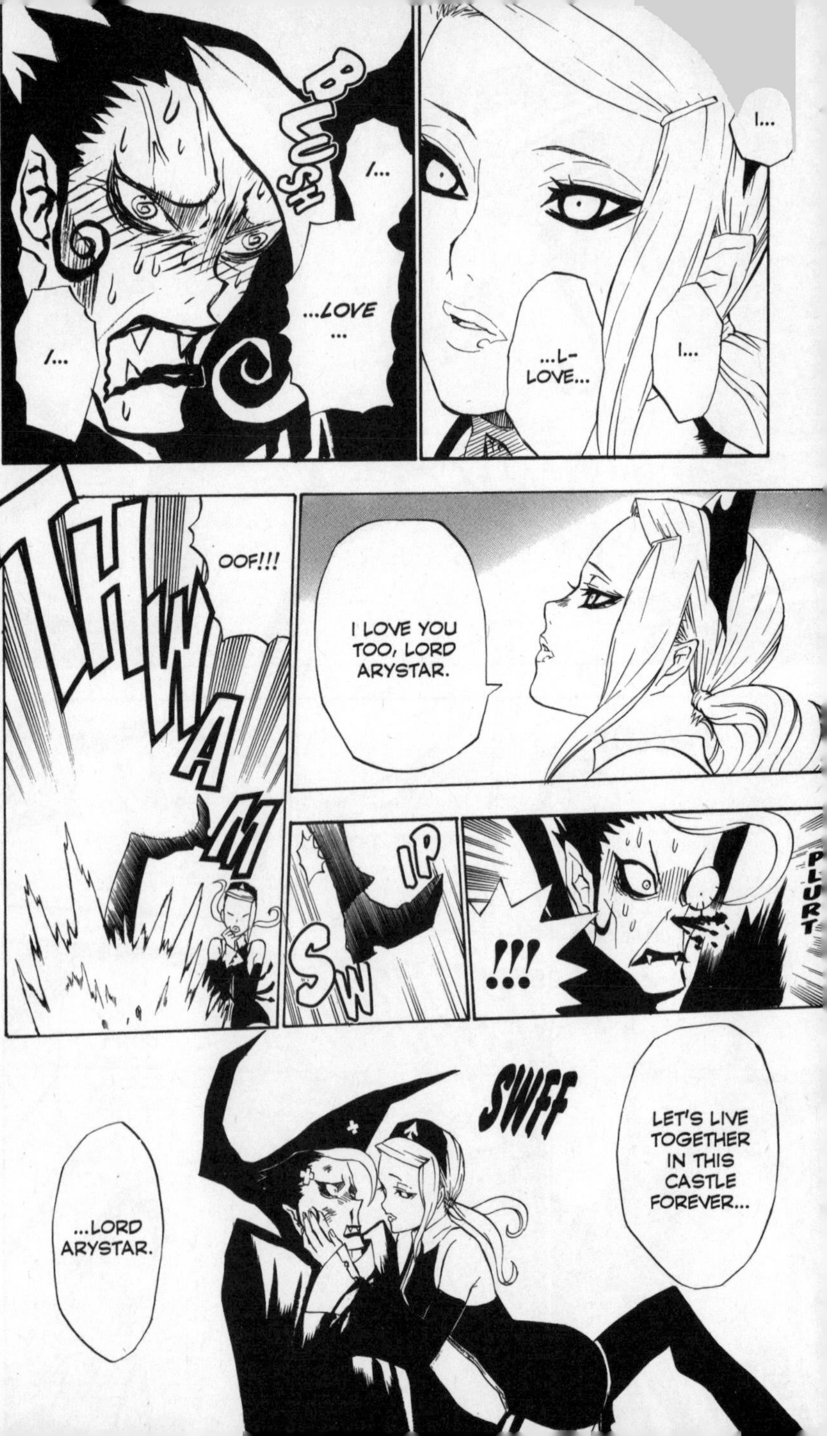
I...
I...
...L- LOVE...
BLUSH
I...
...LOVE ...
I...
I LOVE YOU TOO, LORD ARYSTAR.
PLURT
!!!
SWIP
OOF!!!
THWAMM
LET'S LIVE TOGETHER IN THIS CASTLE FOREVER...
SWFF
...LORD ARYSTAR.

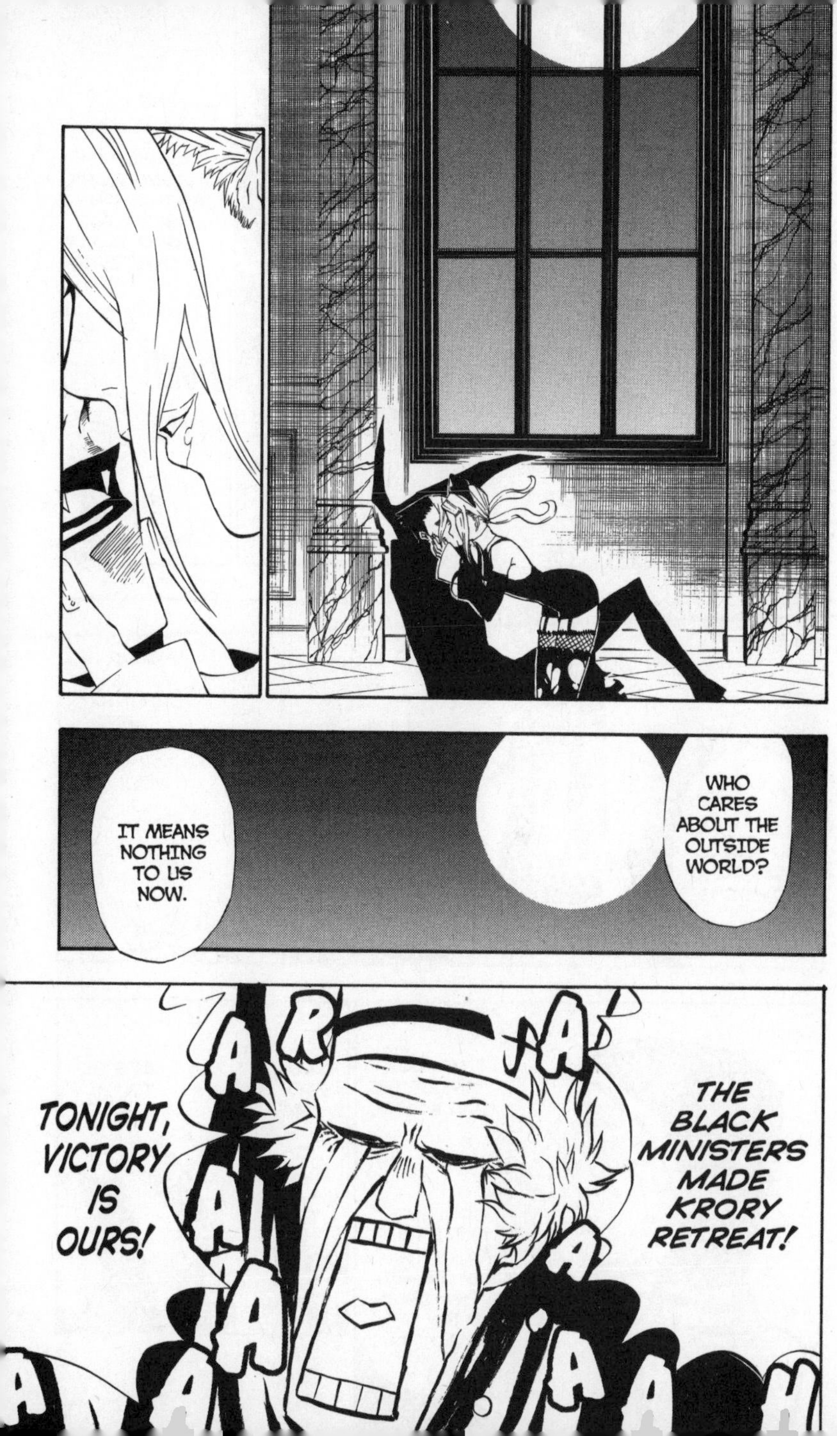
WHO CARES ABOUT THE OUTSIDE WORLD?
IT MEANS NOTHING TO US NOW.
THE BLACK MINISTERS MADE KRORY RETREAT!
TONIGHT, VICTORY IS OURS!

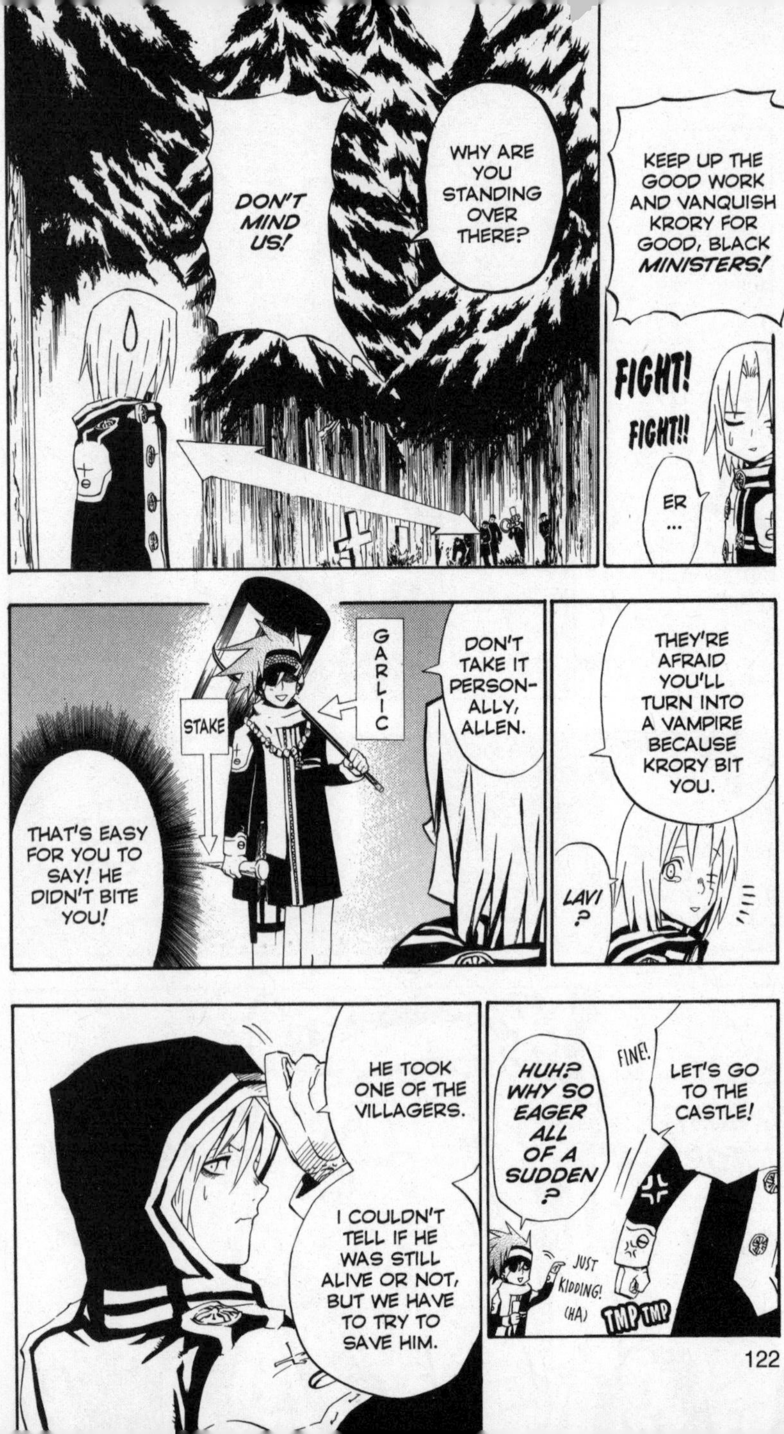
KEEP UP THE GOOD WORK AND VANQUISH KRORY FOR GOOD, BLACK *MINISTERS!*
FIGHT!
FIGHT!!
ER ...
WHY ARE YOU STANDING OVER THERE?
DON'T MIND US!
THEY'RE AFRAID YOU'LL TURN INTO A VAMPIRE BECAUSE KRORY BIT YOU.
LAVI ?
DON'T TAKE IT PERSON-ALLY, ALLEN.
GARLIC
STAKE
THAT'S EASY FOR YOU TO SAY! HE DIDN'T BITE YOU!
LET'S GO TO THE CASTLE!
FINE!
HUH? WHY SO EAGER ALL OF A SUDDEN ?
JUST KIDDING! (HA)
TMP TMP
HE TOOK ONE OF THE VILLAGERS.
I COULDN'T TELL IF HE WAS STILL ALIVE OR NOT, BUT WE HAVE TO TRY TO SAVE HIM.

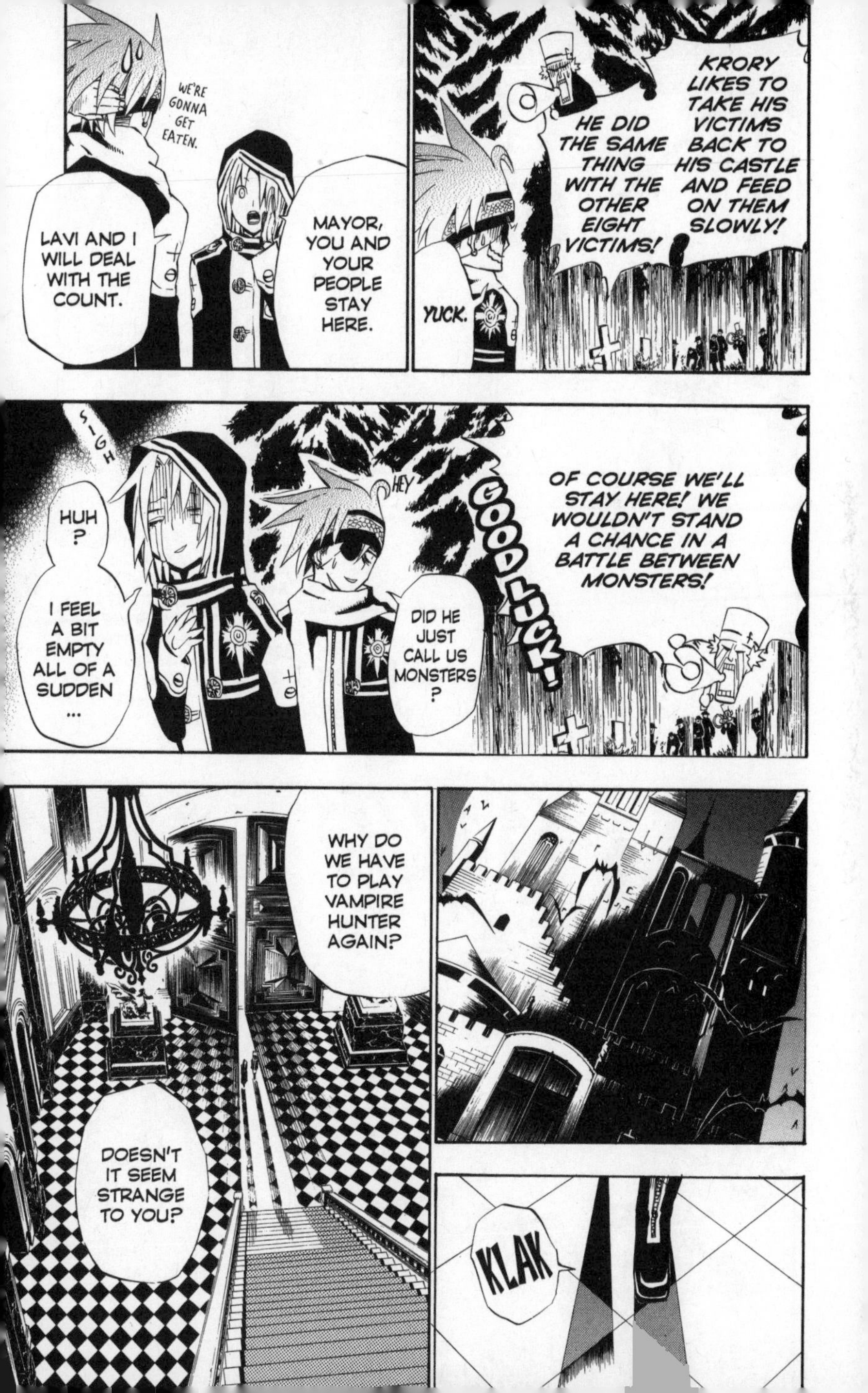
KRORY LIKES TO TAKE HIS VICTIMS BACK TO HIS CASTLE AND FEED ON THEM SLOWLY!
HE DID THE SAME THING WITH THE OTHER EIGHT VICTIMS!
YUCK.
WE'RE GONNA GET EATEN.
MAYOR, YOU AND YOUR PEOPLE STAY HERE.
LAVI AND I WILL DEAL WITH THE COUNT.
OF COURSE WE'LL STAY HERE! WE WOULDN'T STAND A CHANCE IN A BATTLE BETWEEN MONSTERS!
GOOD LUCK!
HEY
DID HE JUST CALL US MONSTERS?
SIGH
HUH?
I FEEL A BIT EMPTY ALL OF A SUDDEN...
KLAK
WHY DO WE HAVE TO PLAY VAMPIRE HUNTER AGAIN?
DOESN'T IT SEEM STRANGE TO YOU?

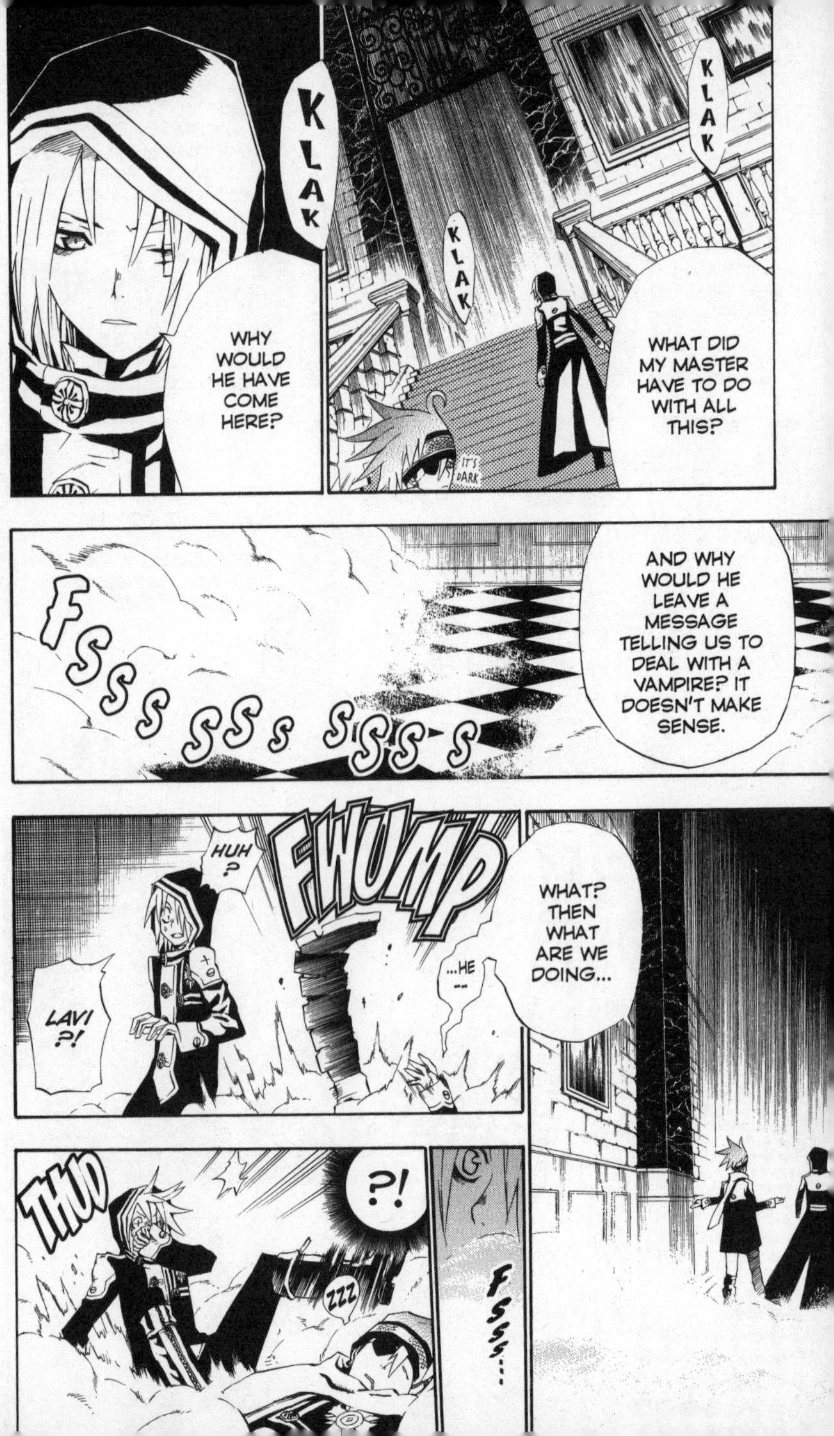
KLAK
KLAK
WHAT DID MY MASTER HAVE TO DO WITH ALL THIS?
IT'S DARK
KLAK
WHY WOULD HE HAVE COME HERE?
AND WHY WOULD HE LEAVE A MESSAGE TELLING US TO DEAL WITH A VAMPIRE? IT DOESN'T MAKE SENSE.
FSSSS SSS SSSS
WHAT? THEN WHAT ARE WE DOING...
FWUMP
...HE --
HUH?
LAVI?!
FSSS...
?!
ZZZ
THUD

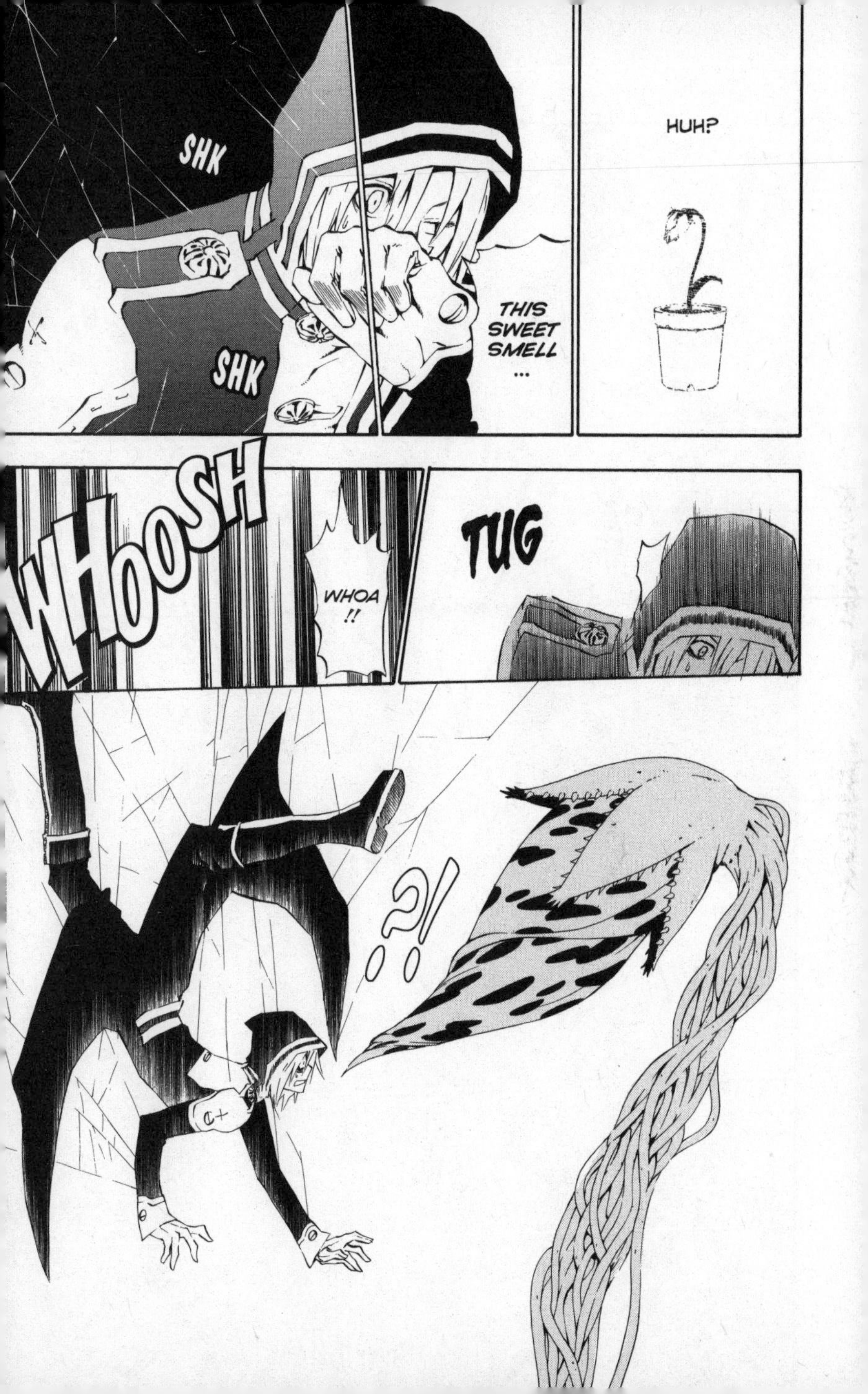
HUH?
SHK
SHK
THIS SWEET SMELL ...
TUG
WHOOSH
WHOA !!
?!

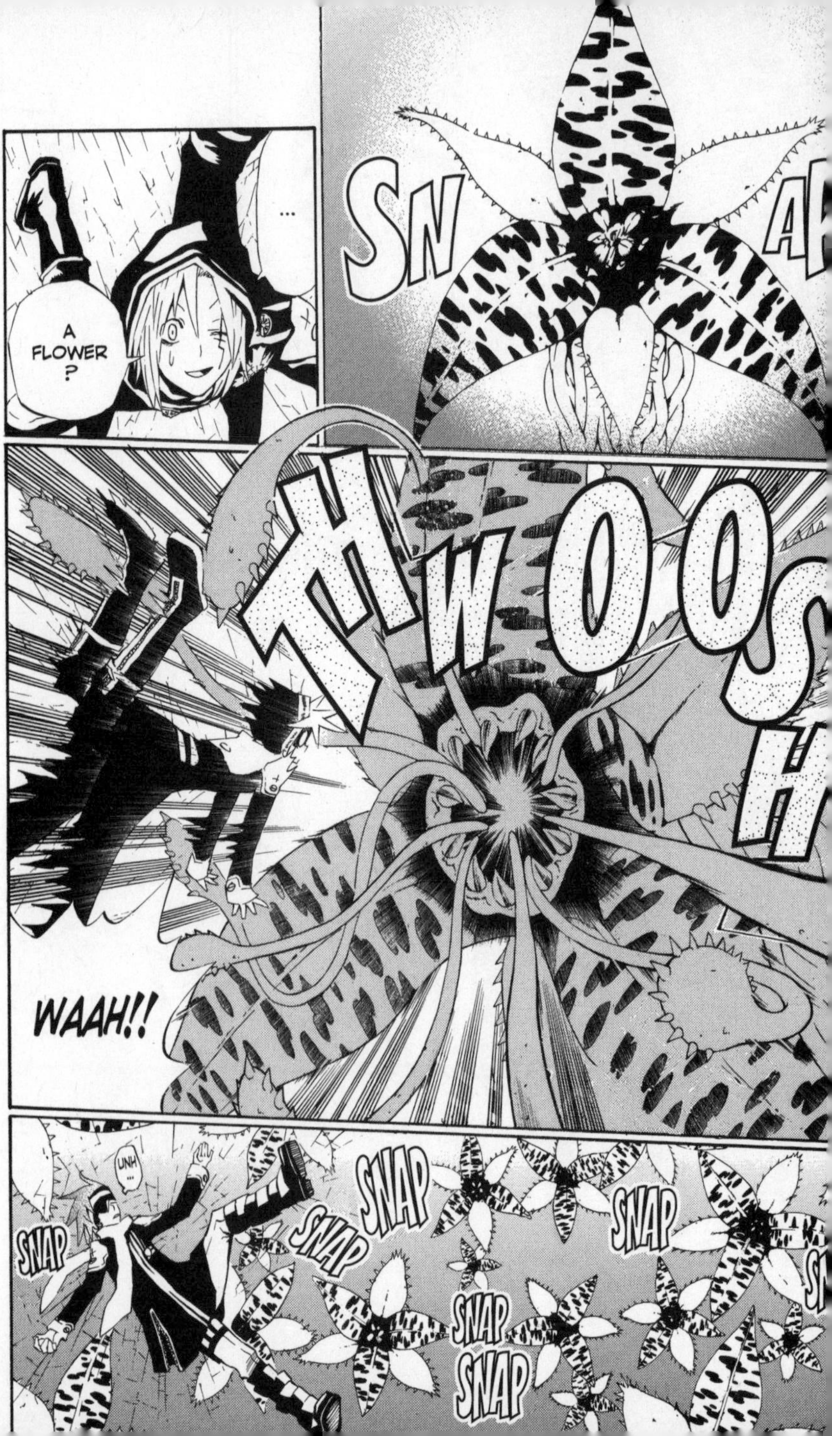
SN
...
A FLOWER?
THWOOSH
WAAH!!
SNAP
SNAP
SNAP
SNAP
SNAP
UNH...
SNAP

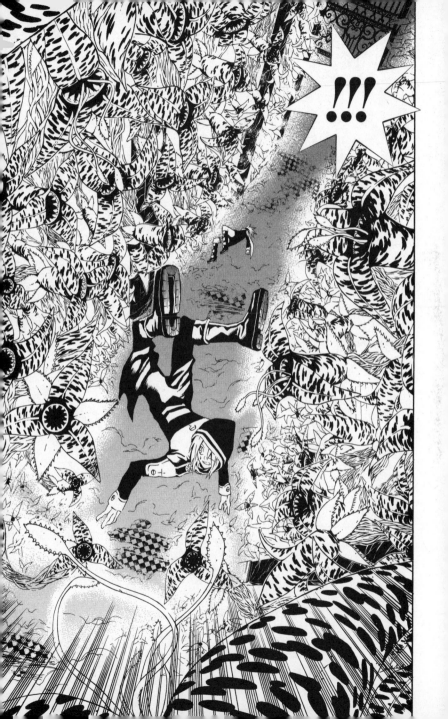

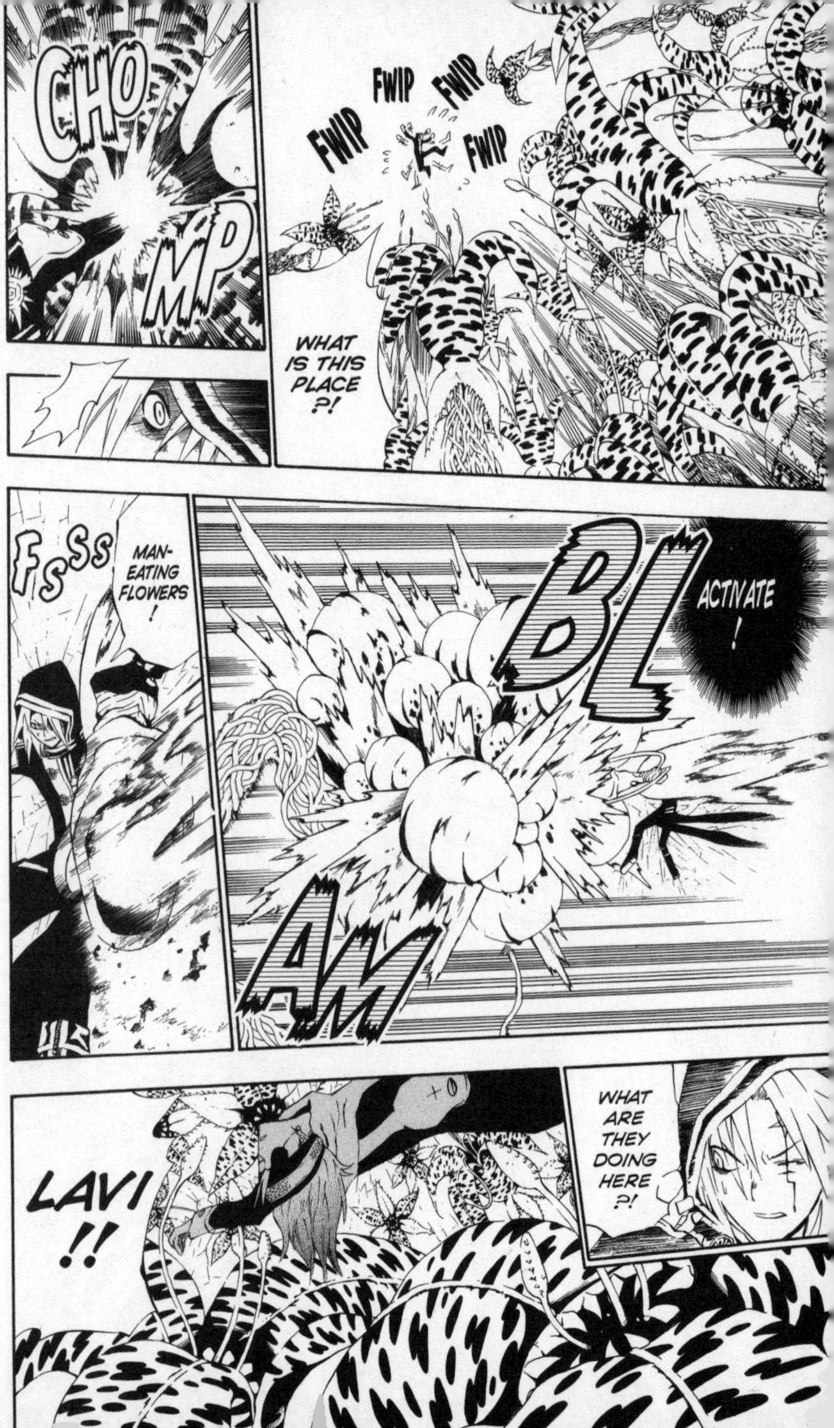

FWIP
FWIP
FWIP
FWIP
WHAT IS THIS PLACE ?!
CHOMP
ACTIVATE!
BLAM
FSSS
MAN-EATING FLOWERS!
WHAT ARE THEY DOING HERE?!
LAVI!!

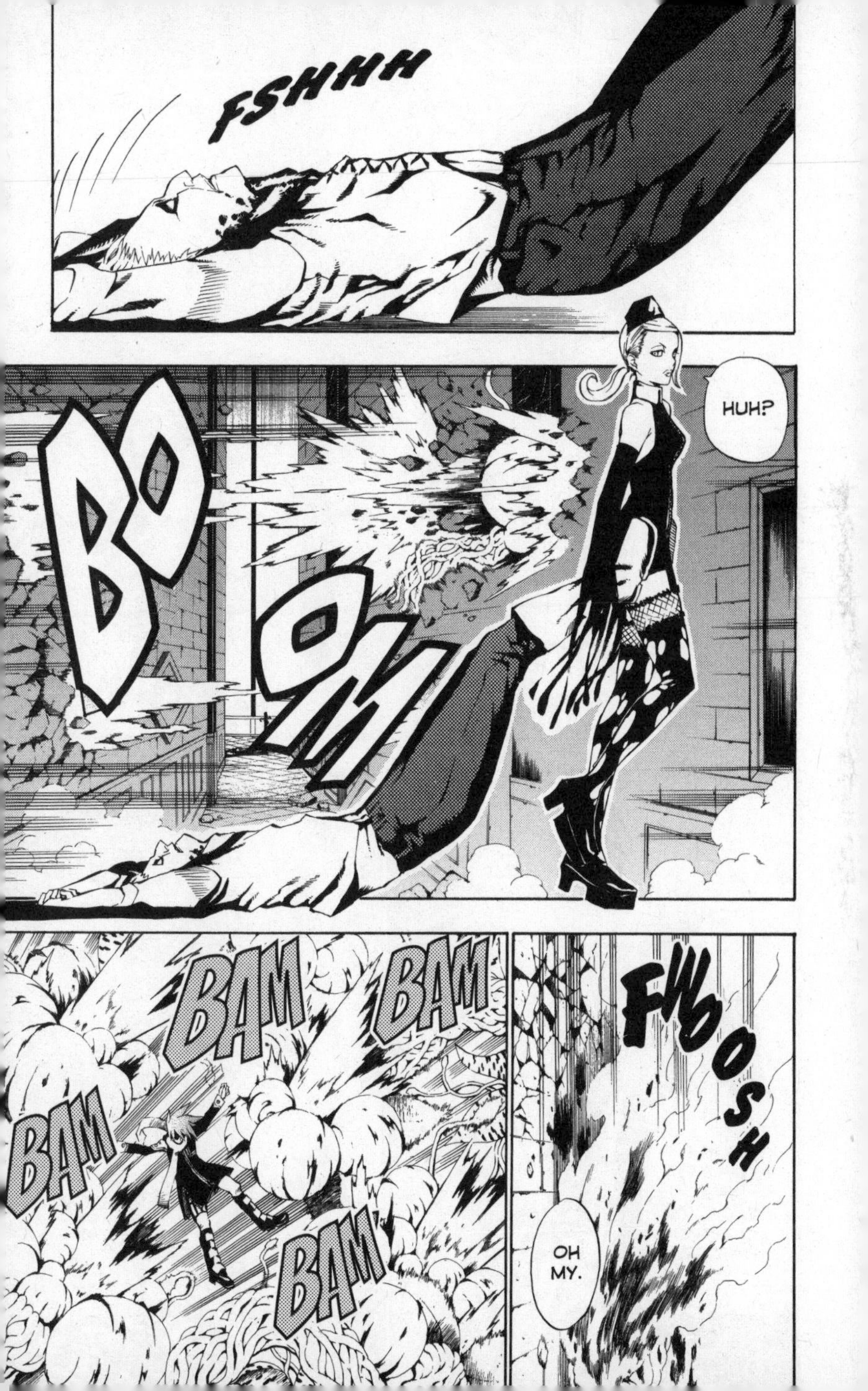
FSHHH
HUH?
BOOM
FWOOSH
OH MY.
BAM
BAM
BAM
BAM

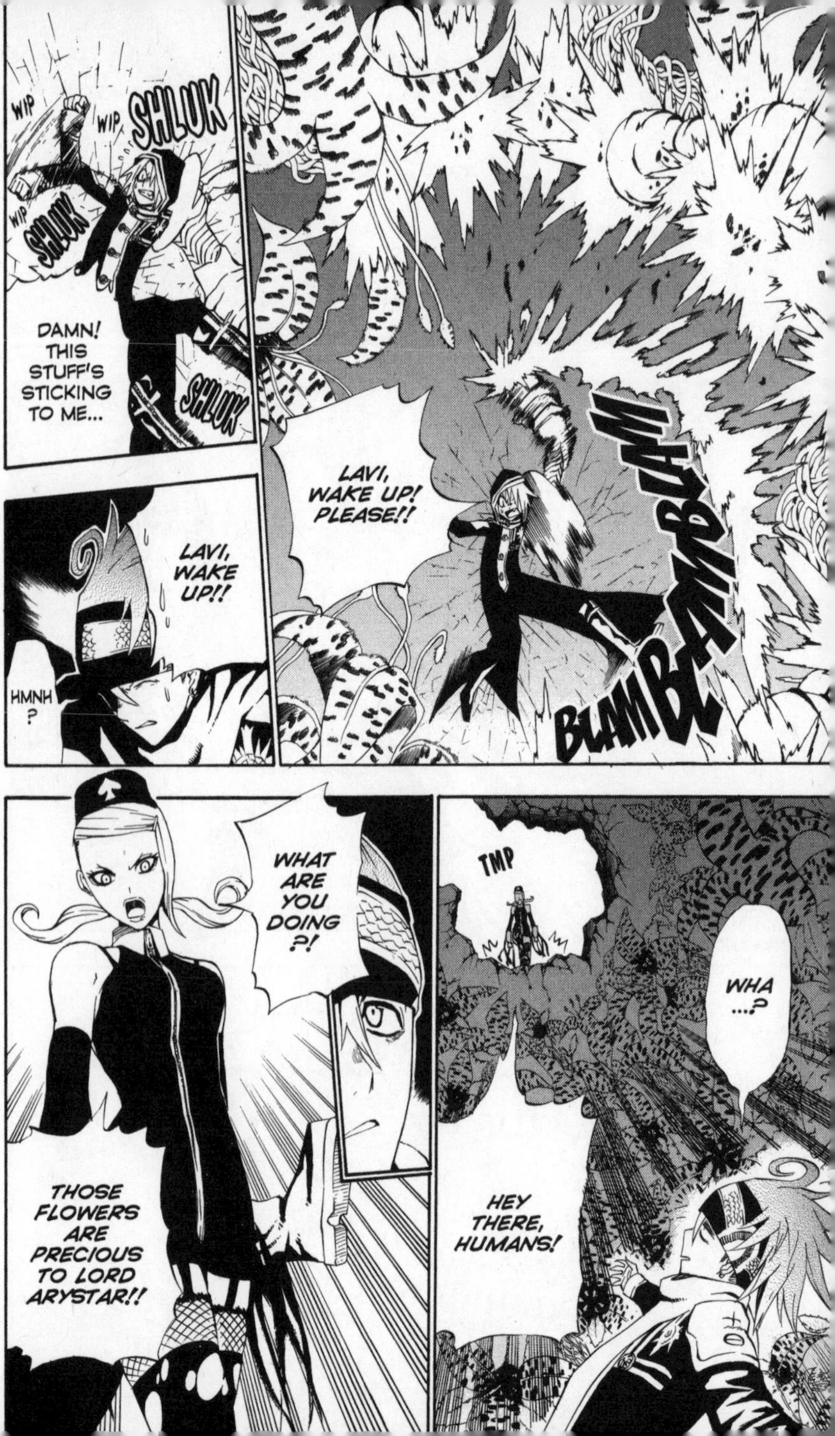
BLAMBLAMBLAM
LAVI, WAKE UP! PLEASE!!
WIP
WIP
SHLUK
WIP
SHLUK
DAMN! THIS STUFF'S STICKING TO ME...
SHLUK
LAVI, WAKE UP!!
HMNH?
TMP
WHA...?
HEY THERE, HUMANS!
WHAT ARE YOU DOING?!
THOSE FLOWERS ARE PRECIOUS TO LORD ARYSTAR!!

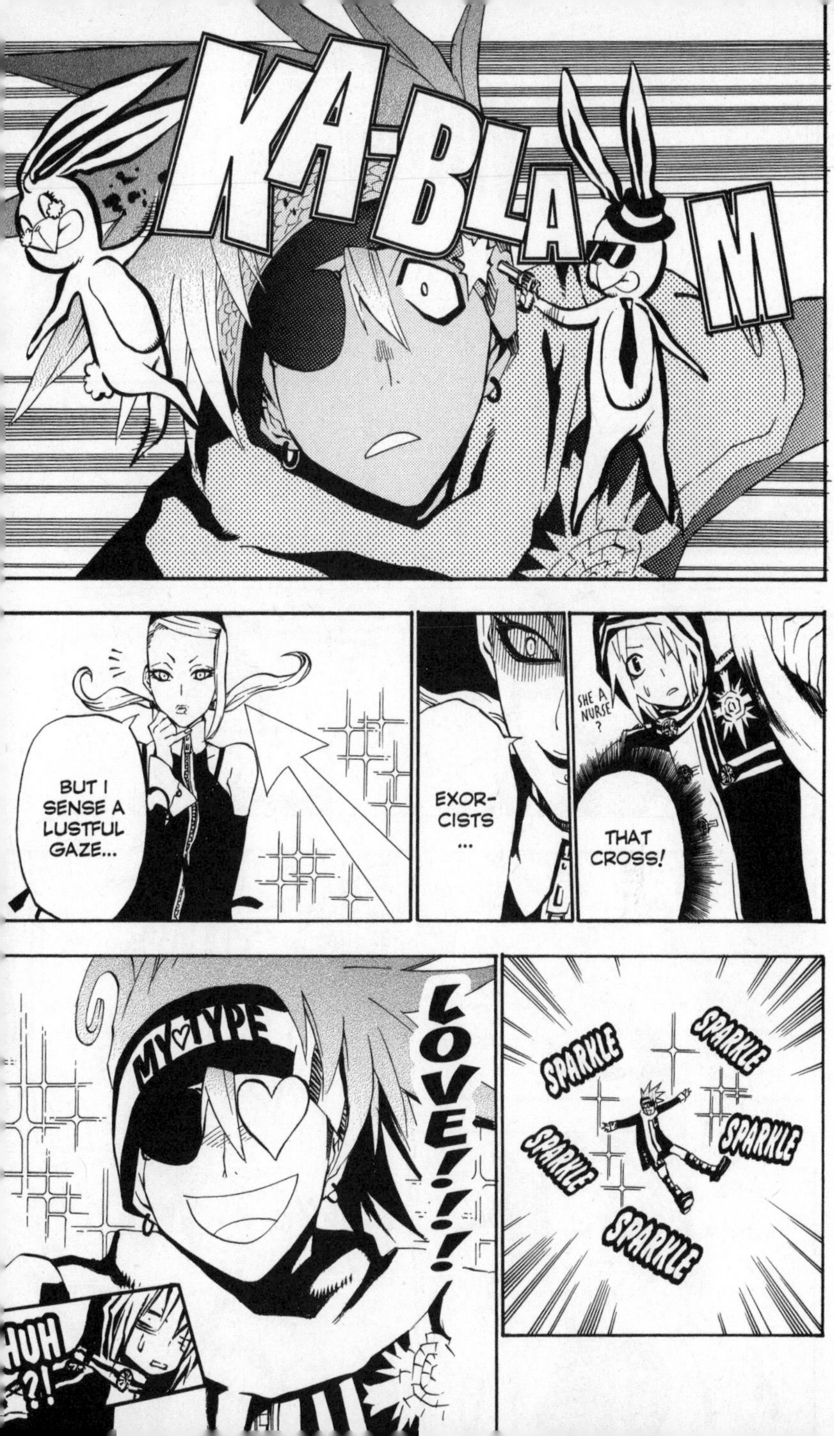
KA-BLAM
SHE A NURSE?
THAT CROSS!
EXOR-CISTS...
BUT I SENSE A LUSTFUL GAZE...
SPARKLE
SPARKLE
SPARKLE
SPARKLE
SPARKLE
MY♡TYPE
LOVE!!!!
HUH?!

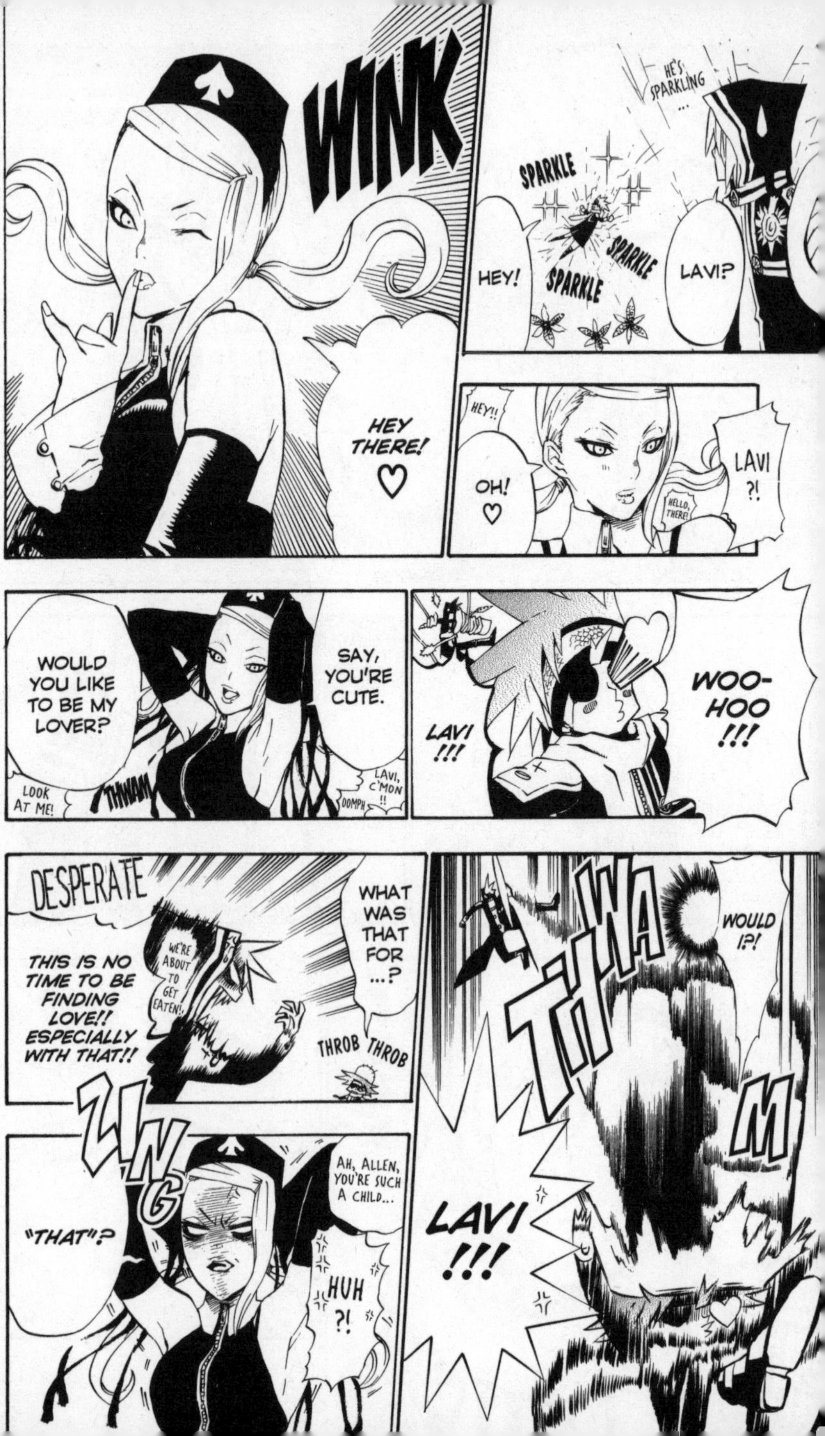

HE'S SPARKLING ...
LAVI?
SPARKLE
SPARKLE
SPARKLE
HEY!
LAVI ?!
HELLO, THERE!
HEY!!
OH! ♡
WINK
HEY THERE! ♡
WOO-HOO !!!
LAVI !!!
SAY, YOU'RE CUTE.
LAVI, C'MON !!
DOOMPH
WOULD YOU LIKE TO BE MY LOVER?
THWAM
LOOK AT ME!
WOULD I?!
THWAM
LAVI !!!
WHAT WAS THAT FOR ...?
DESPERATE
WE'RE ABOUT TO GET EATEN!
THIS IS NO TIME TO BE FINDING LOVE!! ESPECIALLY WITH THAT!!
THROB THROB
AH, ALLEN, YOU'RE SUCH A CHILD...
HUH ?!
ZING
"THAT"?

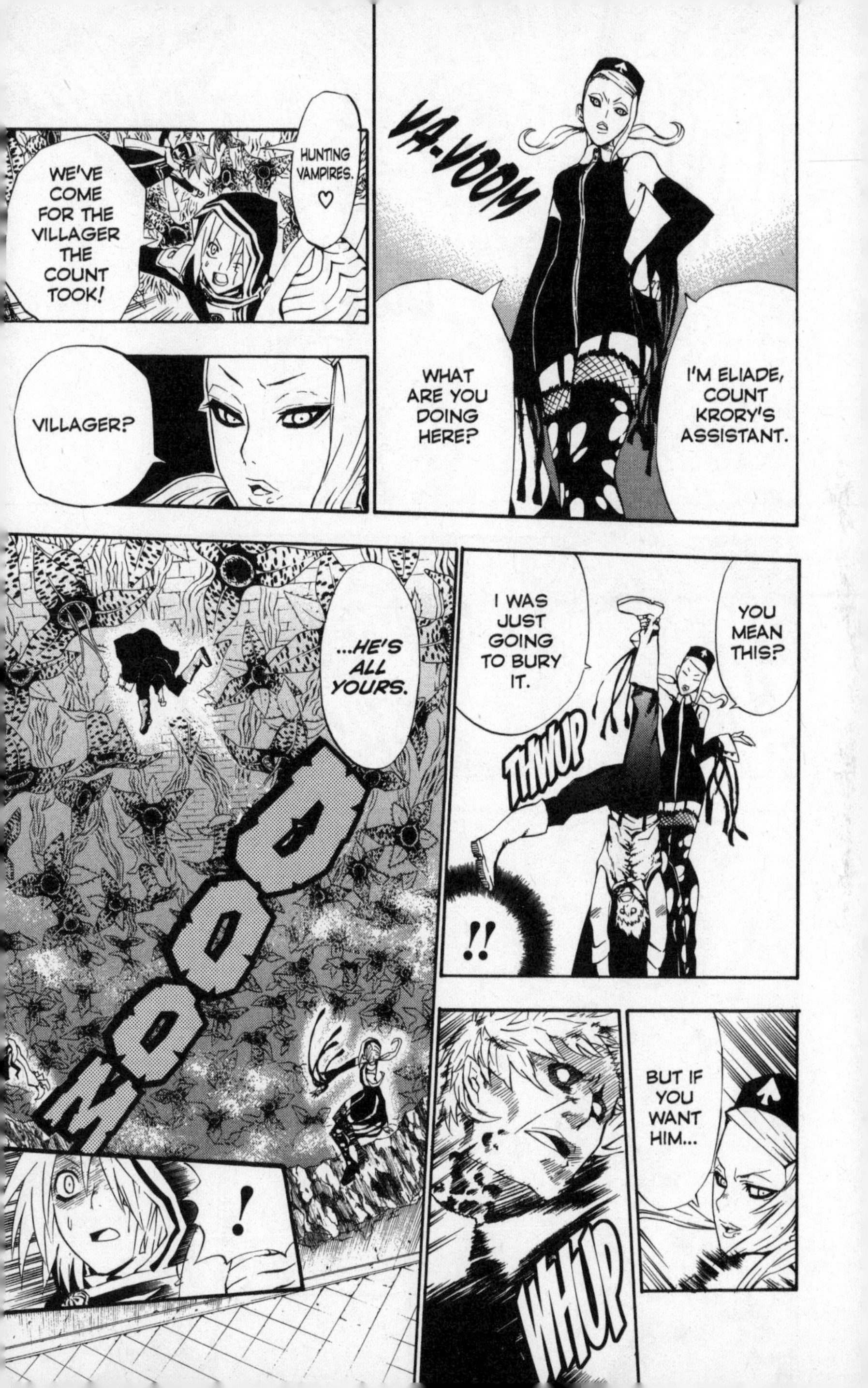
VA-VOOM
I'M ELIADE, COUNT KRORY'S ASSISTANT.
WHAT ARE YOU DOING HERE?
HUNTING VAMPIRES. ♡
WE'VE COME FOR THE VILLAGER THE COUNT TOOK!
VILLAGER?
YOU MEAN THIS?
I WAS JUST GOING TO BURY IT.
THWUP
!!
BUT IF YOU WANT HIM...
WHUP
...HE'S ALL YOURS.
!

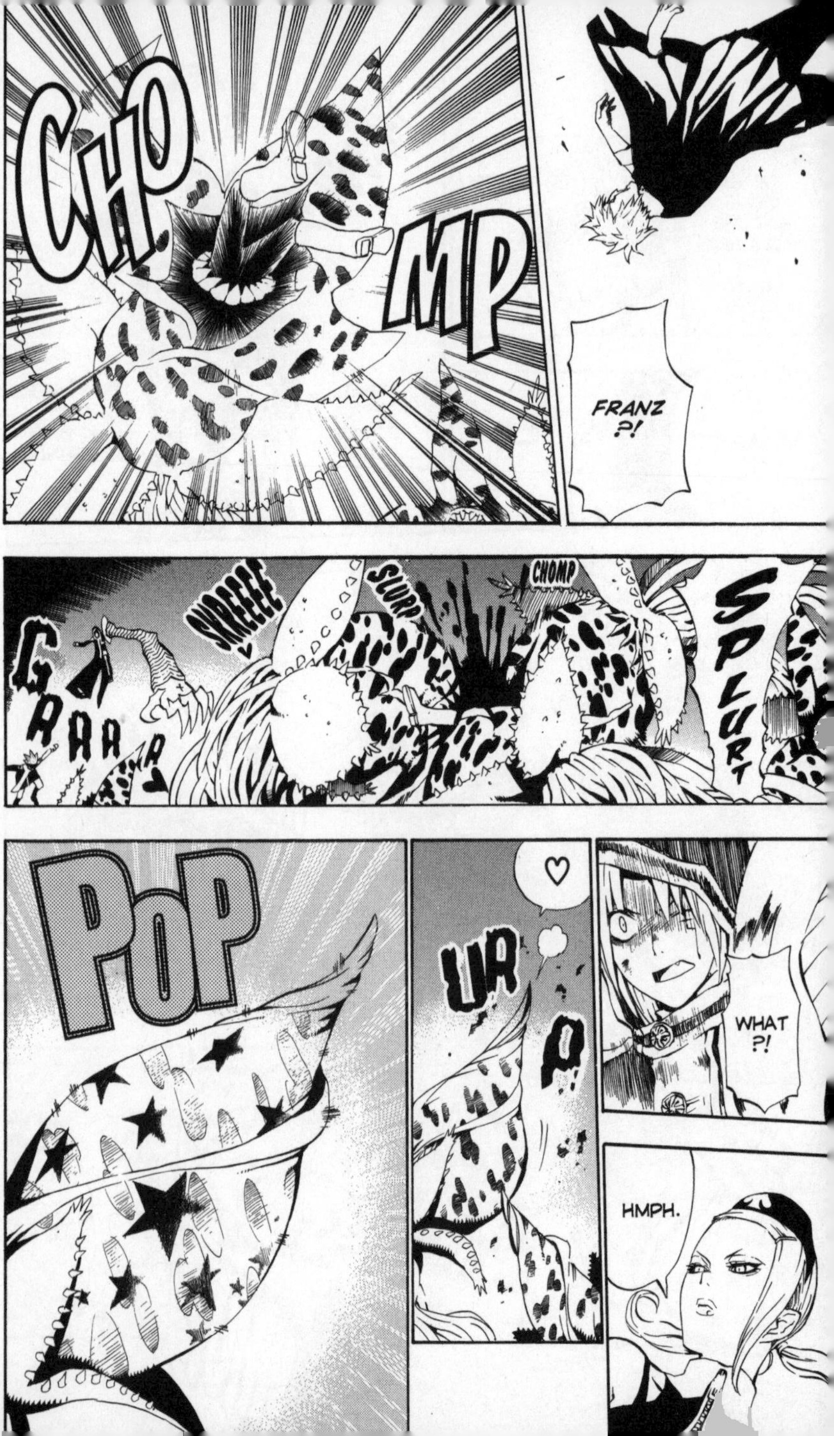
FRANZ ?!
CHOMP
SPLURT
CHOMP
SLURP
SKREEEE
GAAAA
WHAT ?!
HMPH.
♥
URP
POP

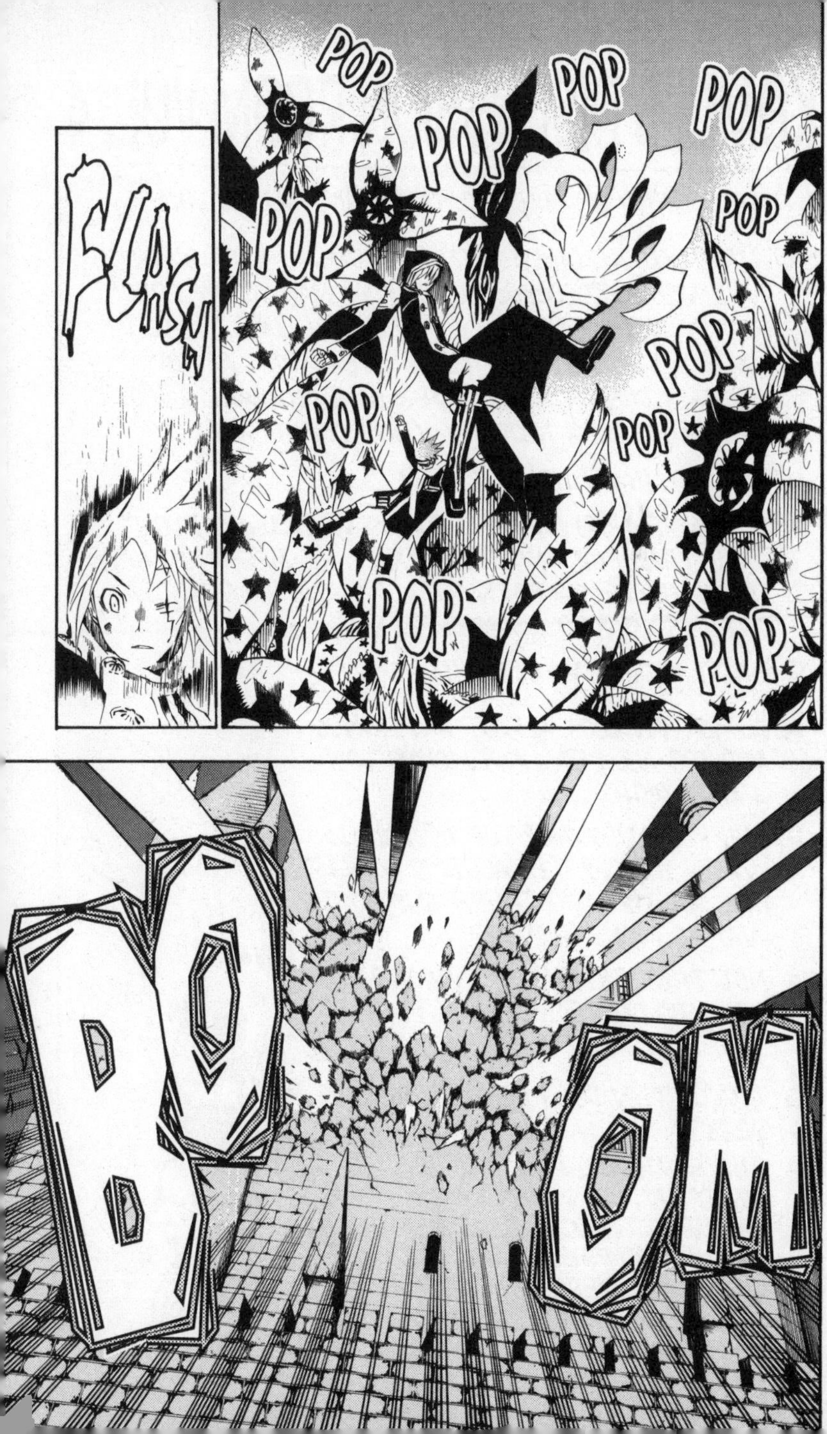
POP
POP
POP
POP
POP
POP
POP
POP
POP
POP
POP
FLASH
BOOM

KOMUI'S DISCUSSION ROOM VOL. 4

Q. WHAT KIND OF GIRLS DO KANDA AND ALLEN LIKE?

A. HUH?! (BLUSH) GIRLS? I DUNNO. UM... I LIKE GIRLS WHO ARE GOOD COOKS. I LOVE A WOMAN IN AN APRON. (HAPPY SIGH) I MIGHT EVEN FALL IN LOVE IF SHE'D MAKE ME SWEET DUMPLINGS EVERY DAY. AS FOR KANDA, I DON'T KNOW. MAYBE SOMEONE WHO'S GOOD AT MAKING SOBA NOODLES? (NONCOMMITTAL)

Q. DO THEY HAVE GIRLFRIENDS?

A. OF COURSE NOT! (WAVING HANDS VIGOROUSLY) I DON'T HAVE TIME FOR THAT WITH ALL THE MISSIONS I HAVE TO COMPLETE. AS FOR KANDA, I THINK HE'S IN LOVE WITH HIS SWORD. (NONCOMMITTAL)

Q. WHAT FOODS CAN JERRY COOK?

A. JERRY CAN COOK ALMOST ANYTHING. AND IT'S ALL REALLY DELICIOUS TOO! (HAPPY SIGH)

Q. CHIEF KOMUI WAKES UP INSTANTLY WHEN YOU SAY "LENALEE IS GOING TO GET MARRIED." IS THERE ANY OTHER WAY TO WAKE HIM UP?

A. NOT THAT I KNOW OF. WHICH MUST BE HARD ON REEVER AND THE OTHERS. I WISH THEM THE BEST.

Q. HOW OFTEN DOES KOMUI CLEAN HIS DESK?

A. I HAVE NO IDEA. I DON'T GO SEE HIM EVERY DAY, BUT WHEN KOMLIN RAMPAGED THROUGH HEADQUARTERS (SEE VOL. 3) REEVER AND THE OTHERS CLEARED KOMUI'S DESK IN THE CLEAN UP. BUT THE VERY NEXT DAY, IT WAS A MESS AGAIN.

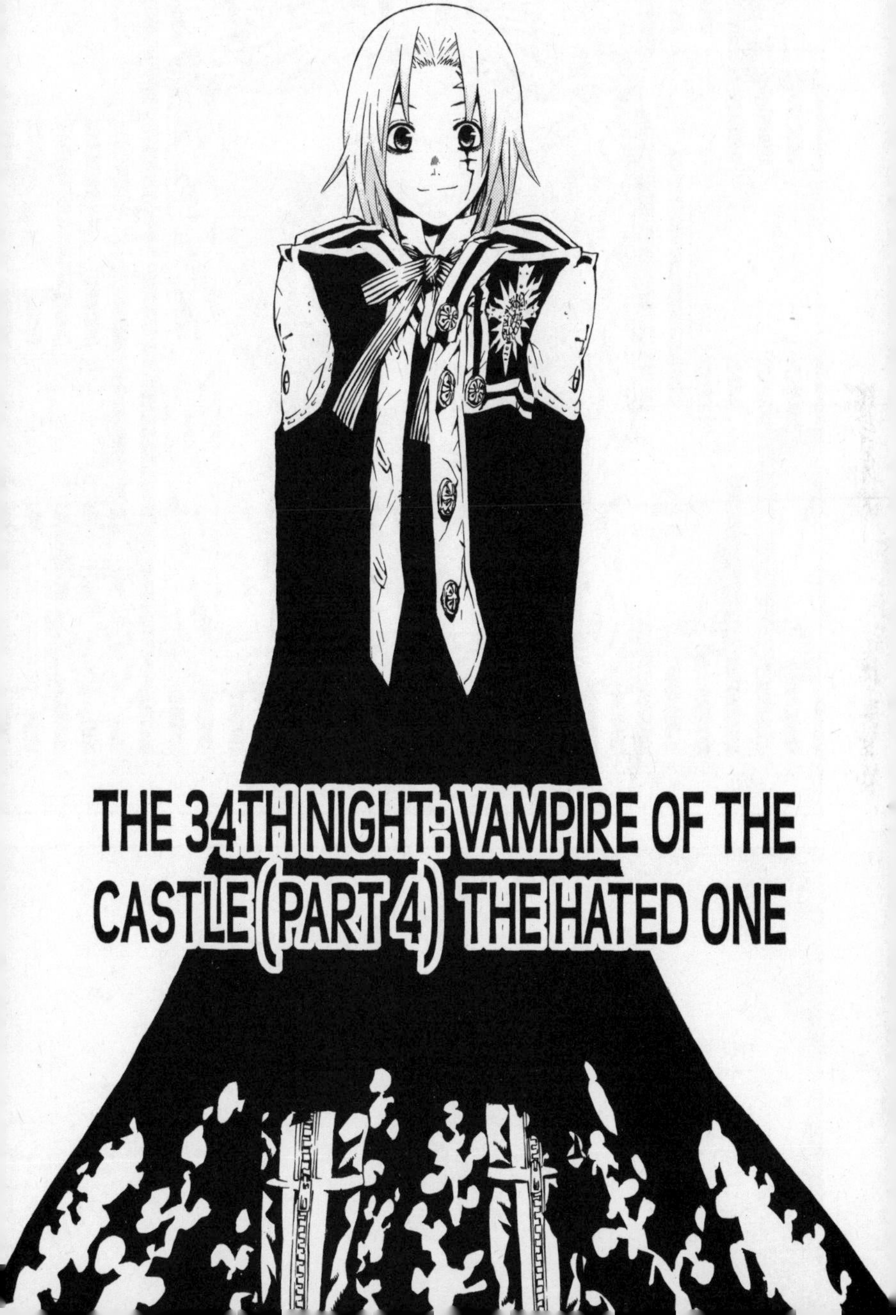
THE 34TH NIGHT: VAMPIRE OF THE CASTLE (PART 4) THE HATED ONE

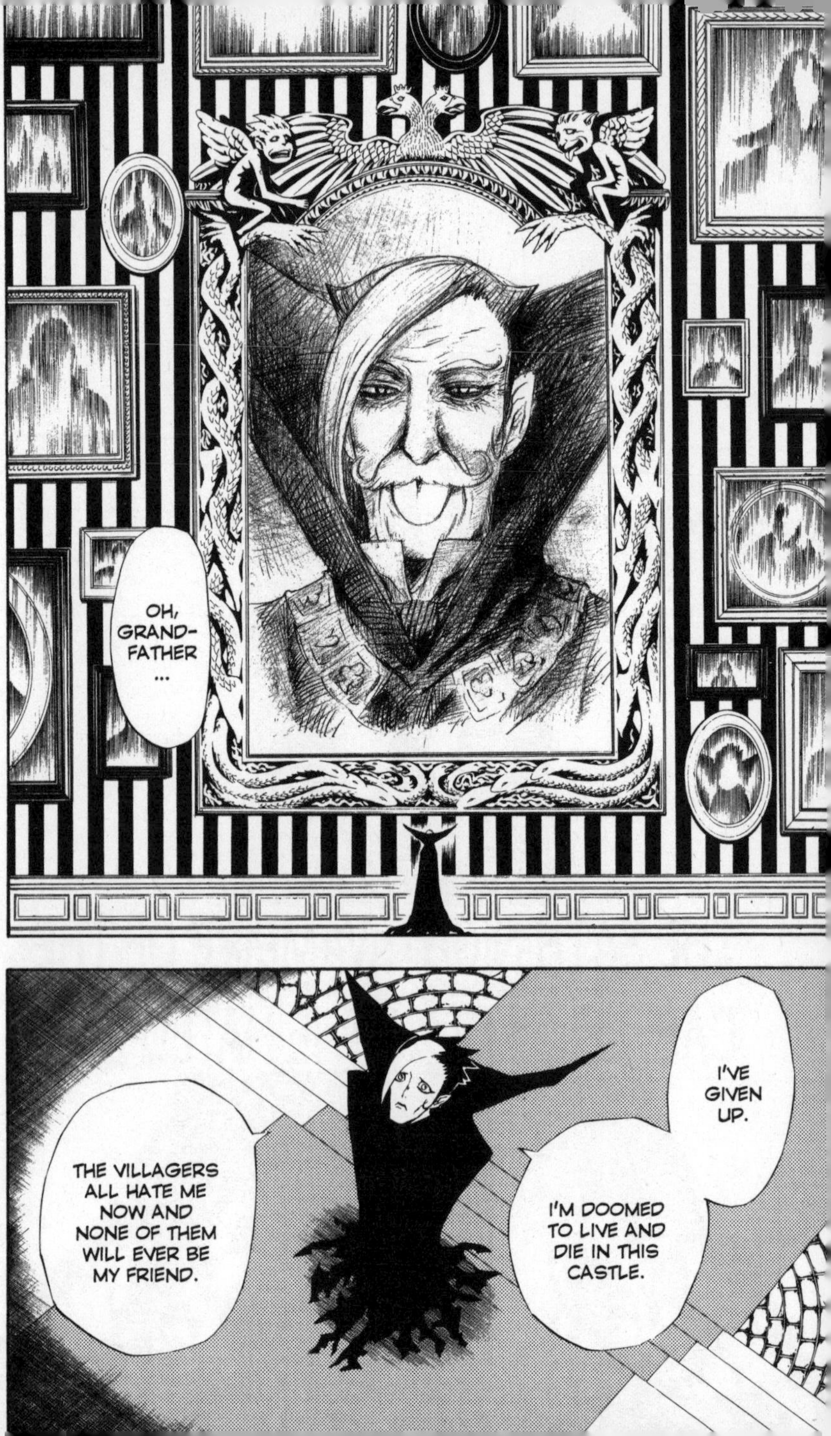
OH, GRAND-FATHER ...
I'VE GIVEN UP.
I'M DOOMED TO LIVE AND DIE IN THIS CASTLE.
THE VILLAGERS ALL HATE ME NOW AND NONE OF THEM WILL EVER BE MY FRIEND.

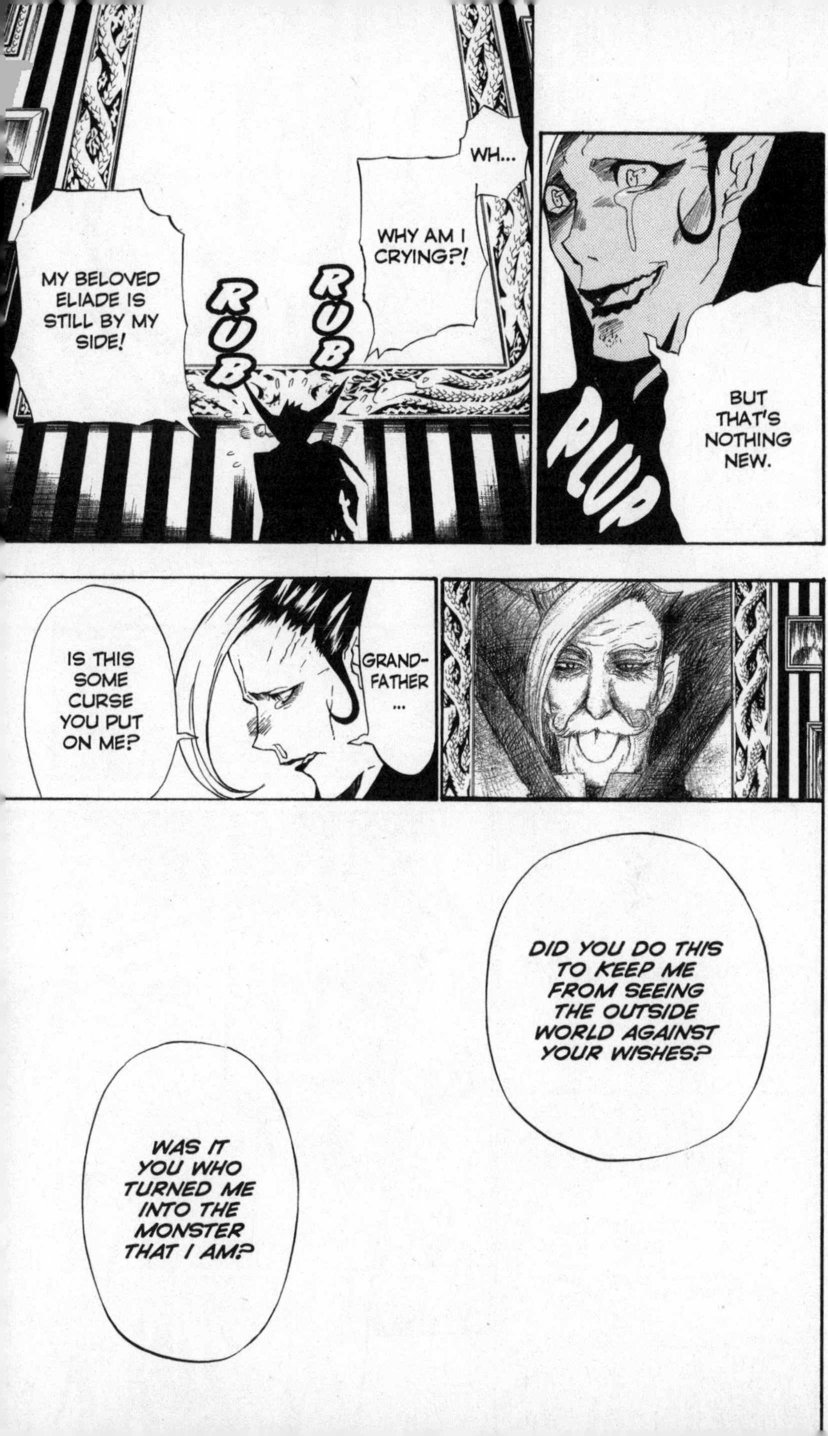
PLUR
BUT THAT'S NOTHING NEW.
WH...
WHY AM I CRYING?!
RUB
RUB
MY BELOVED ELIADE IS STILL BY MY SIDE!
GRAND-FATHER ...
IS THIS SOME CURSE YOU PUT ON ME?
DID YOU DO THIS TO KEEP ME FROM SEEING THE OUTSIDE WORLD AGAINST YOUR WISHES?
WAS IT YOU WHO TURNED ME INTO THE MONSTER THAT I AM?

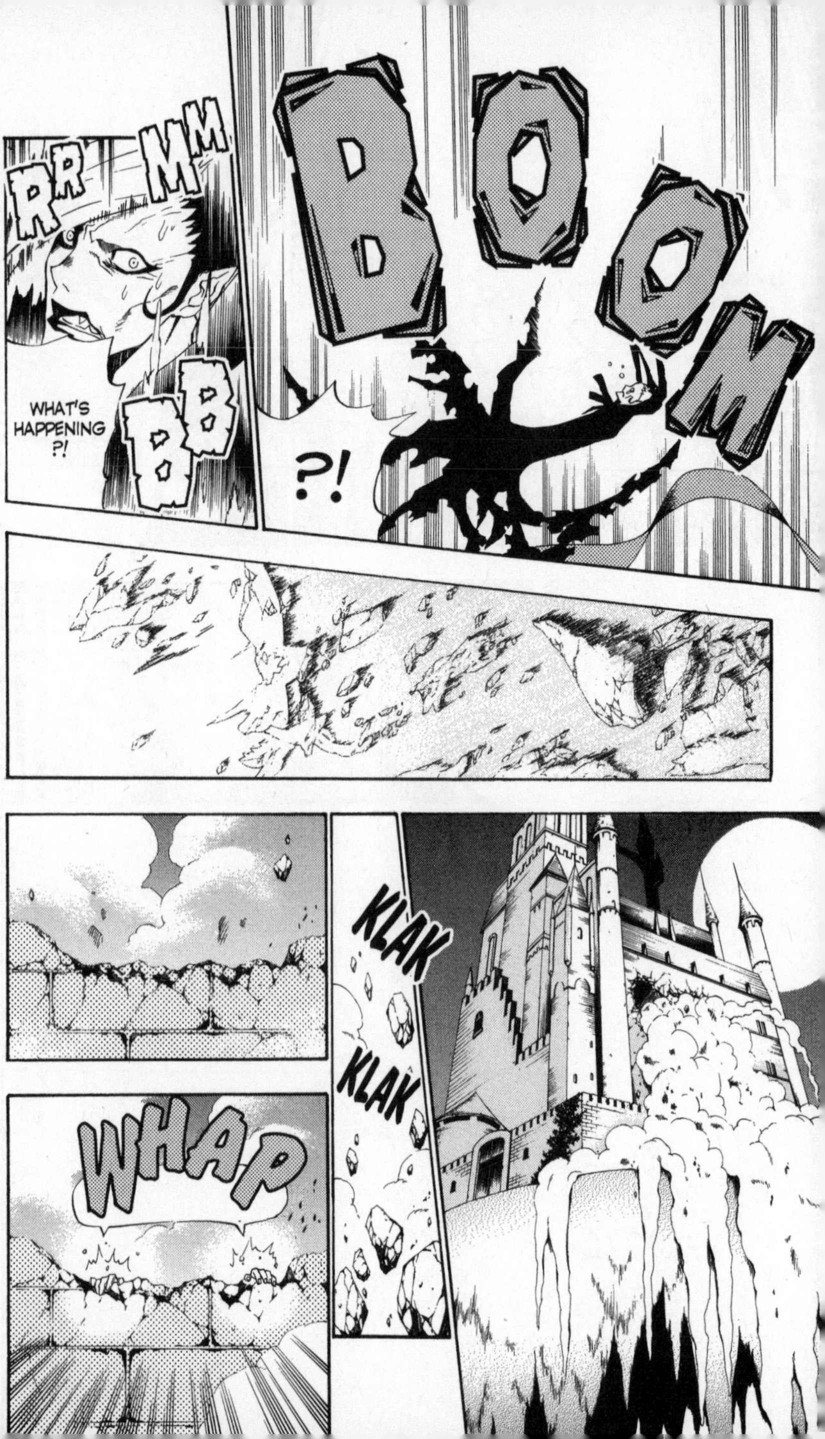
BOOM
?!
RRMM
WHAT'S HAPPENING ?!
BB
KLAK
KLAK
WHAP

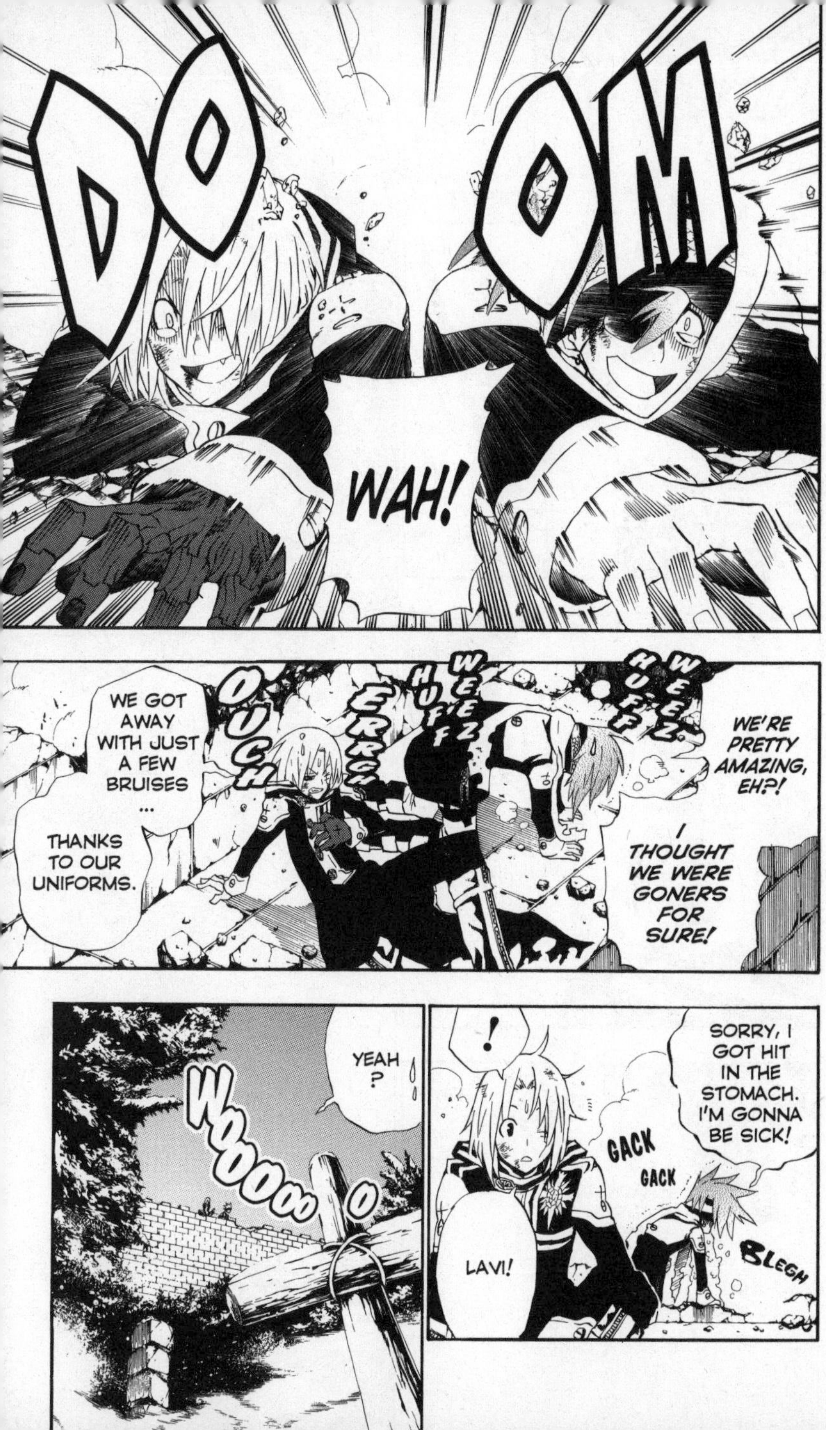
DO
OM
WAH!
WHEEZ
HUFF
WE'RE PRETTY AMAZING, EH?!
I THOUGHT WE WERE GONERS FOR SURE!
WHEEZ
HUFF
ERRGH
OUCH
WE GOT AWAY WITH JUST A FEW BRUISES ...
THANKS TO OUR UNIFORMS.
!
SORRY, I GOT HIT IN THE STOMACH. I'M GONNA BE SICK!
GACK
GACK
BLEGH
LAVI!
YEAH ?
WOOOOO O

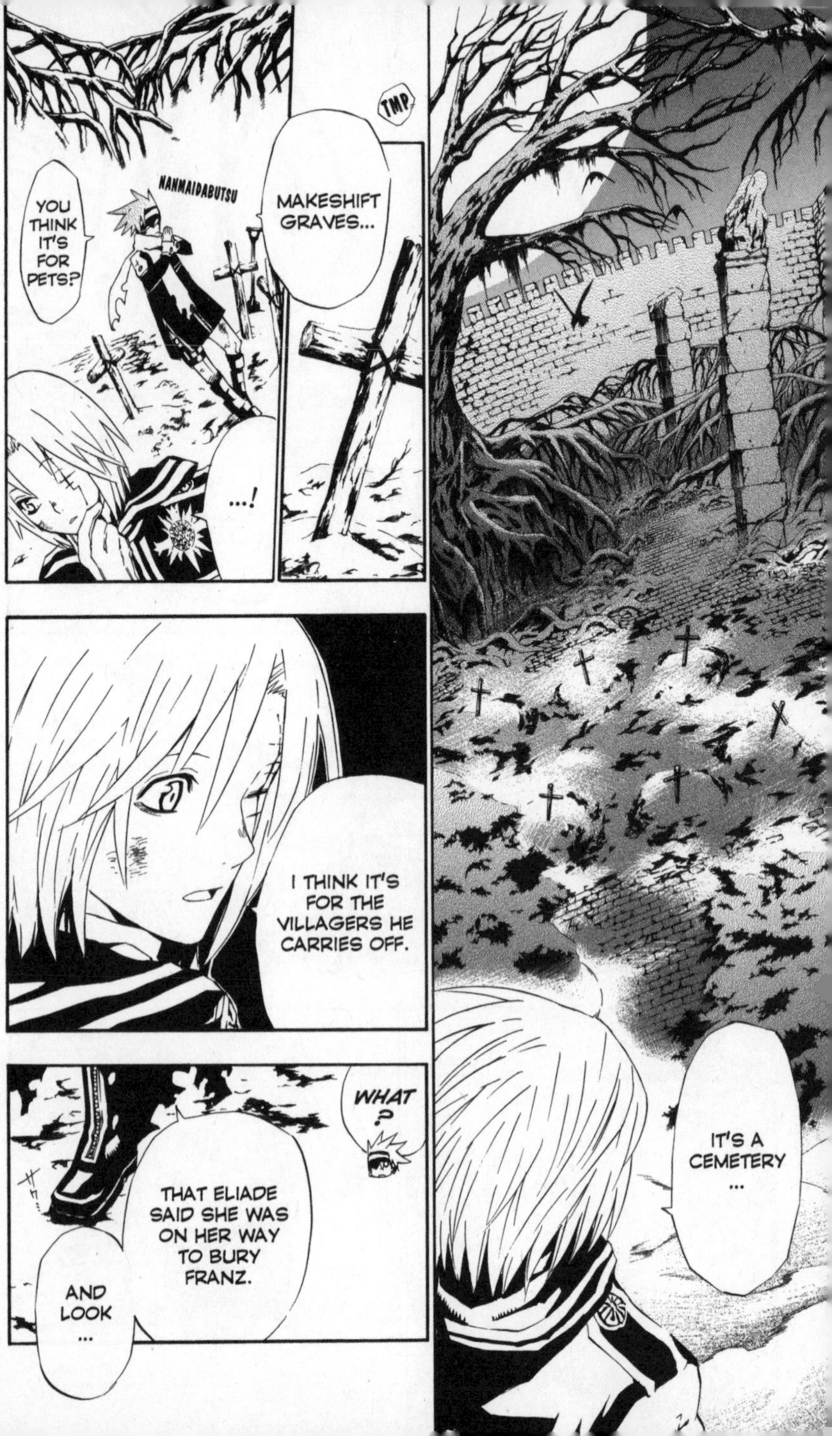
IT'S A CEMETERY...
TMP
MAKESHIFT GRAVES...
NANMAIDABUTSU
YOU THINK IT'S FOR PETS?
...!
I THINK IT'S FOR THE VILLAGERS HE CARRIES OFF.
WHAT?
THAT ELIADE SAID SHE WAS ON HER WAY TO BURY FRANZ.
AND LOOK...

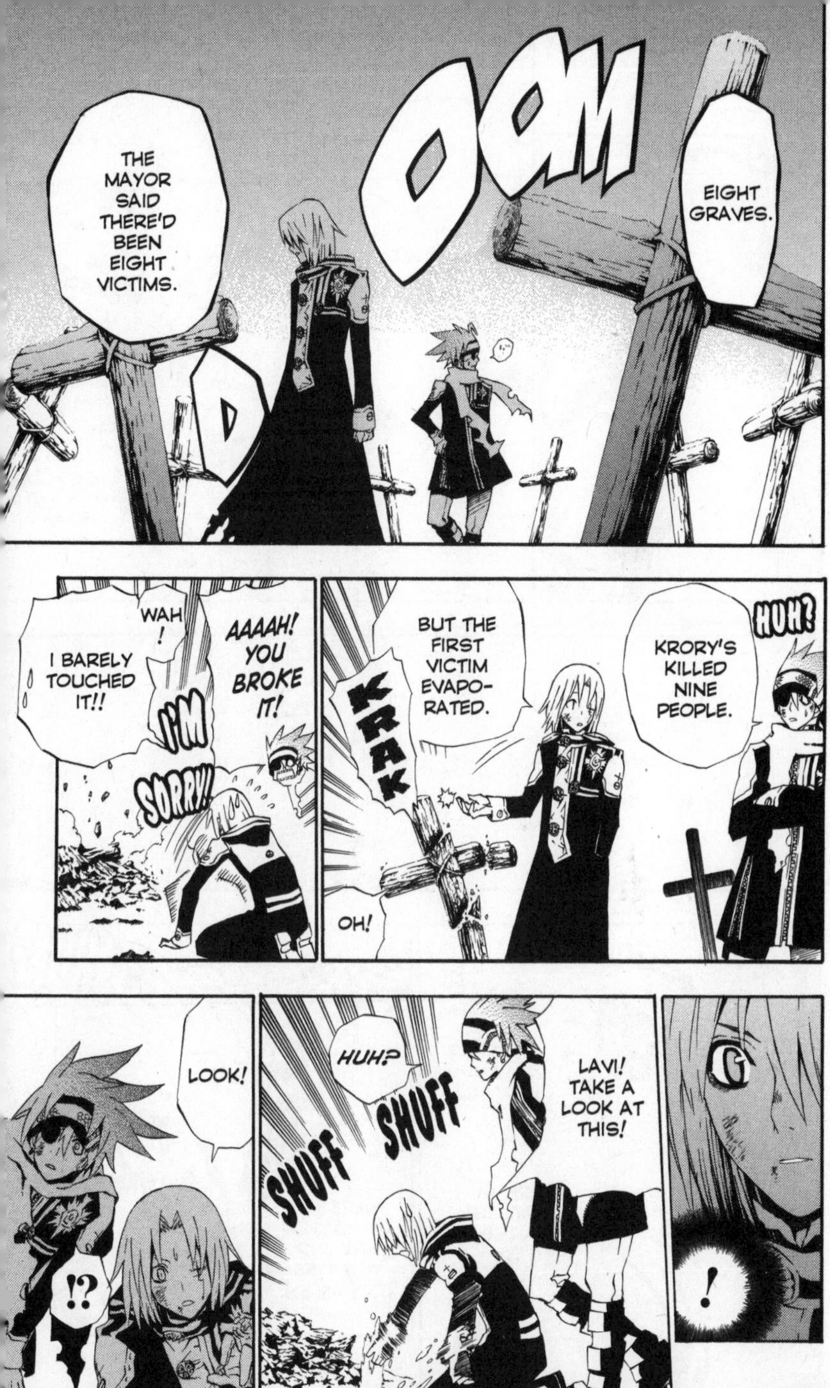
EIGHT GRAVES.
THE MAYOR SAID THERE'D BEEN EIGHT VICTIMS.
DOOM
HUH?
KRORY'S KILLED NINE PEOPLE.
BUT THE FIRST VICTIM EVAPO-RATED.
KRAK
OH!
AAAAH! YOU BROKE IT!
WAH!
I BARELY TOUCHED IT!!
I'M SORRY!!
!
LAVI! TAKE A LOOK AT THIS!
HUH?
SHUFF
SHUFF
LOOK!
!?

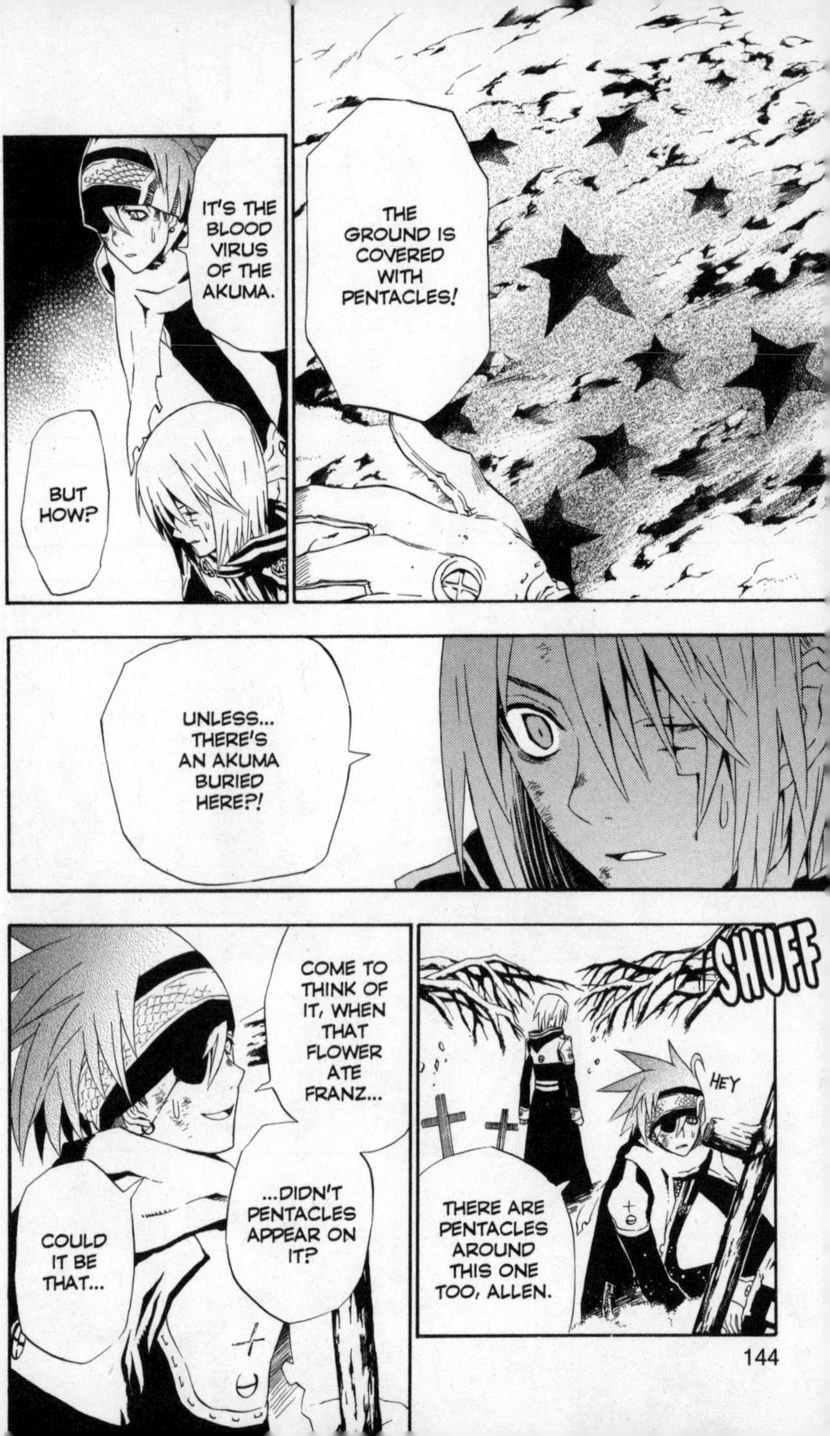
THE GROUND IS COVERED WITH PENTACLES!
IT'S THE BLOOD VIRUS OF THE AKUMA.
BUT HOW?
UNLESS... THERE'S AN AKUMA BURIED HERE?!
SHUFF
HEY
THERE ARE PENTACLES AROUND THIS ONE TOO, ALLEN.
COME TO THINK OF IT, WHEN THAT FLOWER ATE FRANZ...
...DIDN'T PENTACLES APPEAR ON IT?
COULD IT BE THAT...

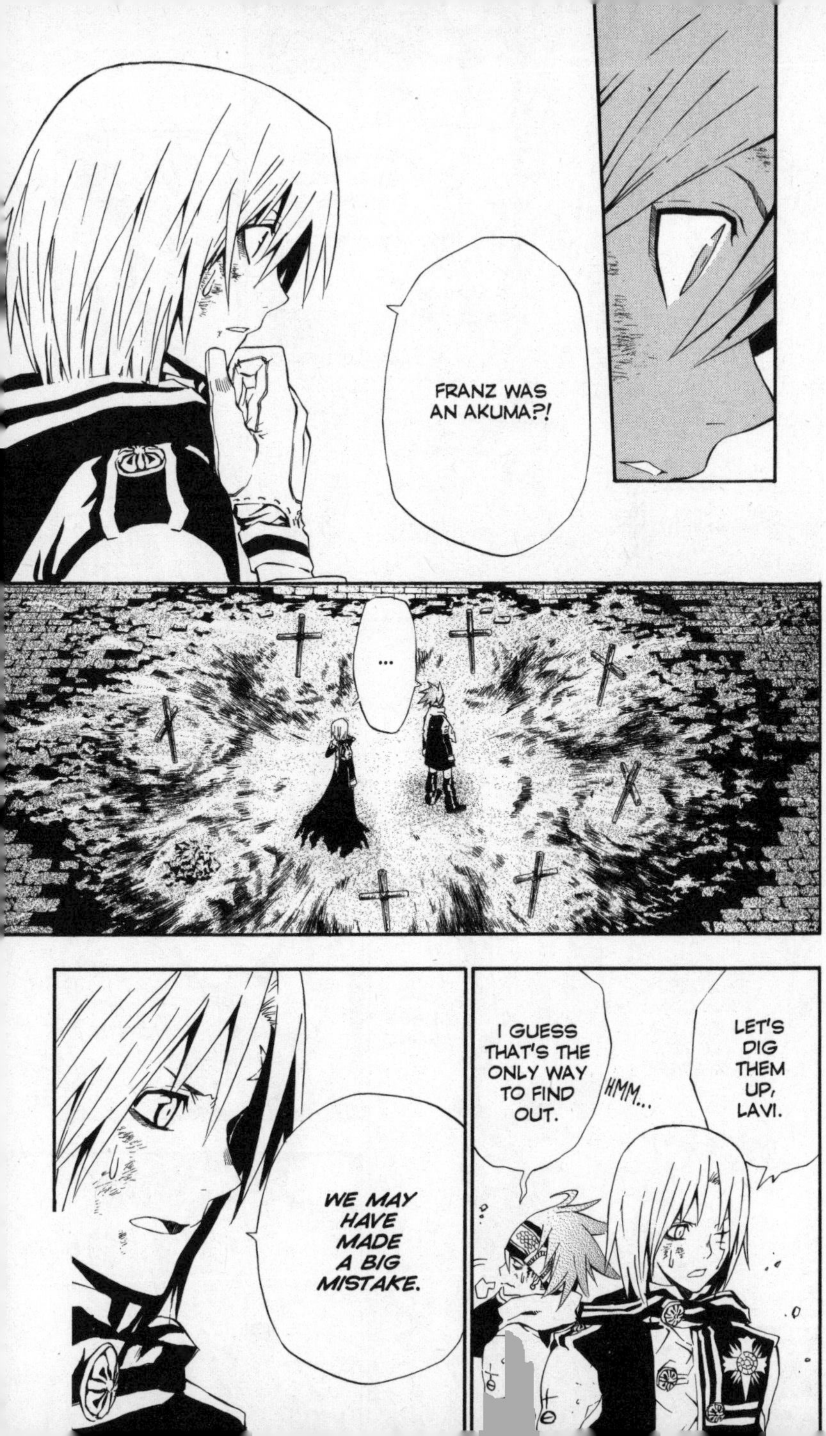
FRANZ WAS AN AKUMA?!
...
LET'S DIG THEM UP, LAVI.
HMM...
I GUESS THAT'S THE ONLY WAY TO FIND OUT.
WE MAY HAVE MADE A BIG MISTAKE.

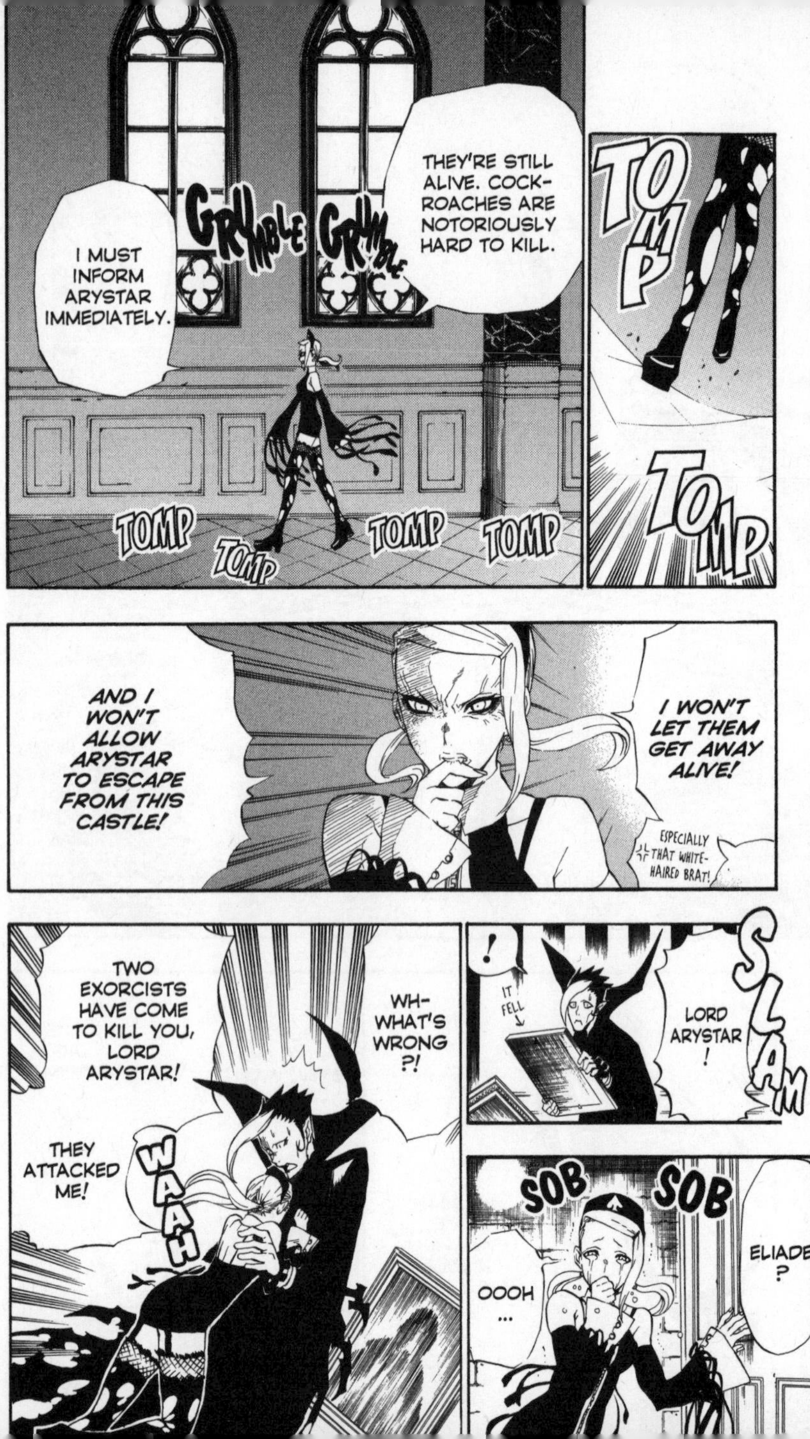
TOMP
TOMP
TOMP
THEY'RE STILL ALIVE. COCKROACHES ARE NOTORIOUSLY HARD TO KILL.
GRUMBLE GRUMBLE
I MUST INFORM ARYSTAR IMMEDIATELY.
TOMP
TOMP
TOMP
TOMP
I WON'T LET THEM GET AWAY ALIVE!
ESPECIALLY THAT WHITE-HAIRED BRAT!
AND I WON'T ALLOW ARYSTAR TO ESCAPE FROM THIS CASTLE!
SLAM
LORD ARYSTAR!
!
IT FELL
ELIADE?
SOB SOB
OOOH...
WH-WHAT'S WRONG?!
TWO EXORCISTS HAVE COME TO KILL YOU, LORD ARYSTAR!
WAAH
THEY ATTACKED ME!

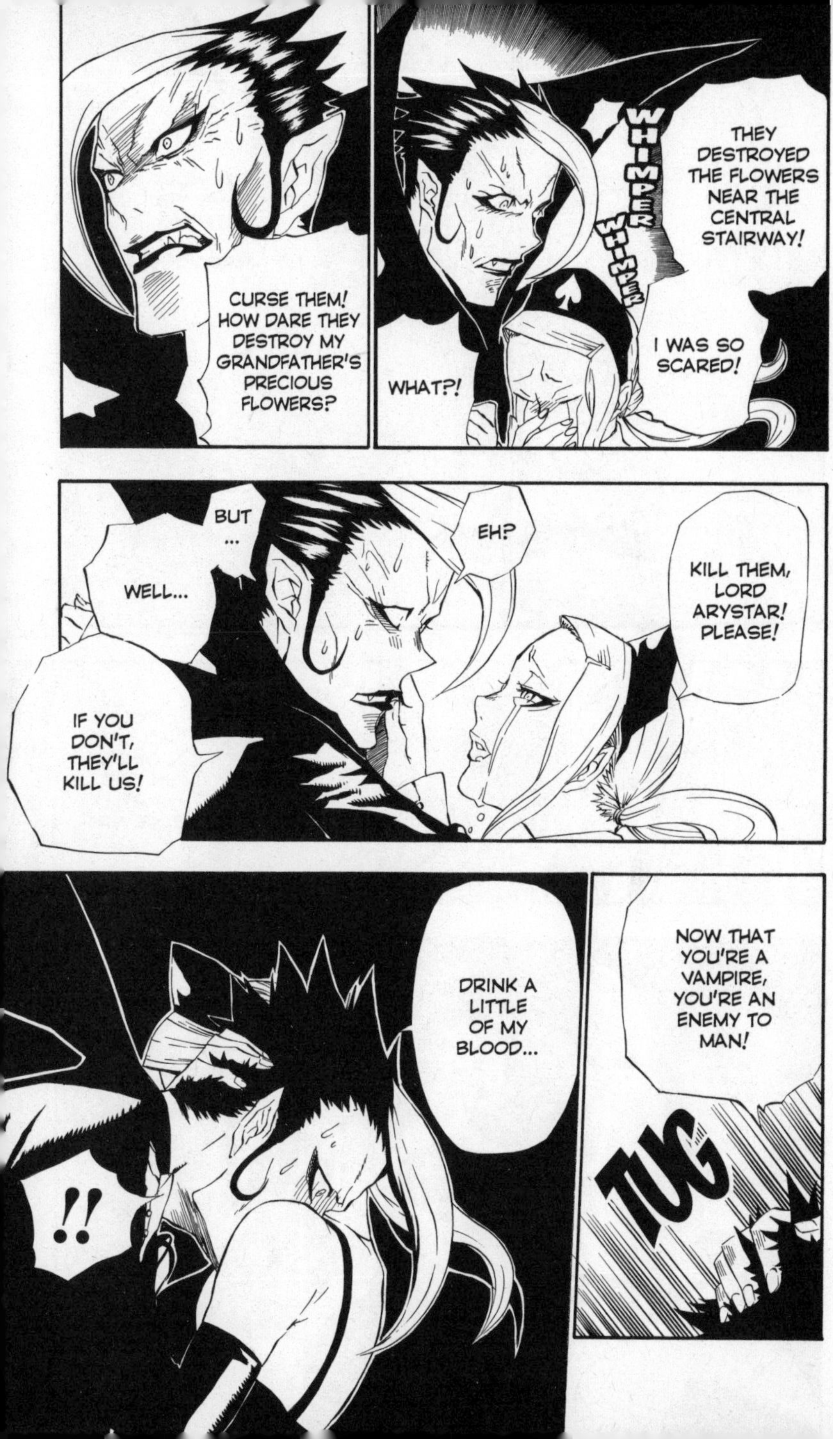
WHIMPER
WHIMPER
THEY DESTROYED THE FLOWERS NEAR THE CENTRAL STAIRWAY!
I WAS SO SCARED!
WHAT?!
CURSE THEM! HOW DARE THEY DESTROY MY GRANDFATHER'S PRECIOUS FLOWERS?
KILL THEM, LORD ARYSTAR! PLEASE!
EH?
BUT ...
WELL...
IF YOU DON'T, THEY'LL KILL US!
NOW THAT YOU'RE A VAMPIRE, YOU'RE AN ENEMY TO MAN!
TUG
DRINK A LITTLE OF MY BLOOD...
!!

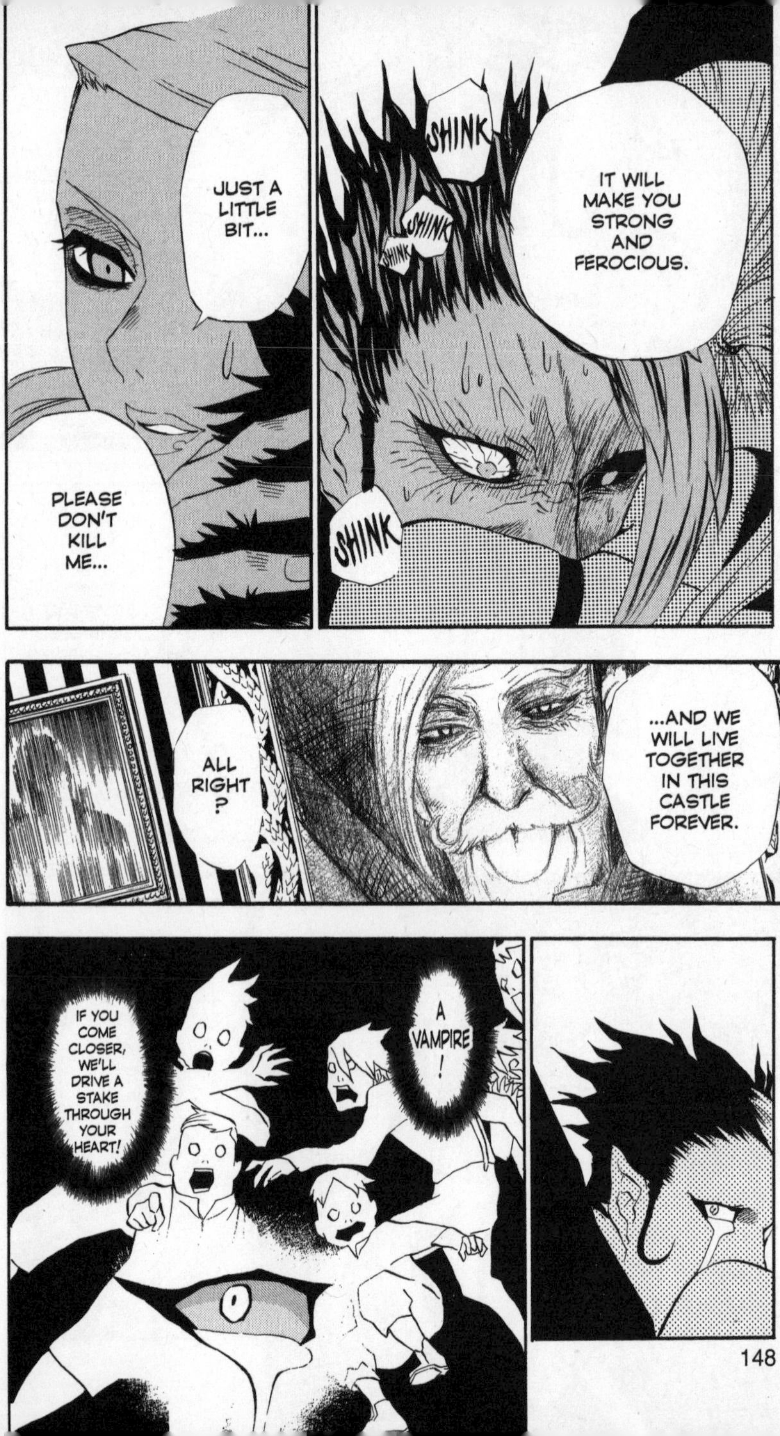
IT WILL MAKE YOU STRONG AND FEROCIOUS.
SHINK
SHINK
SHINK
SHINK
JUST A LITTLE BIT...
PLEASE DON'T KILL ME...
...AND WE WILL LIVE TOGETHER IN THIS CASTLE FOREVER.
ALL RIGHT?
A VAMPIRE!
IF YOU COME CLOSER, WE'LL DRIVE A STAKE THROUGH YOUR HEART!

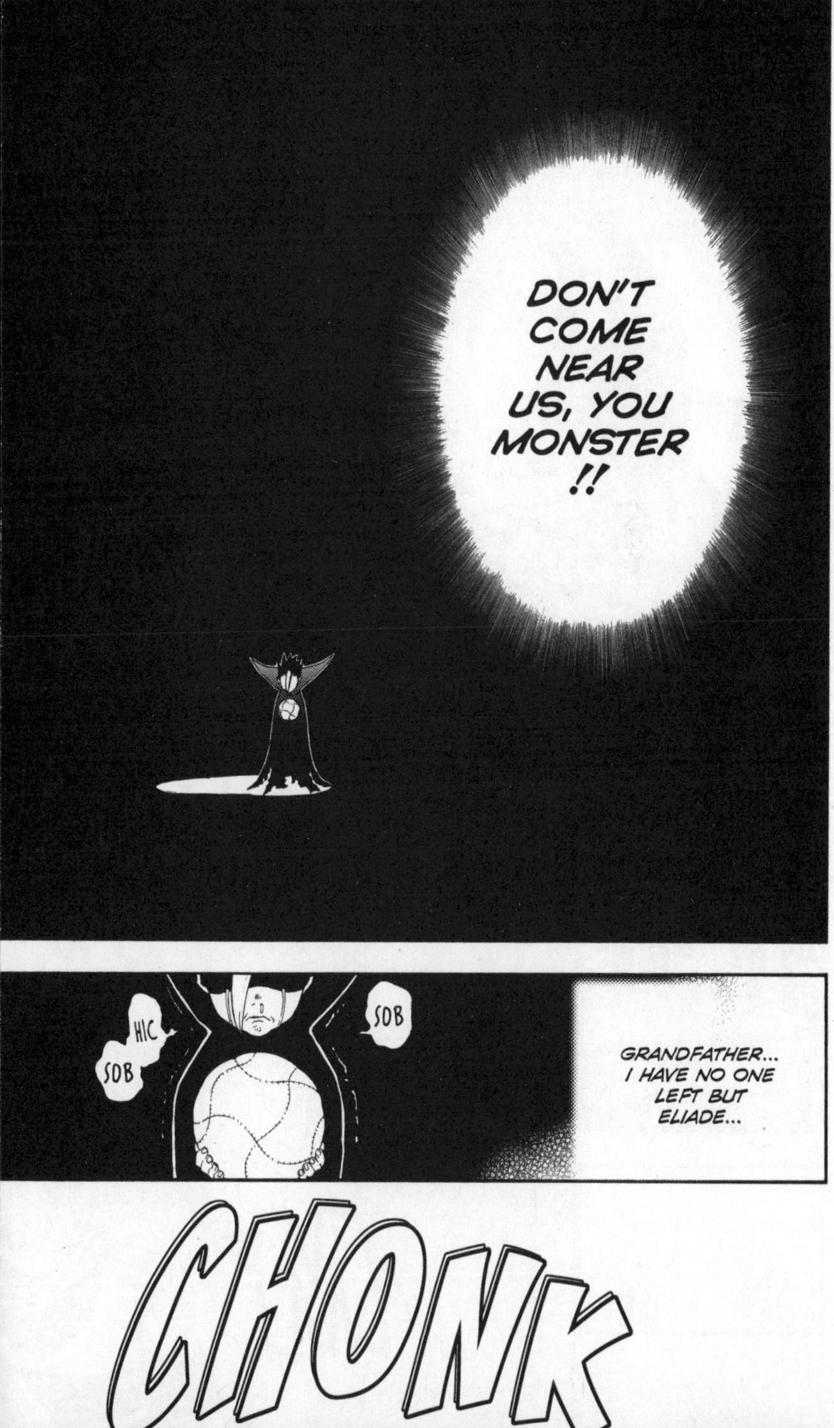
DON'T COME NEAR US, YOU MONSTER !!
GRANDFATHER... I HAVE NO ONE LEFT BUT ELIADE...
SOB
HIC
SOB
CHONK

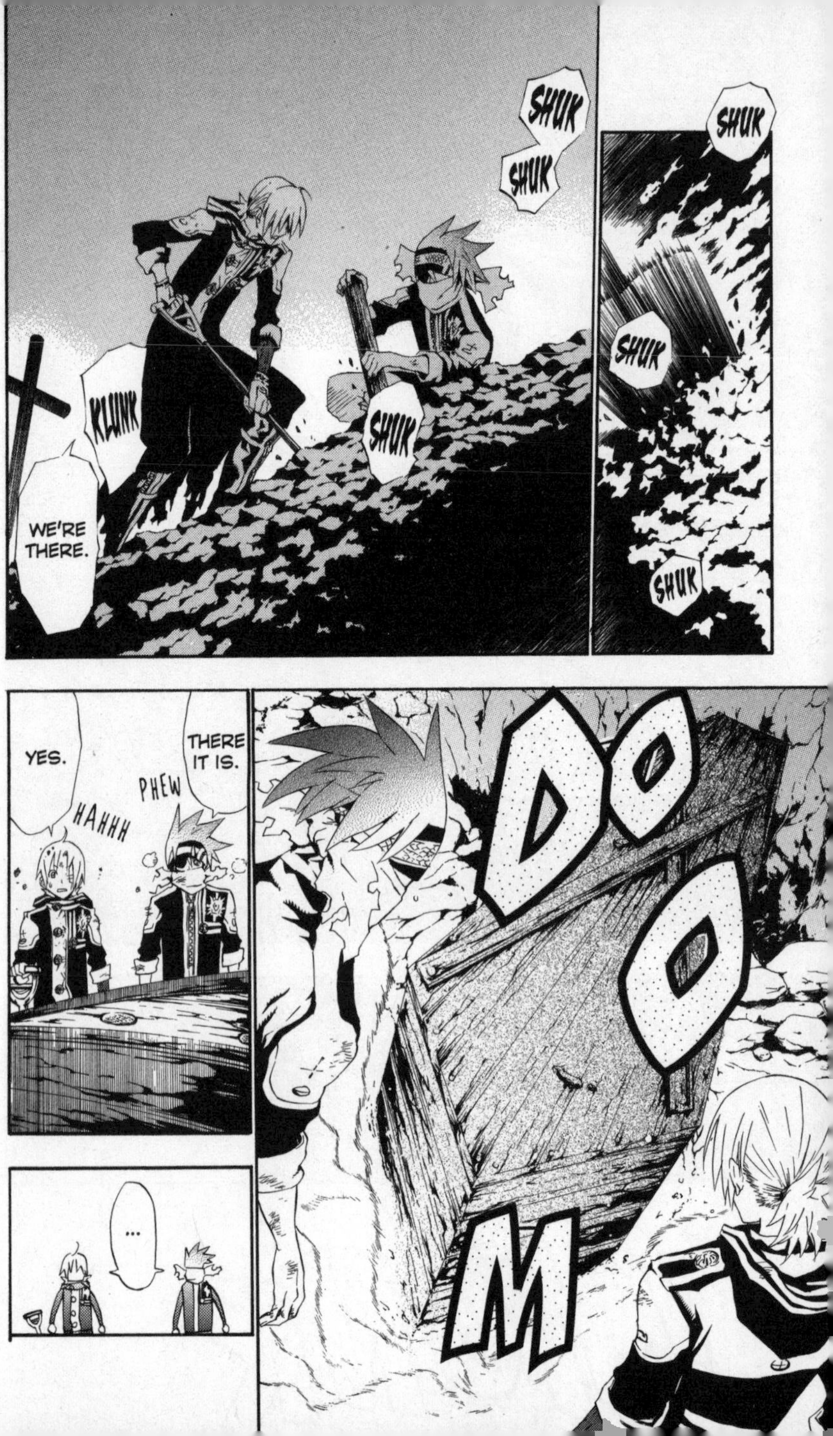
SHUK
SHUK
SHUK
SHUK
SHUK
SHUK
KLUNK
WE'RE THERE.
DOOM
THERE IT IS.
PHEW
YES.
HAHHH
...

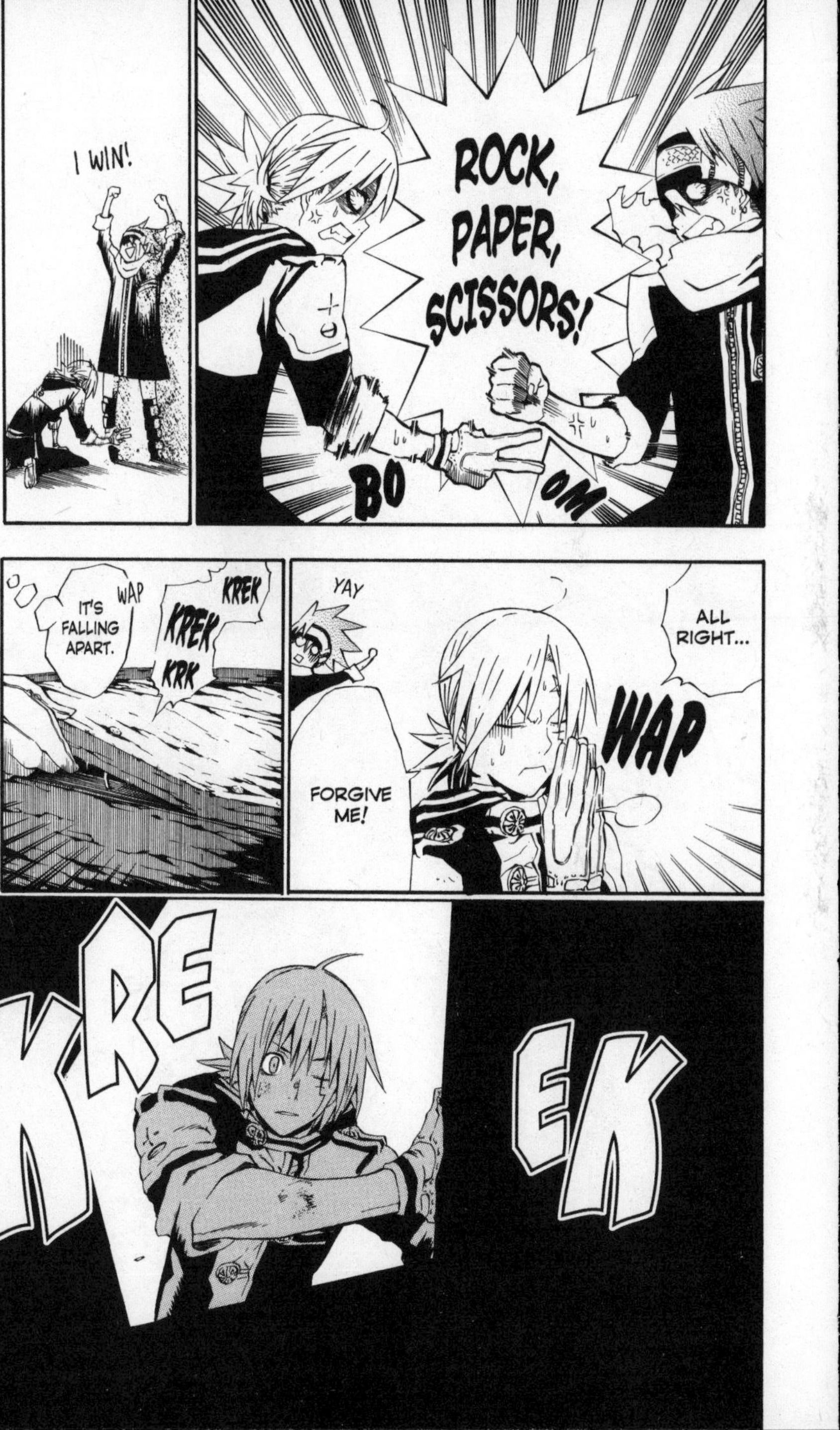
ROCK, PAPER, SCISSORS!
BO
OM
I WIN!
ALL RIGHT...
WAP
YAY
FORGIVE ME!
KREK
KREK
KRK
WAP
IT'S FALLING APART.
KREK

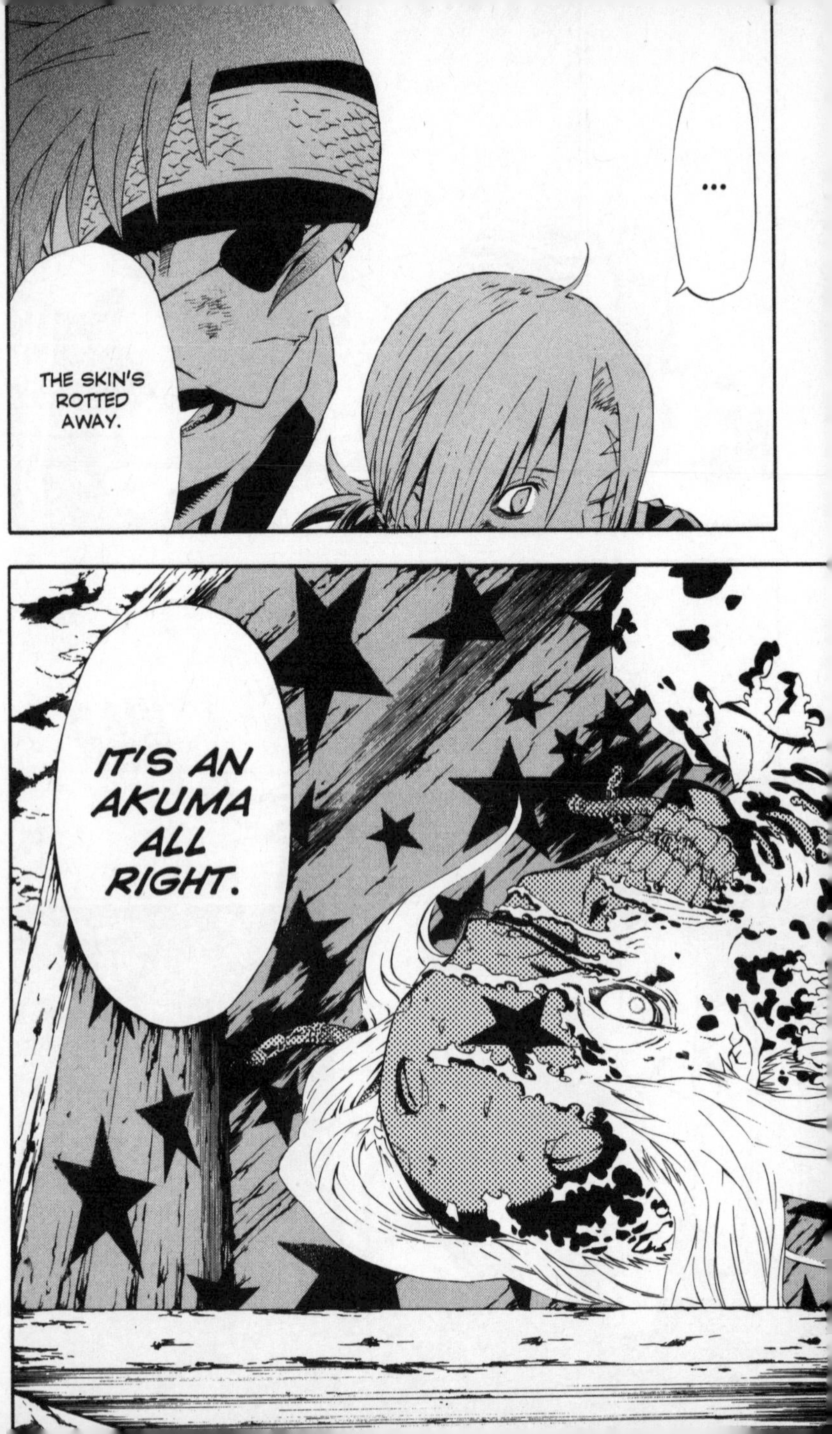
...
THE SKIN'S ROTTED AWAY.
IT'S AN AKUMA ALL RIGHT.

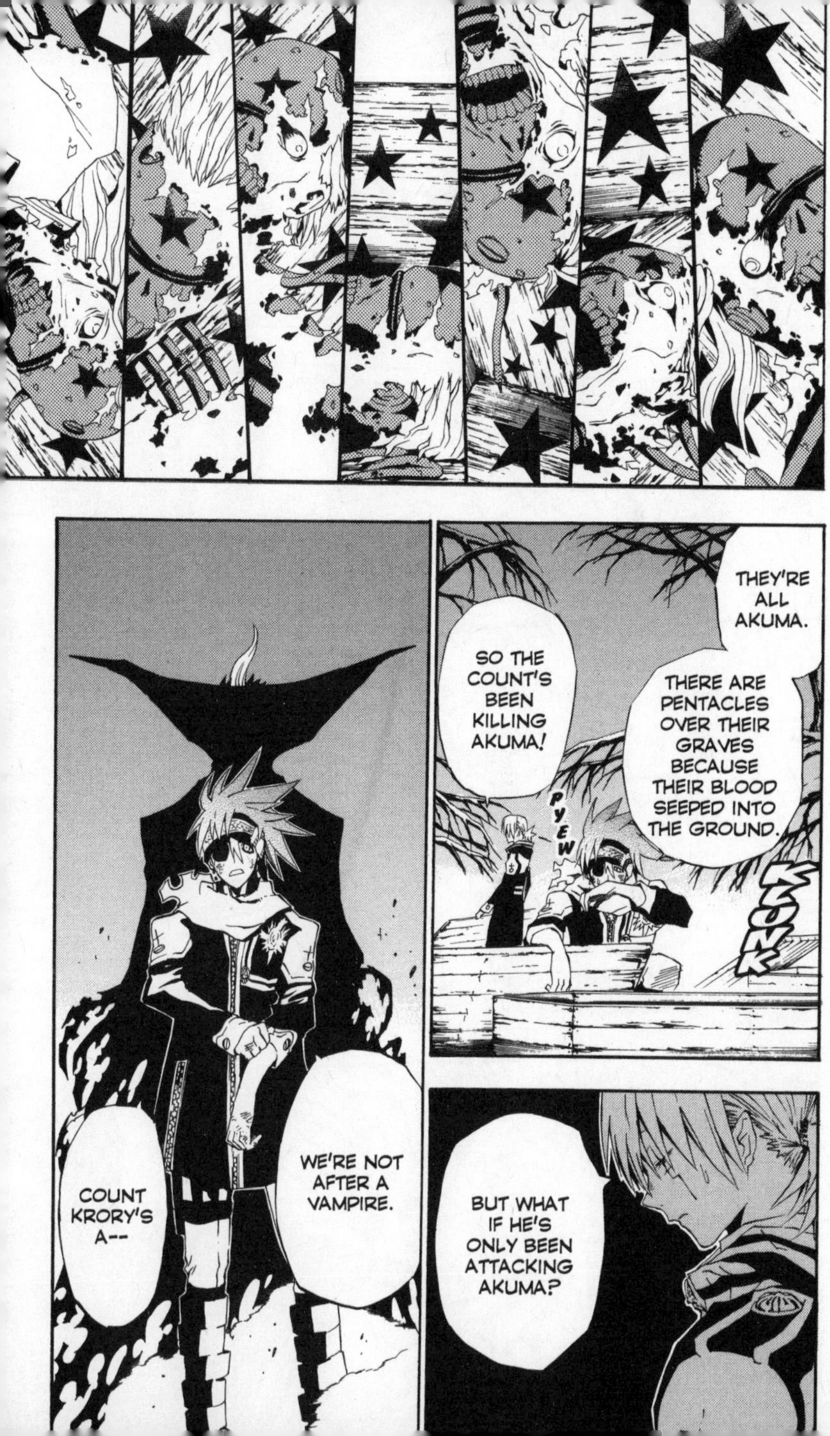
THEY'RE ALL AKUMA.
SO THE COUNT'S BEEN KILLING AKUMA!
THERE ARE PENTACLES OVER THEIR GRAVES BECAUSE THEIR BLOOD SEEPED INTO THE GROUND.
PYEW
KLUNK
BUT WHAT IF HE'S ONLY BEEN ATTACKING AKUMA?
WE'RE NOT AFTER A VAMPIRE.
COUNT KRORY'S A--

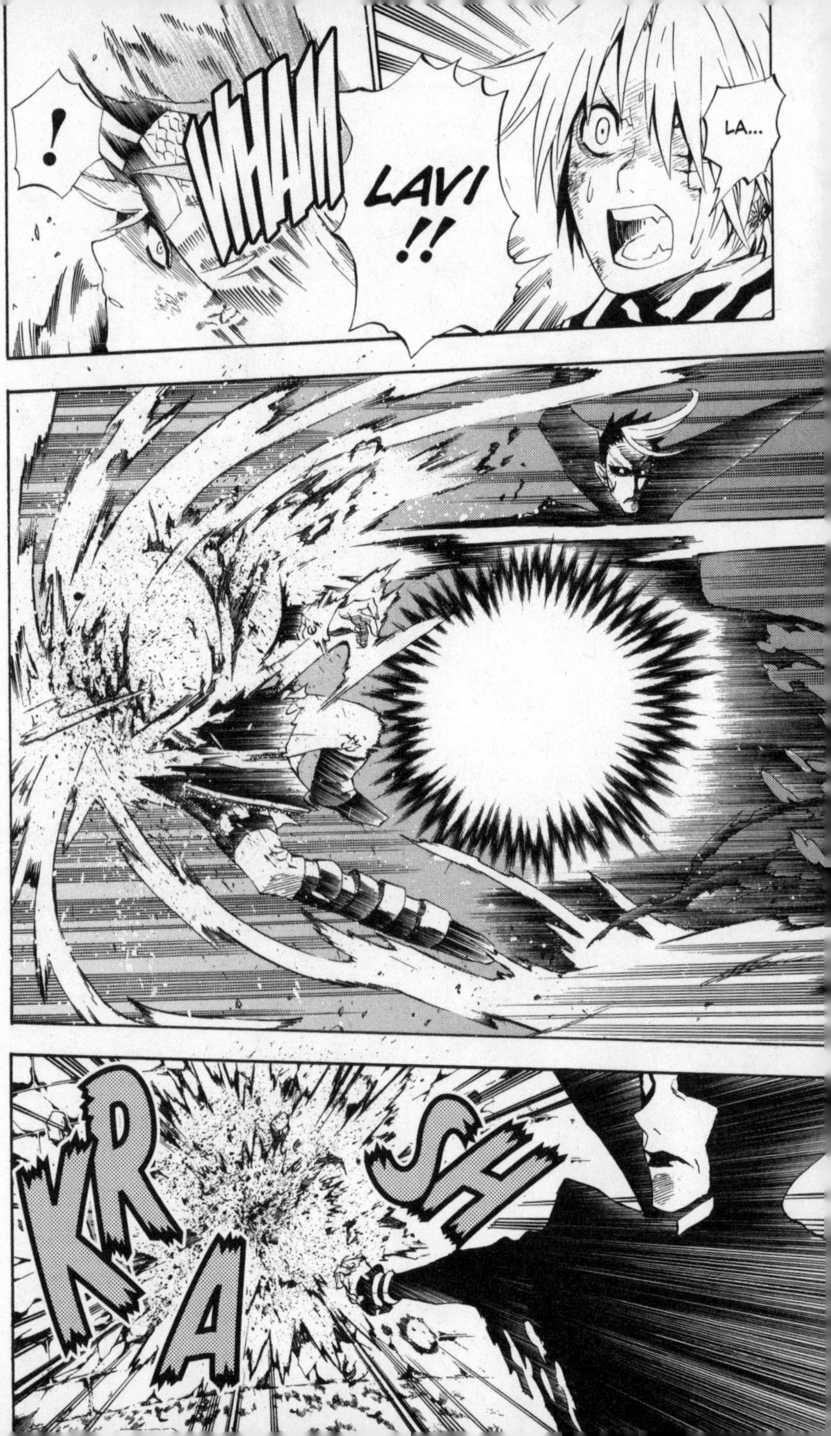

LA...
LAVI !!
WHAM
!
KRASH

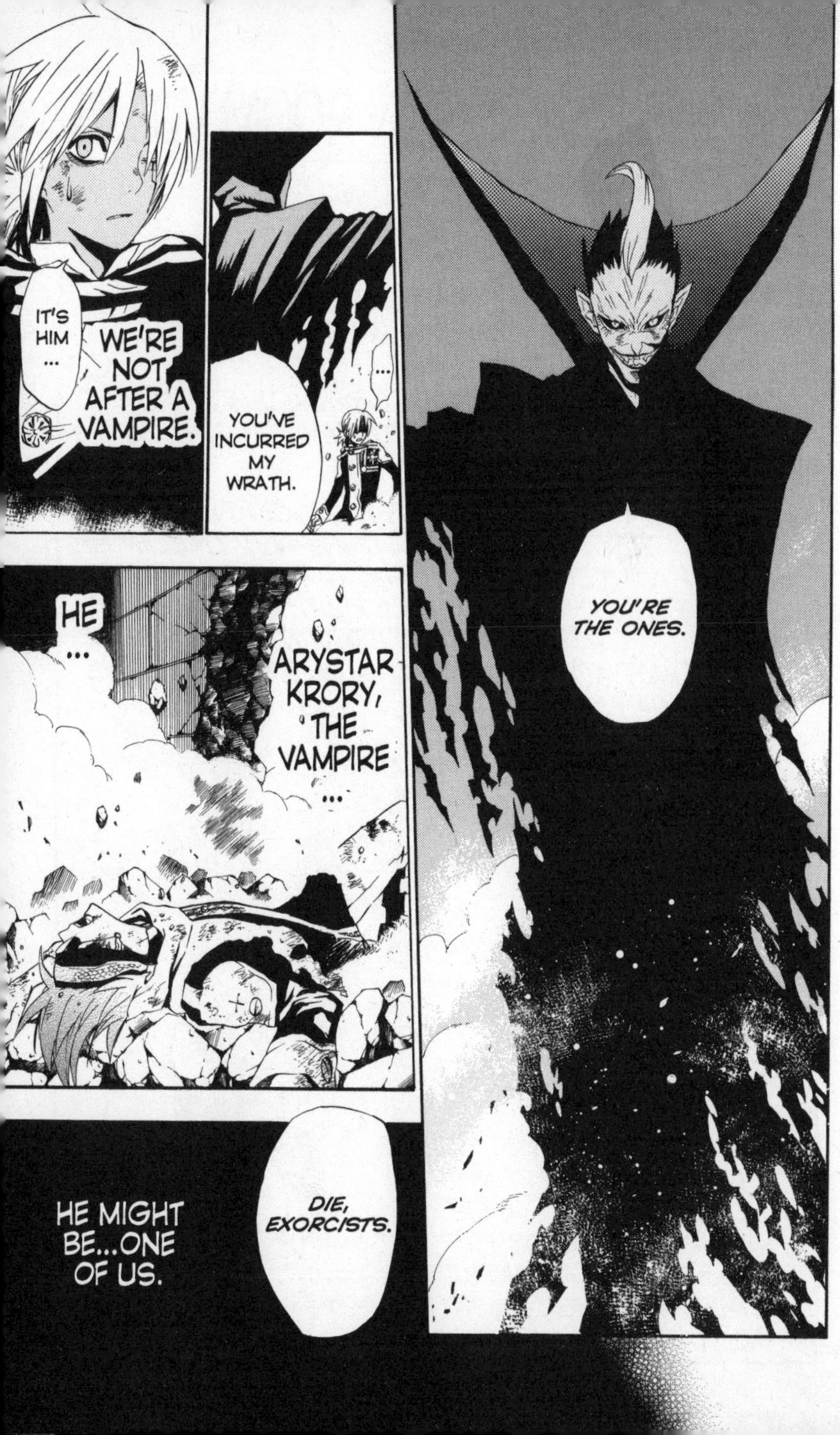
YOU'RE THE ONES.
...
YOU'VE INCURRED MY WRATH.
IT'S HIM ...
WE'RE NOT AFTER A VAMPIRE.
HE ...
ARYSTAR KRORY, THE VAMPIRE ...
DIE, EXORCISTS.
HE MIGHT BE...ONE OF US.

KOMUI'S DISCUSSION ROOM VOL. 5

Q. WHAT DOES ALLEN THINK OF LENALEE'S TANTALIZINGLY SHORT SKIRT?

A. I THINK ALL MEN LIKE MINISKIRTS. BUT I WONDER IF IT DOESN'T GET A BIT COLD SOMETIMES.

Q. THE UNIFORMS OF THE BLACK ORDER SEEM TO VARY CONSIDERABLY. ARE THEY ALL CUSTOMIZED?

A. I SUPPOSE SO. THE SCIENCE TEAM MAKES THEM FOR US, BUT THEY ASK US WHAT DESIGNS WE'D LIKE. IN MY CASE, I WANTED A HOOD SO THAT I'D HAVE SOMEPLACE TO HIDE TIMCANPY. IT WAS ALL RIGHT WHEN HE WAS LITTLE, BUT HE'S GETTING SO BIG THAT HE'S STARTING TO ATTRACT ATTENTION. (*ACTUALLY, IT'S TO HIDE THE WHITE HAIR.)

Q. IN THE AUTHOR'S COMMENTS AT THE BEGINNING OF VOLUME 2, WHAT'S THE NAME OF THE KITTEN THAT'S GOT TIMCANPY?

A. OH, THAT CUTE LITTLE KITTY? (HAPPY SIGH) THAT'S HOSHINO'S BELOVED KORO.

Q. HOW MANY VALENTINE'S DAY CHOCOLATES DID YOU RECEIVE? WHO GOT THE MOST?

A. I GOT THE MOST--115. (SMILES) THANK YOU ALL VERY MUCH. WELL, THAT'S IT FOR THE DISCUSSION ROOM FOR THIS VOLUME. I HAD A WONDERFUL TIME, THANK YOU. SO, UNTIL NEXT TIME.

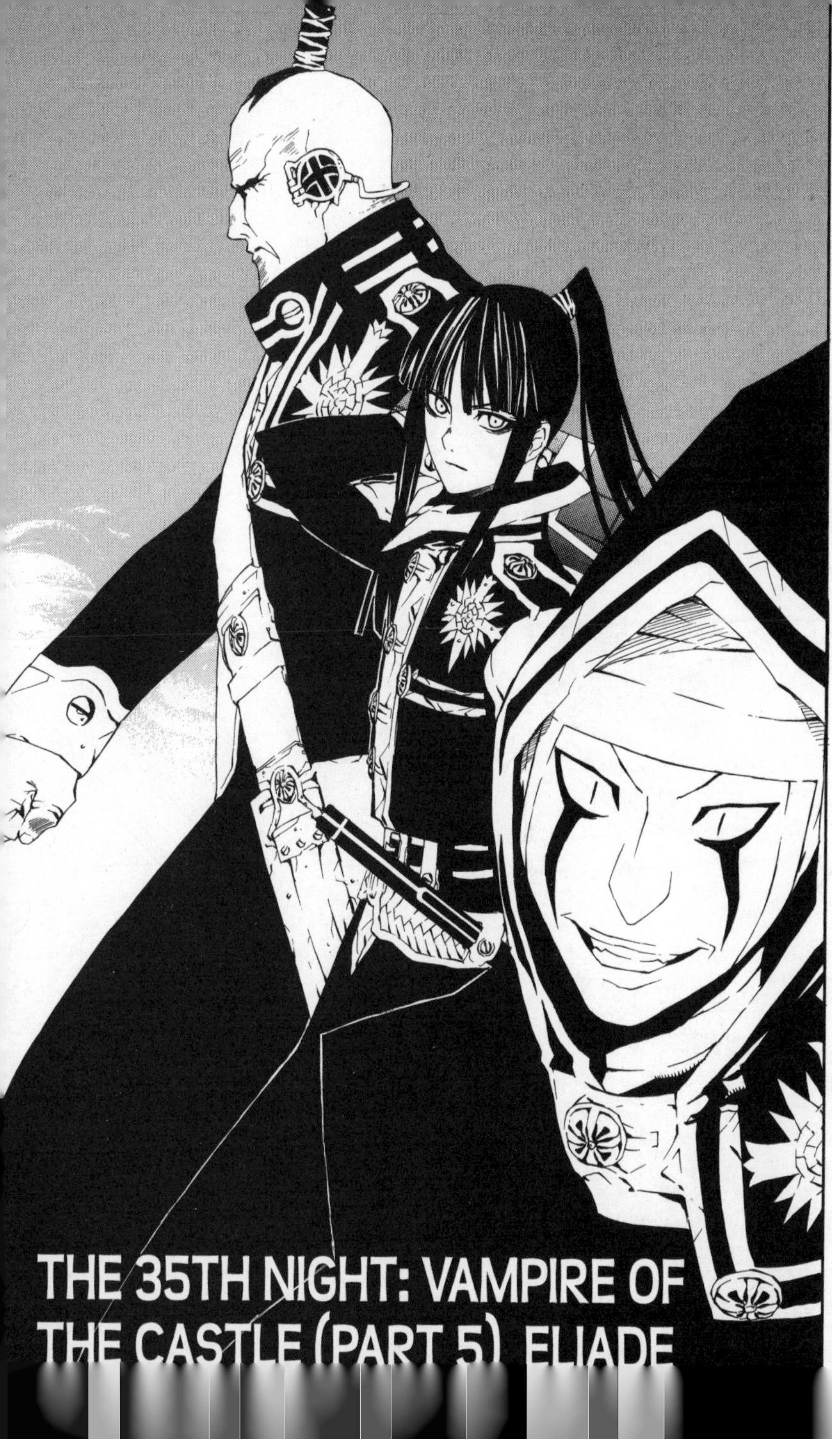
THE 35TH NIGHT: VAMPIRE OF THE CASTLE (PART 5) ELIADE

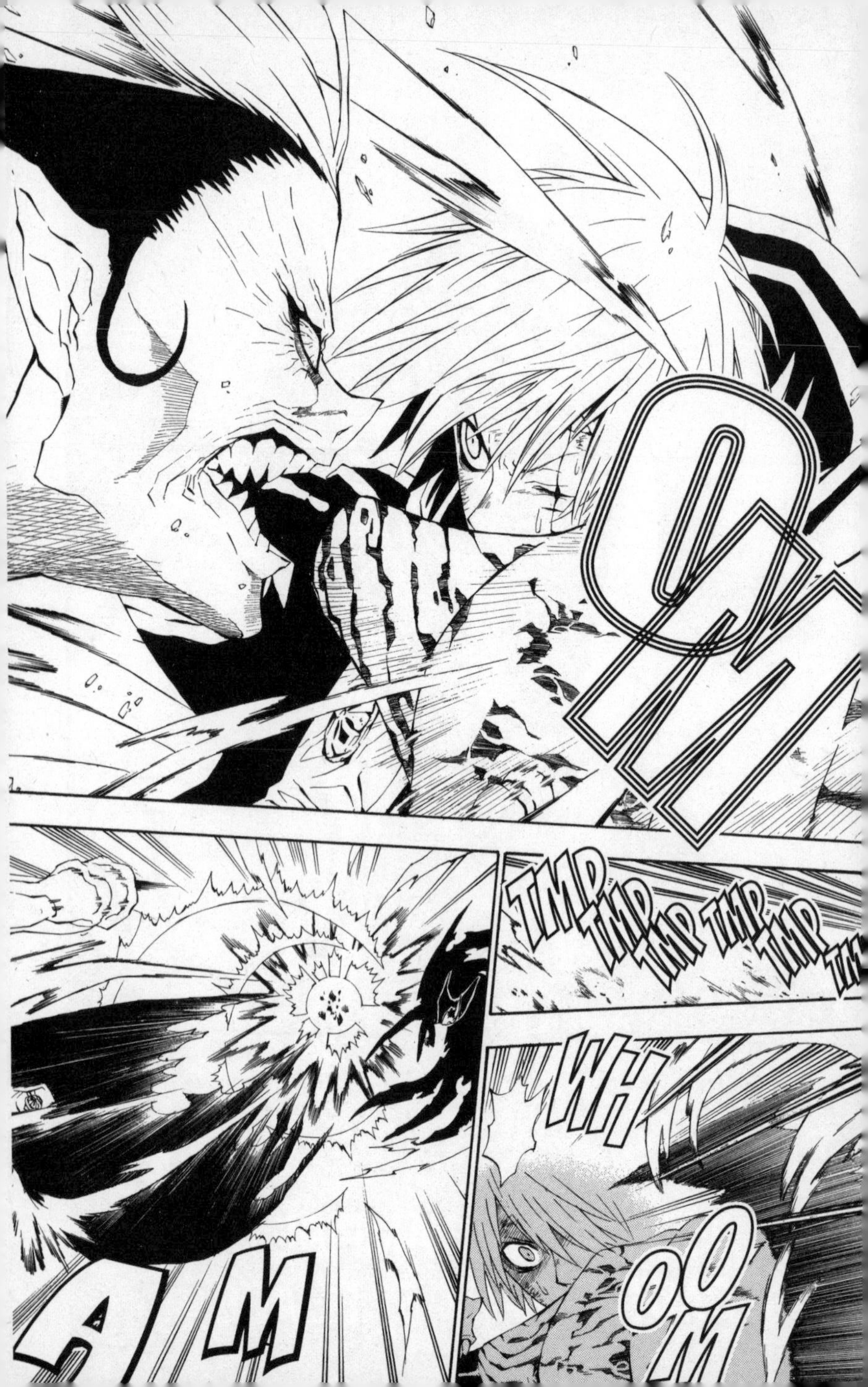
TMP TMP TMP TMP TMP
WHOOM

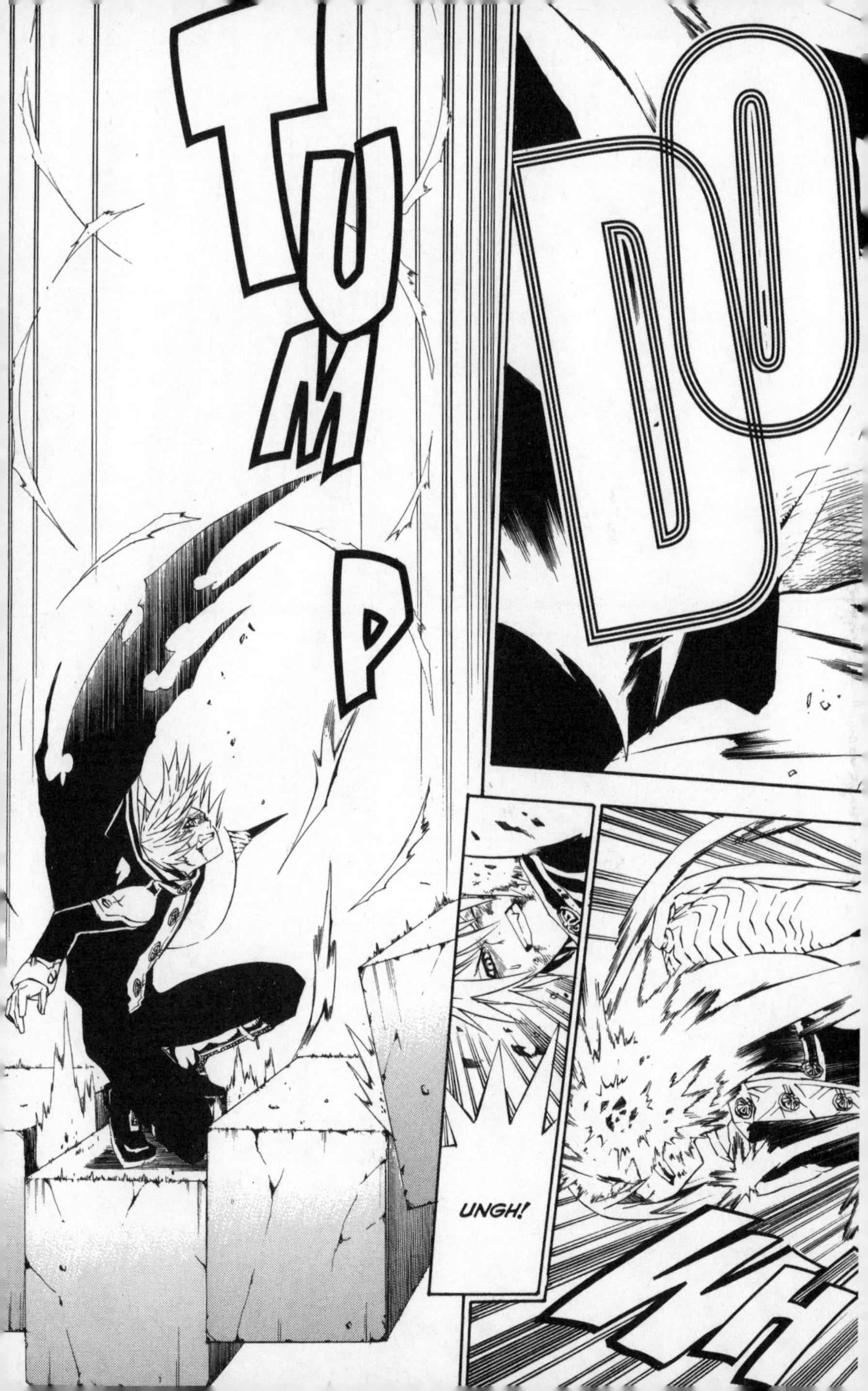
UNGH!
TUMP

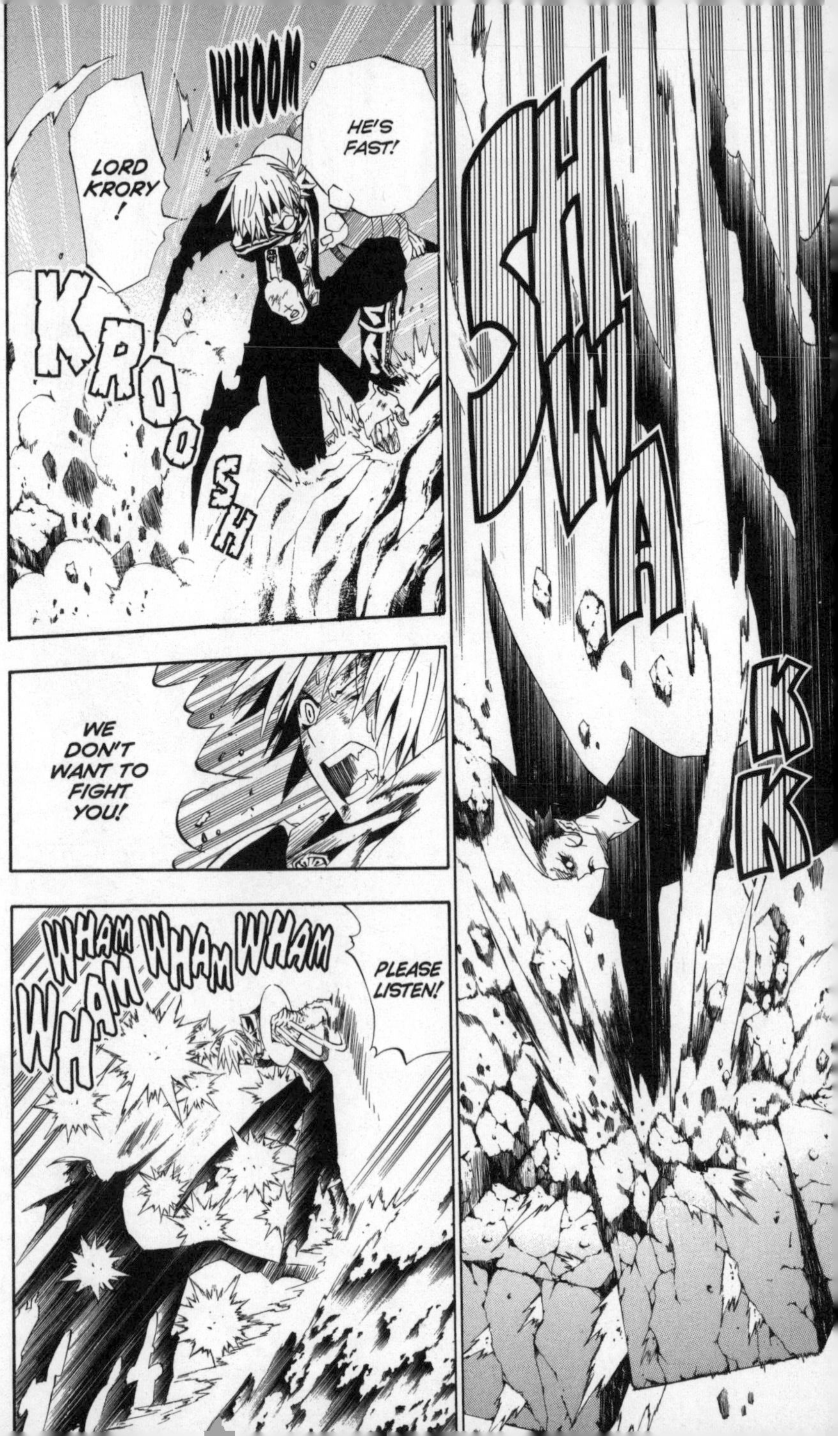
SHWAKK
WHOOM
HE'S FAST!
LORD KRORY!
KROOSH
WE DON'T WANT TO FIGHT YOU!
PLEASE LISTEN!
WHAM WHAM WHAM WHAM

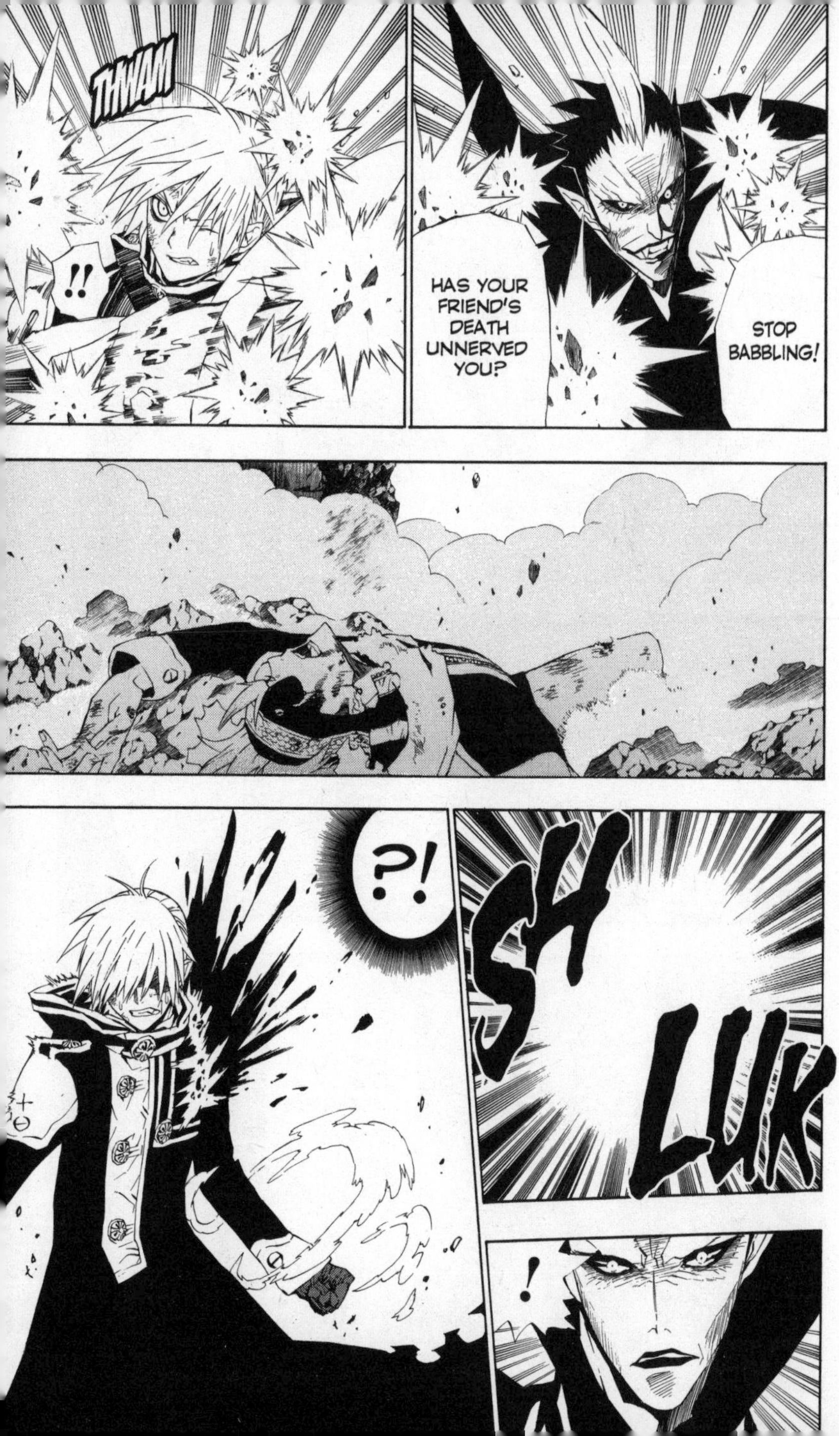

HAS YOUR FRIEND'S DEATH UNNERVED YOU?
STOP BABBLING!
THWAM
!!
SHLUK
!
?!

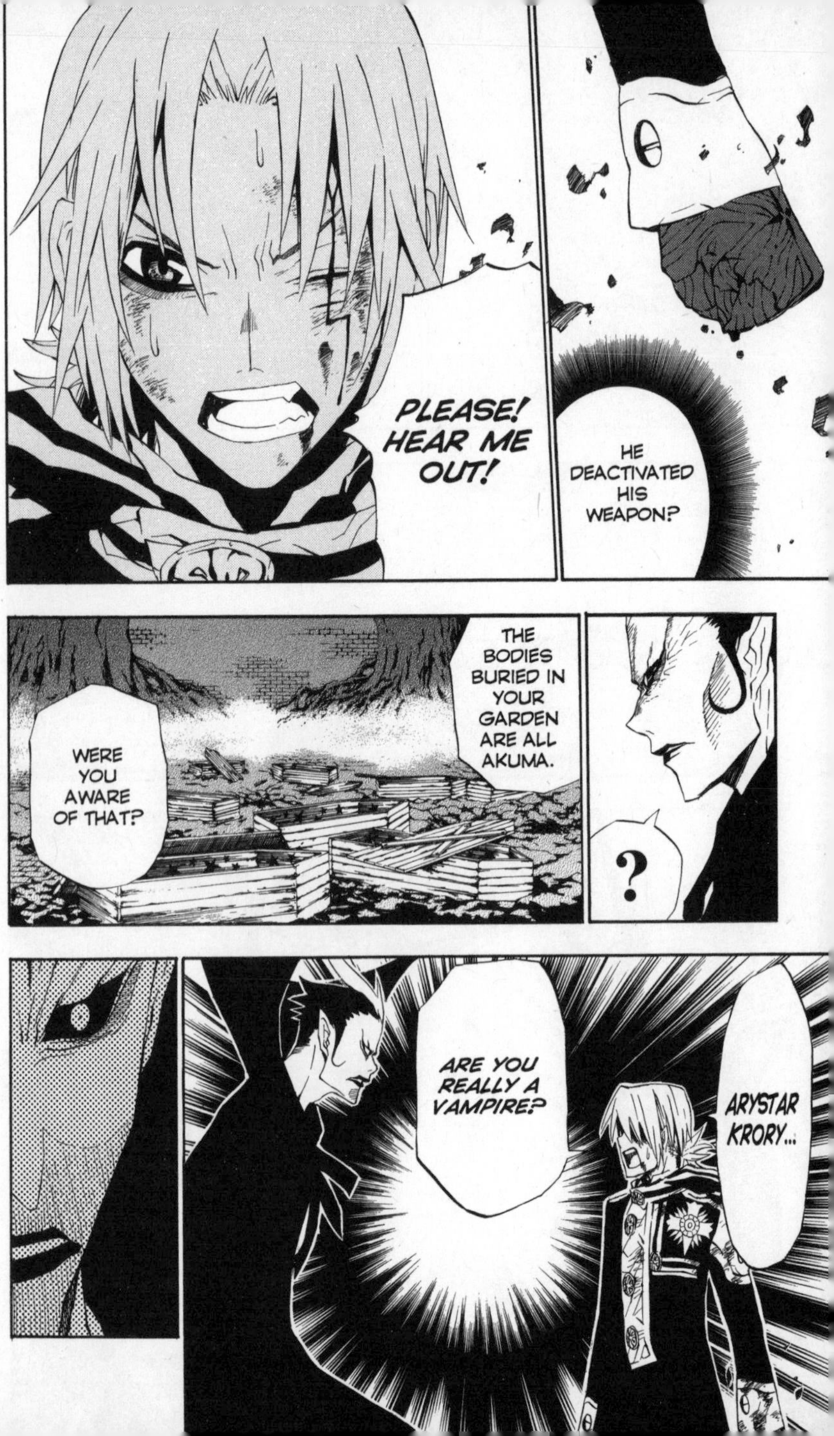
HE DEACTIVATED HIS WEAPON?
PLEASE! HEAR ME OUT!
?
THE BODIES BURIED IN YOUR GARDEN ARE ALL AKUMA.
WERE YOU AWARE OF THAT?
ARYSTAR KRORY...
ARE YOU REALLY A VAMPIRE?

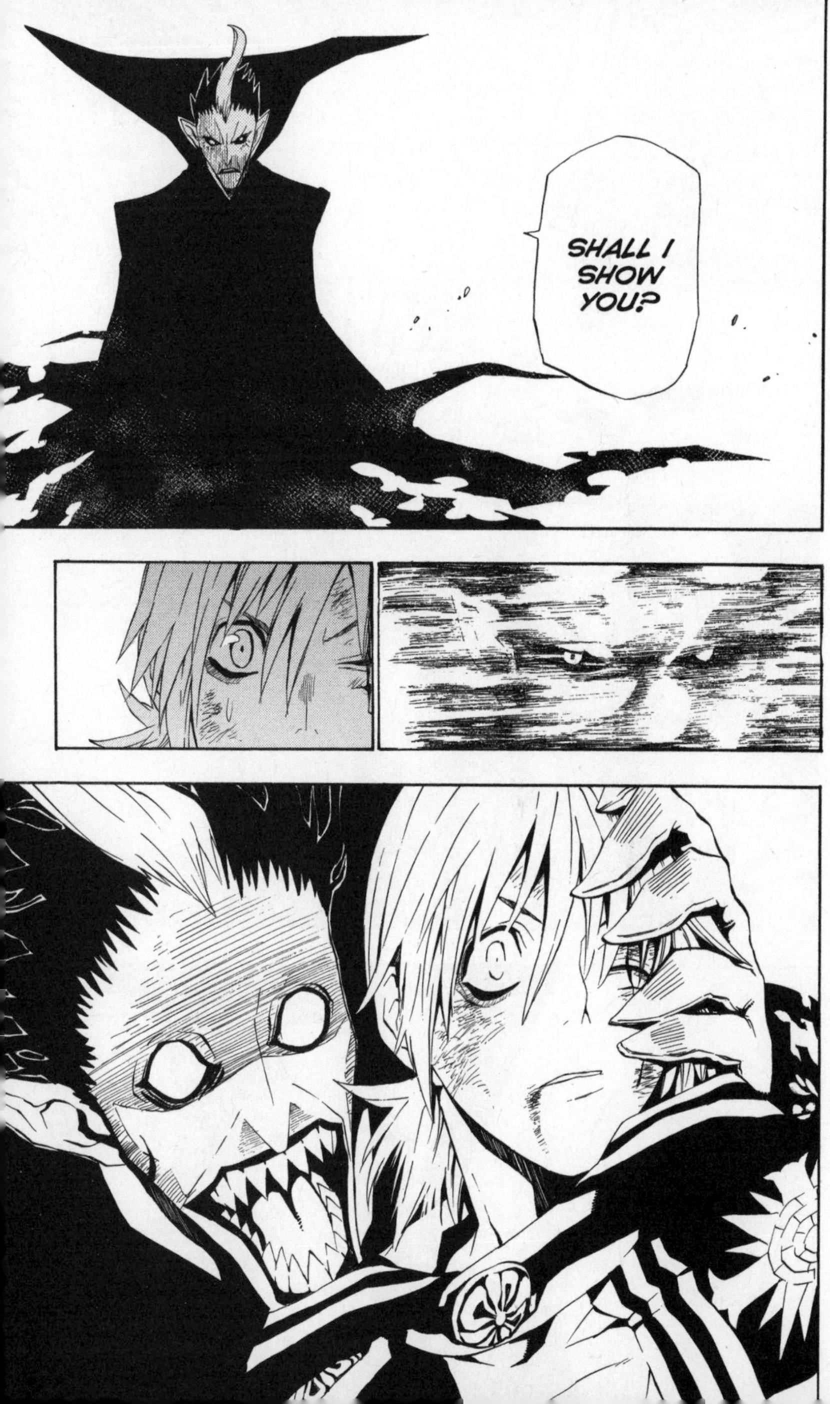
SHALL I SHOW YOU?

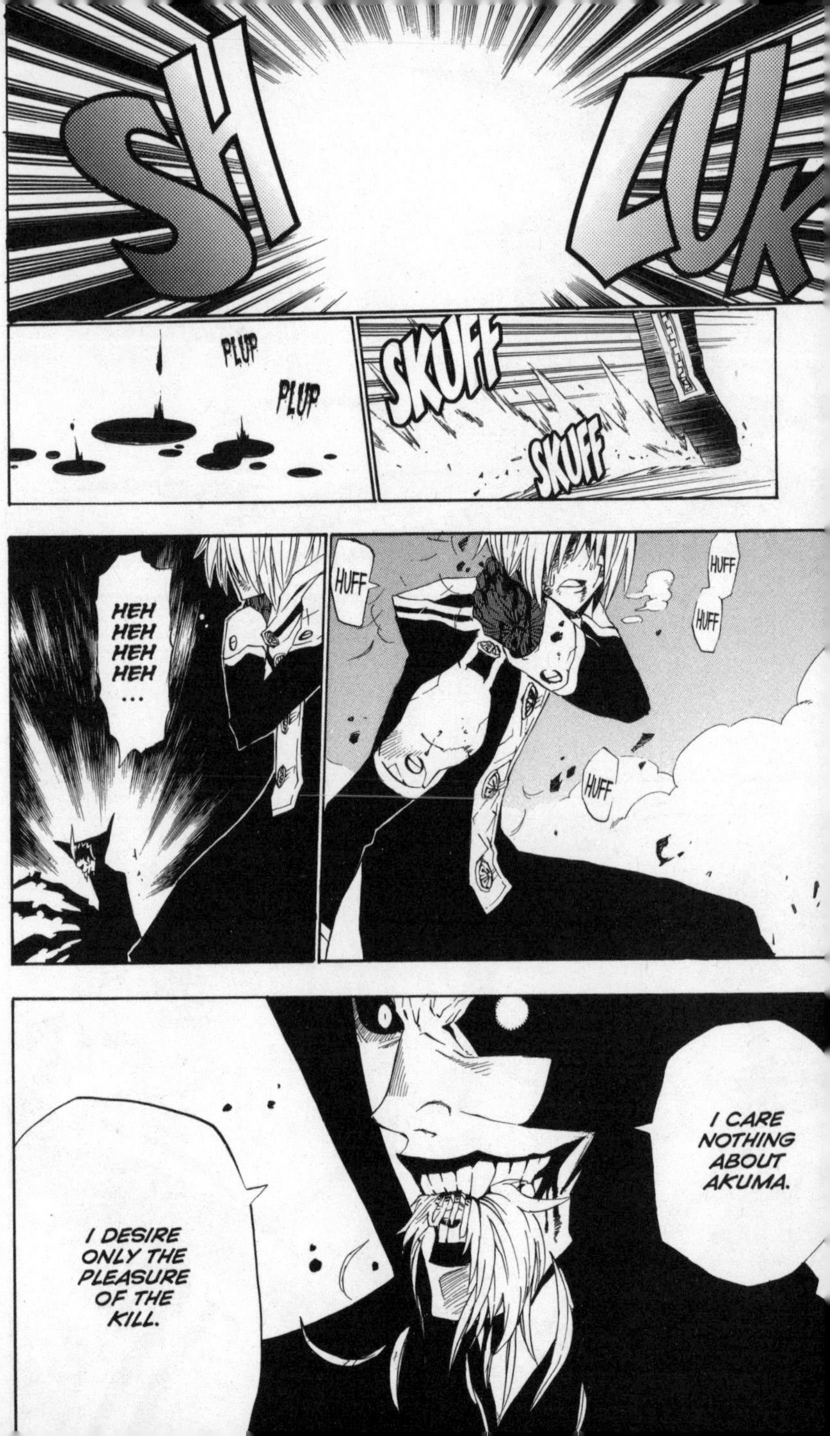
SHLUK
SKUFF
SKUFF
PLUP
PLUP
HUFF
HUFF
HUFF
HUFF
HEH HEH HEH HEH ...
I CARE NOTHING ABOUT AKUMA.
I DESIRE ONLY THE PLEASURE OF THE KILL.

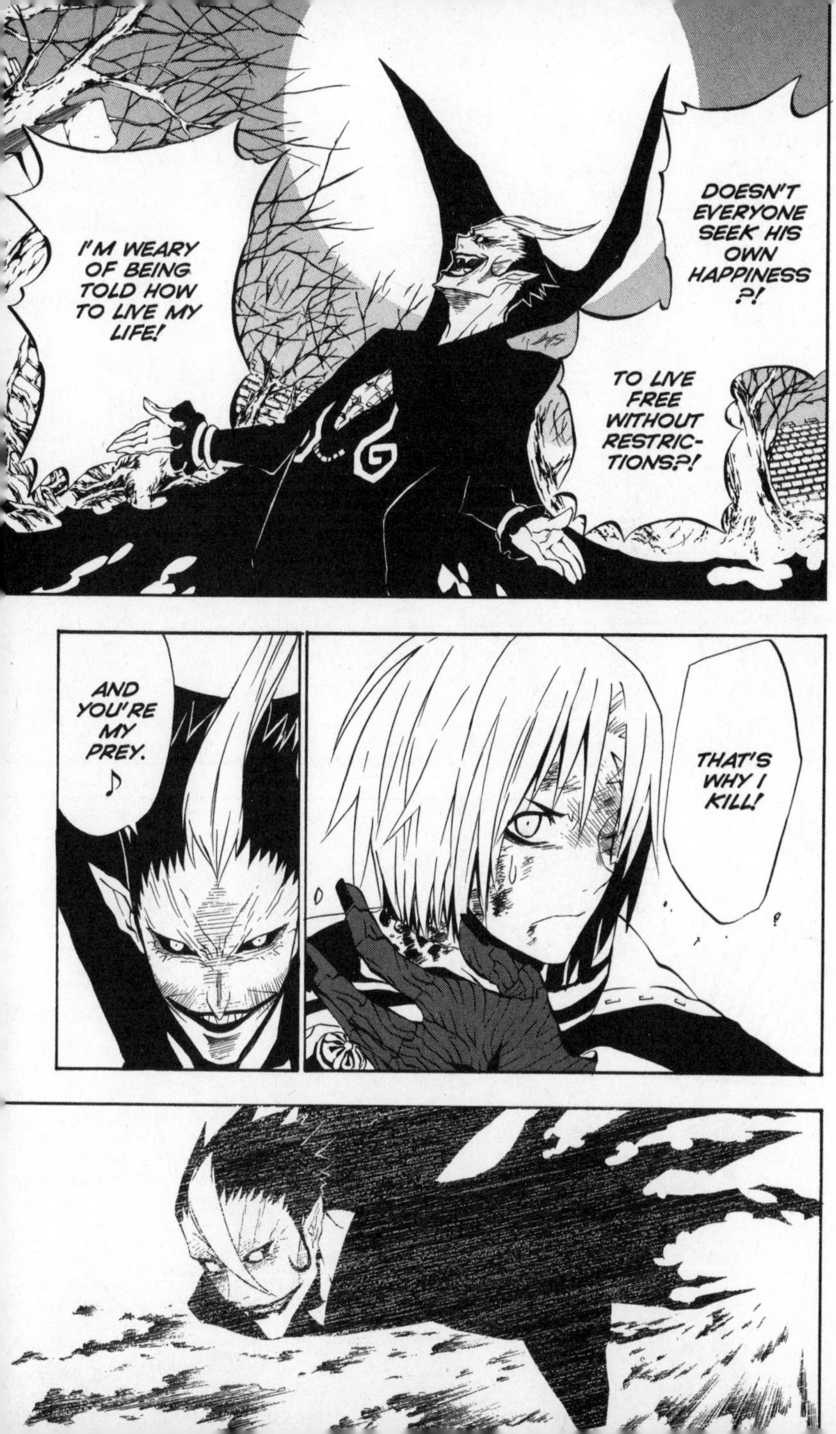
DOESN'T EVERYONE SEEK HIS OWN HAPPINESS?!
TO LIVE FREE WITHOUT RESTRICTIONS?!
I'M WEARY OF BEING TOLD HOW TO LIVE MY LIFE!
THAT'S WHY I KILL!
AND YOU'RE MY PREY. ♪

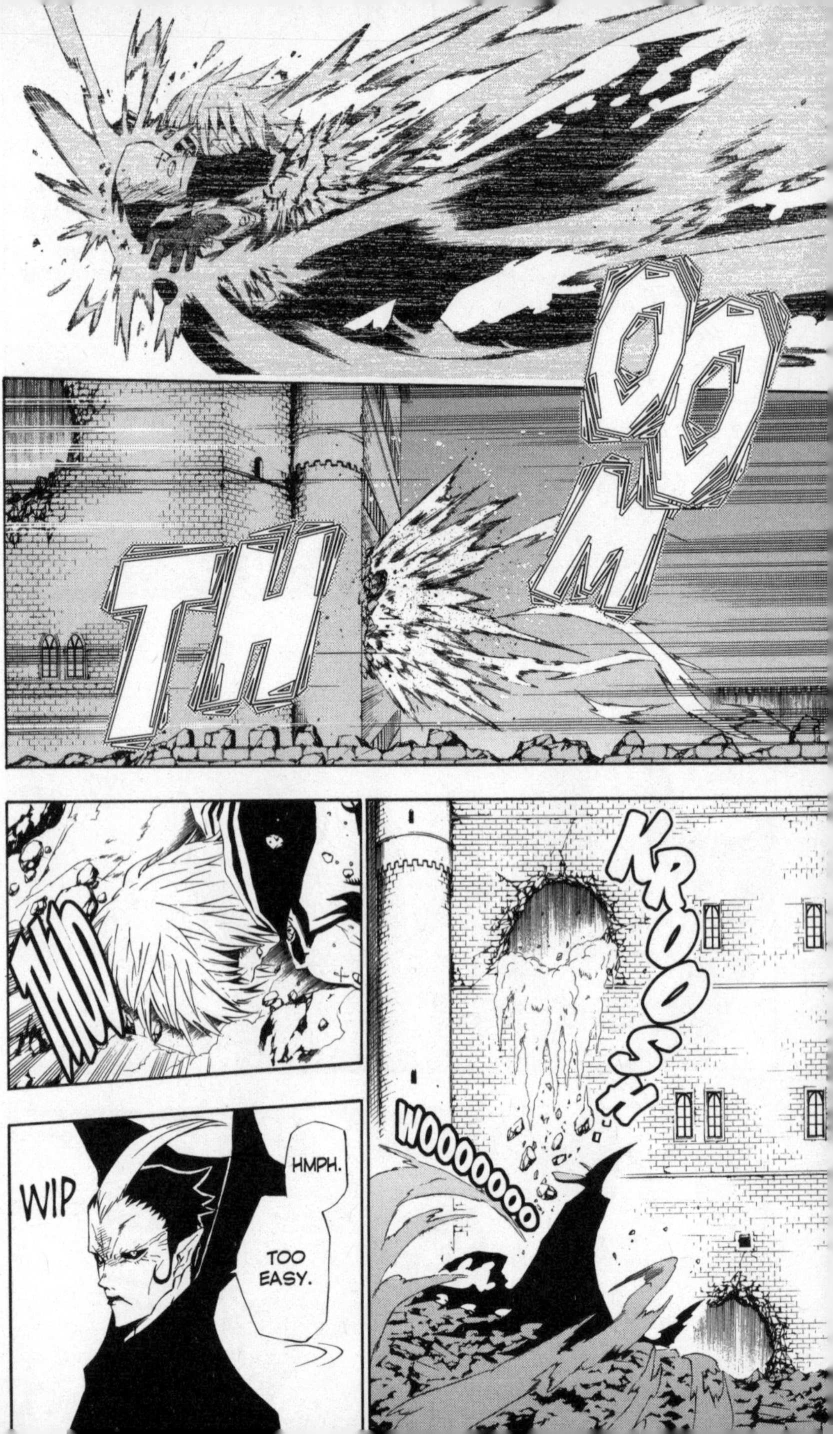
THOOM
KROOSH
WOOOOOOOO
THO
HMPH.
WIP
TOO EASY.

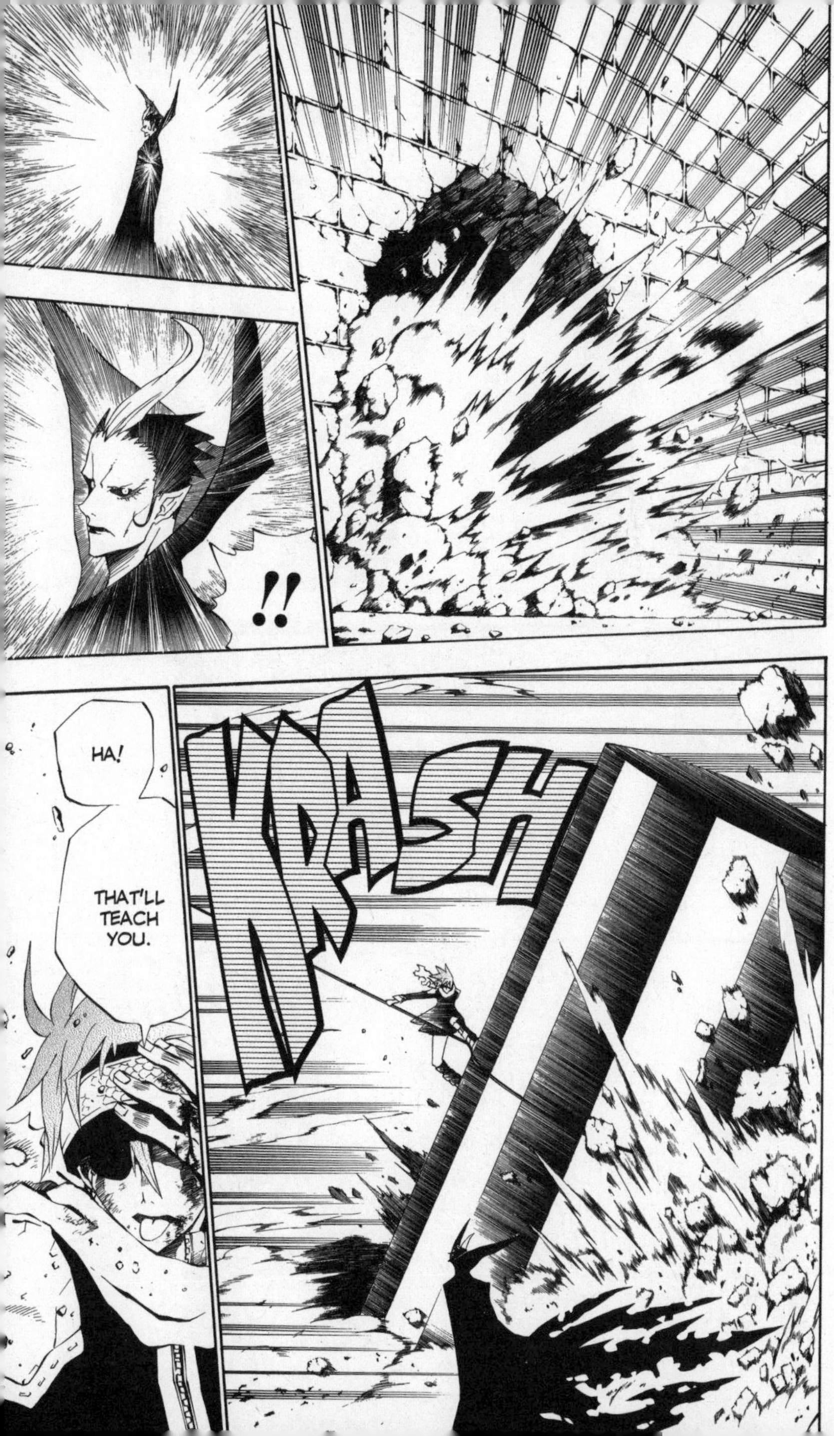
!!
KRASH
HA!
THAT'LL TEACH YOU.

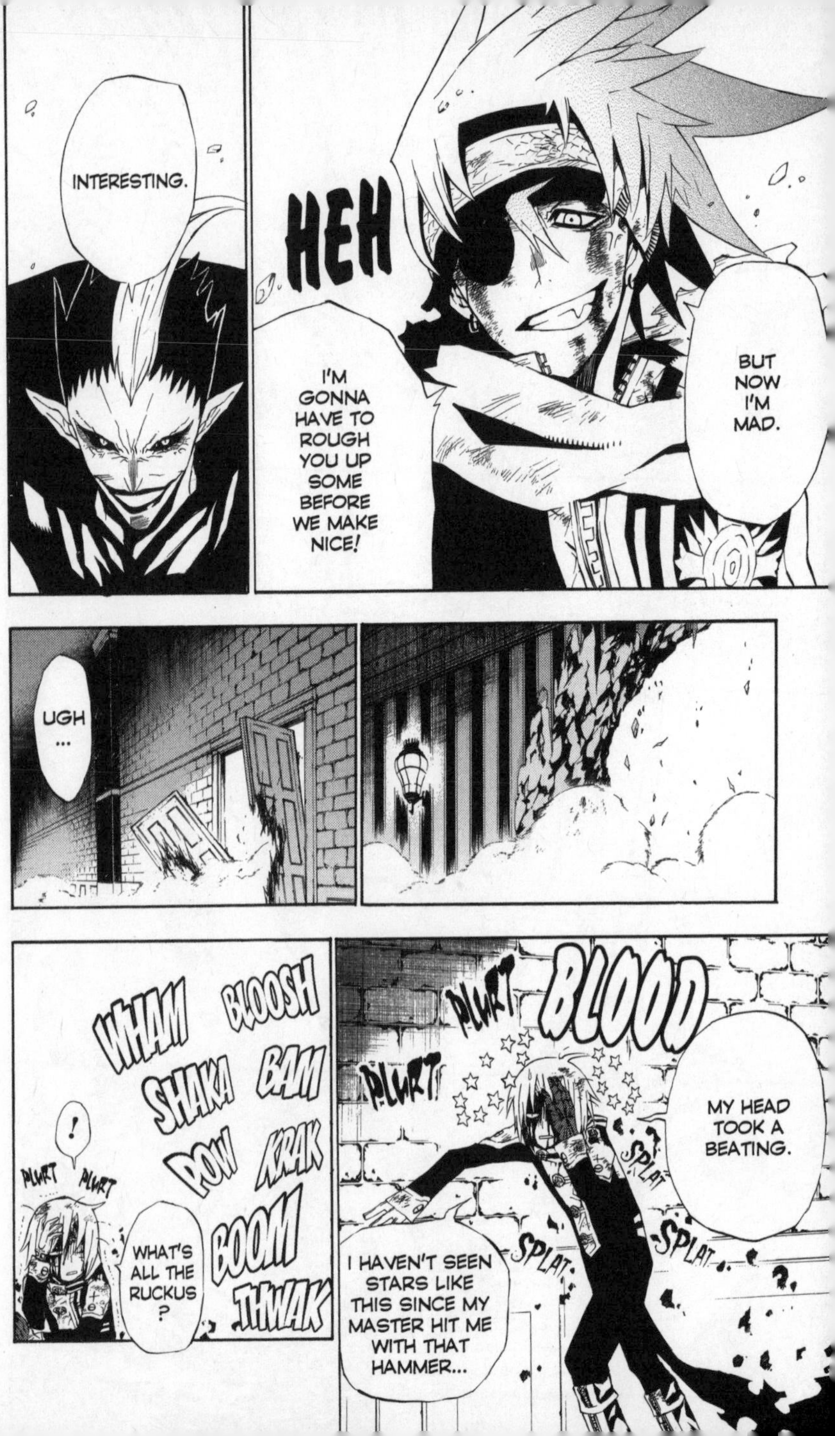
HEH
BUT NOW I'M MAD.
I'M GONNA HAVE TO ROUGH YOU UP SOME BEFORE WE MAKE NICE!
INTERESTING.
UGH ...
BLOOD
PLURT
PLURT
MY HEAD TOOK A BEATING.
SPLAT
SPLAT
SPLAT
I HAVEN'T SEEN STARS LIKE THIS SINCE MY MASTER HIT ME WITH THAT HAMMER...
BLOOSH
WHAM
BAM
SHAKA
KRAK
POW
BOOM
THWAK
!
PLURT
PLURT
WHAT'S ALL THE RUCKUS?

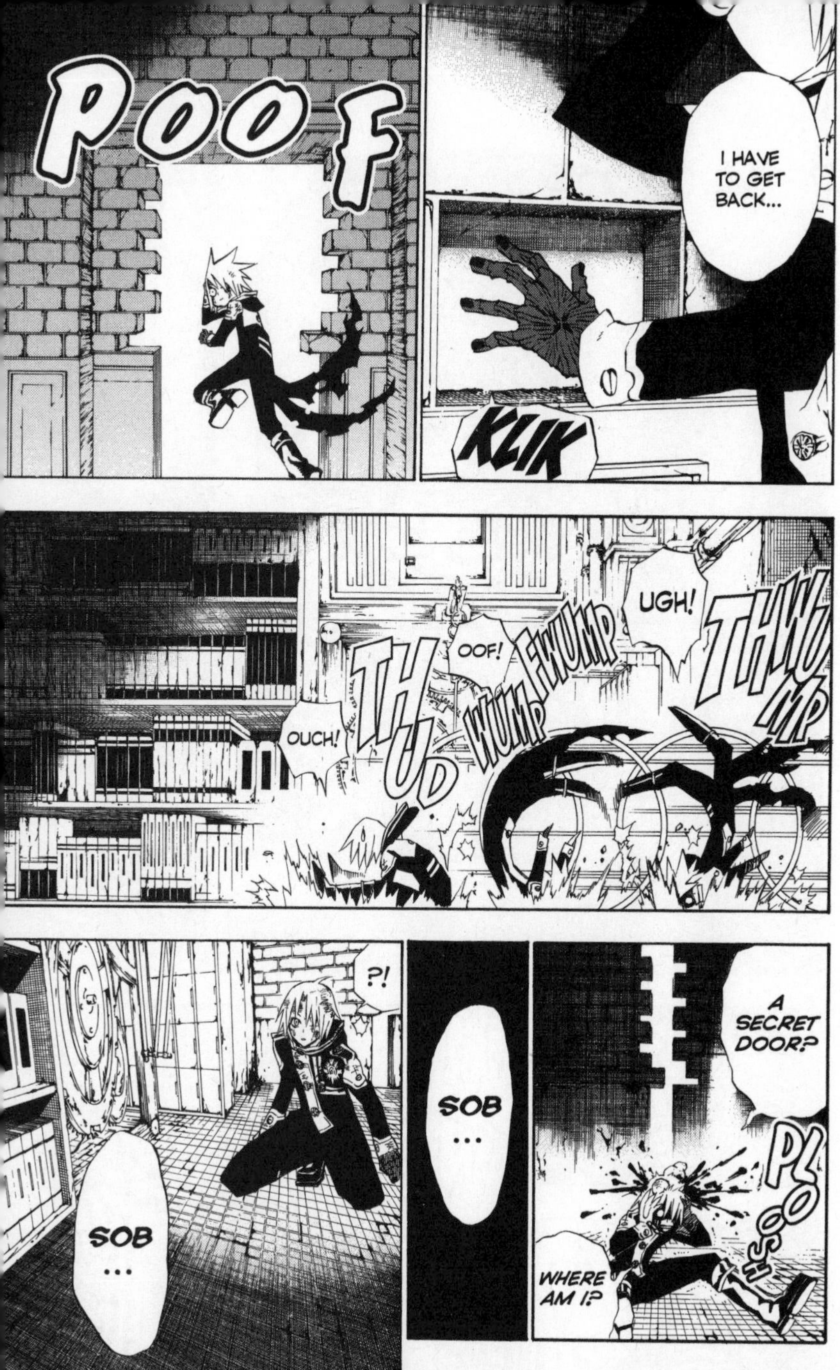
I HAVE TO GET BACK...
KLIK
POOF
THWUMP
UGH!
FWUMP
WUMP
OOF!
THUD
OUCH!
A SECRET DOOR?
PLOOSH
WHERE AM I?
SOB...
?!
SOB...

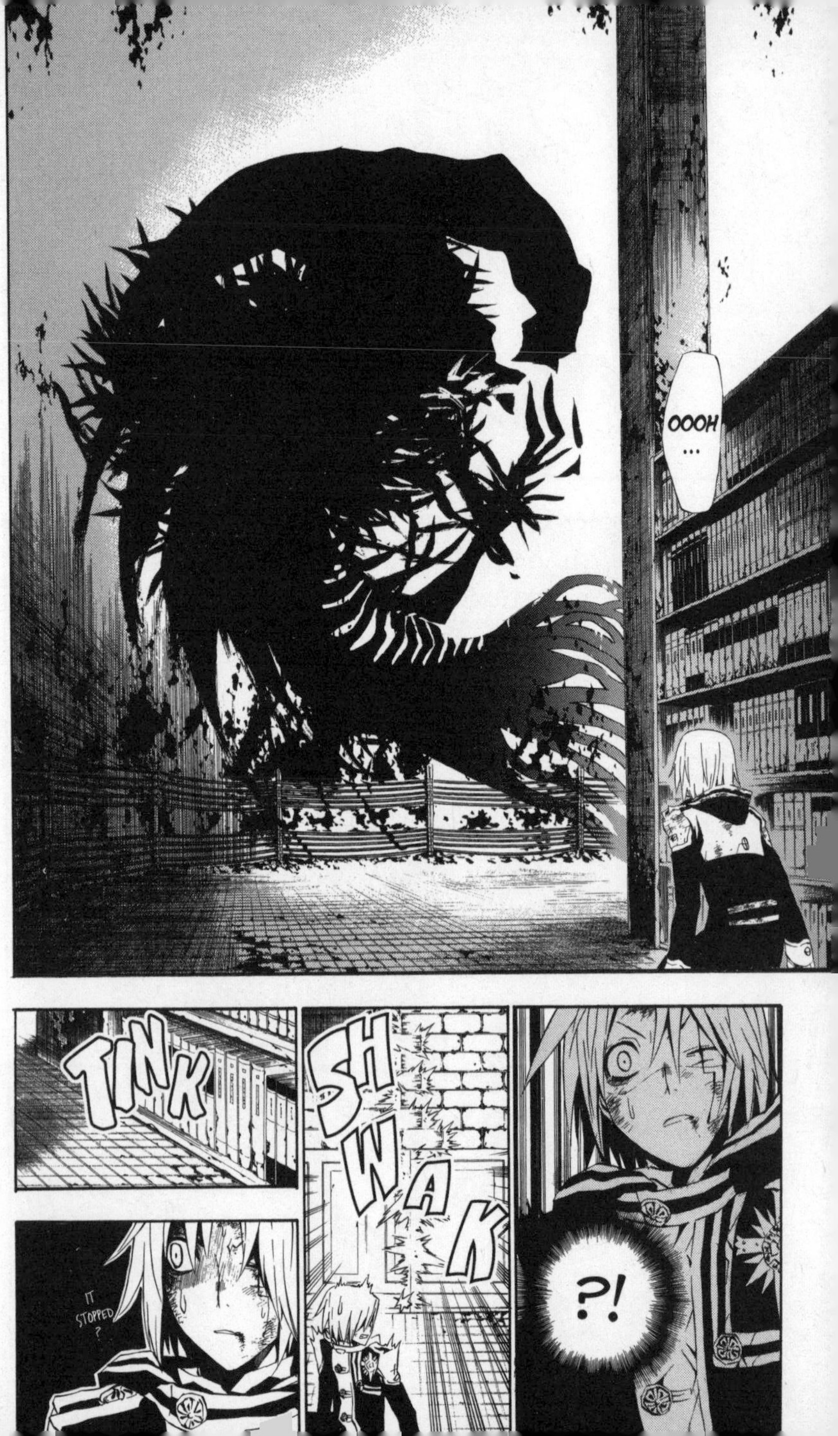
OOOH ...
?!
SHWAK
TINK
IT STOPPED?

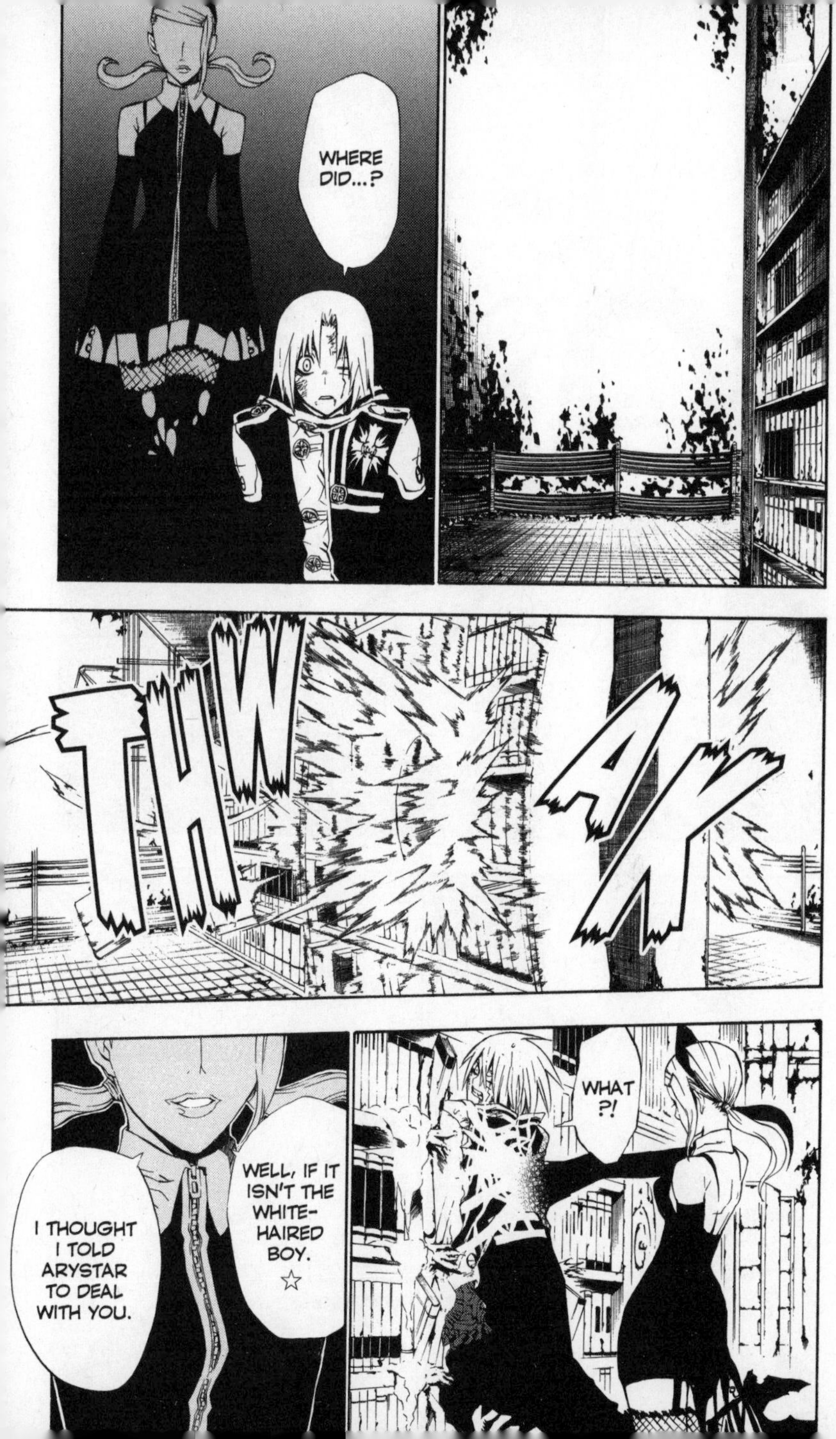
WHERE DID...?
THWAK
WHAT?!
WELL, IF IT ISN'T THE WHITE-HAIRED BOY. ☆
I THOUGHT I TOLD ARYSTAR TO DEAL WITH YOU.

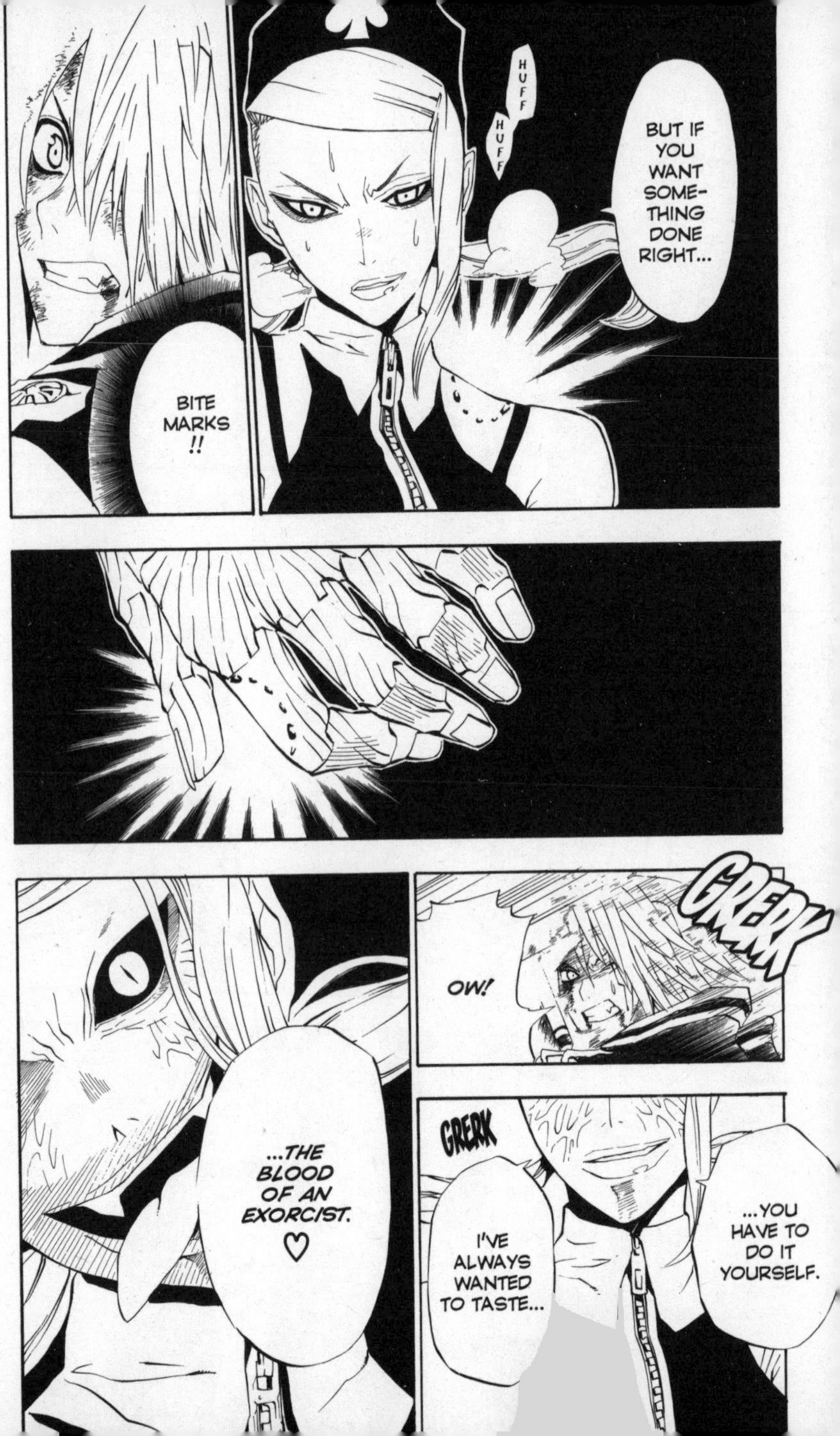
HUFF HUFF
BUT IF YOU WANT SOMETHING DONE RIGHT...
BITE MARKS!!
GRERK
OW!
GRERK
...YOU HAVE TO DO IT YOURSELF.
I'VE ALWAYS WANTED TO TASTE...
...THE BLOOD OF AN EXORCIST. ♡

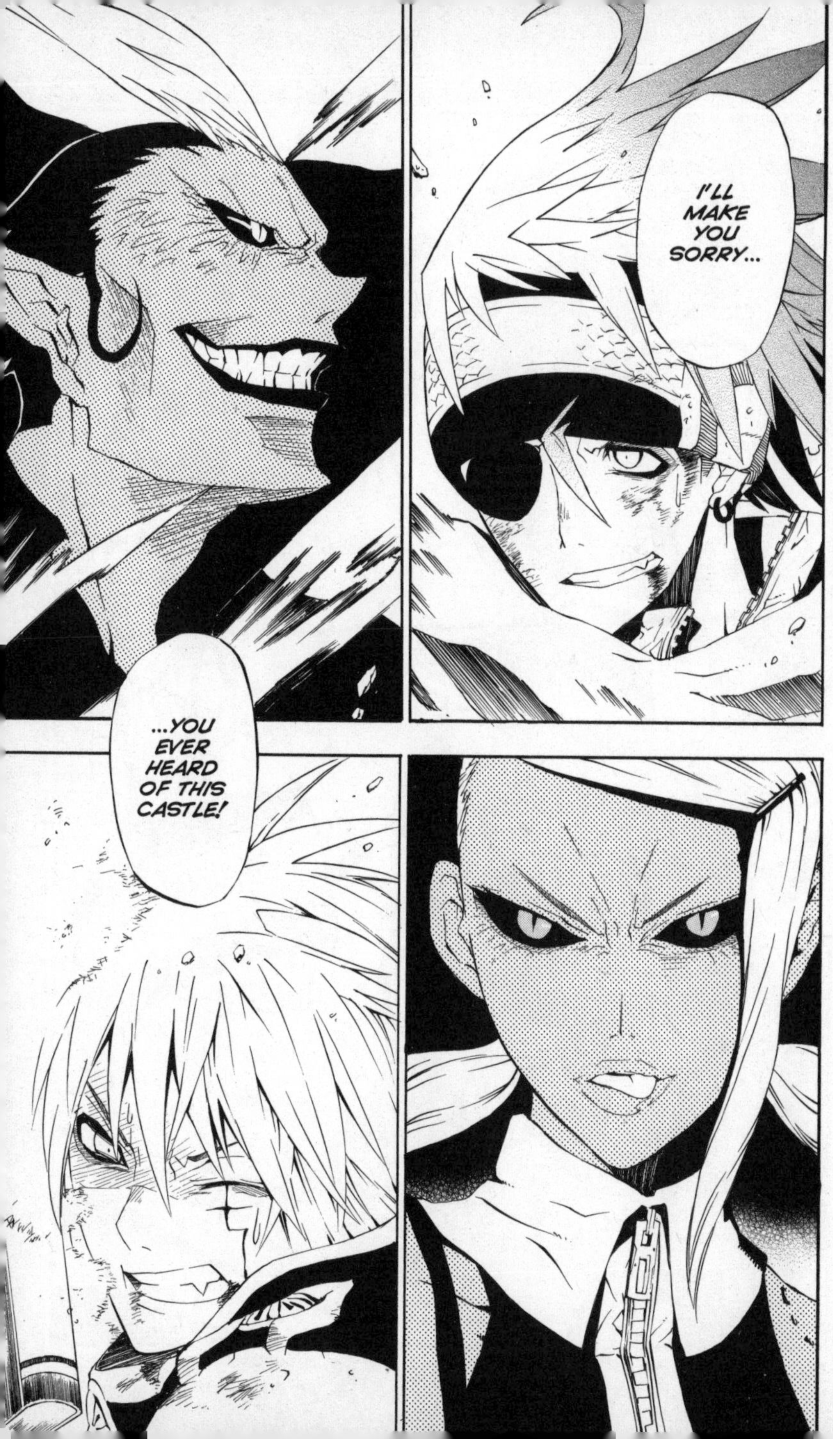
I'LL MAKE YOU SORRY...
...YOU EVER HEARD OF THIS CASTLE!

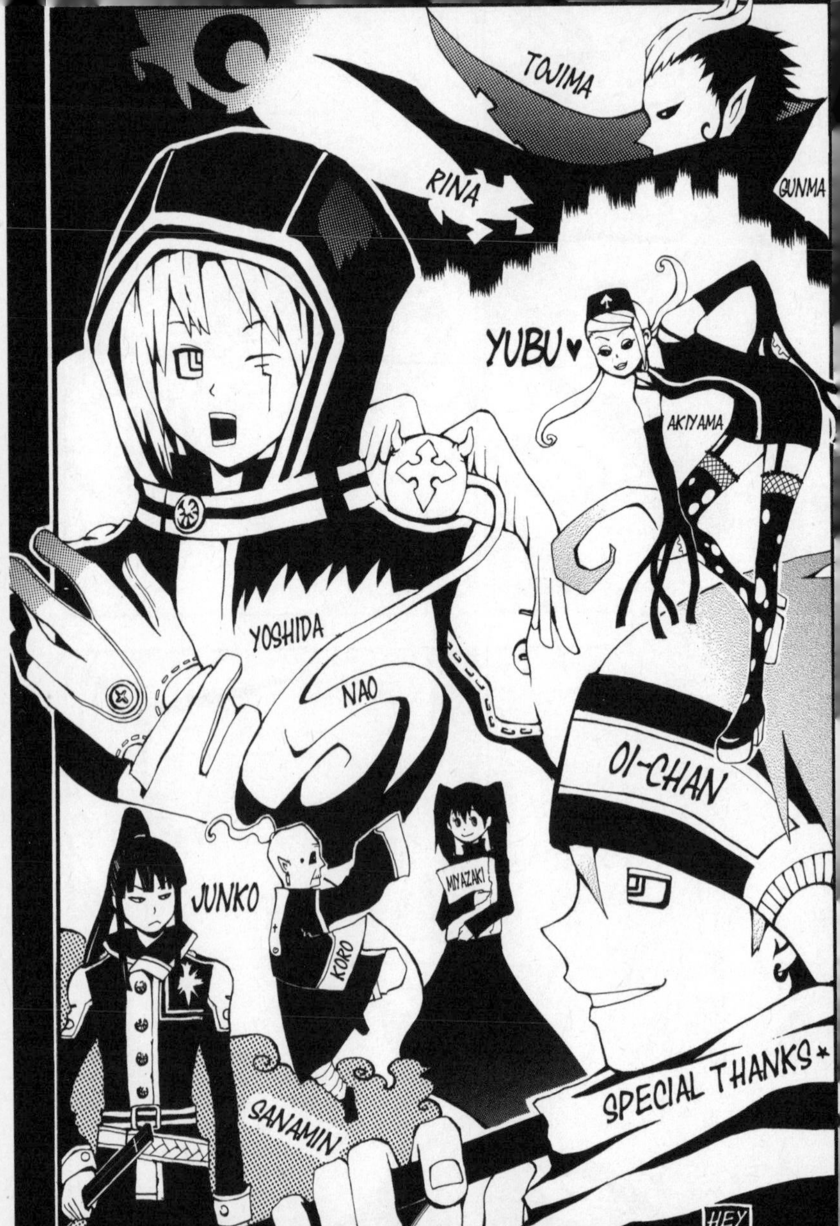
TOJIMA
RINA
GUNMA
YUBU♥
AKIYAMA
YOSHIDA
NAO
OI-CHAN
JUNKO
MIYAZAKI
KORO
SANAMIN
SPECIAL THANKS★
HEY

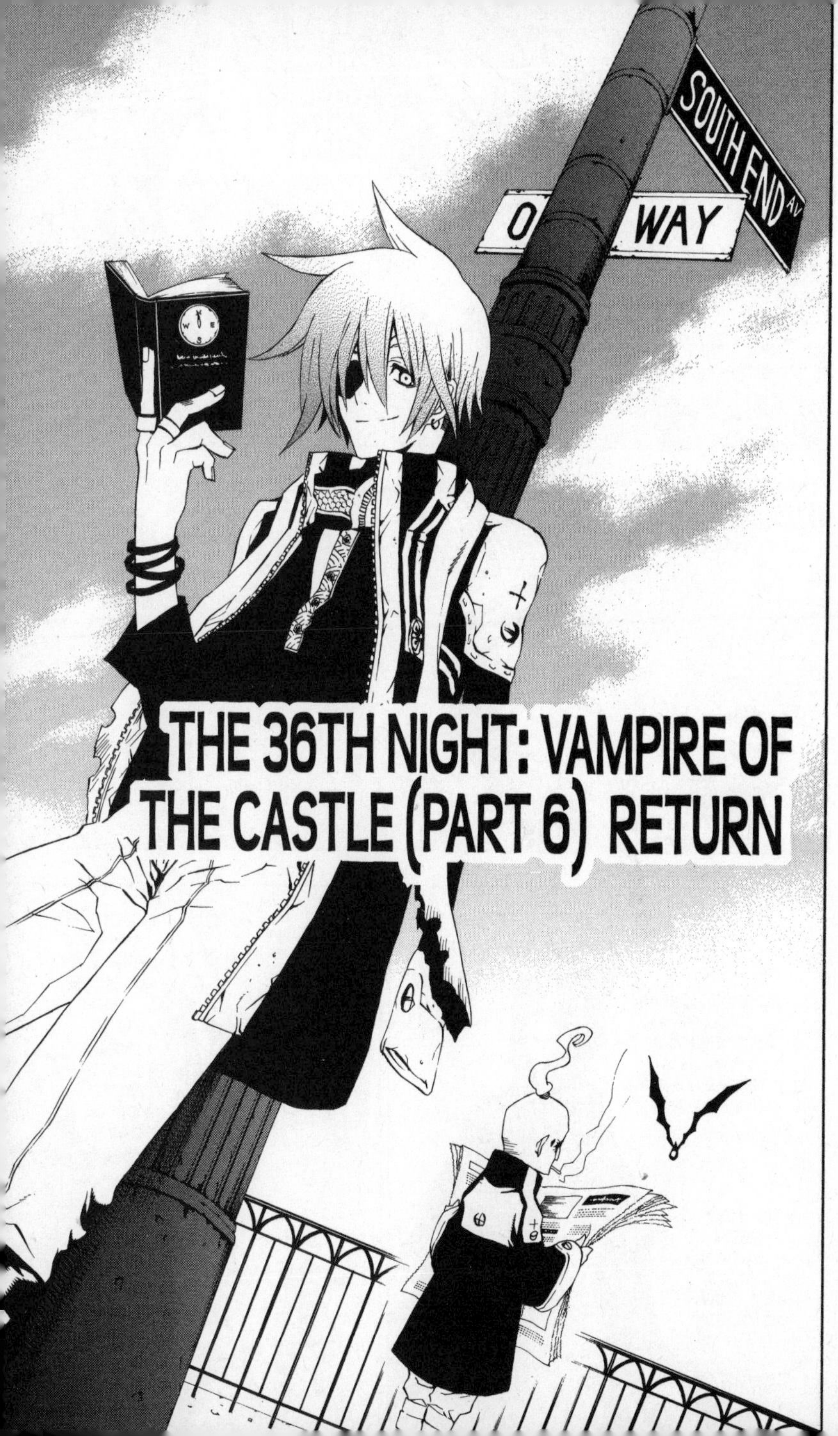
SOUTH END AV
O WAY
THE 36TH NIGHT: VAMPIRE OF THE CASTLE (PART 6) RETURN

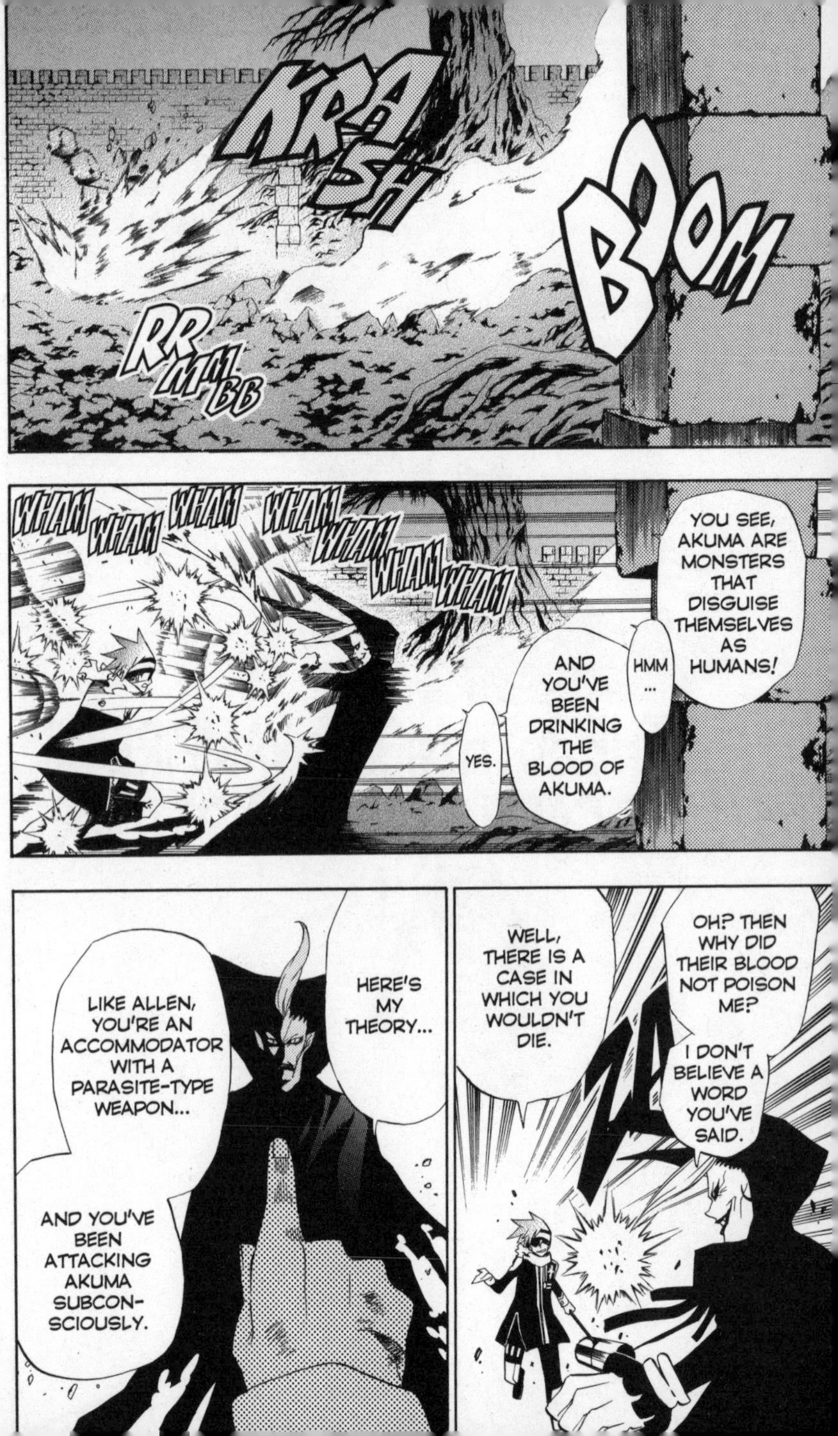
BOOM
KRASH
RRMMBB
YOU SEE, AKUMA ARE MONSTERS THAT DISGUISE THEMSELVES AS HUMANS!
HMM...
AND YOU'VE BEEN DRINKING THE BLOOD OF AKUMA.
YES.
WHAM WHAM WHAM WHAM WHAM WHAM WHAM
OH? THEN WHY DID THEIR BLOOD NOT POISON ME?
I DON'T BELIEVE A WORD YOU'VE SAID.
WELL, THERE IS A CASE IN WHICH YOU WOULDN'T DIE.
ZA
HERE'S MY THEORY...
LIKE ALLEN, YOU'RE AN ACCOMMODATOR WITH A PARASITE-TYPE WEAPON...
AND YOU'VE BEEN ATTACKING AKUMA SUBCON-SCIOUSLY.

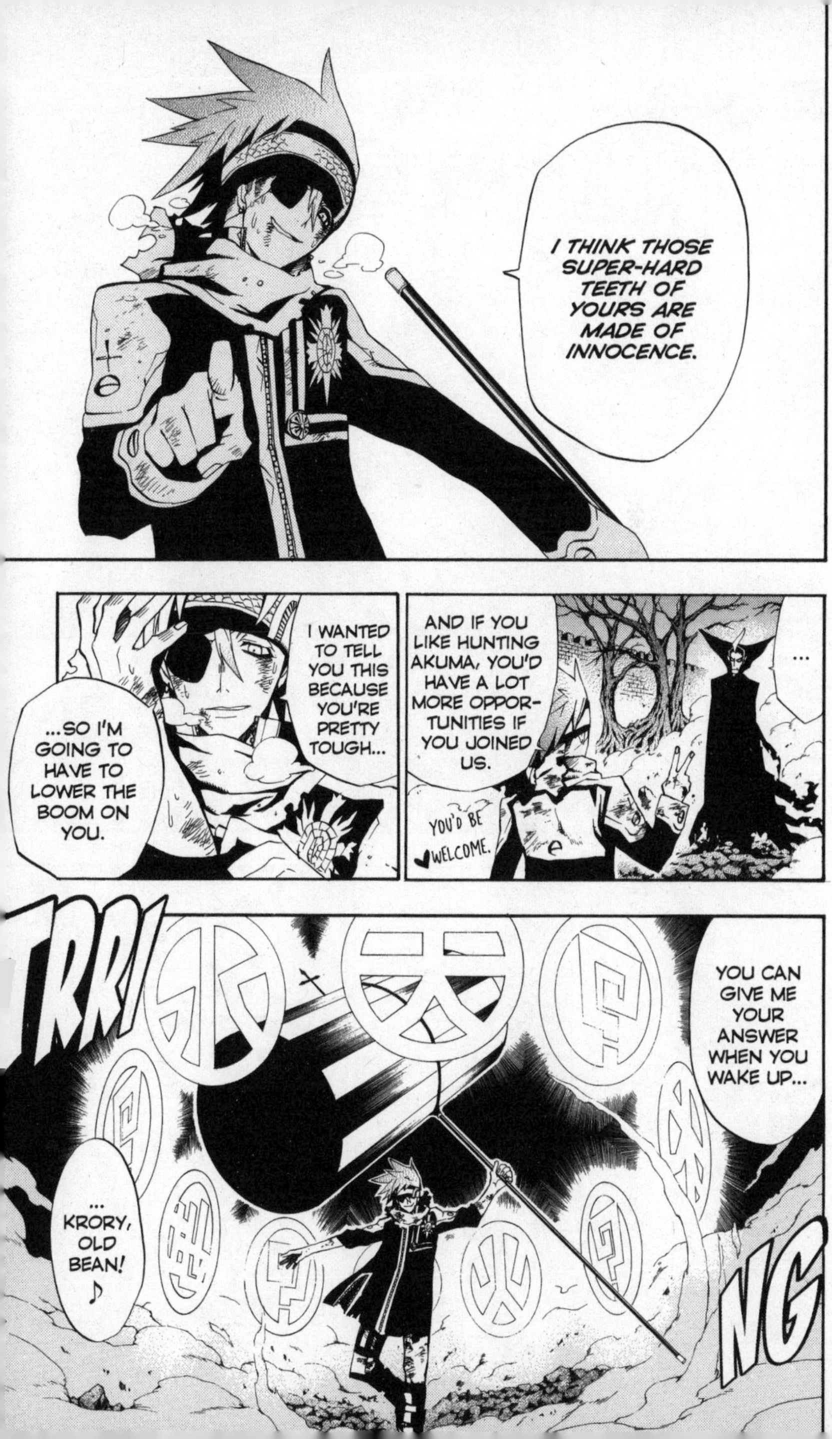
I THINK THOSE SUPER-HARD TEETH OF YOURS ARE MADE OF INNOCENCE.
...
AND IF YOU LIKE HUNTING AKUMA, YOU'D HAVE A LOT MORE OPPOR-TUNITIES IF YOU JOINED US.
YOU'D BE WELCOME.
I WANTED TO TELL YOU THIS BECAUSE YOU'RE PRETTY TOUGH...
...SO I'M GOING TO HAVE TO LOWER THE BOOM ON YOU.
YOU CAN GIVE ME YOUR ANSWER WHEN YOU WAKE UP...
TRRI
NG
... KRORY, OLD BEAN! ♪

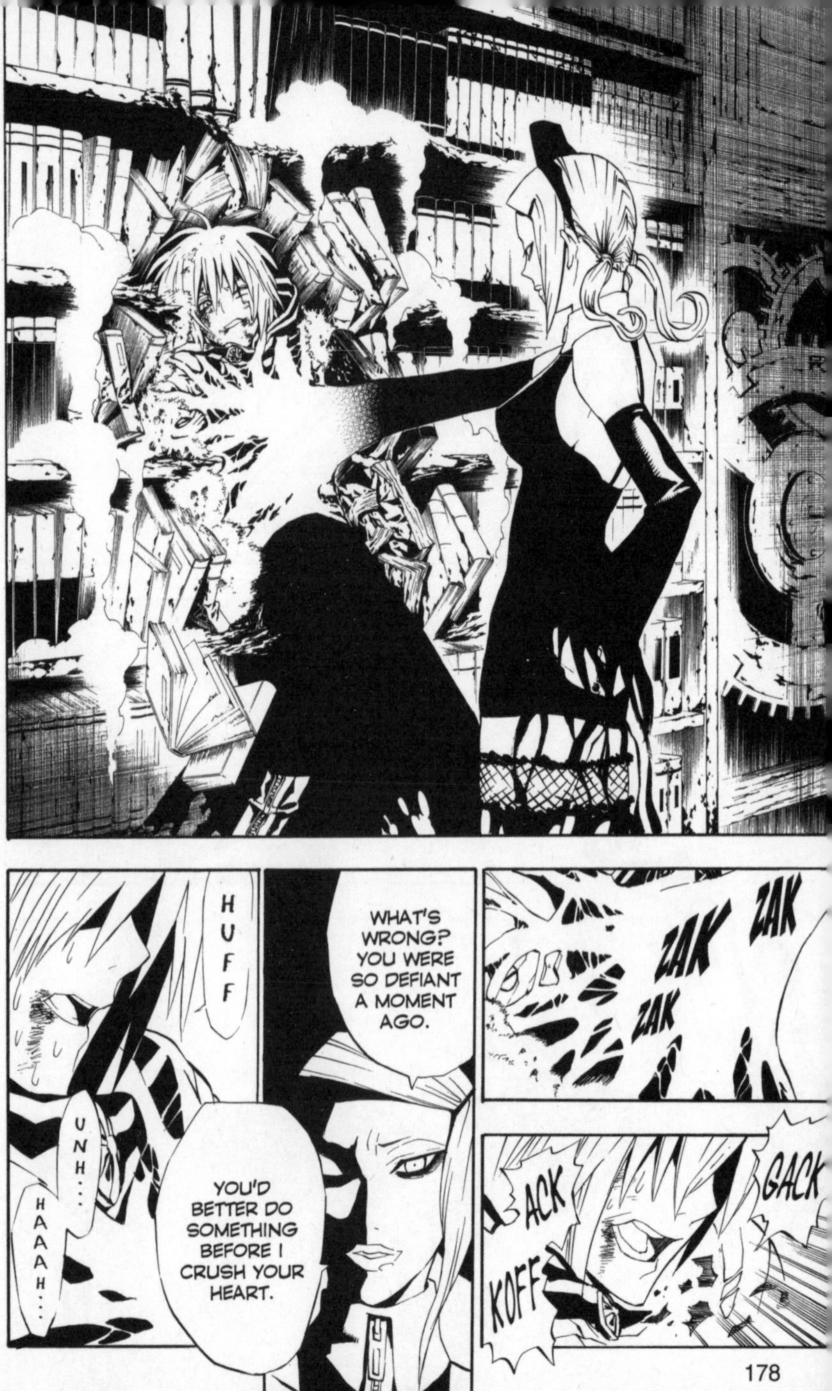
ZAK ZAK ZAK ZAK
GACK
ACK
KOFF
WHAT'S WRONG? YOU WERE SO DEFIANT A MOMENT AGO.
YOU'D BETTER DO SOMETHING BEFORE I CRUSH YOUR HEART.
HUFF
UNH...
HAAAH...

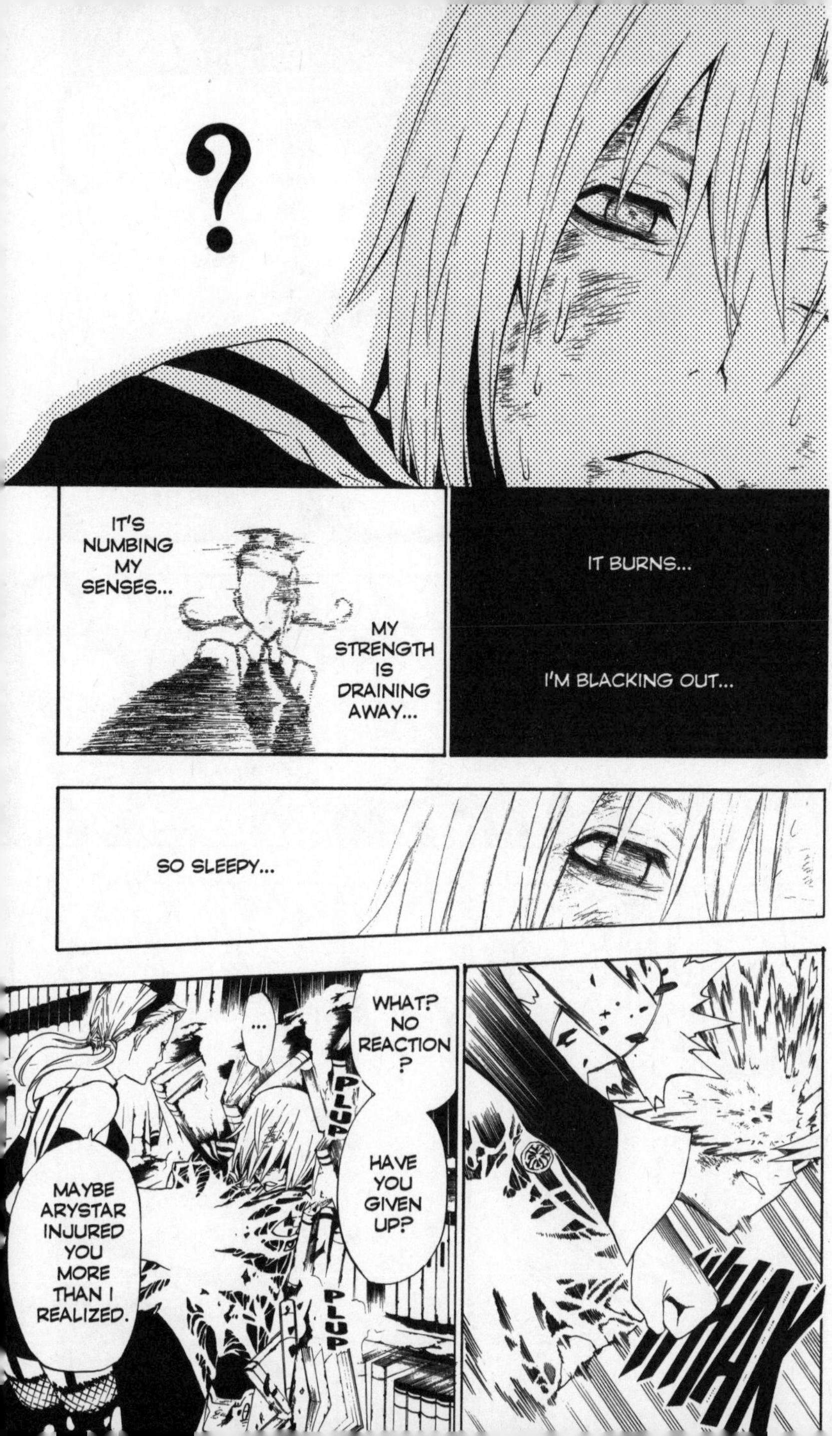
?
IT BURNS...
I'M BLACKING OUT...
IT'S NUMBING MY SENSES...
MY STRENGTH IS DRAINING AWAY...
SO SLEEPY...
WHAT? NO REACTION?
...
PLUP
HAVE YOU GIVEN UP?
PLUP
MAYBE ARYSTAR INJURED YOU MORE THAN I REALIZED.

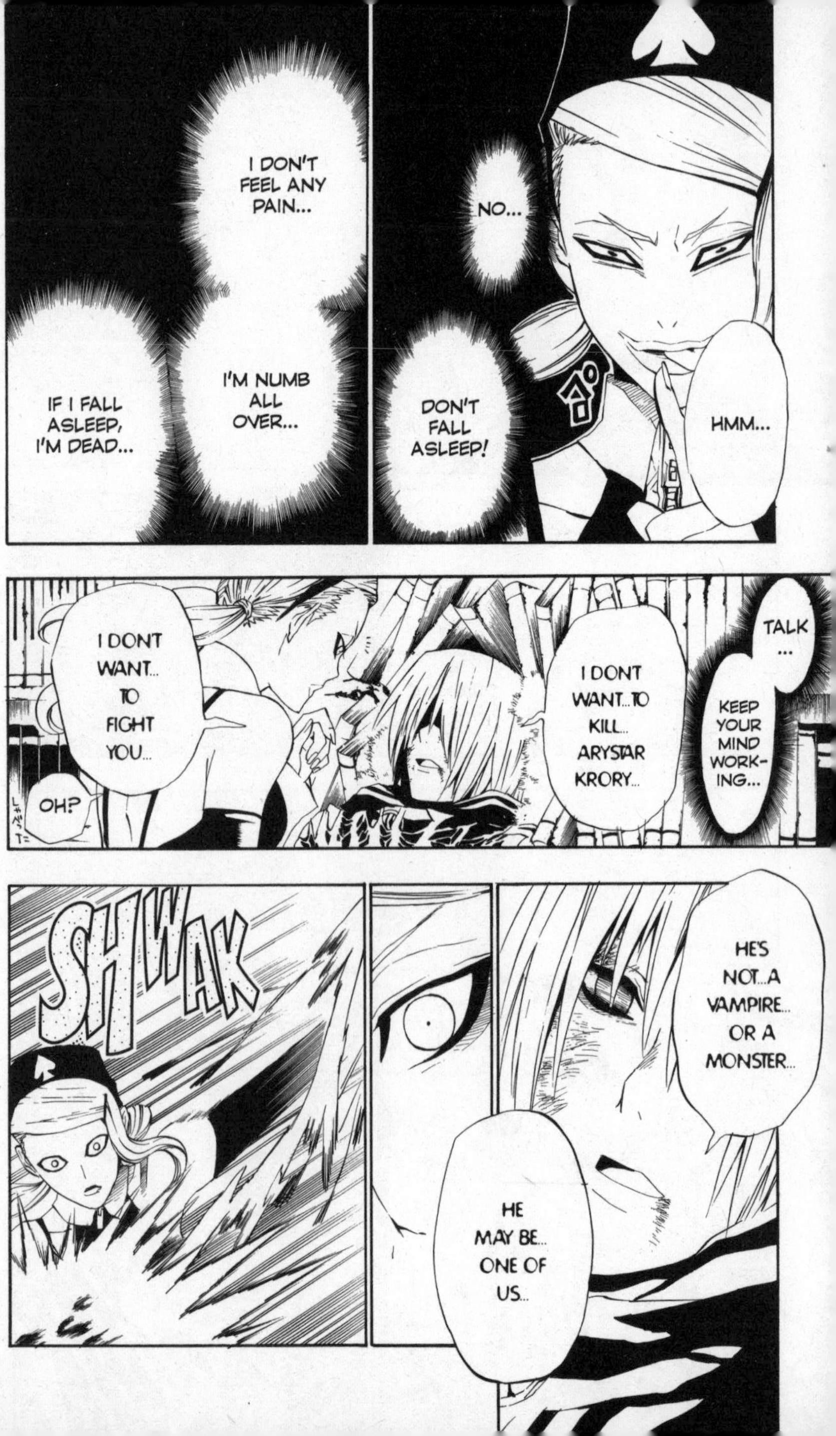
HMM...
NO...
DON'T FALL ASLEEP!
I DON'T FEEL ANY PAIN...
I'M NUMB ALL OVER...
IF I FALL ASLEEP, I'M DEAD...
TALK...
KEEP YOUR MIND WORKING...
I DONT WANT...TO KILL... ARYSTAR KRORY...
I DONT WANT... TO FIGHT YOU...
OH?
HE'S NOT...A VAMPIRE... OR A MONSTER...
HE MAY BE... ONE OF US...
SHWAK

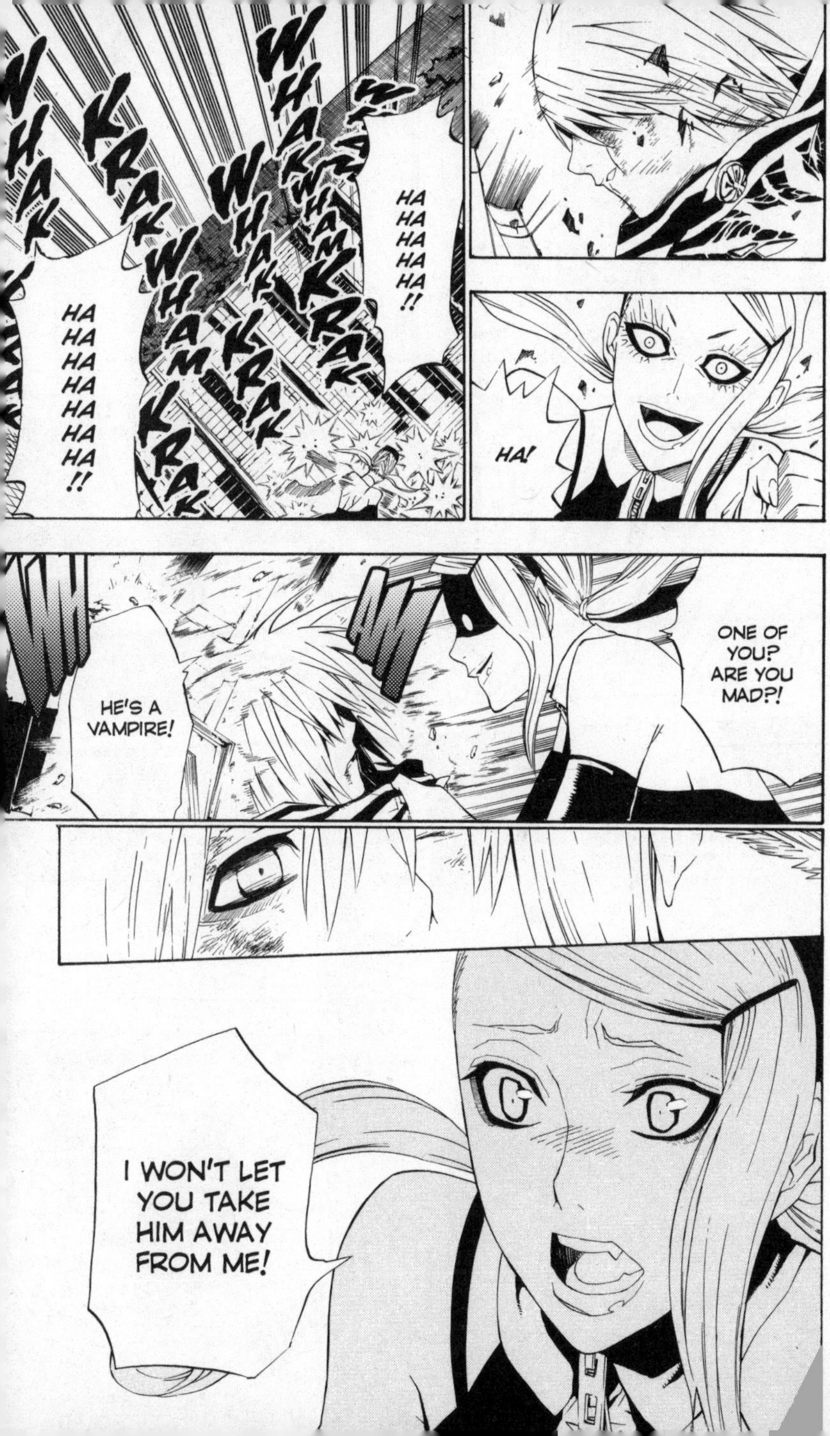
HA!
HA HA HA HA HA!!
HA HA HA HA HA HA HA HA!!
ONE OF YOU? ARE YOU MAD?!
HE'S A VAMPIRE!
I WON'T LET YOU TAKE HIM AWAY FROM ME!

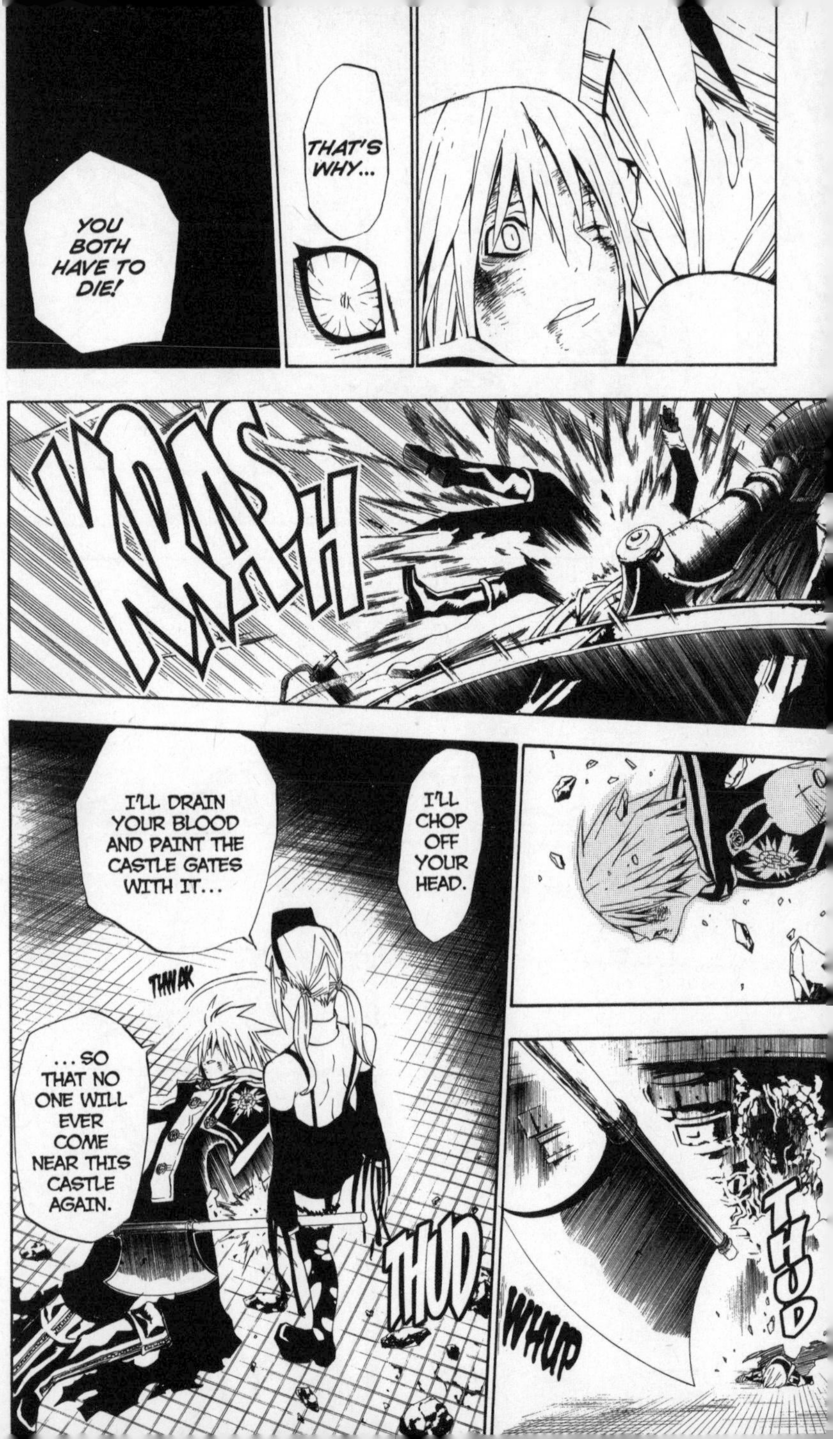
THAT'S WHY...
YOU BOTH HAVE TO DIE!
KRASH
THUD
WHUP
I'LL CHOP OFF YOUR HEAD.
I'LL DRAIN YOUR BLOOD AND PAINT THE CASTLE GATES WITH IT...
THWAK
...SO THAT NO ONE WILL EVER COME NEAR THIS CASTLE AGAIN.
THUD

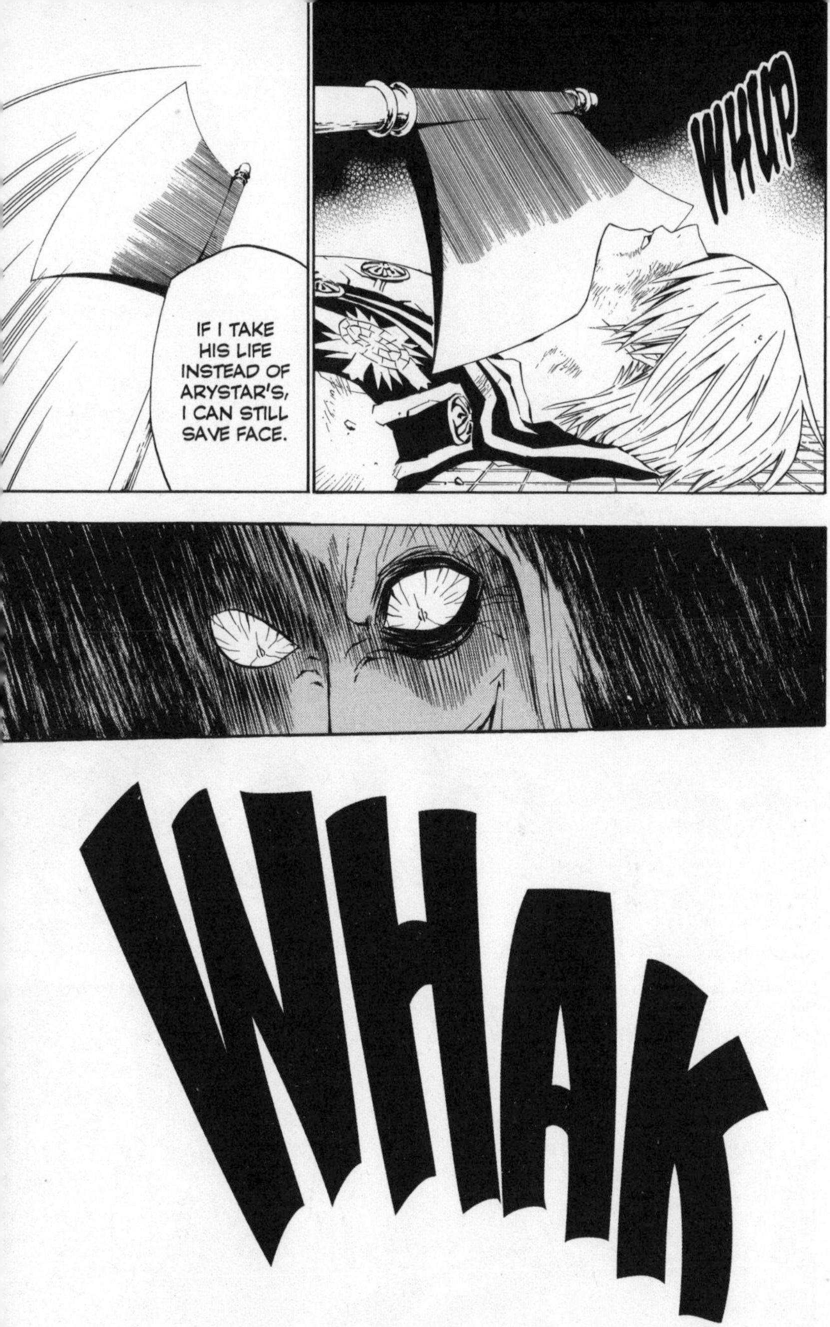
WHUP
IF I TAKE HIS LIFE INSTEAD OF ARYSTAR'S, I CAN STILL SAVE FACE.
WHAK

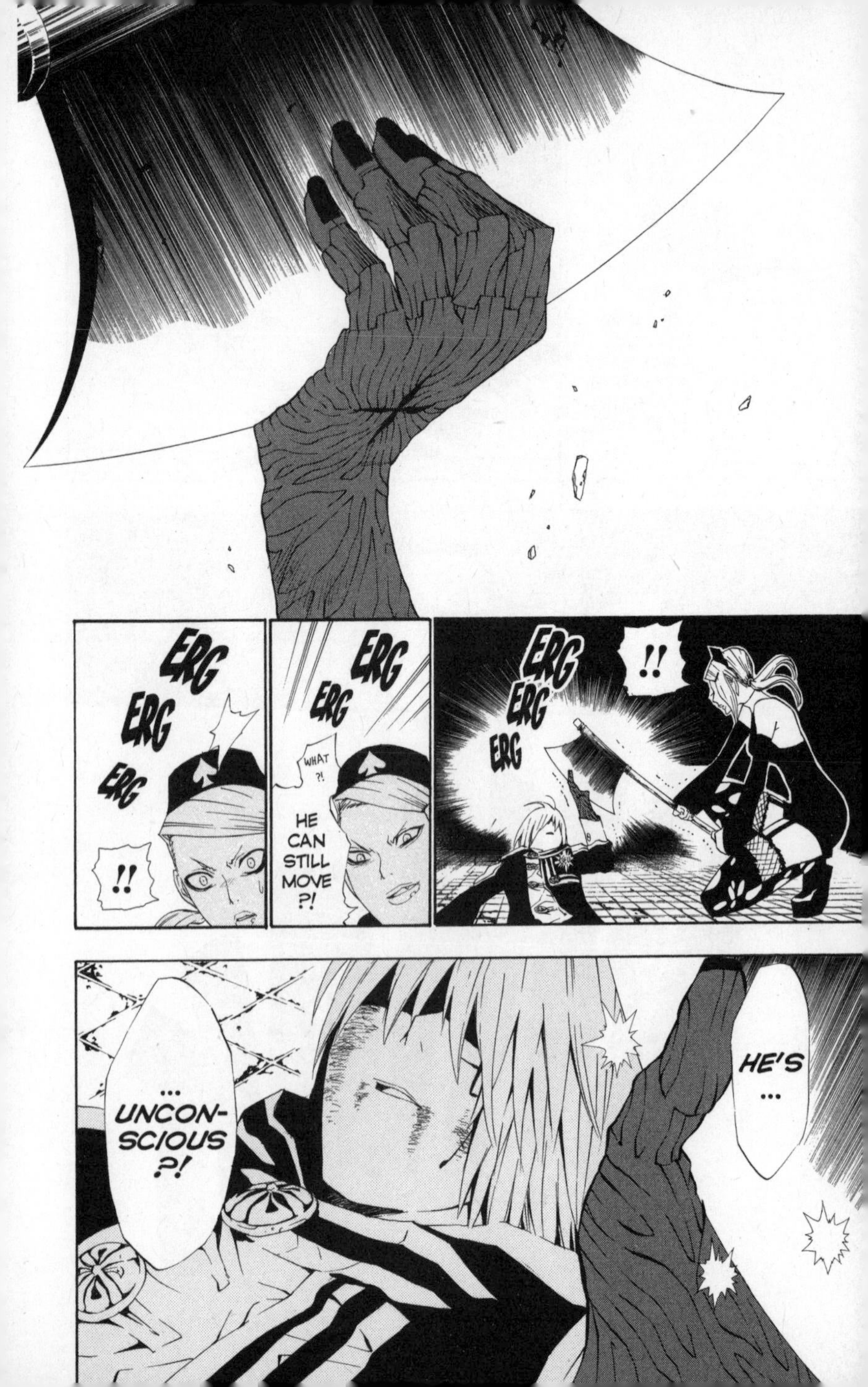
ERG
ERG
ERG
!!
ERG
ERG
WHAT ?!
HE CAN STILL MOVE ?!
ERG
ERG
ERG
!!
HE'S ...
... UNCON-SCIOUS ?!

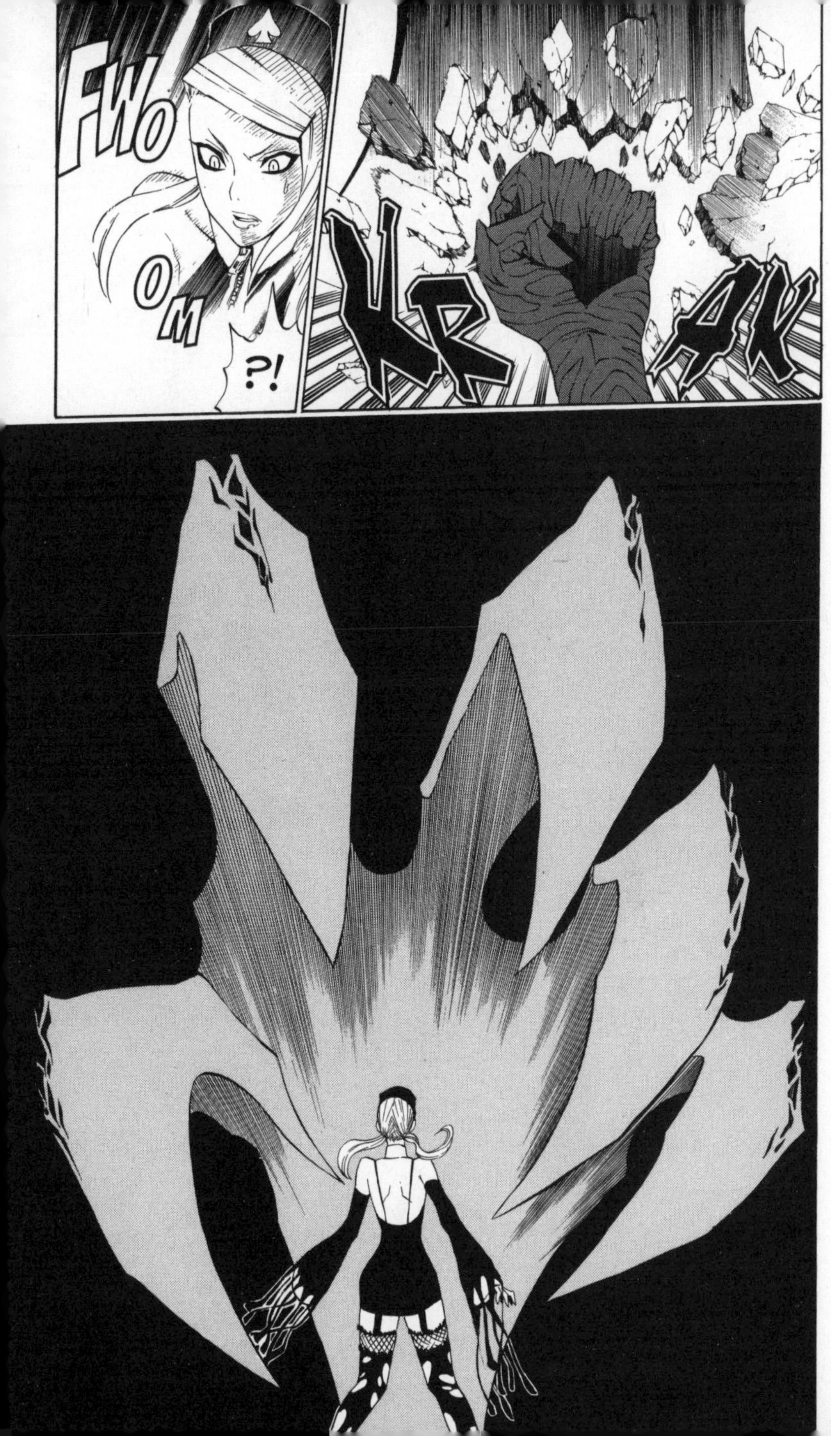
KRAK
FWOOM
?!

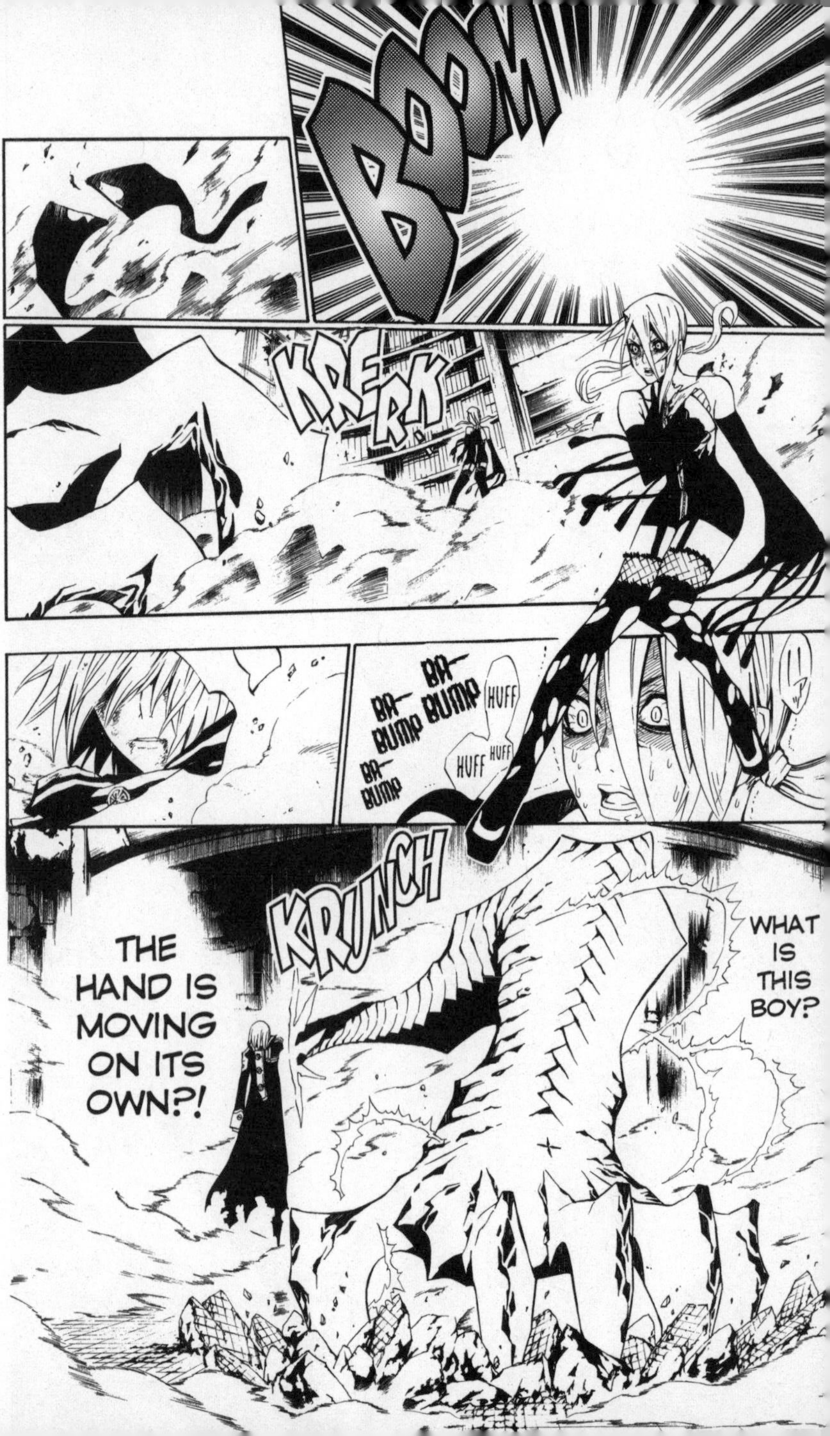
BOOM
KRERK
HUFF
BA BUMP
BA BUMP
HUFF HUFF
BA BUMP
KRUNCH
WHAT IS THIS BOY?
THE HAND IS MOVING ON ITS OWN?!

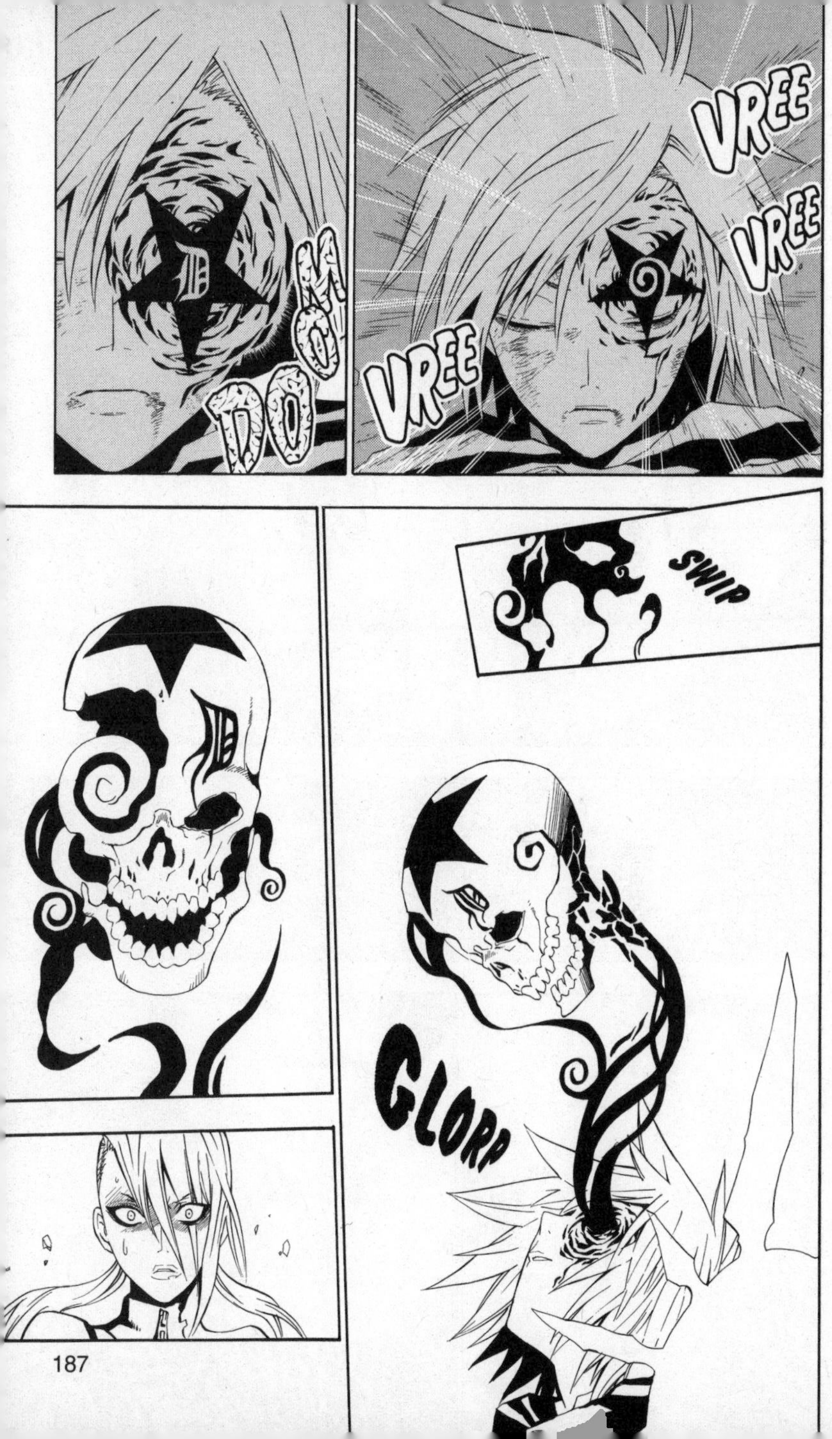
VREE
VREE
VREE
DOOM
SWIP
GLORP

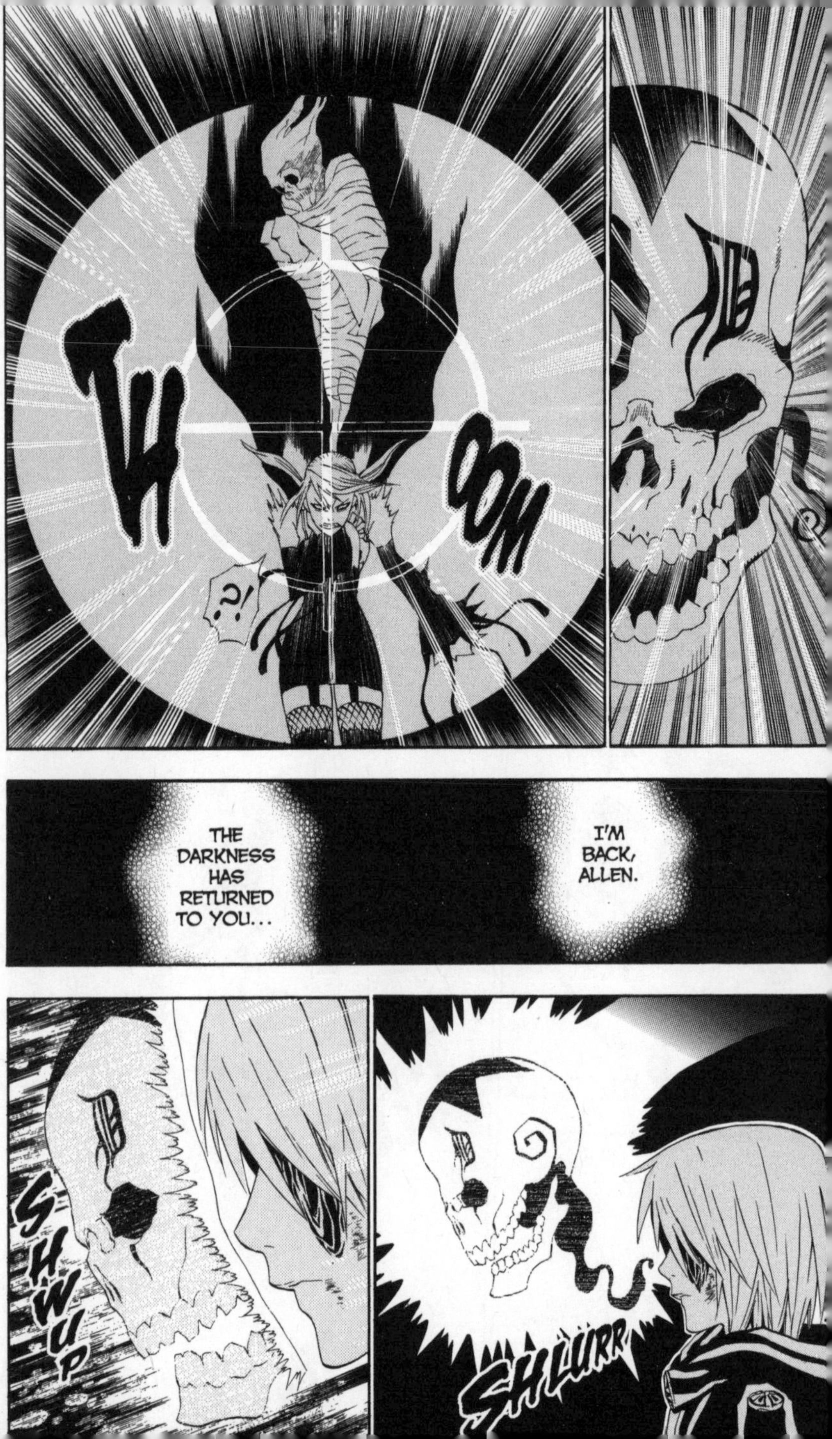
THOOM
?!
I'M BACK, ALLEN.
THE DARKNESS HAS RETURNED TO YOU...
SHLURR
SHWUP

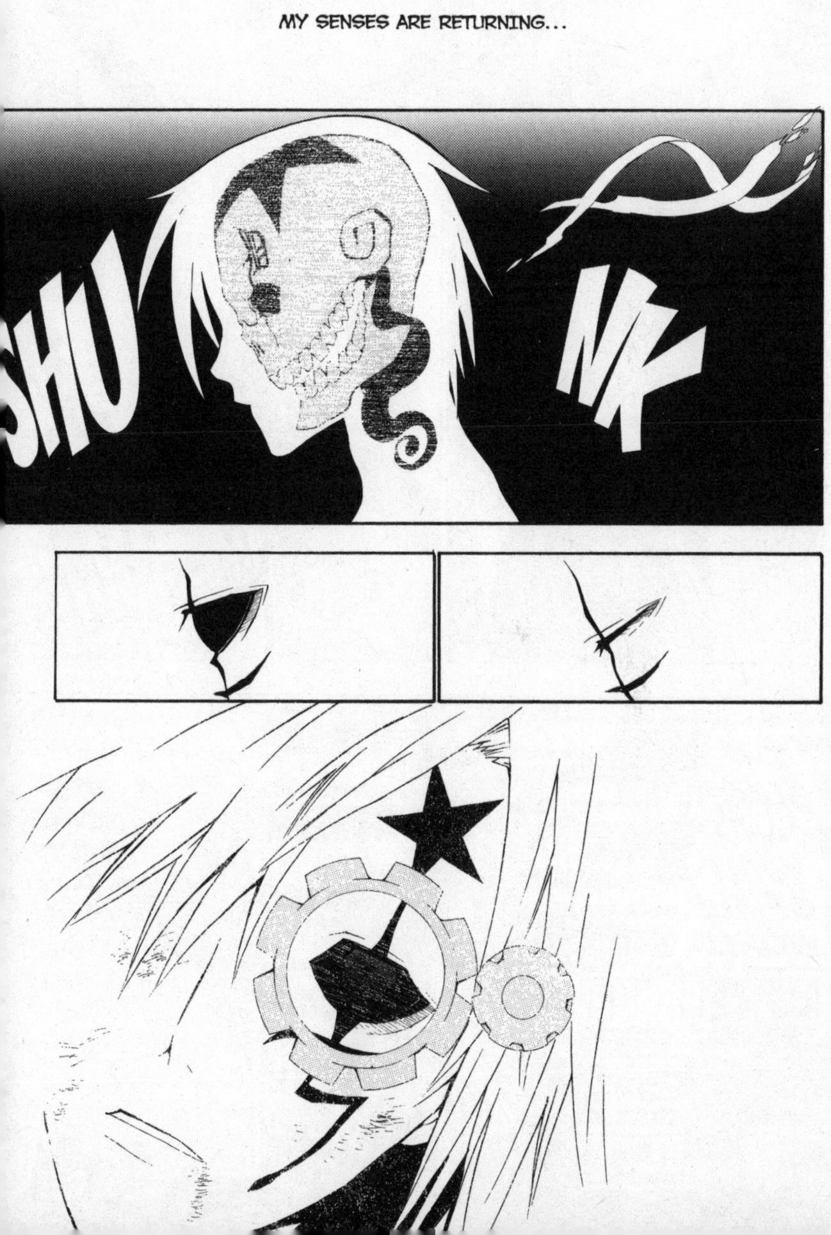
MY SENSES ARE RETURNING...
SHUNK

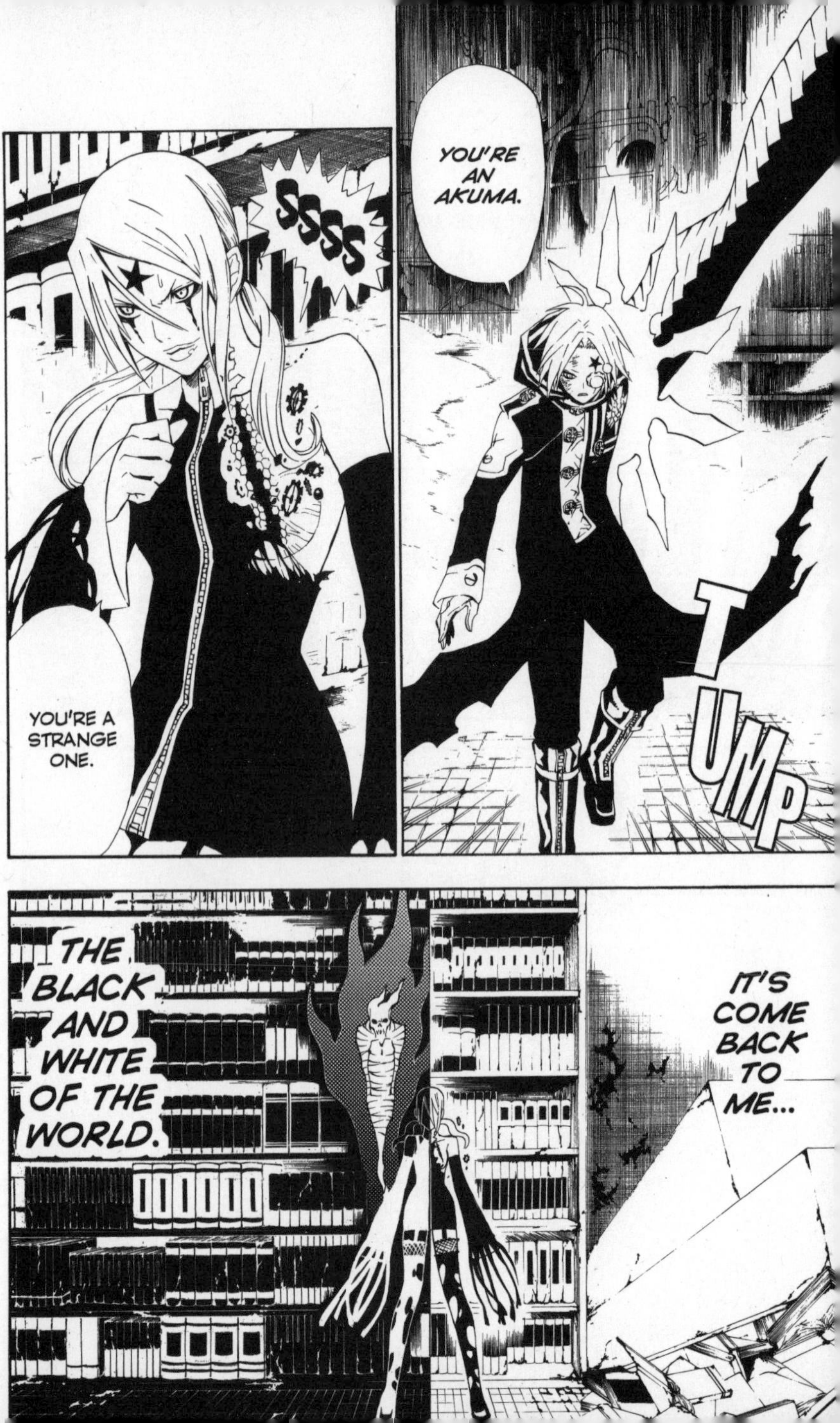
YOU'RE AN AKUMA.
TUMP
SSSS
YOU'RE A STRANGE ONE.
IT'S COME BACK TO ME...
THE BLACK AND WHITE OF THE WORLD.

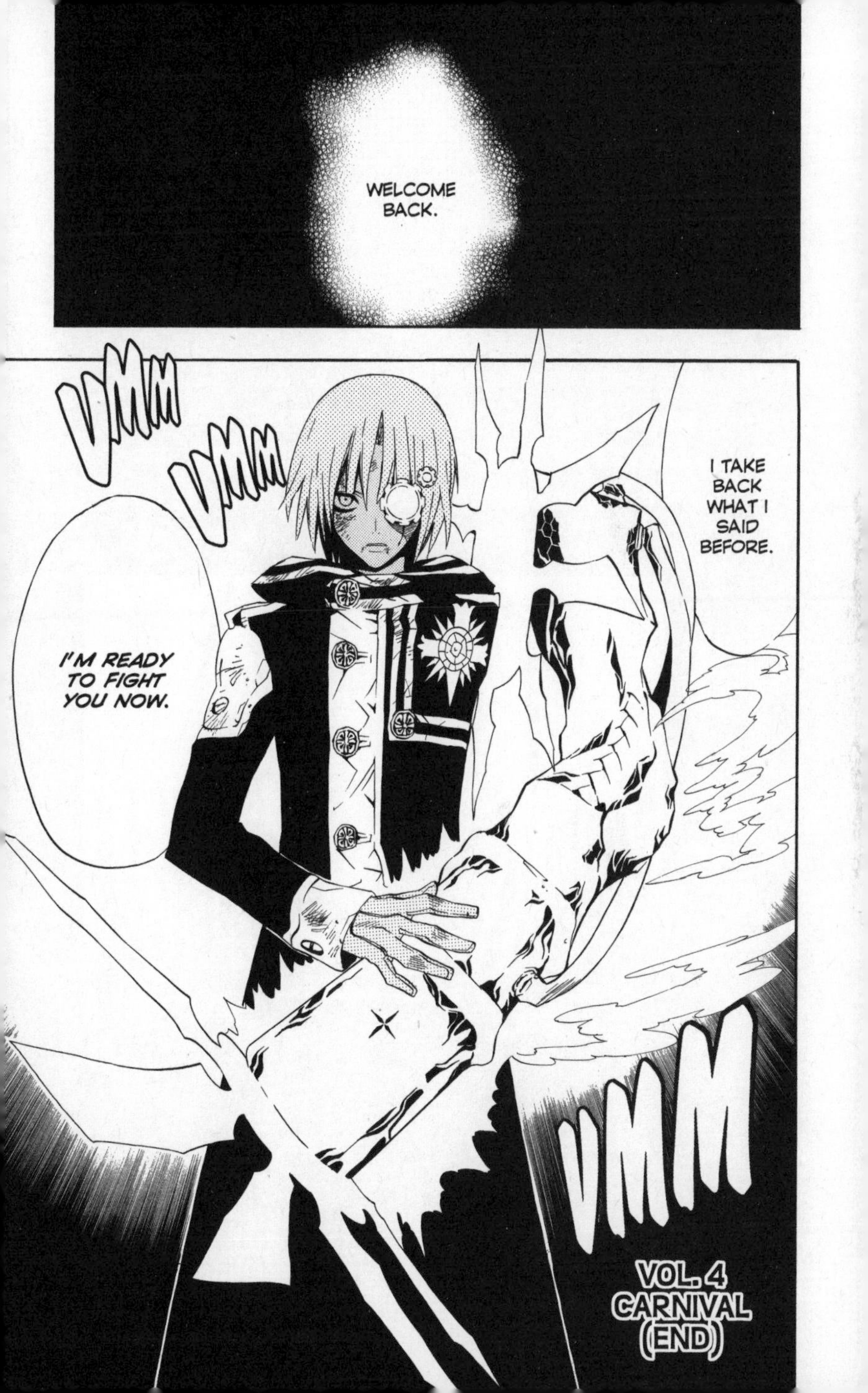
WELCOME BACK.
VMM VMM
I TAKE BACK WHAT I SAID BEFORE.
I'M READY TO FIGHT YOU NOW.
VMM
VOL. 4 CARNIVAL (END)

IN THE NEXT VOLUME...

The battle rages on against Arystar Krory and Eliade. Allen's eye is now healed and strange truths begin to reveal themselves. Allen's companion Lavi realizes that Arystar might not be a vampire but something else entirely. Plus Allen and Lavi find themselves with an unexpected traveling companion—but who could it be?

Available now!

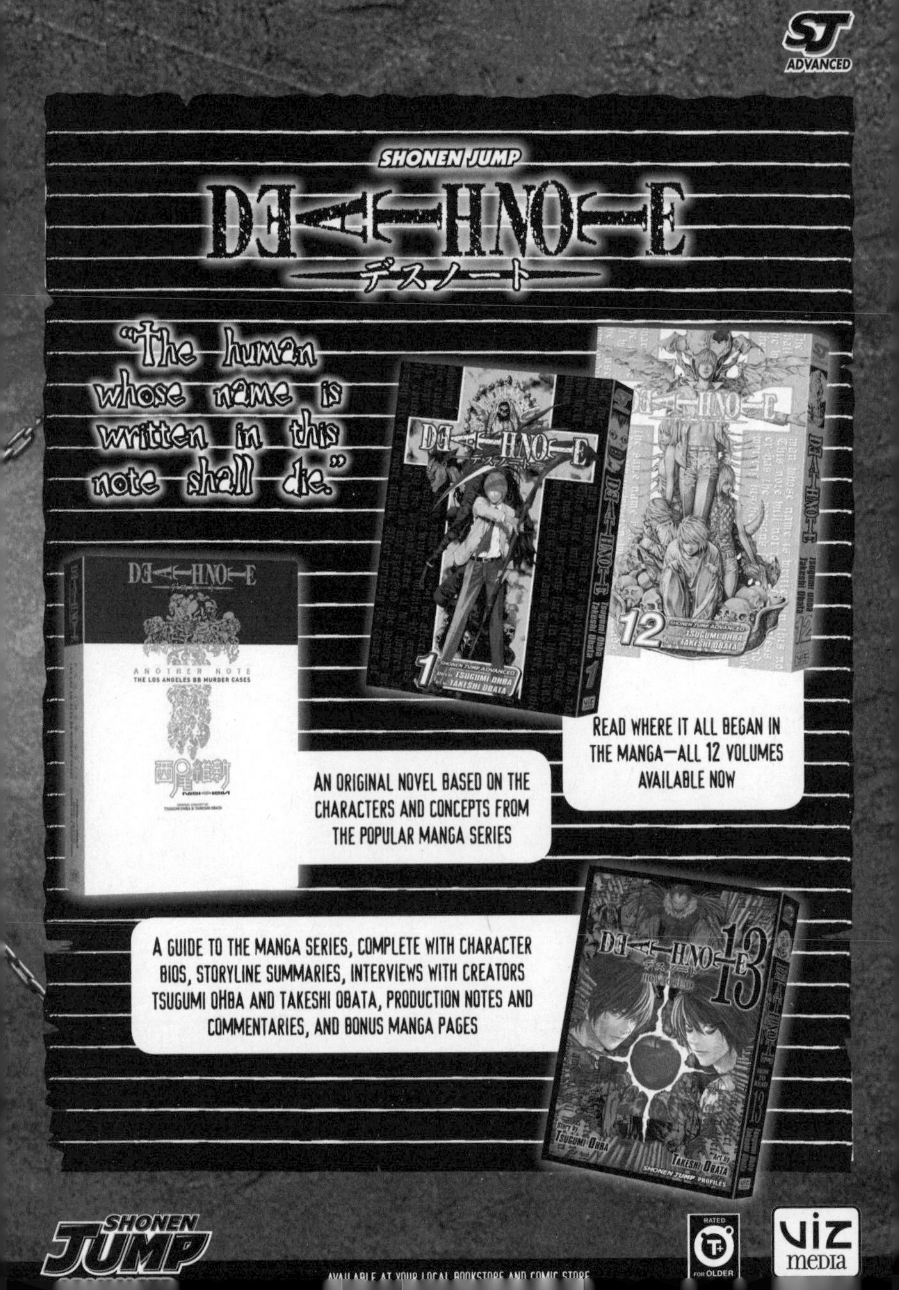
SJ ADVANCED
SHONEN JUMP
DEATH NOTE
デスノート
"The human whose name is written in this note shall die."
ANOTHER NOTE
THE LOS ANGELES BB MURDER CASES
AN ORIGINAL NOVEL BASED ON THE CHARACTERS AND CONCEPTS FROM THE POPULAR MANGA SERIES
READ WHERE IT ALL BEGAN IN THE MANGA—ALL 12 VOLUMES AVAILABLE NOW
A GUIDE TO THE MANGA SERIES, COMPLETE WITH CHARACTER BIOS, STORYLINE SUMMARIES, INTERVIEWS WITH CREATORS TSUGUMI OHBA AND TAKESHI OBATA, PRODUCTION NOTES AND COMMENTARIES, AND BONUS MANGA PAGES
SHONEN JUMP
AVAILABLE AT YOUR LOCAL BOOKSTORE AND COMIC STORE
RATED T+ FOR OLDER
VIZ media

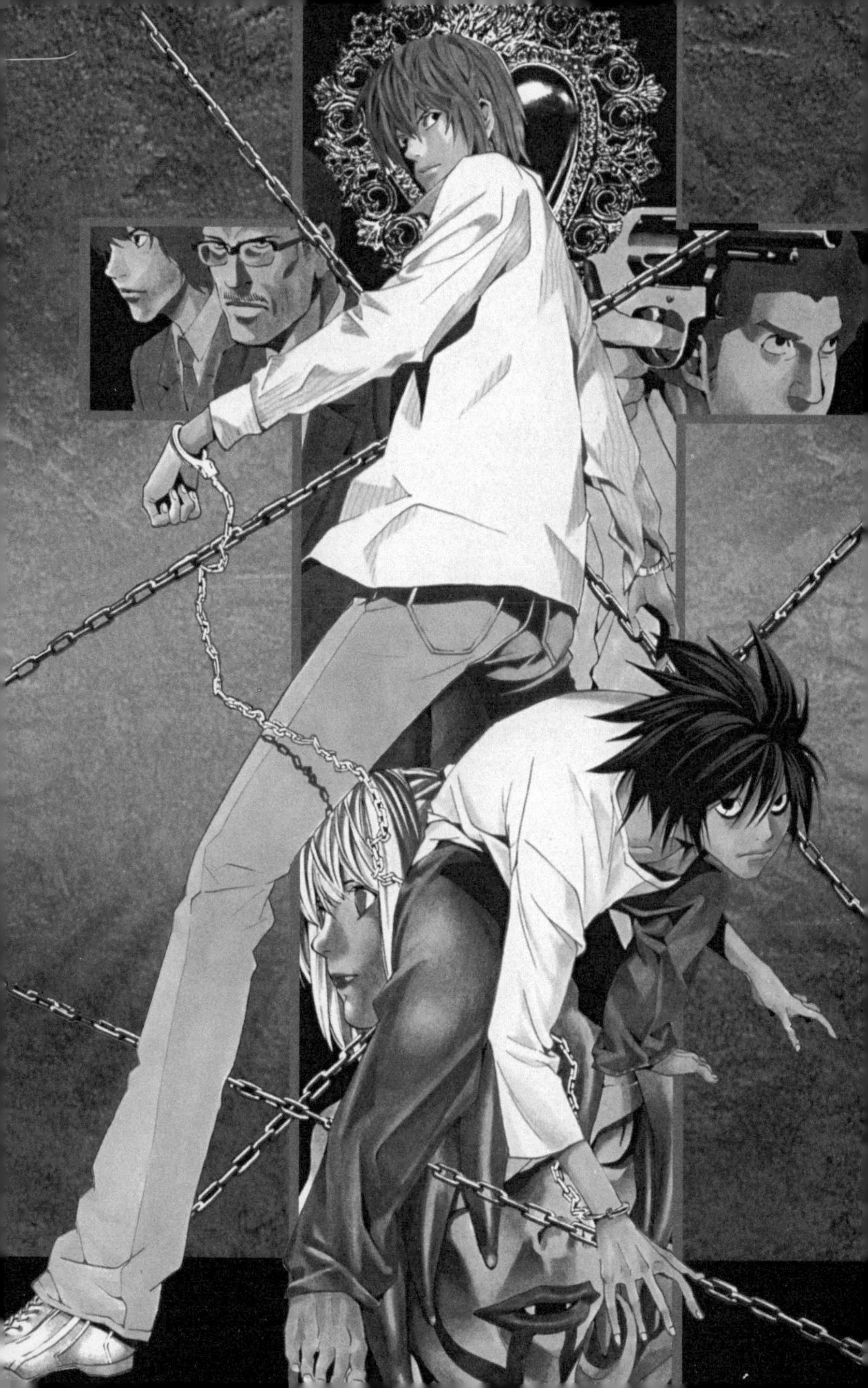

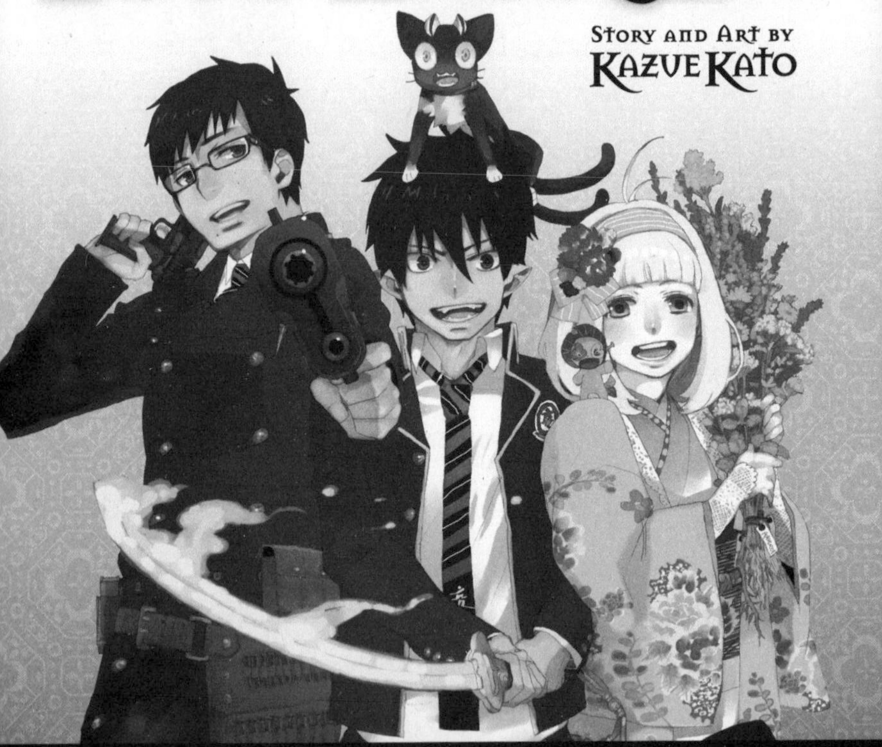

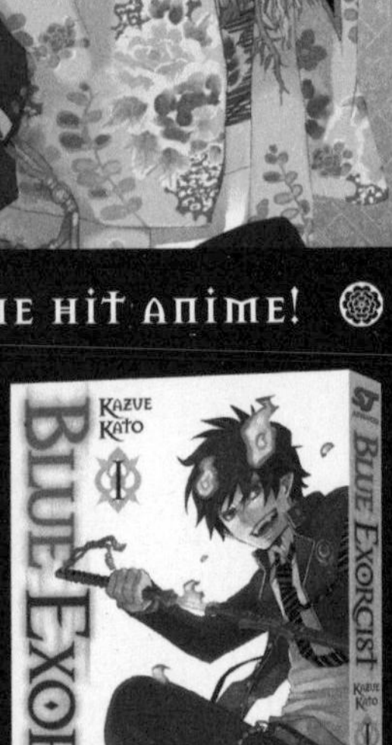

KAZUE KATO
BLUE EXORCIST
1

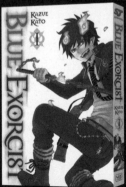

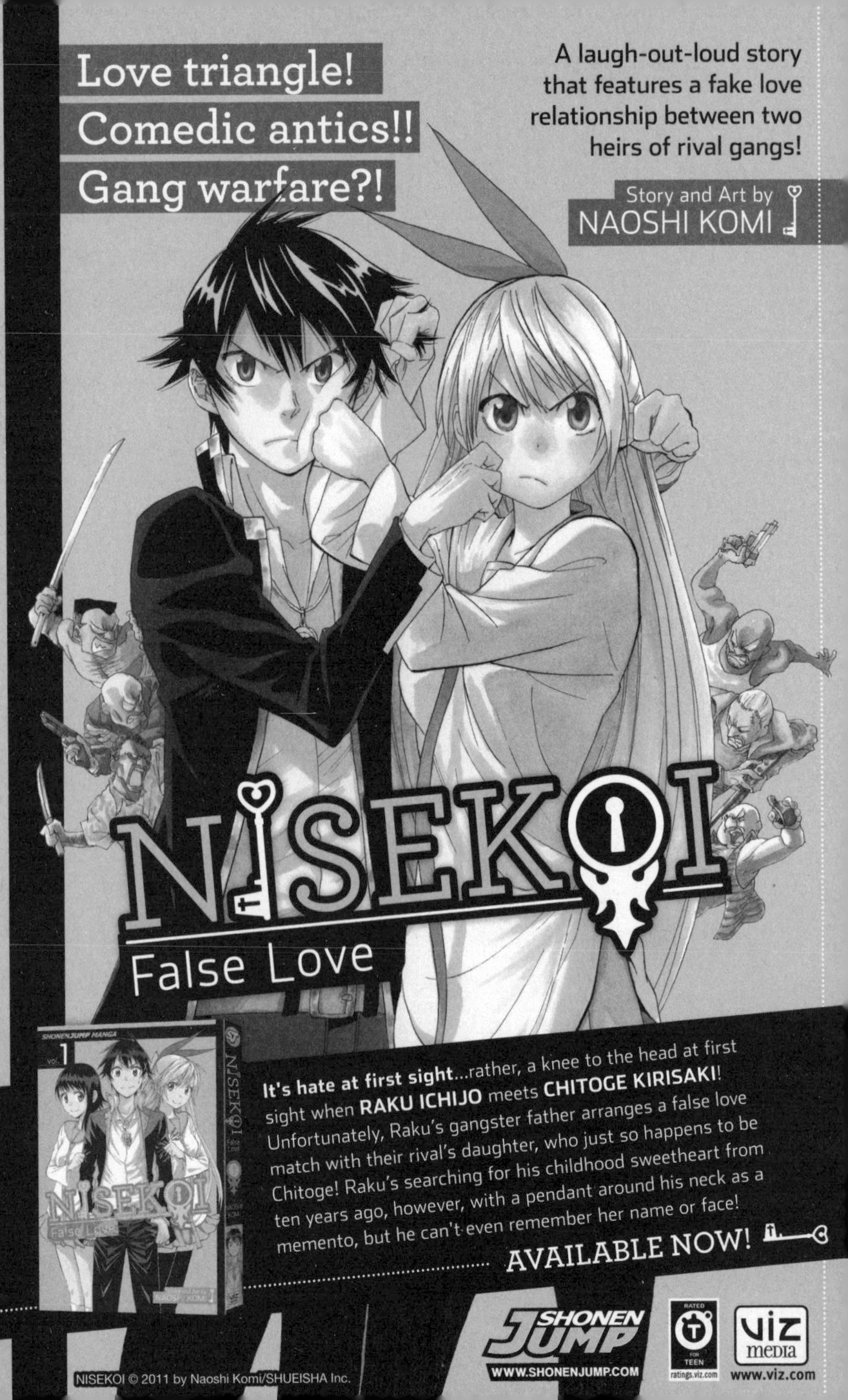
Love triangle!
Comedic antics!!
Gang warfare?!
A laugh-out-loud story that features a fake love relationship between two heirs of rival gangs!
Story and Art by NAOSHI KOMI
NISEKOI
False Love
SHONEN JUMP MANGA
vol. 1
It's hate at first sight...rather, a knee to the head at first sight when RAKU ICHIJO meets CHITOGE KIRISAKI! Unfortunately, Raku's gangster father arranges a false love match with their rival's daughter, who just so happens to be Chitoge! Raku's searching for his childhood sweetheart from ten years ago, however, with a pendant around his neck as a memento, but he can't even remember her name or face!
AVAILABLE NOW!
SHONEN JUMP
WWW.SHONENJUMP.COM
RATED T FOR TEEN
ratings.viz.com
VIZ media
www.viz.com
NISEKOI © 2011 by Naoshi Komi/SHUEISHA Inc.